Lighthouses
of the Pacific

Jim A. Gibbs

4880 Lower Valley Road, Atglen, PA 19310 USA

Since this photo was taken several years ago changes have taken place on the grounds surrounding Oahu's Barbers Point Lighthouse. Note the Stars and Stripes flying from the lantern balcony. U.S. Coast Guard photo.

Published by Schiffer Publishing Ltd.
4880 Lower Valley Road
Atglen, PA 19310
Phone: (610) 593-1777; Fax: (610) 593-2002
E-mail: Info@schifferbooks.com
Please visit our web site catalog at **www.schifferbooks.com**

This book may be purchased from the publisher.
Include $3.95 for shipping. Please try your bookstore first.
We are always looking for people to write books on new and related subjects.
If you have an idea for a book please contact us at the above address.
You may write for a free catalog.

In Europe, Schiffer books are distributed by Bushwood Books
6 Marksbury Avenue Kew Gardens
Surrey TW9 4JF England
Phone: 44 (0) 20-8392-8585; Fax: 44 (0) 20-8392-9876
E-mail: info@bushwoodbooks.co.uk
Free postage in the UK. Europe: air mail at cost.

Introduction

Watchman, what of the night?

Where have all the lighthouses gone? Many have vanished. One day there's a bonfire, and from the ashes rise a skeleton tower, or an ugly pole with a light on top. The Coast Guard's *Notice to Mariners* informs us only after the building has been eliminated.

Shades of gloom; a century of history, a storehouse of memory, a seamark, a landmark. Constructed on remote capes, patches of sea-girt rock, unique expressions of human creativity, architectural genius, complex solutions to triumphant engineering problems, colorful personalities uniformed and dedicated; all gone in a puff of wind.

Lighthouses are noble human achievements, the material from whence comes drama, poetry, artistry, peril and rescue. They are guideposts marking watery highways leading to everywhere. They came in different shapes, sizes, colors and characteristics. In many cases today, residents and tourists no longer ogle the architectural symmetry of an active light tower but must be satisfied with navigation lights on stark pedestals that do nothing for the imagination. Though at night men of the sea seek the safest means of navigation which reduces lights to a secondary role, many lament the passing of the traditional lighthouse and the warm glow of the Fresnels. Acryllic lenses or airway type beacons just don't look the same nor do they possess the scintillating qualities of hand-ground, polished glass prisms. To the sailors of old, lighthouses were like personal friends tenanted by faithful keepers and their families, totally dedicated to their humanitarian roles.

Lest the blame fall on the United States or Canadian Coast Guard, responsible for aids to navigation, let it be said that they are not funded to maintain historic attractions or public parks. So much money is alloted only for the purpose of safeguarding navigable waterways in the most economical and practical method. It is not their responsibility to maintain lighthouses that are unmanned or obsolete. Wherever possible they keep the lights burning, but when it becomes more economical to utilize a utilitarian form of navigation aid, the old structures often are put out to pasture. Public pressure and demands have saved some of the better known landmark towers. Increasing public interest and funding has also been a prime factor in making practical use of former lighthouse reservations. A remarkable awareness of historical things has swept the country in recent years and at last the citizenry has been awakened to the importance of retaining the lighthouses that mark the outer limits of our coasts, our bays and our rivers. Though too little, too late, many of the old relics have been brought back to life for one purpose or another. Some hopes have been dashed.

Take the case of an old Canadian who had a love affair with an abandoned lighthouse. He purchased it from the Crown for a song, but with the understanding he'd remove it by the start of the navigation season. That year, drift ice was unusually thick. Unable to get equipment there to take the lighthouse from its foundation and tow it to a nearby village, he requested an extension, but was refused. The day before the deadline, he reached the site and torched the frame structure to save his $500 performance bond. He watched his long time dream go up in smoke. Then to add to his misery, a construction crew arrived with components to erect a utilitarian aid to navigation with none of the charm of the old structure. It was high enough to have been visible over the former tower which lay on the ground a heap of ashes.

Nobody can turn back the pages of time. Maybe someday people will regret the fact that navigation lights in any form will have become obsolete. Our computer world is making us all number conscious instead of human conscious, and none can argue that the innovative radio electronic navigation devices have replaced the basic lighthouse. But never will they merit the human affection, artistry and beauty of the lighthouses of old. The sentinels that remain are getting a new lease on life and many in their sunset years have finally gotten the respect due their humanitarian role, even in the nuclear age.

This book is not a detailed technical effort on lighthouse engineering, but an effort to convey some of the romance, drama and nostalgia in word and photograph involving the watch towers that have been so much a part of western America and Canada for decades. Hopefully, many of the old lighthouses will remain so coming generations will have a chance to see the way it used to be when the old Fresnels were illuminated by oil flames, or blasted their big brass steam whistles to warn seafarers of the perils along the coastlines. Though shipwrecks have been legion along the shores of North Pacific, the toll would have been astronomical without the lighthouses.

And God said, "Let there be light; and there was light."

Jim A. Gibbs
Cleft of the Rock Lighthouse
Yachats, Oregon

Acknowledgments

Special thanks must go to Captain Robert Blackburn, who retired from the U.S. Coast Guard in the summer of 1985 after a brilliant career which terminated as Group Commander, headquartered at North Bend, Oregon. Another helpful individual was Bob DeRoy of Vallejo, California, son of the late Frank DeRoy, longtime Civil Service lighthouse keeper. Wayne Wheeler, president of the U.S. Lighthouse Society, aids to navigation assistant for the 12th Coast Guard District, (Alameda) San Francisco, and ex Coast Guardsman Ken Black, who heads the Shore Village Museum in Rockland, Maine, are two individuals who have done more to promote lighthouse lore in the country than just about anyone else. Sam Foster, Media News Service, Seaside, Oregon is always most helpful as is Michael Naab, Director of the Columbia River Maritime Museum, Astoria, Oregon, as well as his assistant, Larry Gilmore.

Further, I would like to thank the Commandants of the 11th, 12th, 13th, 14th, and 17th Coast Guard districts and their staffs for assistance in the writing of this book. Individuals within those districts that were of considerable help were Glenn E. Rosenholm, 17th District, Juneau; Tom Pierson, 13th District, Seattle; Jimi Chiunate, 11th District, Long Beach; R.F. Massey, 12th District, Alameda and Bob Jones, and Todd H. Parker, 14th District, Honolulu.

Up Canada way, considerable assistance was rendered by Rex Pendrill "Pen" Brown and L.E. Slaght of the District Office in Victoria, B.C. for the Canadian Coast Guard, and B. Bomben of the Prince Rupert, B.C. District.

Geri Manthe of Reedsport was helpful as was my wife Cherie. In fact, a ten gun salute goes to numerous others who down through the history of our nation have been instrumental in making lighthouses the outer humanitarian guardians of our shores.

Contents

*Port of no return—the foreward section of the **Blue Magpie**, ill-fated Japanese freighter, wallows in its death agonies in November 1983 off the north jetty of the Yaquina Bay bar. U.S. Coast Guard photo.*

*Her holds full of water,, the **Blue Magpie** comes to an ignominious end, but only after a daring rescue effort by the Coast Guard in saving her 19 man crew. Her master failed to heed the warnings against crossing the bar. U.S. Coast Guard photo.*

CHAPTER ONE

Man's Control Stops at the Shore

The mariner remembers when a child,
On his first voyage, he saw it fade and sink;
And when, returning from adventures wild,
He saw it rise again o'er Ocean's brink.
....Henry Wadsworth Longfellow

The concentration of light into powerful beams counts for nothing when fog settles upon the sea, dropping a mantle of white that closes down the world. The multimillion candlepower rays are of little more value than a single candle, nor are the blaring foghorns with their mournful, guttural sounds of more than token assistance to the navigator feeling his way along a fog—shrouded shore. And then there are those howling gales with driven sheets of rain, sleet and snow which next to fog have been the bane of countless men who have gone down to the sea in ships. That shocking, aweful roar of breakers as a ship scrapes ironbound outcrops, unseen traps in areas darker than the inside of a pocket.

Ah, but alas! the dreadful chapters of the past, when the grim toll in men and ships was legion, is over. Modern ingenuity has rung in a new era of remarkable aids to navigation that penetrate the thickest weather—sonar, radio beacons, radio direction finders, loran, radar radio telephones, depth finders, etc., have brought about a fantastic era of high—tech ocean and inland water navigation. But despite it all, the human eye cannot be replaced, and capable operators must be alert at all times to see that the equipment performs properly.

And what about the lighthouse, a symbol of hope to the sea—weary mariner for more than 2000 years? Relegated to a secondary role today, many have passed into oblivion, while others have defiantly clung to their perches defying time and decay. Created from stone, brick, rivet, concrete, staunch timbers and iron, skilled artisans of another age took pride in their beauty and grace. Now, they have caught the eye of an appreciative public and many of these old monuments are being restored, with or without government assistance. Other lighthouses have managed to survive the 20th century advances on their own, due to their strategic locations and familiarity to seafarers and "landlubbers" as well. Like silver—haired statesmen or elderly women of royalty, such monoliths stand regal and splendid, in many shapes, sizes and colors, each distinctive in their own right, each with a peculiar light sequence, and sometimes foghorns with various ear—piercing voices. In most cases, the fulltime attendants have departed the premises replaced by silent partners known as automation. Some stations' grounds have been opened to tourists and campers, only the navigation aids being off limits to the public. Though, the traditional lights and foghorns are no longer the main source of safe navigation, their role is by no means negated; the maritime world still depends on these friendly old beacons. Whenever the Coast Guard *Notice to Mariners* suggests an economy move to close one of the old sentinels, a howl goes up from both land and sea factors; preserve the tower and its surroundings if only for historical purposes. And rightfully so, for they are every bit as much of America as baseball and apple pie.

Shipwreck sometimes occurs within the shadow of a lighthouse, and due to human error, ships equipped with every modern radio aid to navigation can and do meet with tragedy. A prime example occurred just a couple of miles from a major seacoast lighthouse on a stormy November night in 1983. But lest it be forgotten, the blame was not due to lighthouse failure, but lack of communication; the ship's captain unable to understand nor heed radio warnings from the Coast Guard.

The cargo vessel *Blue Magpie,* Japanese flag, Korean—manned, fought her way along the Oregon coast as night came on . Winds were blowing up to 44 knots and the sea was filled with pulsating greybeards raising swells of 18 feet. In the murk, her masthead lights were barely visible as she worked her way north a few miles off Cleft of the Rock Lighthouse at Cape Perpetua. Void of cargo, the vessel rode high, rolling and pitching enough to alarm Korean Captain Kim Gab Bong. He sought entrance into Yaquina Bay as the nearest harbor of refuge, but the bar was a dangerous caldron of breakers. The Yaquina Coast Guard Station answering Bong's request to enter, warned him the bar was impassible that he must stand offshore until a pilot could come alongside the following morning.

Piercing the storm—filled night, Yaquina Head light flashed to the north; if only the ship's master would take a bearing and change course. Confusion and fear plagued the skipper and his 19-man Oriental crew. Captain Bong appeared determined to cross the bar, but suddenly the freighter was swept behind the north jetty. In a moment of terror, steel plates smashed against huge boulders, grinding action that sliced open the hull and left the ship in grave peril. Thirty-eight hundred tons of steel were no match for the immovable jetty rocks. She had reached her port of no return.

The old sentinel on Yaquina Head, a sea and landmark since 1873, seemed to mourn its ineffectiveness as the freighter writhed in its death agonies. Action was quick. A Coast Guard priority message went out over the airwaves, Mayday! Mayday! Senior Chief Boatswain's Mate Ron Garrison, officer-in-charge of the Yaquina Station took charge. The North Bend Coast Guard Air Station dispatched a rescue helicopter ordered out by Group Commander, Captain Bob Blackburn. A second copter was ordered to standby. Contact was suddenly lost with the *Blue Magpie's* radio operator. Garrison then ordered two 44 foot motor lifeboats out with orders to remain in the bay for further instructions. A beach crew was also dispatched. Giant seas were creaming the jetty rocks, and the freighter was breaking up.

Somewhat mysteriously, an erroneous call was relayed from the Canadian Coast Guard that the impaled ship's crew was in the water. Garrison had no choice but to order his motor lifeboats to cross the bar and direct searchlights on the wreck.

Temporary radio contact was then reestablished between the Yaquina Station and the *Blue Magpie.* Terrified, the crew was still aboard but the deck was breaking up under their feet. Inside the bar lay the city of Newport, so near and yet so far away.

In the raging night, chopper 1444 arrived from the North Bend station nearly 100 miles from its home base. Below, grinding against the jetty rocks the *Blue Magpie* had buckled amidships and listed dangerously. The moment was tense. An hour had passed since the stranding. Lieutenant Commander Lou Dunn had maneuvered his Sikorsky HH-52 into a perilous hovering position above the disassembled masts and cargo booms of the broken freighter. In the glow of the searchlights, faces grim, the Koreans clung desperately for handholds and footholds inside the wheelhouse. Quick action was necessary, for the ship could break apart at any moment. Aviation Machinist Brian Smith readied the rescue gear. Shuddering against the wind gusts the copter maintained direct contact with the Yaquina station. Lieutenant Steve Holferty handling the chopper's radio could see the Korean seamen who appeared frozen in their tracks. However, when the rescue line dangled nearby they finally left the confines of the wheelhouse.

Dunn was playing a game of Russian roulette. The ship's masts and antennas were bucking, the hull splitting into three sections. One blow from the cargo gear could knock the copter from the sky. With a hoistline only 100 feet long, just slightly above the height of the masts, Dunn had to rely on Smith's judgement while virtually flying blind in the murk. Smith stood at the open door latching on to two five pound shot bags which he secured to the end of the dragline and dropped to the Koreans. With much difficulty they managed to haul in the hoistline and rescue basket. Instructed to man the basket one at a time, they instead came up in two's. Fortunately the gear was able to handle the extra weight. Every moment was precious, and Dunn took a chance in exceeding the load limit. Taking ten survivors in the first lift (lift load, four plus crew) he made a direct run to the Newport airport to offload his passengers and then hastened back to the wreck for the others. Again the Sikorsky resumed its holding pattern while motor lifeboats and beach rescue crews stood by. In rapid succession eight others were airlifted, leaving but one solitary figure on the wreck. There was concern, for the dragline could not be left to dangle loose lest it get fouled. As the basket came up, the line could latch onto the ship's cargo gear and knock out the chopper's tail rotor. The dragline nevertheless was lowered, the waiting crewman coiled it and flung it into the basket in front of him and up he came at precisely 9:25 p.m.

Off into the night the last survivor was carried to the airport to join his shipmates. Victory with a capital V had been accomplished under the most trying circumstances. The Sikorsky fueled up and the crew returned to homebase for a long overdue dinner. It is foregone conclusion that there was no lack of conversation at the table that night. For their heroic act, Lou Dunn and Brian Smith were presented the Distinguished Flying Cross and Steve Holferty the Air Medal, among the Coast Guard's highest awards.

The Yaquina Bay Coast Guard Station work had only begun, for the broken freighter was spewing an estimated 92,000 gallons of fuel oil and diesel into the immediate area, much of which was being swept into the bay. Under Garrison's direction a massive clean up effort was underway both by government and private sources. Containment booms were rigged. A fishery resource was at stake. The cost of the cleanup ran about a quarter of a million dollars, far less than the estimated $1 million. During the following weeks, the Coast Guard reasoned about 11,000 gallons were cleaned up from the beaches and the bay, plus another 300 cubic yards of oily debris. The service agency awarded several commendations for a job well done, by both service personnel and civilians.

In the interim, the *Blue Magpie* irretrievably lost, was battered to pieces, leaving only a grim tombstone protruding above the water at low tide. Ageless Yaquina Head Light continued to shine.

Don't let anyone ever tell you if you've seen one lighthouse you've seen them all. The qualities of a lighthouse are just short of human. They each have their distinctive personalities, and stories that vary in every detail. Of course, through automation, considerable romance and drama are missing, as the colorful old keepers who kept their respective stations operating at top efficiency are around no more. When the U. S. Coast Guard absorbed the U. S. Lighthouse Service in 1939, an era ended. Though the Coast Guard has maintained aids to navigation since that year, the civil service attendants gradually dropped out and short-term Coast Guardsmen took over the duties, sometimes lacking the devotion so prevalent among the career lighthouse keepers. In the decade of the 1960's most of America's lighthouses bowed to automation, and attendants were removed leaving only maintenance crews to make periodic checks on lights

and foghorns. Manicured grounds went to seed, towers fell into disrepair; vandals marked the areas with ruin. Years passed before the public began to realize the historical importance of lighthouses. The fact that an airport beacon could be placed atop an ugly pole with the same efficiency as a prismatic Fresnel lens inside a graceful tower, saddened the lighthouse buff, but the mariner at sea was only interested in the characteristic of the light by night and little concerned with the tapering beauty of a lighthouse. They call it progress and time marches on. There's no turning back except in memory and the written word which alone preserve the thrilling events of another era when the lower lights were kept burning for those in peril on the sea. Then there was the joy of that first friendly landfall light after many weary weeks on the open ocean; home is the sailor, home from the sea.

In memory, look back through the eons of time and give a thought to that peculiar breed of men, and women too, who once manned the lighthouses of America.

Take the 1881 unexplained mystery of the Columbia River pilot schooner *J. C. Cousins*. Probably the last to sight her crew were the lighthouse keepers at Cape Disappointment and Point Adams. Intrigue and mystery surrounded the 87 foot two-masted vessel when those who peopled her decks seemed to vanish into infinity. Built in San Francisco as a schooner-yacht, her owner spared no expense in getting a quality vessel featuring a copper plated hull, and a generous portion of mahogany and teak in her interior.

As a pilot vessel, her homeport was Astoria, where she engaged in cutthroat competition, and price wars. Area of operation was a treacherous graveyard of ships, the Columbia River bar, which had gained a sinister reputation for marine casulties. It was during her second year of service, that the morning dawned bright and clear on October 6, 1881. Skipper Alonzo Zeiber cast off from the Astoria pilot dock. The drama that followed was to rival the mystery surrounding the disappearance of the crew of the infamous *Mary Celeste* in the Atlantic a decade earlier. Zeiber, with a cook and two seamen aboard was under orders from the owners to proceed over the bar and await the arrival of a French barkentine from the Far East. At noon, the *Cousins* dropped her hook off Point Adams Lighthouse, where Keeper Munson observed her presence in the river near the entrance. He assumed the vessel was waiting for the tide to ebb for easier transit over the bar. The light keepers at Cape Disappointment also observed the actions of the schooner as did those aboard the pilot vessel *Mary Taylor,* lying off Ilwaco.

At about 5 P.M. when the lamp at Point Adams Lighthouse sent its red beam seaward, the *Cousins* upped anchor and rode the tide out to sea, her movements accordingly being logged at the shore station.

At dawn on October 7, the blue sky was flecked with small puffs of cloud; there was a light breeze and a ground swell. The lighthouse keepers again noted the schooner maneuvering under sail off the bar, supposedly awaiting her charge.

When her movements became somewhat erratic, the boat keeper at the U. S. Lifesaving Station at Fort Canby was alerted. In the interim, the schooner came about and headed directly for Clatsop Spit. Onshore, watchers looked on in bewilderment as the vessel entered the outer breakers off the dreaded spit, plowing headlong into the barrier of sand with canvas flapping. She came to a jarring halt wrenching the fittings in her wooden hull. Her hooks remained at the catheads. No distress signals were sighted, no lowering of canvas. The schooner's boat remained lashed, no individuals were seen struggling in the water.

Out went the lifesaving craft, backs and arms of the surfmen straining. When abreast of the wreck their shouts and hailings went unanswered, so they ran the breakers and straddled the spit. Swarming aboard the schooner, the surfmen found it void of life. Further inspection showed everything in proper condition, the boat

Semper paratus is their guide—North Bend helicopter 1373 hovers over Umpqua River's 44 foot motor lifeboat 44331 in practice drill in preparation for the real thing. U.S. Coast Guard photo.

securely lashed, the galley stove still warm, potatoes boiled dry in the pot, a meal little touched. Crew quarters were in reasonable order. A final entry in the log made by Zeiber in mid-river at sunrise indicated no problems.

All through the previous night the beacons at Cape Disappointment and Point Adams were in view of the *Cousins*. Search for the missing men now turned toward the sea. Nothing was found by the diligent surfmen, nothing at all.

Zeiber was known to be of good character, nor was there any evidence that relationship with his crew was anything but good. Subsequent boardings of the schooner found her, for the most part, shipshape, the rudder and helm in proper working order. Nothing could account for the vessel's strange antics. Despite all efforts, the weeks passed affording no evidence of the missing men. They were never seen nor heard from again.

As in all unexplained mysteries of the sea, theories were numerous. Hints of barratry, murder, bribes etc. all ran their courses. Nothing concrete came forth. All efforts were now turned toward salvaging the derelict. Despite persistent efforts, the shoal refused to release its prisoner and the salvagers could do no more than remove equipment

and fittings. With winter coming on, storm-lashed seas and giant breakers reduced the *Cousins* to kindling.

Lengthy litigation followed. The insurers stuck by a claim that the schooner had been purposely grounded for insurance money. They, however, could produce no proof and finally agreed to pay the owners a meager $4,000, far short of the vessel's true value. Rumors continued for years that Zeiber had been seen in Far Eastern ports, in Africa and in Latin America, rumors with no solid foundation. In the saloons along Astoria's little Barbary coast the *Cousins* case was a familiar topic, but was destined to go into the maritime history books as unsolved.

And again, it was the lighthouse keepers who were last to see the ill-fated HMS *Condor* after she rounded Cape Flattery Lighthouse (on Tatoosh Island) and vanished forever with her entire complement of well over 100 officers and enlisted men of the British Navy. It was one of the most baffling mysteries in the annals of the Pacific.

It was on December 2, 1901 that the HMS *Condor,* a barkentine-rigged steam sloop of 980 tons departed Esquimalt, British Columbia for a cruise to Honolulu and the South Pacific islands. Composite constructed—wooden planking on iron frames, she was copper-sheathed. On her first commission, in command of Commander Clifton Scalater (Sclater) RN, she carried a complement of 110 Royal Marines and seamen. (accounts of the number aboard have also varied from 104 to 140).

Heavily-armed, the fighting ship carried ten 4 inch guns and four 3 pounders. She put to sea in company with the HMS *Warpite* which was under orders to return to England. The weather bode well for a good Pacific crossing. The two ships parted company as the *Condor* broke off in the Strait of Juan de Fuca to engage in gunnery practice. Thus the day was well spent when she passed close to Cape Flattery Lighthouse (Tatoosh) where the keepers accepted her signal and logged her passing. Pursuing a southwesterly course, the ship, contrary to early reports headed into turbulent weather. That was the last anybody ever saw of the *Condor* or her crew, and the irascible sea was stingy in rendering clues. Weeks later, reports from the *Warspite* told of encountering extremely heavy seas that caused damage on her decks, and she, at 8,400 tons, was a much larger vessel than her ill-fated counterpart.

After 35 days and no report of the *Condor's* whereabouts, the HMS *Egeria* was ordered out to conduct a thorough search of the west coast of Vancouver Island. All that was found was a flag locker and a grating, reputably from the missing vessel. Close coastal probing caused the *Egeria* to strike an outcrop of rock and rip off a large section of her keel, necessitating her return to Esquimalt for repairs.

Lending assistance to the search a U. S. Revenue Cutter Service vessel in command of Commander Tozier learned that a dinghy and

*The vanishing HMS **Condor** that was lost with her entire company after rounding Cape Flattery Lighthouse in 1901, one of the tragic Pacific disasters. She is seen here steaming in Queen Charlotte Sound a few weeks before her loss. Courtesy Provincial Archives, Victoria, B.C.*

The original Umatilla Reef Lightship first stationed off the dreaded reef in 1898. She is seen here about 1914 coming in for repairs suffered in a storm. Her long time master, Captain Eric Lindman claimed she was the greatest little ship in the world.

*In June 1916, the SS **Bear** of the San Francisco and Portland Steamship Company ran aground in the fog near Cape Medocino, and became a million dollar loss. The Blunts Reef Lightship **No. 83** took aboard 155 passengers and crew members who put to sea in lifeboats after the stranding.*

bits of other wreckage, presumably from the *Condor,* was among the Indians at the village of Ahousat. The commander bargained with the chief for return of the goods, but the shrewd old Indian leader turned out to be a seasoned trader. He claimed anything swept up by the sea belonged to the finder, but, on eying the dress sword worn by Tozier his eyes lighted up. The commander, reluctantly traded his handsome saber in the hope the recovered goods might shed further light on the tragic loss of the *Condor.*

His sacrifice received little attention until two decades later after his retirement from government service. While in the hospital, he was visited by the British Ambassador who presented him with a shining new sword from King George V. Inasmuch that an American officer was not permitted to accept a gift from a foreign nation, a special Act of Congress was required before the weapon could be accepted. (In 1915 the U. S. Lifesaving Service and the U. S. Revenue Cutter Service were combined to form the U. S. Coast Guard).

As in all such tragedies, theories concerning the disappearance of the *Condor* were numerous. The *Umatilla Lightship,* stationed off the northwestern coast of Washington was blown off course at the time the *Condor* went missing, but the incident was dismissed as having no bearing on the case.

In 1949, when the American trawler *Blanco,* dragging for sole, snagged a teredo-encrusted binnacle off Cape Beale. It was thought to be from either the *Condor* or the British steamship *Matteawan* which was also lost with all hands off the Strait of Juan de Fuca. Up in the net with the binnacle came a battered clinker-built British lifeboat, but it broke loose and sank again. Its identity might have solved the mystery of where the *Condor* lies asleep in the deep. Ironically the binnacle's serial number could still be distinguished. Contact with the British Admiralty failed to positively identify it as belonging to the *Condor*

but it was determined that the maker had supplied the ship with the same type navigation instrument, and that it might well be presumed to be either from the SS *Matteawan* or the *Condor.* The Flattery light keepers logged the southwesterly courses of both the *Condor* and the *Matteawan,* the latter a British-built collier laden with 5,000 tons of coal. Ironically, no bodies from either ship were ever recovered. The two vessels were two of several deepsea ships that vanished around the turn of the century after signalling the keepers on Tatoosh Island. Though each presented an unsolved mystery, the common theory was that the ships involved were overloaded, battling their way in severe Pacific storms that raised seas of tremendous proportions. Giant acclivities frequent in the north Pacific are aroused by winds sometimes exceeding 100 knots.

The disappearance of the *Condor* must be left to speculation pending some ambitious underwater recovery effort. Until then, the tragedy is recalled at the St. Paul's Church in Esquimalt, B. C. where hangs a lifering and a plaque which reads: "To the memory of the commander, officers, and men of the HMS *Condor* which was lost at sea with all hands in December 1901 off the coast of Vancouver Island. Out of the deep have I called unto thee: O Lord hear my voice." It was erected by the officers and men of the Pacific Squadron.

In many tragic events of the past, the light keepers were the last to view a vanishing ship, but likewise were they frequently the ones who sent warnings resulting in the saving of lives, nor were they personally remiss in saving lives themselves, often in heroic acts performed at great risk.

Lightships are no longer positioned at perilous spots along the west coast, but before the electronic revolution in navigation aids, they played a vital role in guiding seagoing vessels, and in addition served as a conveyance for castaways.

*Columbia River Lightship **No. 88** spent many years as a prime aid to navigation off the river entrance. Many shipwreck castaways found refuge aboard her.*

In the black, fog-filled early morning hours of a June day in 1916, the lookout of Blunts Reef Lightship No. 83 stationed off the northern California coast detected the sound of human voices echoing over the water. The plaintiff cries seemed to come out of nowhere. Until that moment only the mournful cry of the vessel's foghorn pierced the darkness. Taken aback, the watchman spotted a lifeboat barely visible in the glow of the lightship beacon, so startled was he that his hand pulled the emergency bell arousing his shipmates from a sound sleep. Up the companionway they came, some in their night clothes fearing that a ship on collision course was bearing down on them. The lifeboat came alongside filled with survivors of the coastal steamship *Bear,* which had run aground near Cape Mendocino. Rather than risk the fearsome breakers the lifeboats had launched out on the open sea. The survivors were removed from the lifeboat, bundled in blankets and taken below. No sooner were they comforted than another lifeboat appeared followed by several more. The lightship was transformed into an overcrowded passenger vessel though shackled to the ocean bottom. Eventually, some 155 survivors from the *Bear* were packed aboard—men, women and children, and despite the overcrowding not one complaint was heard, for the crowdedness of the lightship far exceeded the bitter cold of an open lifeboat.

Trailing astern of the Lightship were no less than nine lifeboats. Captain Henry Pierotti, master of the No. 83, wasted no time digging into the ship's stores and food lockers to see that his passengers were as comfortable as possible under the circumstances.

By 3 P.M. when the Coast Guard motor lifeboat *Liberator* arrived at the lightship to confer with Captain Pierotti, it was learned that two of the boats from the *Bear* were still missing. Fortunately the remaining survivors had been plucked from their miserable confines by the tug *Relief.*

The immediate problem was what to do with the survivors. Eventually wireless contact was made with the steamer *Grace Dollar* which made a quick response. By 7:30 A.M. she was standing by, and the transfer of passengers commenced. An hour and 15 minutes later the evacuation, without injury or delay, was completed. Grateful passengers waved a fond farewell to the lightship crew.

It was not quite the happy ending on the *Columbia River Lightship No. 88* on January 7, 1913. She took aboard the only survivors of the oil tanker *Rosecrans* which was mangled on dreaded Peacock Spit with the loss of 33 lives. The rescue craft from the Point Adams station battled mighty seas as she made her way through an area known as the graveyard of ships, but could only find three survivors and one corpse. Sea conditions worsened to such an extent that the lifeboat sought out the lightship, the bar, a pulsating mass of foam-ridged breakers. With great difficulty the boat came alongside, its occupants soaked to the skin and numbed by the cold. Despite the rise and fall of the seas the lightship crew managed to get them aboard, and then endeavored to secure the lifeboat. Despite a tenacious effort, the craft broke loose, drifting away, the corpse astride the bilgeboards. Many hours passed before the survivors and the surfmen could be removed from *No. 88.*

The incident was just one of many when the lightship afforded refuge for the tempest-tossed.

Today the lightship off the entrance to the Columbia River is no more. In its place bobs a sizable navigational buoy complete with light, fog signal, radiobeacon and Racon signal. It rises 42 feet above the sea, anchored in 210 feet off the river entrance rangeline. Its light flashes white every two seconds. A similar conveyance marks the offshore entrance to San Francisco's Golden Gate, also the former location of a lightship.

11

Augustin Jean Fresnel, the man who made the great breakthrough in lighthouse optics. Born in France in 1788, he died on Bastille Day 1827, at the age of 39, but his genius lived on.

Centuries of Light

O' sparkling jewel
in lantern's crown
You guide the mariner's way
Across the boundless, rolling deep
A light thru night till dawning day.
JAG

Scintillating and sparkling, the first order Fresnel lens of French manufacture has often been described as one of the most beautiful creations made by the hands of man. Though some lighthouses still retain their jewels of polished glass in frames of brass or bronze, they are gradually becoming relics for museums, replaced by acrylic lenses or by aero-marine type beacons typical of those so familiar at airports around the world.

To Augustin Jean Fresnel goes credit for the great breakthrough in lighthouse optics. This genius was appointed a member of the French Lighthouse Commission in 1811. Totally aware of the shortcomings of the former catoptric form of lighting, he found a way of negating the loss of light. When a lamp is lighted, the luminous rays are diffused on every side, horizontally as well as vertically. In the lantern of a lighthouse, the beam has to be thrown in a horizontal line only, while the light which is shed towards the top and bottom must be diverted so that the proportion of waste luminosity can be minimized. Though parabolic reflectors achieved a portion of the goal, it fell well short of the ultimate. Fresnel found a means of condensing the entire rays into a horizontal beam. He took a central piece of rounded, magnified glass, often referred to as a bullseye, and around it disposed numerous concentric rings of glass, each of the rings projecting beyond another. Each constituted the edge of a lens, which, while its radius differed from the other, owing to its position, yet was of the same focus in regard to the source of illumination. Each part was of hand-ground, polished glass delicately shaped and held by fish glue in a metal frame. The result was dazzling. The comparatively thin lenses allowed only one-tenth of the light passing through to be absorbed, compared to a loss of one half in the old parabolic reflectors. This revolution in lighting came to full fruition in 1822, and its principal still holds in numerous forms of lighting into the atomic age. The old Fresnel lenses, of course, were developed well before the advent of commercial electricity and were designed to take a small oil flame and fan it into a beacon of brilliance seen many miles seaward. It was the biggest step forward in optics in 2000 years of pharology. Lighthouses the world over switched to the new method giving greater hope to men of the sea.

Lighthouses go back into antiquity. Perhaps the first regularly maintained lighthouse was at Sigeum (Cape Incihisari) in the Troad, mentioned by the Greek poet Lesches in 660 B.C. The celebrated Colossus at Rhodes has been supposed by many to have served as a lighthouse, a cauldron of burning coals being raised skyward in its giant hands. The structure was reputedly 105 feet high, its feet resting upon the two moles which formed the harbor entrance, allowing ships to pass under the arc of the legs. A winding staircase spiraled upward to the top by which slaves carried fuel to maintain the flame. Erected in 278 B.C. by Chares, it was destroyed by a severe earthquake in 224 B.C. which broke it off at the knees. According to history, the remains were sold to a Jewish merchant in 684 A.D., who in turn hauled away so much brass that it required the loading of 900 camels.

None can deny, however, that the greatest of all lighthouses, past or present, from the standpoint of its massive structure was the giant Pharos of Alexandria, erected in 270 B.C., for Ptolemy Philadelphus, on the eastern summit of a small island in the Bay of Alexandria,

seven miles from the mainland. Fourteen years later Dexiphanes built a causeway to the giant structure which became known as one of the Seven Wonders of the World. Built of white marble, it rose pyramidically in a number of receding stories and was adorned with pillars and galleries. Its height has been estimated as anywhere from 350 up to 600 feet, with fire beacons kept burning by night that could be seen, as estimated by Josephus, 40 miles at sea. Sostratus, (the Cnidian) the architect was so impressed with his creation that he engraved his name on the structure's stone and then filled the hollow with mortor so that in the course of time after King Ptolemy's inscription had worn off, his would be uncovered, preserving his name for eternity. But all in vain. An earthquake again was the villian of destruction in 1350 A.D.

Many lighthouses followed, such as the pharos built by Emperor Claudius at the port entrance to Ostia in 50 A.D., and others at Pozzuola, Messina and Ravenna, all magnificent structures. The early lighthouses that marked the Mediterranean shores soon had counterparts as far away as England and France. One of the first, if not the first, was the Tour de Corduan which stood on a flat rock in the Bay of Biscay off the mouth of the River Garonne. It was constructed by Louis le Debonnaire in 805 A.D.

Many generations were to pass before the north Pacific was to be illuminated by anything resembling a lighthouse. Not until the early 1800's did the Spanish or the Russians consider aids to navigation along the western rim of the north Pacific, and they were at best feeble. On northern shores, New Archangel (Sitka), Russian Alaska was the site of the first structure recognized as a lighthouse, constructed in 1837 atop the government house, often referred to as Baranof's Castle.

At the old Hawaiian whaling port of Lahaina on the island of Maui, a small light structure was established as early as 1840. The light under the old Hawaiian monarchy was the only beacon in the Pacific for thousands of miles.

Though America's initial lighthouse, Boston Light was erected on Little Brewster Island in 1716, a century and a half passed before the U. S. government set up lighthouse keeping on the Pacific Coast. Along the entire shoreline from the Mexican border to the Strait of Juan de Fuca there was not a single lighthouse by the mid 1800's, nor was there a lighthouse from the southern border of British Columbia to the North Pole, except for the one at New Archangel. The acquisition of California, with the termination of the Mexican War, and the possession of the Oregon Territory as a result of the treaty with England in 1846, posed a formidable task for the U. S. government in establishing aids to navigation at pivotal points for growing Pacific commerce. Congress was somewhat nervous about allocating funds for what they considered the wild and mutable west.

As early as 1848 government surveys had recommended and underlined the need for a lighthouse on Cape Disappointment at the entrance to the Columbia River, an area that had already earned the reputation of being a ship killer. With the discovery of gold in California in 1849, however, most attention was focussed on San Francisco. Commerce from the world over entered the Golden Gate and there were no navigation safeguards to prevent shipwreck. Quick

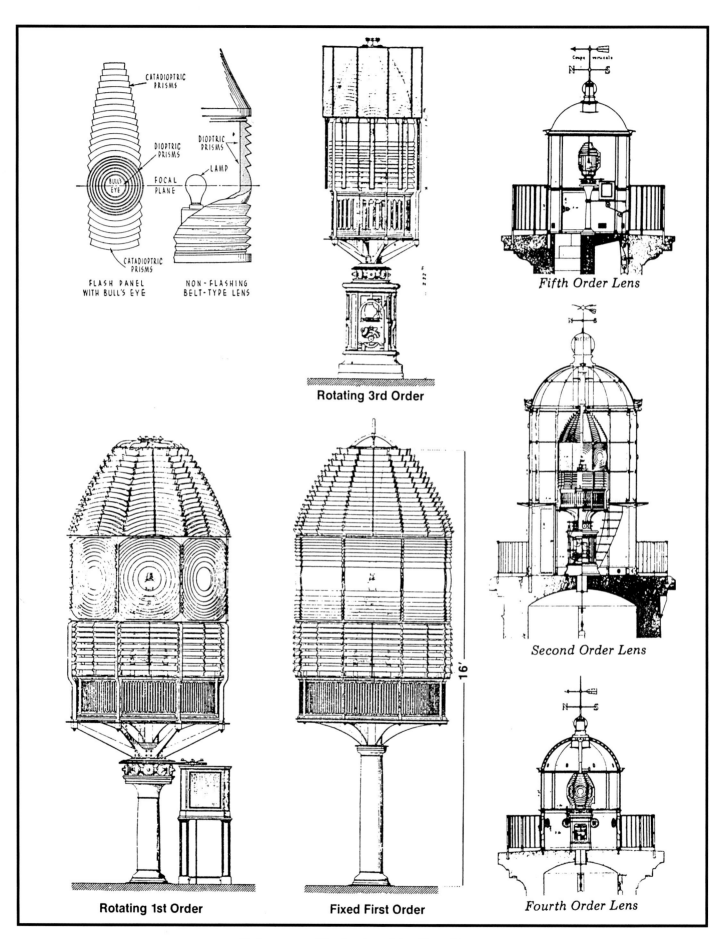

CATADIOPTRIC PRISMS

DIOPTRIC PRISMS

DIOPTRIC PRISMS

LAMP

BULL'S EYE

FOCAL PLANE

CATADIOPTRIC PRISMS

FLASH PANEL WITH BULL'S EYE

NON-FLASHING BELT-TYPE LENS

Rotating 3rd Order

Fifth Order Lens

Second Order Lens

16'

Rotating 1st Order

Fixed First Order

Fourth Order Lens

Various types of fixed and revolving Fresnel lenses.

14

April 27th. 1793.

Approved, so far as it respects the new chain; but is there an entire loss of the old one?

G. Washington

Two great Americans played a role in America's early lighthouses—The upper document was signed by George Washington regarding acquisition of chain. The center one, a document concerning Thomas Jefferson's opinion on dismissal of a keeper. Lower photo, is an artist's drawing of America's first lighthouse, Boston Light on Little Brewster Island, built in 1716 and destroyed by the enemy in the Revolutionary War.

I think the keepers of light hou-
-ses should be dismissed for small
degrees of remissness, because of
the calamities which even these pro-
-duce, & that the opinion of Colo.
Newton in this case is of sufficient
authority for the removal of
the present keeper.

Th. Jefferson

Dec. 31. 06.

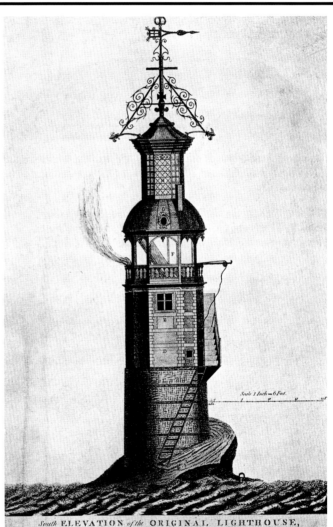

South ELEVATION of the ORIGINAL LIGHTHOUSE, Built upon the EDYSTONE ROCK, according to the first Design of Mr WINSTANLEY. Taken from a Perspective Print, drawn at the Rock, by Jaaziell Johnston, Painter. —— Original by Rev. Roberts 1761.

Jaaziell Johnston drew this picture of the original Eddystone Lighthouse in England in 1761. The structure was built in 1699 and was torn out by the terrible tempest that struck the English coast in 1703. The present Eddystone Light bears little resemblance to its predecessors that have marked the dangerous sea-girt barrier, nor to the later sentinels that have marked the shores of the Pacific.

An artist's depiction of the Pharos of Alexandria, largest and tallest lighthouse ever built, one of the wonders of the ancient world. Reputedly built between 331 and 280 B.C., it was believed to be 350 to 400 feet high. Drawing by Hashime Murayama, Illustrated London News.

The cupola atop the old Russian Governor's Mansion (Baranof's Castle) is seen here as depicted by artist Whymper who drew it for the Bulkley Telegraph Expedition in 1867-68, the time of the purchase of Alaska by the United States. The lighthouse was the first official light between the Mexican border and the Arctic Circle. It was built in 1837.

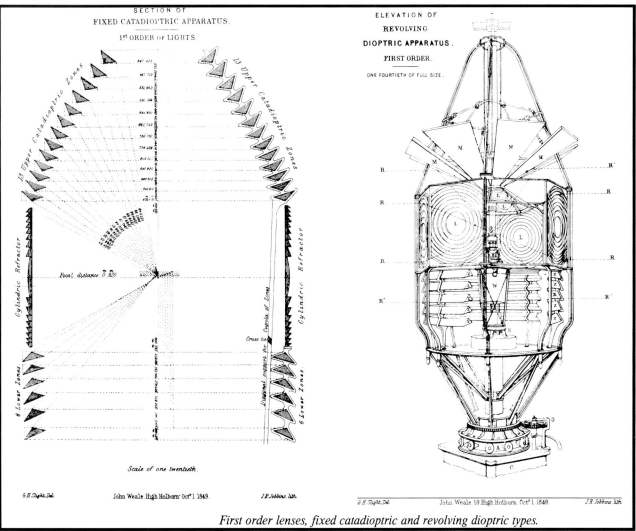

SECTION OF
FIXED CATADIOPTRIC APPARATUS.
1ST ORDER OF LIGHTS

ELEVATION OF
REVOLVING
DIOPTRIC APPARATUS.
FIRST ORDER.
ONE FOURTIETH OF FULL SIZE.

13 Upper Catadioptric Zones

Cylindric Refractor

Focal distance 0.920

6 Lower Zones

Cross tie

Diagonal support for Cupola of Zones

Scale of one twentieth.

G.H.Slight.Del.   John Weale. High Holborn Oct.r 1.1849.   J.R.Jobbins, lith.

G.H.Slight.Del.   John Weale 59 High Holborn, Oct.r 1.1849.   J.R.Jobbins, lith.

First order lenses, fixed catadioptric and revolving dioptric types.

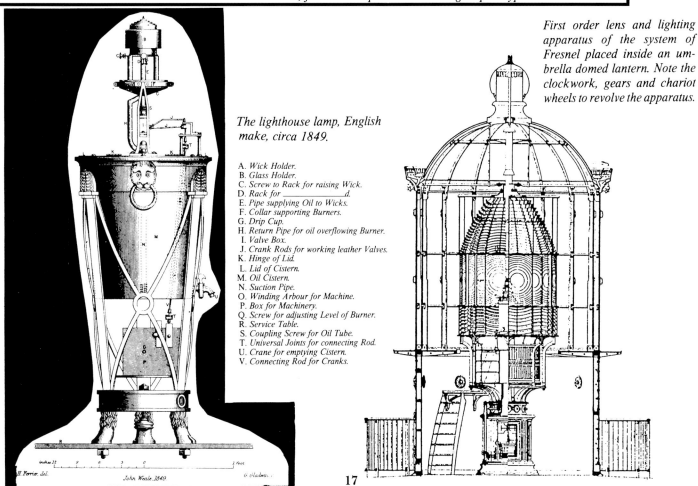

First order lens and lighting apparatus of the system of Fresnel placed inside an umbrella domed lantern. Note the clockwork, gears and chariot wheels to revolve the apparatus.

The lighthouse lamp, English make, circa 1849.

A. Wick Holder.
B. Glass Holder.
C. Screw to Rack for raising Wick.
D. Rack for _____ d.
E. Pipe supplying Oil to Wicks.
F. Collar supporting Burners.
G. Drip Cup.
H. Return Pipe for oil overflowing Burner.
I. Valve Box.
J. Crank Rods for working leather Valves.
K. Hinge of Lid.
L. Lid of Cistern.
M. Oil Cistern.
N. Suction Pipe.
O. Winding Arbour for Machine.
P. Box for Machinery.
Q. Screw for adjusting Level of Burner.
R. Service Table.
S. Coupling Screw for Oil Tube.
T. Universal Joints for connecting Rod.
U. Crane for emptying Cistern.
V. Connecting Rod for Cranks.

H. Ferrier, del.   John Weale. 1849.   G. Gladwin.

17

action was necessary. The U. S. Coast Survey made recommendations for navigation aids at several points on the coast, and by 1852, Congress had authorized construction of 16 lighthouses and some additional buoyage. Of that total the majority were for strategic locations in California waters including Fort Point, Alcatraz, Farallons, and Point Bonita, in or near the San Francisco Bay area. Other locales in the Golden State were at Point Loma, Point Pinos, Santa Barbara, Point Conception, Humboldt Harbor and Crescent City. Recommended for the Pacific Northwest were Umpqua River, Cape Disappointment, Willapa Harbor, Cape Flattery, New Dungeness and Smith Island.

The usual government red tape followed. The administration of navigation aids was finally moved from the ineffective efforts of the Fifth Auditor of the Treasury and placed under a nine member Lighthouse Board composed of military officers and scientists. It came at a time when the government was making the transition from the old Argand lamps and parabolic reflectors to the hightly efficient Fresnel lenses and smokeless lighting equipment.

The Baltimore firm of Gibbons and Kelly won the initial bid to build the first West Coast lighthouses. The Treasury Department had elected to take the various monies appropriated to that period and let a contract to erect eight lighthouses, following some rather questionable ethics on behalf of the government body. Finally Francis X. Kelly and Francis A. Gibbons wound up with the contract and in 1852 dispatched the bark *Oriole* from Baltimore with men and materials for lighthouses at Point Loma, Point Conception, Point Pinos, Farallon Islands, Fort Point, Alcatraz, Humboldt Bay and Cape Disappointment.

After a long voyage around the Horn, the vessel arrived in San Francisco in December of 1852. The construction crew commenced laying the foundation for Alcatraz Lighthouse on an island in the middle of San Francisco Bay, and even while the work was underway, the secretary of the treasury, directly related in the operation of lighthouses, turned that responsibility over to the newly appointed Lighthouse Board. In the interim, part of the work force shifted to Fort Point to erect a lighthouse there. By March, part of the crew were transported south to begin work on Point Pinos Light near Monterey, the erstwhile Spanish seaport. Next, some of the workers eyed craggy Southeast Farallon and made plans to build a tower at the crest of the highest hillock in that smattering of desolate islets. Until that time, the lighthouses had retained the basic design devised by a well known architect named Ammi B. Young, who was under the employ of the Treasury Department, a simple economical, design with the tower rising from the center of the dwelling. Not so with the Farallon Light. There was only enough room at the summit of the monticule to build a tower. The dwelling would have to be placed at the lowest elevation.

Next, the *Oriole,* was dispatched to the Columbia River, but on making her entrance, ran onto a reef and began breaking up, ironically within clear view of the site where the Cape Disappointment Lighthouse was to be built. Though all hands survived after a miserable experience, the *Oriole* was a total loss as was her cargo— the building materials for the remaining four lighthouses. Disheartened, but by no means ready to give up, the experienced contractors within a few months continued construction on the remaining lighthouses, replacing lost supplies with local materials.

Though the *Oriole* had offloaded a fair share of her cargo at California ports, the wreck presented a stumbling block and seriously delayed construction of Cape Disappointment Lighthouse which previously had been on the priority list. The cape appeared jinxed, for not only had it kept the secret of the Columbia River as the last plum of discovery in the American west, but had also cast its shadow over the ship with supplies to cap its crown with a lighthouse. The cape was properly named.

But the Columbia was not the only trouble spot, for work on Farallon light was delayed by the famous "egg war." Egg pickers, furnishing the gourmet restaurants of San Francisco, refused at first to let the lighthouse construction crew land for fear they would drive the birds away from the island. After guns, knives and fists were openly displayed, the laborers retreated for a legal counterattack. On enlisting the aid of the Collector of Customs in San Francisco, who also served as the local superintendent of lights, he in turn dispatched a Coast Survey steamer to the island, heavily-armed. The egg pickers became passive and no more eggs were thrown at the newcomers.

In seven months the contractors erected four lighthouses. Unfortunately, one of the first four, Fort Point, had to be dismantled before it was fitted with lighting equipment. The U. S. Army decided that its strategic location was ripe for gun emplacements and down came the lighthouse.

By the end of 1854, the initial lighthouses were completed and officially turned over to the government. Lighting apparatus, however, was long overdue, and at that date only two lighthouses were displaying their lights. The keeper at Alcatraz touched the lucerne to the oil wicks June 1, 1854, becoming the first U. S. Government lighthouse to be commissioned on the Pacific Coast. Runner-up honors went to Point Pinos where the other available lens was fitted. By order of Major Hartman Bache, the district inspector, the lighting apparatus intended for Fort Point was sent to Point Pinos and was officially lighted on February 1, 1855.

Problems of another nature arose after the additional lighting equipment arrived from France aboard the ship *St. Joseph* in December of 1854. The importers appeared far more interested in the large cargo of French wines discharged at dockside for rowdy San Franciscans. The problem was not the lenses nor the wine but the fact that the towers had been built to the wrong dimensions to handle the lighting apparatus. Costly alterations were necessary. Farallon, Conception and Disappointment towers had to be dismantled brick by brick and be rebuilt.

In the interim, a second Fort Point lighthouse was erected and commissioned on March 21, 1855, and a local contractor was hired to construct Point Bonita Light at San Francisco's north portal. Its lamp was lit on August 9, 1855.

After some alterations, Point Loma was fitted with a third order lens and lighting apparatus and illuminated November 15, 1855. On the slopes of ageless Point Conception the light was commissioned on February 1, 1856, one month after Farallon Light was placed in operation, 23 miles westward of San Francisco.

Finally, long delayed Cape Disappointment Lighthouse which was supposed to have been the coast's initial beacon became operational on October 15, 1856, ending a turbulent and frustrating construction period.

In the following months, local contractors were employed to finish lighthouses at California's Santa Barbara and Crescent City, while in Oregon Territory towers were built and commissioned at Umpqua, Cape Flattery, Willapa (Shoalwater) Bay, New Dungeness and Smith Island. The Pacific Northwest lighthouses were established in 1857-58, and with their completion the Pacific Coast had come of age in the maritime world. A new breed of keepers, affectionately referred to as "wickies," became a well respected fraternity.

Within a few months, Canadian lighthouses were constructed at Fisgard and Race Rocks on the British Columbia side of the Strait of Juan de Fuca.

The life of the traditional principal lighthouse keeper in the old days was to a degree similar to being captain of a ship. Though his command was stationary, it was operated with precision, and everything was expected to be in immaculate condition at all times. Polishing brass, bronze and glass was a daily chore especially when the oil flames tended to smut up the lamp chimneys and the lens

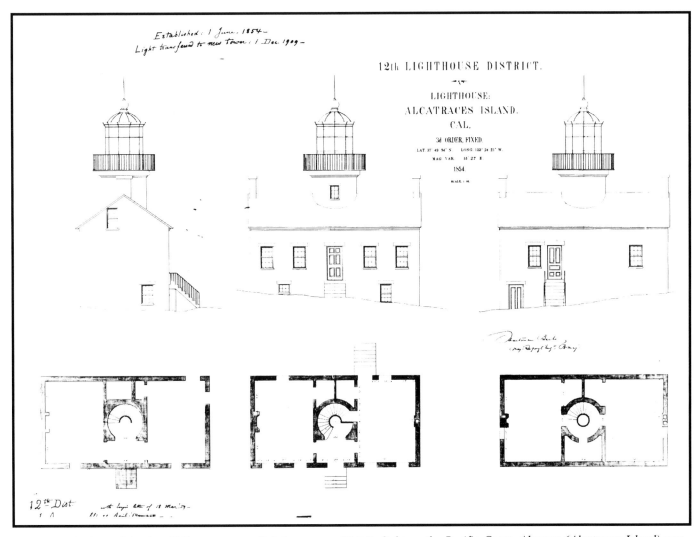

12th LIGHTHOUSE DISTRICT.

LIGHTHOUSE:
ALCATRACES ISLAND.
CAL.

3d ORDER, FIXED.

LAT. 37° 49' 54" N.   LONG. 122° 24' 21" W.

MAG. VAR.   15° 27' E

1854.

12th Dist

Structural plans of the first U.S. government lighthouse to exhibit its light on the Pacific Coast. Alcatraz (Alcatraces Island) was commissioned June 1, 1854. Courtesy Wayne Wheeler, Keeper's Log.

The pioneer Alcatraz lighthouse, probably taken sometime after the advent of the great San Francisco earthquake of 1906, and before the walls of the prison demanded the building of a new, much more elevated lighthouse. Note the keeper's dwelling and the fallen rock from the isle cliffs.

Polishing the brass on a steam fog whistle, was a vital part of the lighthouse keepers duties. Most attendants preferred stations not equipped with fog devices. Courtesy Wayne Wheeler, Keepers' Log.

*Built in Philadelphia in 1857, the lighthouse tender **Shubrick** came to the Pacific Coast the following year as the west's first supply and service vessel for aids to navigation.*

Hartman Bache's sketch of Cape Disappointment Lighthouse made for the office of the 12th Lighthouse District, San Francisco in 1857. The lighthouse, commissioned in 1856, at the north portal of the Columbia River was scheduled to be the first government light on the coast, but delays prevented its completion.

Earliest known drawing of Alcatraz Island Lighthouse, sketched by Hartman Bache in the 1850's, in the wake of the California goldrush.

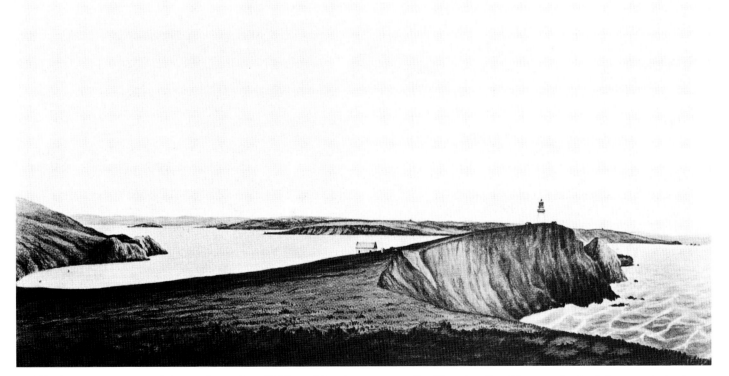

The first Point Bonita Lighthouse, dating from 1855, marking the entrance to San Francisco Bay. The reproduction is from a painting by Major Hartman Bache, district lighthouse inspector responsible for the supervision of construction of the pioneer West Coast light towers.

prisms. The chore of cleaning a smaller fourth or fifth order lens was not nearly as difficult as cleaning a first, second or third order lens, the former sometimes having in excess of 1,000 prisms. The lamps had to be trimmed, the oil fountains filled, machinery oiled, weights checked, lantern panes cleaned and every sector of the tower and quarters kept spotless. The exterior of the lighthouses had to be kept painted and all metal work on the galleries and doors kept rust free. Duty entries had to be made in the station logbook on each watch denoting weather and sea conditions and comments of unusual occurrences. All visitors were required to sign the guest register. In addition, the grounds had be be manicured, and in the stations without women, which the majority were, each keeper took his turn as cook.

The writer can remember hearing some of the old civilian keepers say they preferred the isolated or sea-swept stations to the more domestic lighthouses because inspectors didn't drop in unexpectedly. It was a misdemeanor to be caught out of uniform or having neglected a routine chore. The atmosphere was more relaxed at the isolated stations. Keepers however, often had to be a jack-of-all trades, especially in emergencies.

The basic gripe of all the old keepers was the endless hours spent polishing brass, and that demanding duty prompted the following poem written decades ago, by Fred Morong. Nobody told it better.

Oh, what is the bane of a lightkeeper's life,
that causes him worry and struggles and strife,
that makes him use cuss works and beat up his wife?
   It's Brasswork.
What makes him look ghastly, consumptive and thin,
What robs him of health and vigor and vim,
And causes despair and drives him to sin?
   It's Brasswork.
The Devil himself could never invent
A material causing more world-wide lament
And in Uncle Sam's service 'bout ninety per cent
   It's Brasswork.
The lamp in the tower, reflector and shade,
The tools and accessories pass in parade
As a matter of fact the whole outfit is made
   Of Brasswork.
The machinery, clock-work, and fog signal bell,
The coal-hods, the dustpans, the pump in the well,
Now I'll leave it to you, mates, if this isn't—well
   Brasswork.
I dig, scrub and polish, and work with a might,
And just when I get it all shining and bright,
In comes the fog like a thief in the night,
   Goodbye Brasswork.
Oh, why should the spirit of mortal be proud
In this short span of life that he is allowed
If all of the lining in every darn cloud
   Is Brasswork?
And when I have polished until I am cold,
And I'm taken aloft to the Heavenly fold,
Will my harp and my crown be made of pure gold?
   No, Brasswork.

Today, most of the brasswork chores are memories of the past. Modern fixtures in lighthouses have no exposed brass, and when they do, its painted over. Cast aluminum, or other non-corrosive metals, fiberglass and acryllics are the main materials. The old Fresnels still in operation often go for months and sometimes years before anyone bothers to polish the brass. The oil flames replaced by clean electricity, no longer smut up the glass and metal as in days of yore.

As the Fresnels are slowly relegated as museum pieces, so have the colorful foghorns of other days been removed or replaced by modern counterparts. Foghorns have always been the mark of dismal depression to most, but music to some. They warn of dangers in gray, blinding fogs, each with a distinctive voice most of which remind the hearer of a spiney sea monster roaring from the depths. Nearby residents of some lighthouses send out howls of protest when their slumber is disturbed.

Some have gone so far as to state that foghorns remind them of impending death which probably inspired the following lines by Browning, "Fear death?—to feel the fog in my throat,
The mist in my face."

Foghorns have never had the glamour of scintillating Fresnel lenses, often broadcasting their messages through big trumpets or ugly standards, but it goes without saying that before modern aids to navigation came into use they were extremely essential. The old-time keepers were often kept busier maintaining the fog signal than at any other lighthouse chore. Especially was it difficult when they had to get up a head of steam in the boiler in order to sound the big diaphones, diaphragms, steam whistles and sirens. When the foghorns failed to work it often required the manual ringing of a standby fogbell at intervals through a cold, clammy night. Its a far cry from the air horns today that work by automated electric impulse.

Diaphones produce sound by means of a slotted reciprocating piston actuated by compressed air. Blasts may consist of two tones of different pitch, one high the other low, often the inspiration for deodorant soaps. Diaphragm horns produce sound by means of a diaphragm vibrated by compressed air, steam or electricity. Duplex or triplex horn units of differing pitch produce a chime signal. Sirens produce sound by means of either a disk or a cup shaped rotor actuated by compressed air or electricity. Whistles produce sound by compressed air emitted through a circumferential slot into a cylindrical bell chamber. Bells are sounded by means of a hammer electrically actuated, a descending weight, compressed gas or manual. The oldest form of fog signal, the gong, produces sounds of varying tones activated by motion.

Diaphones are probably the most powerful and earthshaking. The one at the Point Reyes Lighthouse when installed decades back was so powerful that the resultant vibration caused tons of rock to tumble down the steep cliff on which it was situated 130 feet below the light. There was such concern over the continuing landslide that it was feared the lighthouse itself would be undermined. The government spent large sums of money reinforcing the precipitious cliff and making alterations on the signal.

At Destruction Island Light Station, off the Washington coast many years ago the islet's lone bull went on a rampage knocking down all the fences thinking that the newly erected fog signal was a rival for the cows grazing nearby.

There were few tears shed in 1919 at the Grays Harbor Light Station when the fog signal house burned down. It housed a huge steam boiler and required a big head of steam before it went into operation. The building had a huge smokestack almost half as high as the light tower, and two lengthy trumpets. By that period, most of the stations were equipped with compressors and generators for powering the fog signals. Many times foghorns and bells were not dependable because of dead spots that occur on the ocean. Such phenomenon is sometimes due to the geographical formations along the shore.

A woman light keeper who tended the Angel Island fog signal on San Francisco Bay, Mrs. Juliet E. Nichols, was rewarded for her tenacity on July 2, 1906 when a thick fog draped itself over the area. When the mechanical striking mechanism for the fogbell broke down, she employed a household hammer and pounded the giant bell continually by hand for 20 hours and 35 minutes to prevent a possible

Completed and accepted by the U.S. government in August 1854, old Point Loma lives on today restored as a memorial of the past. An original sketch by Hartman Bache as he viewed the highly elevated sentinel guarding the Silver Gate and the open Pacific.

Hartman Bache depicts the transport of the big fog bell up to Point Conception Lighthouse on the rugged California coast in the 1850's.

Farallon Islands Lighthouse was commissioned January 1, 1856 atop the Southeast Farallon. The rugged trail is pictured winding up the precipitous hill. The keepers dwelling is shown at the foot of the monolith while egg poachers below rob bird eggs for the restaurants of San Francisco. Hartman Bache sketch.

shipwreck. Before her stiff arm had healed, the bell mechanism broke down again two days later and she repeated her prior performance all through another night. One can't imagine what the constant gonging of a 1,500 pound bell can do to the ears and the nerves over a 24 hour period when standing beside it.

Fog signals today, whether they be large or small are mostly activated by electric impulse, those on buoys usually powered with batteries. The Pacific Coast's first fog signal was an Army surplus cannon placed at Point Bonita Light Station at the entrance to San Francisco Bay. The cannon was officially placed in service on August 8, 1856, and during foggy periods was fired every half hour. The 24 pounder taken from the Benicia Arsenal was placed in charge of Sgt. Maloney, who had retired from the Army. With an average of 1,000 hours of fog annually, the old vet wore himself out, often working 24 hours around-the-clock with no relief. The inspector finally had mercy and sent him an assistant. The troublesome weapon was terminated on March 18, 1858 when a fogbell was installed. The old firing piece still survives as a museum attraction, its role having pioneered thousands of fog signals of gradually improving caliber that have honked their dismal cries at stations all along the Pacific rim.

A facet of lighthouse life on the lighter side, were the gab sessions at isolated light stations where lonely men would discuss everything from sex to storms, and were never lax at stretching the truth. Many had put in time at sea and had brought with them the proverbial yarn. Each one had caught a larger fish or had survived a worse ordeal than the others. Exotic stories of foreign intrigue and sometimes spicey encounters with women became hot subjects. Generally, they steered away from politics and religion but lest one think that this special breed of man was a cut above those in other professions, think again. Isolated personalities in confined quarters day after day sometimes have serious arguments, usually involving neglect of duty, unacceptable meals or other less important complaints. Occasionally the result was total abstinence from conversation, threats, or in isolated cases fisticuffs, all of which were followed by letters of request for transfer. Generally the principal keeper was in total authority, and unless he suffered mental breakdown or injury, the inspectors took his word over any of his assistants.

In some of the isolated Alaska stations, disagreements could bring months without social intercourse, a serious situation that might cause one to become mentally unstable.

For the most part, however, the keepers of the lights were quiet, self-reliant, industrious and slow to anger. Conversations were generally friendly and informative and tension could be broken when laughter prevailed. Stretching the truth was a code word for good relations. The writer remembers one recitation repeated by a keeper who had formerly made his life from the sea. It was entitled: *I Wish I Could Tell A Lie.*

I stood one day on a breezy bay, watching the ships go by,
When an old tar said, with a shake of his head, I wish I could tell a lie.
I have seen some sights what would jigger your lights as they figgered mine for sooth.
But I ain't worth a darn at telling a yarn, when it wanders away from the truth.
I was on a bark, called the Nancy Stark, a league and a half at sea,
When Captain Snook with a troubled look, he came to me and said:
Now boatswain Smith, make haste forthwith and hemstitch the foremain sail,
Accordian pleat the spanker sheet, for she is gonna blow a gale.
I straightaway did as the Captain bid, and no sooner the job was through,
When a North wind crack, set us dead aback and murdering lights how she blew.
She blew the tars right off the spars, and the spars right off the masts;
Anchors and sails, and kegs of nails, went by on the wings of the blast.
The galley shook, when it blew the cook right out through the starboard glim;
Pots and pans, kettles and cans, went clattering after him.
It blew the fire right out of the stove and the coal right out of the bin,

And he cried alack when it blew the beard right off the Captain's chin.
Then the old man said, with a shake of this head, and the words they blew out of his mouth;
We are lost I fear, if the wind don't veer and blow awhile from the South.
Now wiggle me dead, no sooner he said the words that blew out of his mouth,
When the wind hauled around with a hurricane sound, and blew straight from out of the South.
It blew the tars back onto the spars and the spars back onto the masts,
Anchors and sails and kegs of nails onto the ship stuck fast.
The galley shook when it blew the cook right back on the starboard poop;
Pots and pans and kettles and cans, without even spilling the soup.
It blew the fire back into the stove and the coal back into the bin.
And we cried hurrah; When it blew the beard right back on the skipper's chin.
There's more to my tale, said the sailor hale, that would jiggle your lights for sooth;
But I ain't worth a darn, at telling a yarn, when it wanders away from the truth.

Santa Barbara Lighthouse was one of the original California sentinels, established in 1856. For 35 years it was tended by beloved grandmother Julia F. Williams. On June 29, 1925, a severe earthquake leveled the building. This Hartman Bache sketch made in 1857, shows it as designed by Ammi B. Young, Treasury Department architect.

Standing through the ages, Point Pinos Lighthouse near Monterey is little changed from its establishment on February 1, 1855. Though the structure was basically completed in the summer of 1853, it had to await its lighting apparatus to arrive from Paris. Though the surrounding area has undergone a transition, Point Pinos stands as a monument. Hartman Bache drawing.

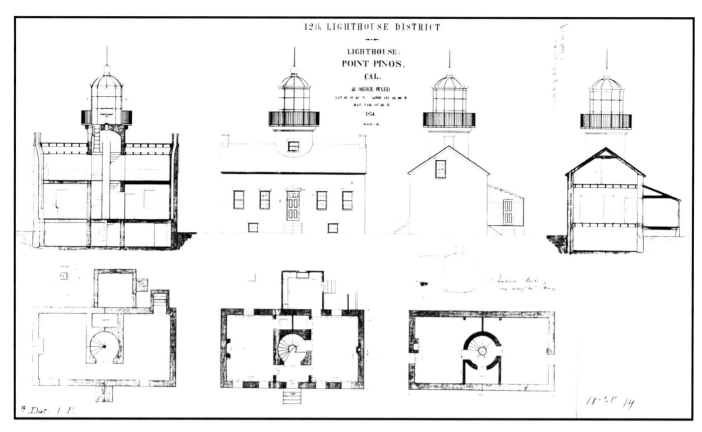

12th LIGHTHOUSE DISTRICT

LIGHTHOUSE:
POINT PINOS,
CAL.
3d ORDER FIXED
1854

The First 16 West Coast Lighthouses
Constructed in the 1850's (from south to north)

Station (Series)	Year	Lens	Comments	Station (Series)	Year	Lens	Comments
Point Loma (1)	1855	3rd	Discontinued in 1891, presently under the jurisdiction of the National Park Service open to the public.	Fort Point (1)	1855	5th	Original building razed months after construction. Present skeleton tower on the parapets of Fort Point was discontinued when the Golden Gate Bridge began construction in 1934.
Point Conception (1)	1855	1st	Reconstructed in 1889. Not accessible to the public.	Alcatraz (1)	1854	3rd	Reconstructed in 1908. Only tower of 2nd lighthouse remains. 1st lens transferred to Cape St. Elias, AK. 2nd (Fourth order) in Alcatraz museum.
Santa Barbara (2)	1856	4th	Destroyed by an earthquake in 1926.				
Point Pinos (1)	1854	3rd	Only one of original eight basically unchanged with original optic still in operation. Under jurisdiction of City of Pacific Grove, has excellent interpretive museum in building. Open on weekends. Hours erratic. Call (408) 372-4212 for information.	Humboldt Bay (1)	1856	4th	Discontinued in 1891. Replaced by Table Bluff. Structure razed sometime in the 1930's.
				Crescent City (2)	1856	4th	Discontinued in 1951. Presently under jurisdiction of Del Norte County Historical Society. Nicely interpreted, open to public in summer at low tide. Active as a private aid to navigation. Has old Fresnel lens in museum. Call (707) 464-3089 for information.
Farallon I. (1)	1855	1st	Original house razed, tower decapitated, original lens in Navy-Marine Corps-Coast Guard Museum on Treasure Island in San Francisco Bay. Museum open to public daily from 10 a.m. to 4 p.m.				
				Umpqua River (2)	1856	3rd	Destroyed in 1861.
				Cape Disappointment (1)	1856	1st	Still in existence and operation. Not open to the public.
Point Bonita (2)	1855	2nd	Original lanternroom and lens relocated to present structure in 1877. Still operational and open to limited tours through NPS Golden Gate National Recreation Area by reservation. Call (415) 331-1540. Original tower and house razed.	Shoalwater Bay (2) or Willapa Bay	1858	4th	Destroyed by erosion 1941.
				Cape Flattery (2)	1857	1st	Still in existence. Not original lens. Very difficult to visit.
				New Dungeness (2)	1857	4th	In St. of Juan de Fuca. Rebuilt in 1927.
				Smith Island (2)	1858	4th	In St. of Juan de Fuca. Rebuilt in 1957

Structural plans of the Point Pinos Lighthouse, one of the original sentinels on the Pacific Coast. Thumbnail history of the first 16 lighthouses constructed on the Pacific Coast, as contracted for under the U.S. Light-House Board. Courtesy Wayne Wheeler, Keeper's Log.

Ghosts, Apparitions, Unsolved Mysteries and Tragedy

Millions of spiritual
creatures walk the earth,
Unseen both when we wake,
and when we sleep.
....Milton

Strange as it may seem, every traditional lighthouse has its peculiar ghost. The writer never met a lighthouse keeper who didn't believe his lighthouse had a ghost by solemn resolve or with tongue-in-cheek, and there was no desire to put the ghost to rest whether it be of good character or bad. There have been keepers who approached the subject from a scientific standpoint, like the one who mentally put the apparition aside although it was seen again and again at California's Point Vicente lighthouse. After considerable study he came to the conclusion that the shape of a ghostly maiden appeared only because of the reversed parenthesis of the shaft of light flashing from the revolving beacon. His fellow keepers refused to accept his theory no matter how hard he tried to persuade them.

Dismissing something as the figment of imagination never completely satisfies, for there is something inherent in all of us that enjoys unsolved mysteries, stories that defy logic and the aura of the unknown. From the beginning, ghosts and apparitions have somehow been associated with lighthouses.

Probably no other structure built by man produces the strange sounds of a light tower. Such buildings are usually in exposed places where strong winds (often of hurricane force), pea soup fogs, sleet, rain or snow are frequent occurrences. A pyramidal, rounded or tapered tower causes howling winds to play strange tricks, creating numerous weird noises that under the right circumstances could scare the socks off the most tempered keeper. Then the spiral staircases associated with many lighthouses make echoing noises when one ascends or descends on the iron grates. The heavy metal storm doors that open onto the exposed galleries, or the creaking window frames, all produce low moans and groans on a stormy night.

When there was no running away from ghosts or apparitions because of the isolated location of a lighthouse, the keeper of old in many cases considered them to be nothing more than friendly wraiths looking for a good place to roost.

On windy nights, the perimeter below a seagirt light tower is often littered with dead seabirds, a common fact that has baffled ornithologists for years. Whatever mystery causes the birds to meet their Waterloo in such strange fashion has always been subject to speculation, but some superstitious keepers of old tried to tie the phenomenon in with spectral influence. Undoubtedly, a wave-swept lighthouse with a brilliant, revolving beacon located in the flight path of migrating seabirds has an affect on their mental processes, sometimes causing them to attack the light in dive-bomber fashion. Large birds have crashed through lantern panes and on occasion have chipped prisms out of lenses. The writer has seen hundreds of dead seabirds of many species lying below Tillamook Rock Lighthouse when its beacon stabbed gale-filled nights. Even though there is probably logic to the pattern of suicide by these airborne creatures, their mass death is always surrounded in mystery.

And certainly Tillamook Rock, abandoned as a functioning lighthouse in 1957, had its ghost which howled like a banshee especially during driving southwesterly storms. It was an experience to stand on the spiral staircase and listen to its shrill cry and then to feel the moist breeze that passed over as if being brushed by a wet blanket. And today, the ghost of Tillamook has lots of company with little

disturbance from the living. The entire interior of the lighthouse has been gutted down to the bare stone blocks. Racks of urns have been placed to hold the ashes of the dead. Owned by Eternity at Sea, the former lighthouse has become the first islet columbarium of its kind anywhere in the nation.

The ghostly atmosphere of the rock goes back to antiquity, for the early coastal Clatsop Indians looked upon the rock with awe. Long before a lighthouse was built on that upheaval of basalt, the natives associated it with the spirit world, believing that secret under-ocean tunnels, inhabited by spirits, ran out to the rock. When the first white men came they found the local tribesmen had a fearful respect for the rock and never attempted to scale its slimy walls or to land their dugout canoes.

Keepers of old often sat around mess tables at lighthouses and talked about strange happenings. One story frequently spoken of concerned the disappearance of the three-man lighthouse crew of England's Seven Hunters Lighthouse. The beacon had been placed on one of seven rock-bound islets, sometimes known as the Flannan Islands, steep walls of gray, clayish type rock. Seven Hunters Light was constructed near the end of the last century, but not completed till December 1899. Four keepers were assigned to the station, three on duty and one on leave, six weeks on followed by a fortnight off. The link between the station and the mainland was the Northern Lighthouse Board's steamer *Hesperus* that made fortnightly visits to the place, weather permitting. On December 26, 1900 the steamer arrived well behind schedule delayed by inclement weather. Her previous visit to the lighthouse had been on December 6. Bringing back a keeper from leave along with needed supplies, the vessel hove to off the east landing and hoisted the usual signals. To everyone's surprise her presence went unnoticed; none of the usual preparations had been made for her arrival. At first it was thought the ship's long delay had caught the keepers off guard. A boat was manned and put out from the anchored steamer to take the keeper to his destination. In the absence of anyone at the landing, he had difficulty jumping ashore with no one to assist.

As the boat pulled away, the keeper could find none of his counterparts, and thus signaled the boat to return, fearing there might be some kind of plague. A systematic search was made through every sector of the keepers' quarters and the tower. No trace or clue was forthcoming. The last entry in the lighthouse log had been made at 9 a.m. on December 15 offering no hint that anything was other than routine. The morning's chores had evidently been completed as all was in immaculate condition. The big lamps had been trimmed, the oil fountains were full and the lens and machinery had been cleaned and polished. Pots and pans in the galley were all washed.

Whatever claimed the three men must have happened after midnight on December 15, for the master of the passing steamer *Archer* had reported the light shining at midnight on that date. The only items found missing were some sea boots and oil skins, suggesting that the men must have been down at one of the landings. Though traces of the wave action had left a few marks, the crane installed on a concrete platform 70 feet above the sea was undamaged, the boom lowered and secured to the rock, the canvas

Considered an engineering triumph, Tillamook Rock Lighthouse commissioned in 1881, took some terrible punishment from raging storms and giant seas during its active years. The station is pictured here, looking eastward toward Tillamook Head, slightly over a mile away. The above photo was taken about 1929.

covering and wire rope on the barrel, firmly lashed. Could seas of gigantic proporation have leaped up and plucked the three men from their high perch? The ropes that had previously held a lifering at the 100 foot level above the sea were found dangling, but the conveyance was missing.

To this day, the mystery has never been solved, but since that time, a ghostly pall has hung over that lighthouse.

Ghosts never die, they just fade away, or do they? One of the spectral family continues to live on in Alaskan folklore. For years she haunted the corridors in the succession of castles and government houses at the old Russian Alaska capital of Sitka. She continued her vigil when the last of that series of structures was built in 1837, the one erroneously labled Baranof's Castle. Though never lived in by Baranof, it served as the royal residence of the chief managers of the Russian-American Company and was the fourth such structure constructed in the same location. Baranof built the first in 1804-05, and it is claimed that the subsequent units erected under Kuskov and Muravyev respectively, all kept feeble oil ships lanterns burning to guide vessels to port. Only the 1837 building had its own lighthouse, and its keepers frequently complained about the ghostly presence that sometimes caused the oil flame to flicker and go out.

Aleksandr Andreyevich Baranof, 1746-1819, was a shrewd Russian trader, chief figure during the Russian control in Alaska, governor of Russian activities in North America from 1799 till 1817. He ran his little empire like a tough dictator and was ruthless toward any who stood in his way. Scores of Russian-American Company vessels were lost en route to Alaska during his reign, with great loss of life and property. Mother Russia was too involved in her own problems to be deeply concerned with the Alaskan outpost. During one period, Baranof went for five years without supplies from the Czar's storehouse. Often plagued by ill-fortune and ill-health, the natives were frequently victim of his wrath. Finally, he was ousted from his post by a Russian admiral backed by naval guns late in 1816, and while being transported back to the mother country and ultimate public disgrace before the courts, he succumbed in the Indian Ocean, reportedly from depression and failing health.

Almost from its inception the governors residence and lighthouse were claimed to be haunted. Legend insisted that the edifice was visited frequently by a beautiful Russian princess whose untimely death was the result of Baranof's bitter actions. Though the tales have varied, the most accepted version was that the princess returned at six

month intervals to haunt the northwest chamber of the "castle." She was reputedly the daughter of one of the old governors, and was forced to marry into nobility against her will. Suddenly and mysteriously she vanished from the wedding festival and was later found dead in her chamber, casting a dark shroud over the festivities. Deeply in love with a common Russian seaman banished from the colony forever by Baranof, the princess, rather than marry another, took her life. Twice a year following her death the swish of her wedding gown and the wringing of her jeweled hands was heard, always followed by the pungent odor of wild briar roses.

When the United States purchased Alaska from Russia in 1867 for $7.2 million, the visits by the wraith began to subside. The Army contingent assigned to Sitka utilized the structure as headquarters for the commanding officer and his staff. The story of the princess did not die but it was almost as if she had moved on to haunt a place in Siberia near her banished lover. Whatever the case, her haunted corridors went forever up in smoke and flames when the famous "castle," in a rather disreputable condition, was destroyed by fire in 1894. With it went the lighthouse and the sound of the princess mourning the loss of her beloved in sad lachrymose.

The ghost of Muriel Tevenard haunts the old Yaquina Bay Lighthouse, a frame edifice that had one of the shortest active careers of any lighthouse on the Pacific Coast. Though the structure has surprisingly survived to the present day, it served under one keeper, from 1871 till 1874, and was then abandoned in favor of the formidable Yaquina Head Lighthouse, a massive masonry sentinel constructed a few miles to the north. Under the auspices of the Lincoln County Historical Society the old lighthouse was saved from certain demolition. A historical building listed in the National Register, it houses marine memorabilia of the past, but most of its publicity revolves around its ghostly past.

Muriel Tevenard is said to have lost her life at the Yaquina Bay Lighthouse under bizarre circumstances. The legend goes back a century when Muriel arrived with her father on a vessel from Coos Bay which allegedly crossed Yaquina bar to allow the crew to refill the water kegs. Her tall, dark father of gentle breeding, believed by some to have been the ship's captain, left his daughter in care of the hotel landlady while he traveled south. Alone in a strange town, the young girl had somewhat of a solitary existence, wiling her hours away sketching or taking long walks on the beach below the abandoned lighthouse. One day she was befriended by a group of

The ghostly old Baranof's Castle, built in 1837, is pictured here about 1890, long after it had outlived its usefulness. Note the cupola atop the structure, where the Russians established Alaska's first lighthouse. It was in this old structure that it was said the ghost of a lovely maiden of royalty swished about in her flowing gowns mourning the loss of her loved one. The structure burned to the ground in 1894.

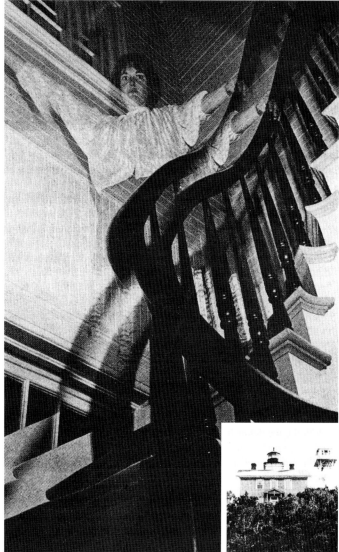

campers. After a few days exploring the area the group decided one dark night to visit the abandoned lighthouse. A mantle of fog dropped its veil over the scene as they approached. Muriel was accompanied by a young man who had been attracted by her charm.

As they entered the dark confines, the circular wooden staircase was before them winding up to the second story. Amid an eerie atmosphere that always pervades an empty structure on a black night, the group spoke in hushed tones, the boys acting bravely and the girls frightened and giddy. On the second landing the group found a closet where a piece of metal covered a dark hole, probably the hollow trunk once used to drop the weights that turned the lens. The discovery led to all kinds of explanations and an accompanying sense of dread. Down the stairs they scurried like frightened rabbits as if a creature from Hell would rise from the black hole.

As they ran out the front door, Muriel remembered she had left her gloves and decided to re-enter the domain. Her beau urged her to forget them but she insisted and went back in by herself.

"Let's get out of here," the others cried, but they held their ground waiting for Muriel. When she didn't return they thought she was playing a trick by leaving through the kitchen door at the rear of the lighthouse. The group questioned one another as to her whereabouts.

Screams were suddenly heard from the edifice, chilling cries that pierced the night air like a sharp knife. Trying to open the front door they found it was latched from the inside. Muriel could be found nowhere. The group left in terror still not certain the young girl wasn't playing on their emotions.

When a search party went up the next day trying to find the girl, pools of blood were evident on the staircase and near the closet with the black hole. Ironically, Muriel was never seen or heard from again, nor did her father ever return for her. Since that time, almost a century ago, claims of Muriel's ghost have been advanced. Many strange events that have occurred around the premises through the years are attributed to her strange disappearance.

The Coast Guard lookout tower stands opposite the old lighthouse, and on occasion men on duty there have mentioned strange lights in the otherwise empty lantern house, perhaps the reflection of the moon, or the figment of the imagination, but nevertheless visible in one form or another. In one instance a Coastguardsman reported seeing the glow of a swinging lamp coming toward the watch tower. As it drew closer it seemed as though a figure held the light in hand. When switching on the watch tower floodlight nothing was there. It is

Ghosts don't show up in a photograph, so the trick photography of Dennis Mavity reproduced the ghost of Muriel which reputedly has haunted the old Yaquina Bay Lighthouse for decades. The wraith is seen on the wooden circular staircase at the lighthouse. Courtesy Newport News Times.

A vintage photo of Yaquina Head Lighthouse at sunset just before the keeper was ready to light the oil lamp. Taken around the turn of the century, all of the original station buildings were still in use.

forbidden to drink on duty so perhaps the report had a modicum of truth. No one has tried to put to rest the story of Muriel and her ghost and as long as the old lighthouse stands, her specter will never die and it will not fade away.

Ghost fever also pervades the nearby Yaquina Head Lighthouse. During its construction in 1872, the story goes, one of the workers fell from the top of the masonry tiers tumbling to his death between the double walls. Rather than recovering the body from the narrow niche, the corpse was allegedly entombed inside, and the vents sealed, closing off any access to that portion of the structure. Ever since, it has been claimed that the ghost of the victim has haunted the tower. Though the story has little foundation, it is no secret that the Yaquina lighthouse is a spooky place on a windy night and certainly condusive to all kinds of weird imaginations of the mind.

Keeper John Zenor, who put in 22 years of duty at Yaquina Head, reaffirmed that the place had its own ghost and that the attendants always accepted it as fact. He and others manning the light said they would frequently hear somebody enter the tower and come up the spiral staircase.

"Everyone heard the specter," said Zenor, "but after the war (WWII), we never heard him again."

Hollywood's Universal Studios perpetuated the ghostly reputation of the lighthouse in 1977 when producers of a Nancy Drew TV production used it as a major attraction. The premises were temporarily taken over by the movie staff after the prop crew gave the formidable tower the haunted look both on the interior and exterior. The transition was remarkably realistic, an aspect that amazed Tom McManus who was at the time chief of the Newport Coast Guard Station, overseers of the lighthouse.

Between the Yaquina Bay Lighthouse and the tower at Yaquina Head a resort hotel was built at Monterey Beach between present-day Nye and Agate beaches in the 1880's. It was constructed by Tom Briggs who was married to an Indian woman. One night, a gale was lashing the seas as he was returning to the hotel by horse. While attempting to cross a rain-swollen creek, a sneaker breaker engulfed him and his mount sweeping them to sea, never to be seen again. His beautiful daughter, a student of music, was torn by the shocking loss of her father and fatally shot herself in her room.

For years after, residents of the area claimed they saw her ghostly figure walking the beach on stormy nights in search of her father.

A factual story involving latter day pirates took place off the Umpqua River Lighthouse in the summer of 1910. This involved the coastwise passenger steamer *Buckman* and two pirates whose nefarious schemes came within an eyelash of succeeding.

French West, a 30 year old sailor, planned his scheme while hanging around the San Francisco waterfront. He conned an old Navy buddy George Washington Wise, a merchant mariner, to be part of his scheme. West had made several trips to Alaska as a seaman and knew that vessels in the trade frequently returned with large amounts of gold bound for the mint in San Francisco. He induced Wise to go to Seattle with him to await a southbound sailing. The plan was to hijack the ship, holdup the crew and make off with the gold. The grandiose plan included knocking out the wireless and running the vessel aground on an isolated section of the Oregon coast.

Carefully, West worked out the details. Traveling north on the SS *Beaver,* the freebooters obtained a double-barreled shotgun, a revolver and 50 short lengths of cord for tying the hands of the crew. They then got steerage accommodations on the southbound sailing of the Alaska Pacific Navigation Company's steamer *Buckman.* With weapons hidden in their gear, they boarded the ship just before sailing time on August 19.

Just after midnight on August 21, the villains struck. The steamer was 20 miles due west of the Umpqua Lighthouse, the maximum range of its powerful Fresnel. West knew that only two men were on duty in the wheelhouse on the midnight to 4 A.M. watch. They crept silently up the companionway to the bridge deck and entered the dimly lit pilot house. Startled by their presence were second mate Fred Plath and quartermaster Otto Kocklmeister.

*Lifting its graceful form, Umpqua Lighthouse built in 1894, was shining its beacon seaward in 1910 when a modern day pirate known as French West, and his cohort, attempted to hijack the SS **Buckman**, purloin the gold she reputedly carried and run the ship aground on a hidden stretch of the central Oregon Coast.*

The famous "Heceta House" which has been the storied abode of mystical happenings down through the years was the former principal keeper's dwelling. The upper photo was taken in the 1920s when there were two keepers dwellings. The one on the left was torn down several years ago. The one on the right still stands and is known as Heceta House, utilized by Lane Community College. In the lower photo the dwelling is pictured through the Needle's Eye. The top of the arc has since eroded away leaving only a rock spike standing. Heceta Lighthouse is pictured at the left. Photos courtesy of Bob DeRoy, whose father Frank DeRoy was former head keeper at Heceta.

"What are you doing here?" snapped the mate.

West whipped out his shotgun and pointed it at Plath. "Stretch out on the deck," he demanded, "or I'll blast your head off!"

The mate had no choice but to obey. The helpless quartermaster stood ridgedly, cursing under his breath as Wise pressed a revolver against the back of his head.

West demanded the whereabouts of the ship's master, Captain Edwin B. Wood, and was told he was asleep in his cabin. West then ordered Wise to hold the two men at bay in the wheelhouse while he found his way to the skipper's cabin on the deck below. Breaking into the captain's cabin, the culprit took the slumbering skipper by surprise. Sensing danger, Wood reached for his revolver, but trigger-happy West emptied both barrels. Blood streaming from his wounds, the shipmaster fell prostrate to the deck, and died.

The loud blast alarmed Wise who stepped out on the bridge wing to see what had happened. Kocklmeister, still at the helm, seized the opportunity to pull the whistle cord. West leaped topside shouting words of profanity, and demanded to know who sounded the whistle. Wise pointed his finger at the quartermaster. Enraged, West rammed his weapon into the man's face and threatened to pull the trigger when suddenly the sound of running feet diverted his attention. Chief mate Richard Brennan rushed in to investigate and in turn was ordered to raise his hands high and stand against the port bridge railing. Plath was then told to stand alongside the chief mate.

Chief engineer John Callfass and other crewmen came running forward but were forced against the railing at gunpoint. The dastardly plot appeared to be succeeding, though the murder of the captain had not been part of the plan. The larger portion of the crew were already immobilized. The situation was grave.

West ordered Wise to go to the wireless room and smash all the apparatus, but the latter lost his nerve, went below and hid himself. West was now a solo act.

"I'll kill every last one of you," he threatened, "I'll take the ship single handed if I have to."

Still another crewman approached the bridge from the starboard side of the wheelhouse and momentarily diverted West's attention. Callfass seized the opportunity and leaped from the bridge deck through the nearby skylight crashing to the galley below. Amid the shattering glass the crew scattered in all directions leaping over rails and down ladders. West pursued them screaming that he would kill them all.

In the darkness, Brennan made his way to the captain's cabin and secured a pistol. In the shadows, he made his way back to the bridge undetected and motioned for the quartermaster to remain silent at the wheel until West returned. They didn't have to wait long.

"Drop your gun and put up your hands!" roared Brennan to the pirate.

Unable to see the chief mate, West fired indiscriminately. His shots missed, but one bullet struck the wheel and knocked out a spoke. The quartermaster stood like a ramrod, but was not hit. Brennan and West then fired at each other. The culprit may have been hit. He bolted out the door, down the ladder, darted aft and flung himself over the side into the black vortex. He was never seen again.

A search of the ship found the accomplice in his bunk whining hysterically. Offering no resistance he was clamped in irons.

Brennan took command and brought the ship into San Francisco Bay the following day. A police launch was standing by to pick up Wise who was later arraigned on a charge of murder and piracy on the high seas which carried a mandatory death penalty. The case, however, never came to trial. On November 4, 1919 George Washington Wise was pronounced insane and placed in a mental institution.

Had it not been for Wise's breakdown under the pressure, West might have succeeded in his hijacking effort. Ironically, on that voyage the *Buckman* carried not a single ounce of gold.

Heceta Head Lighthouse is in an unrivaled setting on a bold promontory of the central Oregon coast. The natural surroundings dispell any ghostly thoughts. However "Heceta House," once the

St. George Reef Lighthouse, the most costly ever built by Uncle Sam, marks the place of many deaths, both on ships and attendants of the light.

abode of the keeper-in-charge, is rated by one nationally known commentator as among the ten most haunted edifices in the country. The gracious old home constructed in the early 1890's is no longer used by the Coast Guard, but is in the National Register and under the auspices of Lane Community College which utilizes it for various functions. The lighthouse, located 700 feet from the dwelling, is maintained by the Coast Guard and continues to show its flashing light over the vast Pacific. Ghosts appear to have spared the tower for the most part, having become associated with the residence.

The ghostly reputation of Heceta House goes back many years and received attention recently when a nationally syndicated television movie production entitled *Cry for a Stranger* was filmed there. Staring several well known personalities, the spooky production centered around Heceta House with many of the scenes filmed in and around the old dwelling.

The late Oswald Allik, who served for several years in the U. S. Lighthouse Service and remained after the Coast Guard took over that service in 1939, was the last keeper of the Heceta station before it was automated in the 1960's. He and his wife Alice spent a large portion of their time conducting courtesy tours for thousands of visitors. Always the subject would turn to the dwelling in which they lived and the stories of its sinister reputation as a haunted house. It had long been rumored by previous occupants that unexplained, mysterious events had taken place in the upper rooms and attic where odd noises were heard from time to time. Doors left ajar would slam shut, closed windows would suddenly open, and tools and other articles would either disappear or be found in some other location. Many believed the dwelling was haunted by one or more ghosts.

Though the dwelling was off limits to the general public, Mrs. Allik was often questioned about the house. She emphatically insisted it was all "hogwash."

"We've lived here for months," she would say, "I'm all over the house everyday and here all night and I've never seen any ghosts or unusual happenings."

Few would believe her because nobody wanted to take intrigue away from the historic mansion. When Ossie was asked the same questions he would neither affirm or deny a ghost's existence, but just left the inquirer dangling. He was a genial man who never liked to deflate anybody. Though he took ghosts lightly, he had spent 20 years out on lonely Tillamook Rock Light and was well aware of the spook that lurked about the premises there. Further he accepted the unwritten tradition that every genuine lighthouse had its special phantom.

Supernatural tales still prevail at Heceta House and, whether true or false, remain in the minds of the hearers.

Harry Tammen, of Yachats, caretaker of Heceta House (1985) reported that while he, his wife and guests were playing cards at the edifice one night, they were shaken up by a shrill scream that sent chills down their spines. On investigation they were unable to find anybody near the place.

On another occasion Tammen discovered that rat poison in the attic had been mysteriously exchanged for a silk stocking.

A worker involved in the remodeling of Heceta House was cleaning an attic window when he caught a strange reflection. On turning around he saw a gray-haired elderly woman in an 1890's style gown. Hastily he left the attic in somewhat of a panic. Later while at work on the exterior of the house he accidently broke an attic window and left shattered glass on the inside. That same night, unaware of the workers mishap, the Tammens were suddenly awakened by a noise in the attic. It sounded as though someone was sweeping up glass. The following day, they found the broken glass swept neatly in a pile.

The lighthouse, (established March 30, 1894) Heceta House, garage and two oil houses have been in the National Register since 1978.

Rising like a medieval castle from the depths six miles off the rugged northern California coast, St. George Reef Lighthouse smacks of intrigue and mystery. The most expensive lighthouse ever constructed by Uncle Sam, its nonconformity architecture, dressed in huge blocks of granite, has made it a phenomenal monstrosity since 1892. The Coast Guard abandoned the tower May 13, 1975, prompted by its high cost of maintenance and danger to personnel. It was left in solitude virtually intact until 1983, when service personnel returned to remove the French-made, first order Fresnel lens, and deliver it to the Del Norte County Historical Society at Crescent City, where it will be displayed for posterity. With considerable difficulty, the gorgeous glass fixture was dismantled and shipped to its new home, only a few chips in the lenses occurring during the operation. The tower was locked up once again to waste away against the punishing elements of nature, sometimes producing waves that inundate the great tower with awesome clout.

Though the St. George sentinel could be the background for a real mystery story, its distance from the mainland and lack of familiarity with the general public has left it one of the hidden secrets of Americana. It was one of the world's great engineering triumphs, built at a cost of three-quarters of a million dollars, taking a decade to complete. To replace it today would demand an outlay of multi-millions of dollars.

Of all the dramatic episodes connected with the lighthouse, one tragic circumstance stands out. It was on April 5, 1951 that the St. George Reef crew was readying the station launch to be lowered by boom and sling, downward to a disturbed ocean. At the boat's wheel was Coastguardsman Stanley Costello; Ross Vandenberg was positioned atop the cabin where he could unhook the craft from the cable once waterborne, and Thomas Mulcahy was at the stern handling the mooring line. Altogether, five station attendants were aboard the motor launch including Coastguardsmen Walker and Becket. Officer-in-charge Fred Permenter at the derrick control on the landing platform eyed the pulsating swells and then lowered away.

The confused seas roared around the inundated reef at the base of the lighthouse. As the boat hit the water it was caught between the trough of two giant waves. In a moment of terror one of the rising walls of brine caught the craft and drove it unceremoniously toward the reef. Backlash from the watery mountain cascaded down like an avalanche, throwing the helpless occupants into the vortex. Though each wore a lifejacket the surging waters canted them about like bits of driftwood.

Those on the landing platform above looked on in horror. Permenter immediately dispatched a Mayday message to the Humboldt Bay Coast Guard Station and then seized the only hope of rescue still available to him, the rubber liferaft. It had broken free from the launch and was drifting about. Without regard for his life, he climbed down the iron ladder to the base of the tower and then jumped 20 feet into the water. Swimming through the turbulence he struggled onto the raft. Awkwardly jockeying the conveyance, he went first to the aid of two victims he thought were drifting away from the reef, but found they had managed to cling to a mooring buoy. Satisfied that they could survive, he struggled toward the other three. One was alive but unconscious. Though nearly exhausted himself, Permenter managed to get the man into the raft. A fourth man was dead, and lacking the strength to get him on the raft he let him drag astern on a rope end. The fifth victim could not be found.

The rescue boat at Humboldt Bay was a considerable distance from the scene so the group commander at the Eureka station solicited the assistance of veteran Coastguardsman Wayne Piland at Crescent City, who with his son Donald, home on leave from the Navy, engaged a fast commercial fishboat to make a run to the reef. Lines were cast loose from the dragger *Winga*, and she pointed her bow seaward into the chop. After a rough trip, the rescue vessel managed

Scotch Cap Lighthouse, a concrete reinforced structure built in 1940 to replace the aging sentinel, was the target of a devastating seismic tidal wave in 1946 that completely destroyed the building and took the lives of its five Coast Guard attendants. U.S. Coast Guard photo.

This was the scene at Scotch Cap before the great wave of 1946 struck. At the far left is the former lighthouse and the new lighthouse. Center right are the three keepers dwellings and other outbuildings, and abutting the dwellings is the wreck of the Japanese freighter **Koshun Maru** *which stranded there in 1930. Everything along the side of the cape was carried into oblivion with the exception of the D/F station at the very top of the cape. The crest of the wave slopped over unto the plateau, 100 feet above the sea. U.S. Coast Guard photo.*

Scotch Cap, after the watery fusillade. Note what remains of the lighthouse, lower right. The beach was swept clean of everything as if the devil had employed an army of supersized bulldozers. U.S. Coast Guard photo.

---

to pluck Permenter and the two clinging to the buoy, Mulcahy and Vandenberg from the water, still conscious. Electricians' mate Beckett was out cold, but still breathing. The other two were dead. Attempts to revive Beckett were continued all the way back to port. An ambulance and doctor were waiting at the Citizen's Dock in Crescent City but the victim was pronounced dead on arrival.

The local newspaper screamed of the awful tragedy. Fear fell upon the men at the lighthouse who had come out to relieve the victims. Would they be next?

Historian Ralph C. Shanks Jr. in his *Lighthouses and Lifeboats On The Redwood Coast,* recounts the accidental death of two other individuals in the early history of St. George Reef Lighthouse, which

with the 1951 tragedy, brought the total to five, the worst in California lighthouse history. In 1952, a year after the tragedy, a keeper had to be removed from the lighthouse suffering a mental breakdown. As it turned out, the winter of 1952 was one of if not the worst ever recorded in the lighthouse log. During one of many gales, winds generated waves of tremendous proportions. Breasting the worst that mother nature could hurl, the fortress-like tower shouldered seas that swept over the top of the tower and lantern house, 146 feet above sea level, knocking out several lantern panes and showering the interior with broken glass.

St. George Reef Light became known as the "sentinel of death," and a public outcry demanded better safeguards for those who manned it. Limited space prohibited the use of a helicopter, and the time of automation had not yet arrived. Thus the transport of attendants still had to be by water, but ever after, a Coast Guard cutter always stoodby during the transfer of personnel.

It happened again in 1958, when the station boat was flipped by the seas, throwing four occupants into the chilling water. Fortunately, the cutter *Ewing* was standing by and hasty action by her skipper saved the lives of the floundering victims.

After 1960, until the station was abandoned, the 95 foot cutter *Cape Carter* stationed at Crescent City, was the standby vessel for St. George Light. A unique method of transferring attendants to and from the lighthouse platform was devised. The *Carter* landed personnel by coming slowly under the long lighthouse boom, as close to the reef as possible. When ensconsed in the "Billy Pugh" net, personnel could be conveyed three at a time. When the cutter rose on a swell, the net was hooked to the boom cable and as the vessel backed off the men would be lifted to the platform above. It took tricky maneuvering but it proved to be a much safer method.

When buoy tenders or larger cutters brought supplies, fuel or water they had to stand well off the reef. Whenever possible moderate sea and weather conditions were sought for transfer of personnel and supplies.

Today, neglected and weather-beaten, awaiting her fate, the tower is so well constructed that it may stand till the end of the age, nuclear attack or not, a fabulous monument of the sea.

It has been said by those on vessels passing the massive St. George tower that the smell of death pervades its sinister presence, yet one can't help but be impressed with this the greatest of American lighthouses. In the depths off the reef lies the wreck of the steamer *Brother Jonathan,* which foundered July 30, 1865 carrying 200 souls to a watery grave.

A terrible tragedy of yet another kind tore a reinforced concrete lighthouse from its foundation and killed its five attendants. Scotch Cap Lighthouse on Alaska's Unimak Island was the victim of a devastating seismic tidal wave on that fateful April Fools Day in 1946.

The two lighthouses on Unimak Island, Scotch Cap and Sarichef, are among the loneliest in the world. When serving as manned stations the duty was subject to severe privation. When automation came there were no tears shed by those who had put in long, dreary months of isolation.

At the time of the Scotch Cap disaster, the light keepers had neighbors atop the 100 foot rocky plateau above the lighthouse. It was a direction finder station (Unimak Radio D/F Station). Those two installations, and the Sarichef Lighthouse at the west end of the island, all Coast Guard-manned, housed the only inhabitants of that basaltic piece of real estate. Situated on the side of a precipitous cliff, Scotch Cap Lighthouse, was 17 miles from its counterpart light across the desolate island where only the most rugged of beasts eked out an existence. In this Aleutian area of volcanic eruptions, landslides and earthquakes, it smacks of an earthly Hell, and that's exactly what it was on that first day of April in 1946.

At the D/F station it was not uncommon to feel small earthquakes, each tremor being logged. On that particular occasion the man on duty looked out into the blackness of the night, the only cheering sight being the beacon from the lighthouse below cutting the night air with its golden glow. Suddenly he felt a tremor of long duration that rattled the loose items about him. His buddy came in to discuss the situation and of course the April Fool concept entered the conversation. A short time later there was a severe shock and the watchman recorded the following entry:

"0130: Severe earthquake felt. Building rocked severely. Objects shaken from locker shelves. Duration approximately 30-40 seconds.

Building creaked and groaned but no apparent damage. Weather clear, calm."

To help pass the time the D/F man made contact by radiophone with the keeper on watch at the lighthouse. He too, reported having felt the tremor but likewise reported no damage. While the two conversed there came still another severe shock and they signed off to check for damage. The D/F log entry read:

0157: Second severe quake felt. Shorter in duration but harder than at 0130...again no apparent damage although buildings shook severely."

By now the officer-in-charge of the D/F station, slightly alarmed by the tremors, put in an appearance. Suddenly the men heard a muffled sound like rolling thunder. It grew louder and louder. Then exploding, almost like a cannon, all hell broke loose. A power-packed watery wall 100 feet high had slammed into Unimak head-on, merciless, awesome, destructive. The barage breached the beach below and climbed up the cliff like an army of 10,000 men bent on total annihilation of the enemy.

Standing in a film of salt-water, the officer-in-charge immediately ordered the remainder of his six man crew to grab warm clothes and head for higher ground, that another wave, even more powerful might erupt and bash in the station walls. Though there was some hesitation, the men reluctantly agreed to go except for the one on watch who felt it his duty to stand by his post. When the door was opened the first man out stopped with alarm. "The light!" he exclaimed. "Scotch Cap Light! It's gone out!"

The men looked down the cliff into dark nothingness. No radio or phone contact could be established. Certainly they reasoned, the five light keepers were all right. After all it was a concrete reinforced structure with walls two feet thick. Built in 1940, it had replaced the former frame lighthouse, constructed in 1903. They could only speculate on the situation till the dawn of April Fool's Day. It came as a terrible shock. Below them, lay the knarled wreckage of broken concrete and twisted steel. The lighthouse had been brutishly destroyed as had the nearby radio beacon tower, the former keepers homes and the rusted steel hull of the Japanese freighter *Koshun Maru* prominent on the beach since being wrecked in 1930. Dante himself could not have painted a more depressing scene of devastation.

The wildest thoughts that passed through the minds of the D/F personnel prior to daybreak were nothing compared to what they now viewed. Their earlier frustrations were evident. At 0218 the D/F officer-in-charge had sent the following message by radio:

"Heard terrific roaring of the sea followed by huge sea immediately. The top of the wave rose above the cliff back of Scotch Cap Light Station and struck D/F Station causing considerable damage. Crew ordered to higher ground. Can't make radio contact."

The building's lights had flickered in eerie pattern. A slight reflection in the distant clouds indicated that the Cape Sarichef Light was still in operation, affording only momentary comfort.

When the telephone rang, the officer grabbed it hoping that it might be from below, but alas, it was the keeper at Sarichef. Members of the D/F crew took turns venturing to the edge of the cliff listening for cries of help, but at 0245, hope having been lost, the following message was dispatched to the Coast Guard headquarters:

"Scotch Cap believed lose; light extinguished and horn silent.

By 3 A.M. when no subsequent quakes or sound of roaring waves were detected, the officer-in-charge thought it safe to return to the D/F station to pick up supplies and necessary equipment. The message sent out at 0345 read: "Sea seems to be moderating. Still no wind but clouding up. Heavy roaring from ocean but seems to be quieting. Light station total loss, all hands."

The dispatch of 0700 told it best. "Went to light station; debris strewn all over place. Piece of human intestine found on hill."

Eldred Rock Lighthouse located on Lynn Canal in Southeastern Alaska appears small beneath high mountain peaks of the Inside Passage. It was there that the remains of the ill-fated steamer Clara Nevada were mysteriously lifted from one location to another in the year 1908, three years after the establishment of the light. The ship was wrecked mysteriously in 1898 with her company of about 100—no survivors. Callarman photo.

At daybreak the Coastguardsmen struggled down the jagged cliff and rummaged through the wreckage but were unable to find any bodies, no equipment, no papers. It was over a week before the sea gave up other pieces of the mutilated bodies—a sickening episode that remained indelible in the minds of the survivors.

For the next two weeks the ground periodically rumbled from small tremors, and to a lesser degree until mid-April, keeping the men constantly on their toes. In the interim, repair crews arrived to inspect the damage and to lay out plans for a new lighthouse at a higher elevation where such a villainous act of nature could not be repeated.

The Coast Guard credited the chief officer of the D/F station with using good sense in ordering his men to higher ground after the wave struck for fear of a second blockbuster.

Spawned by an Aleutian cataclysmic undersea eruption in a deep fissure, the frightful seismic tidal waves that struck Unimak went roaring southward through the Pacific at speeds of 500 miles-an-hour, striking Hawaii, Oahu, Maui and Molokai. No less than 160 lives were lost and numerous other persons were injured, the damage running into the millions of dollars.

An epistle of profound mystery surrounds the Eldred Rock Lighthouse on Lynn Canal along Alaska's inside passage. Lonely and enticing, the lighthouse continues to blink its light at a steady parade of vessels navigating those fabulous and intricate waterways, including scores of summertime luxury cruise ships.

Our story goes back to 1898 and involved the SS *Clara Nevada,* converted from the government survey vessel *Hassler* to a passenger ship for service in the booming Alaska goldrush trade. Though the steamer had seen better days anything that floated during that period was pressed into service to meet the demands. Inspection laws were lax and fares were high.

Departing Dyea, Alaska on the bleak winter evening of February 5, 1898 under the command of Captain C. H. Lewis, the vessel was southbound with officers and crew numbering 39 and an estimated passenger list of about 65, bringing to about 100 the number of persons aboard. Nobody really knows what happened, but hours later in the teeth of a howling gale and rough seas she reputedly caught on fire off Berners Bay and then passed into oblivion for an entire week. Then one day the crew of the steamer *Rustler,* out of Juneau, sighted rigging protruding from the water off Eldred Rock. They could find no survivors and only one body, that of the purser. It was the wreck of the *Clara Nevada.*

Newspaper headlines reported the tragedy. Charges and counter-charges followed. The owners, the newly formed Pacific and Alaska Transporation Company were taunted by the public claiming the ship was unseaworthy. On her earlier departure from Seattle on January 27, the *Clara Nevada* had backed into the Revenue Cutter *Grant.* That incident marked the start of an ill-fated voyage that would be the topic of conversation for months thereafter. One of the passengers that debarked at Skagway before the vessel's disappearance said he "felt the impending disaster in his bones." He claimed on the trip north the steamer rammed every pier where they tried to dock and that three boiler flues blew out before reaching Juneau. The waters were so rough that most of the passengers were seasick, and further he noted intoxication among the ship's officers amid volleys of profanity. Others refuted his claims insisting that the officers were men of good reputation, Captain Lewis, a veteran of 20 years with the Oregon Railway and Navigation Company and Pacific Coast Steamship Company. Sometime later, wreckers moved in where the sunken hulk lay and managed to remove machinery, donkey engines, and other gear, leaving the wreck to rot away in solitude, a grim tombstone to the missing souls that had once peopled her decks. It was theorized that in a desperate attempt to keep the fire from reaching powder and dynamite in the cargo, control of the ship was lost in the blinding storm and she was driven onto the outcrops of Eldred's sharp clutches. Fire hose was found reeled out on the sunken wreck attached to hydrants and coupled to the pumps.

It was an unfortunate fact that no lighthouse had yet been built on Eldred Rock. In fact, it was not until 1905, seven years after the tragic loss of the *Clara Nevada* that a lighthouse was commissioned there. One night in 1908 the keepers of the light were huddled against the station stove in the lighthouse kitchen listening to a howling wind sweeping up Lynn Canal. Unknown to them the rising waters mysteriously lifted the ghostly hull from the rocks and moved it to the south section of the rocky islet. When discovered after the storm, the keepers recovered some human bones inside the weed draped, teredo riddled confines. Ever after, when ghostly subjects were discussed by the keepers of the light, the *Clara Nevada* was involved. Spirits of the dead who perished in the deep seemed to hold a shroud over the forlorn lighthouse on Eldred Rock. Nor was it forgotten that in 1898, at the peak of the goldrush, some 34 shipwrecks occurred in southeastern Alaska sealanes, then virtually unmarked by aids to navigation. It was a regrettable oversight by Uncle Sam that the Inside Passage lacked a major lighthouse until the Southeast Five Finger and Sentinel Island lights were established in 1902.

A true story often mentioned by the old light keepers concerned a tiny lighthouse located on lonely Clipperton Island a few hundred miles off the west coast of Mexico. Clipperton was named for a mutineer—John Clipperton, the first mate of an English sailing vessel who had led 21 confederates in seizing their vessel in 1704. They turned pirate and made the island their stronghold for eight years until Clipperton was captured and hanged by the British.

In 1897, a shipwreck deposited 36 English castaways on the uninhabited island. The wreck's master created chaos among the survivors by spreading a tale that the deposed pirate Clipperton had buried a rich treasure somewhere on the island. During the wild melee that broke out in search of the treasure chest, things got totally out of hand before a British warship finally arrived and put an end to the six weeks of bloody privation.

Mexico attempted to enforce its claim to the island in 1908 by settling 29 men, 13 wives and several children there. In 1914 Mexico was torn by revolution, and the tiny colony was forgotten. Supply ships failed to bring badly needed food. The following year scurvy swept the settlement. The frustrated leader of the group thought he saw a rescue ship, only a mirage, and in turn ordered all the men except the island's lighthouse keeper to row out and intercept it. Those watching from shore saw the men arguing violently, apparently about their leader's hallucination. In the fracas that followed, the skiff overturned throwing its occupants into the sea, riddled with hungry sharks. There was not a survivor among them.

The helpless women on the island were thereafter harassed by the lighthouse keeper who turned them into his private harem, forcing them to submit to his personal desires by threatening their children. His brutal treatment caused such anger among the women that on July 8, 1917, one of their number grabbed a hand ax and crushed in the keeper's skull.

Ironically, the same day, the American gunboat *Yorktown* reached the troubled island and removed the survivors, three women and eight children.

A further irony came in 1930 when Mexico, the only nation to try to colonize the island, lost its claim. Mexico, England and France each put forth their claims, and King Victor Emmanuel of Italy was asked to arbitrate. France got the nod and still holds sway over that remote isle of sorrows.

In what ſtate.	Where ſituated.	Number.	Superintendents.	Keepers.
New Hampſhire	New-Caſtle Iſland, near Portſmouth	One	Joſeph Whipple	Titus Salter
Maſſachuſetts	Nantucket Iſland	One	Benjamin Lincoln	Paul Pinkham
Ditto	Thatcher's Iſland	Two	Ditto	Joſeph Soward
Ditto	Plumb Iſland, near Newbury Port	Two	Ditto	Abner Lowell
Ditto	Portland Head	One	Ditto	Joſeph Greenleaf
Ditto	Light-houſe Iſland, in Boſton bay	One	Ditto	Thomas Knox
Ditto	On the Gurnet, near Plymouth	1 with 2 lanterns	Ditto	John Thomas
Rhode-Iſland	On Conanicut Iſland	One	William Ellery	William Martin
Connecticut	At the mouth of Thames River	One	Jedediah Huntington	Daniel Harris
New-Jerſey	Sandy-Hook, New-York Bay	One	Tho. Randall, of N.Y.	Matthew Ely
Delaware	Cape-Henlopen, Delaware Bay	One	Wm. Allibone, of Ph.	Abraham Hargis
Virginia	Cape Henry, Cheſapeak Bay	One	William Lindſay	Laban Goffigan
North-Carolina	Cape-Fear Iſland (nearly completed)	One		
South-Carolina	Middle-Bay Iſland, near Charleſton	One	Edward Blake	Thomas Holling
Georgia	Tybee Iſland, near Savannah	One	John Haberſham	

State of the Light Houſes[a] erected on the headlands and iſlands of the United States.

* N. B. Theſe, and all the beacons, buoys, public piers, and ſtakeages, for the protection and guidance of ſhips under the ſuperintendence of the Commiſſioner of the Revenue, in the department of the treaſury of the United Sta.

Complete list of lighthouses and keepers, five years after the setting up of the United States government. List is reprinted from the United States Register, circa 1794, more than a half century before the first government lighthouse was established on the Pacific Coast.

CHAPTER FOUR

California Lighthouses, Southern Sector

"...from each projecting cape
And perilous reef along the ocean's verge.
Starts into life a dim, gigantic shape,
Holding its lantern o'er the restless surge.
——Longfellow

California has one of the nation's lengthiest coastlines dotted by numerous aids to navigation. In the heyday of the lighthouse, those sentinels were of paramount importance, especially to the large coastwise fleet that frequently hugged the shoreline. The seacoast of the Pacific states of California, Oregon and Washington under jurisdiction of the 11th, 12th and 13th Coast Guard Districts respectively, cover some 1,810 miles, but when adding the sounds, bays, inlets and rivers up to tidewater, that distance is expanded to 8,900 miles. Southern California's deepsea traffic constitutes some of the heaviest in the Pacific. True, the coastwise shipping that boomed up until World War II has been seriously eroded by land transport, but overseas shipping has expanded in both volume and in size of vessels. Aids to navigation are extremely important to modern shipping, but the radio electronic equipment has stolen the lead role from the traditional lighthouse, though many still survive and carry on a proud tradition that goes back to antiquity.

For decades, both commercial and naval vessels have transited the Silver Gate wherein lies the safe haven of San Diego Bay. Here California maritime history began in 1542. Located ten miles from the Mexican border it was for many years controlled by Spain. In September of the aforementioned year, Juan Rodriquez Cabrillo sailed his command into the bay and claimed it as one of the finest natural harbors in the world, affording excellent protection in all weather, free of excessive tidal currents. A low, narrow sandspit expanding to a width of 1.6 miles at North Island on its northwest end separates the bay from the ocean. Though no official documents survive, it is said that Spain maintained candles in metal frames or small fire braziers as aids to navigation as far back as the late 1700's. An order by ruling governor Jose Joaquin Arrillaga, dated July 2, 1806 provided for a beacon at the Castillo de los Guijarros, place of a battle in 1805 between Spanish San Diegans and Yankee sailors of the *Lelia Byrd,* (first American vessel to anchor there) but the Spaniards established nothing that would qualify as a genuine lighthouse.

Greater San Diego stands out today in broad contrast to the dusty little Spanish mission settlement of the yesteryears. The bay bristles with numerous aids to navigation, and trained pilots take large vessels in and out of the harbor always maintaining constant radio contact.

Two lighthouses have become as much a part of San Diego as are salt and pepper in a kitchen. Old Point Loma Lighthouse, one of the oldest on the coast, attracts lighthouse buffs, while its successor is of primary value to the navigator. The latter is situated 88 feet above the water and is shown from a black lantern house on a 70 foot white square pyramidal skeleton tower at the south end of the point. The station has a radio beacon, fog signal and a radio direction finder calibration station. Unlike most such installations today, a small contingent of Coast Guard personnel are attached to the station. Though great beds of kelp flourish offshore, the setting of the lighthouse is picturesque with well maintained out buildings, palm trees and sea-eroded cliffs with little sea caves. The lighthouse itself is not a classic structure, but has served its purpose well, demanding no major overhaul since its inception. The tower as of March 31, 1891 replaced the pioneer Point Loma Lighthouse atop the bold monolith.

The lower elevation better met navigation requirements, being freer from frequent fogs that obliterated the old lighthouse. Another area lighthouse was established August 1, 1890 at Ballast Point, a low, sandy projection less than a half mile northeast from the east side of Point Loma. That unique, little frame lighthouse whose initial keeper was a colorful old salt named David Splaine, has since been razed, and only a minor light and fog signal are there today. For many years the lantern's green glow kept ships in the proper channel.

Flashing its white light every 15 seconds, Point Loma Lighthouse has never produced great drama, for the most part, a utilitarian station always number one on the duty request list. Now, near the century mark of service, Point Loma Light is San Diego's friendly warden of the Silver Gate.

When it comes to history and color, the old sentinel at the top of the hill steals the show. It has become one, if not the most popular lighthouse attraction in the nation. The restored structure and surrounding park, form Cabrillo National Monument, honoring the discoverer of San Diego Bay. A statue of the renowned Spaniard is located 300 yards northeast of the lighthouse and ironically has been reported by pilots and navigators to be a better daymark than the old lighthouse when fog creeps up to the summit of the headland.

But let us go back to its inception. In the year 1851, the local news sheet reported that the U. S. Coast Survey was actively engaged in the survey of the harbor, preparatory to searching out a location for a government lighthouse. That same year, under the direction of George Davidson, the site was selected. Considerable delay followed, and it wasn't until April 8, 1854 that construction got underway. The contract was held by Gibbons and Kelly, and W. J. McManus who

Like a breath out of the past, old Point Loma Lighthouse, dating from the mid 1850s, lives on amid Cabrillo National Monument at the top of the rugged summit of Loma. Restored to its old condition in recent years, it is one of San Diego's prime attractions. Inset, Robert Decatur Israel, the last official keeper of the light from 1873-1891. The friendly old gentleman passed away in 1908. Courtesy San Diego Historical Society.

Point Loma Lighthouse as it appears today, one of California's most popular tourist attractions. Though its light is no longer an aid to navigation, having been replaced by the Point Loma Light at a lower elevation in 1891, it has been refurbished to appear as it did as one of the state's earliest lighthouses.

Point Loma Lighthouse has been the active beacon at the entrance to San Diego Bay since 1891, when it took over the duties from the pioneer structure atop Point Loma. The station is one of the most desired in the district. At right, the light sends out its friendly glow across the Silver Gate and out to sea. U.S. Coast Guard photo.

Ballast Point in San Diego Harbor was the site of a frame lighthouse built in 1890. After many years of service it was bugled out and eventually razed. Today Ballast Point Light B, is shown from a dolphin with a green and white diamond shaped daymark off the end of the point, less than a mile northeast from the east side of Point Loma. A naval submarine facility is nearby. U.S. Coast Guard photo.

represented the contractors, was in charge of the construction work. He found raw sandstone at Ballast Point and on Point Loma, but bricks, lime and lumber had to be shipped in, mostly from Monterey on the schooner *Vaquero*. The "lanterns and lenses are coming direct from Paris whence they have been ordered and will be of the latest improvement..." so reported the *San Diego Herald*.

An entourage of local folk climbed the hill daily to watch the progress. There was great jubilation when Point Loma's first lighthouse keeper, Captain James Keating, lit the two concentric wicks on November 15, 1855, producing the flame to illuminate the Fresnel lens. A brilliant fixed white light displayed its cheery glow from an elevation of 462 feet, and was reportedly visible 25 miles at sea, then the highest marine beacon in America. One master of a sailing vessel reported seeing its reflection in the clouds 39 miles offshore.

But all wasn't roses. During that first year, the lighthouse inspector, Major Bache, expressed his dissatisfaction. He complained to Captain Edmund Hardcastle, secretary of the Light-House Board in the nation's capital, that the tower was short two courses of brick and that he was compelled to order reconstruction work. Further, he claimed the cistern was too small, that it leaked and needed a cement and brick bottom. Exterior lighthouse bricks were of such poor quality that they had wasted away to a depth of two inches in some places.

It was suggested that McManus, and stonemason, Harvey Ladd may have substituted some mud bricks taken from the remains of the old Spanish Fort Guijarros. All of Bache's demands were met plus a new paint job.

That some of the bricks may have been from the Spanish fort led to the myth for many years that the lighthouse was of Spanish origin. It was, however, typically Yankee in design and construction being completed at a cost of $30,000, the second most costly of the original

California lighthouses. All materials had to be hauled up the steep, chaperal covered cliffs of Loma by beasts of burden which did little to keep the cost down. Originally, a first order lens was to have graced the lamproom, but owing to the diameter of the tower and lantern house, the smaller third order apparatus intended for Humboldt was substituted, negating alternate plans to reconstruct the tower. The first order lens was put in storage and eventually taken to Tatoosh Island for installation in Cape Flattery Lighthouse.

Point Loma Light was an economy structure combining the tower and the living quarters under one roof. There were living quarters for two keepers and their wives. When they had children, things got a bit crowded. To assist in paying for supplies, the personnel often doubled as whale watchers and would raise a flag when the leviathans were spouting. The local whaling vessels would then set to sea from Ballast Point. If a ship was sighted in trouble, the keeper would discharge a gun to alert the volunteer rescue crew.

Captain Robert D. Israel was principal keeper at the station from 1873 till 1891 when old Point Loma was abandoned. As a former Army veteran who fought in the Mexican War he and his Spanish wife Dona Maria Arcadia Alipas de Israel were devoted servants of the light and hosted numerous visitors during their long tenure.

After the old lighthouse was abandoned it fell into disrepair and would have passed into oblivion had not civic minded people in later years recognized the value of the structure. Eventually it was restored to its former status and placed on the National Register. It was also refurbished with period furniture to resemble its original character. Millions of visitors have come to the Cabrillo Monument and most of them have visited the lighthouse and walked up its narrow spiral staircase to the lantern room, where a lens removed from Mile Rocks Lighthouse on San Francisco Bay has been installed.

120 feet above the sea. Point Fermin is the southeast extremity of San Pedro Hill. A prominent pavilion (The Bell of Friendship) is above the light. The attraction in the park, however, continues to be the old lighthouse, one of a kind. It affords a pleasant breath of the past recalling other times when the edifice was in charge of Mary L. Smith, who with her sister, was awarded the job of lighthouse keeper at a time when the area was nothing more than a remote fishing village. They came in 1874 to find peace and healthful living, but after months of privation and loneliness decided that such a life was not for them, and in turn, tendered their resignations.

Despite the lighthouse at Point Fermin, the bay at that early period had many obstructions. The British ship *Respigadera* on a foggy October day in 1888, inbound from Austrilia, draped her frame over an outcrop right below the lighthouse. Salvors bought the hull for $1,200 and after removing deck gear dynamited the wreck as a menace to navigation.

When it comes to popular lighthouses in San Pedro Bay, none is better known than Los Angeles Light. The tower is 69 feet high, cylindrical in shape with black pilasters set on concrete, at the outer end of the San Pedro Breakwater. It is passed by every vessel moving in and out of the busy harbor, by nightfall, winking its green light like a happy sentry on duty. The nationally televised TV series *Love Boat*, nearly always shows the lighthouse as the *Pacific Princess* begins her weekly cruises. Equipped with light, fog signal radio beacon and special radio direction finder calibration station, it is an entity unto itself. A prominent feature since 1913, the lighthouse has had some interesting episodes during its tenure.

Since its early years it has been on a slight tilt due to a severe gale which spawned large breakers that slammed with tremendous force

Long Beach Harbor Light, better known as "the robot light," was built in 1949, as the first non-conformative lighthouse in California. Designed to withstand earthquake, wind and wave forces, it was from the start automated with 36-inch airway beacon, dual two-tone fog signals and radio beacon all incorporated within its monolithic frame. U.S. Coast Guard photo.

Early photo of the Los Angeles Harbor Lighthouse at the outer end of San Pedro Breakwater. It was built in 1913 and has been one of the port's most impressive monuments ever since. Coast and Geodetic Survey photo.

Moving northward along the California coast, is innovative Long Beach Harbor Light, often called "the robot light," a latter day design completed in 1949, featuring a white, rectangular tower on a building set on a columnar base, a total departure from the traditional lighthouse. Its unusual character is designed to hold it firm and safe in a California earthquake and seismic tidal waves. Situated in busy San Pedro Bay at the Middle breakwater, it is just one of numerous aids to navigation that mark the state's premier port, wherein lies the sprawling metropolis of Los Angeles of which San Pedro is the seaport.

Again it was the *Lelia Byrd*, Captain William Shaler, of New Bedford that was the first Yankee vessel to visit the port, in 1805. Nearly a half century later (1852) the steamer *Sea Bird* began regular service between Los Angeles and San Francisco. At that period no major lights marked the harbor, not until the Point Fermin Lighthouse, a Victorian frame structure was built in 1874. The lighthouse now restored as an historical attraction, unfortunately has been replaced by a utilitarian light shown from a pole at an elevation

into the lighthouse. For five days the onslaught continued. When the waters finally abated, the attendants complained of walking difficulties within the confines. Finding the lighthouse slightly out of balance, a plumb line was dropped from the lantern gallery to the ground which proved their suspicions. Not to worry, for the strong pilasters had been designed to give slightly in case of earthquake or tidal wave. Though the tower never resumed its original position, it has remained steady.

High seas have shattered windows in the tower 35 feet above the harbor entrance, nor has the structure been immune from ships that challenged its ramparts. A battleship years ago tried to scrape the tower off the charts when it struck the rocks directly below. The terrible grinding aged the keepers on duty when they looked out the windows and saw the menacing gray bulk only a stone's throw away.

That incident probably inspired Don Newman's tongue-in-cheek lines entitled, *Check your Bearings:*

"First voice: Our radar has you on a collision course with us. You should alter course 10 degrees south.

Second voice: We have you on our radar. Suggest you alter course 10 degrees north.

First voice: We have Admiral Goodman aboard. Strongly suggest you bear 10 degrees south, this is a battleship!

Second voice: This is seaman Farnsworth. Still suggest you bear 10 degrees north. This is a lighthouse!"

Prior to the erection of the lighthouse, the San Pedro Entrance Light was demolished on May 7, 1912 when the steamer *Roanoke* plowed through it like a seagoing bulldozer.

From the top of Los Angeles light tower, rising above the breakwater, a fantastic view presents itself both seaward and

Point Vicente Lighthouse is a familiar sight to those living in the greater Los Angeles area. Since 1926 it has played its guardian role and has been the backdrop for many movies and TV series. Coast Guard photo.

Greeter light for greater Los Angeles to the steady parade of ships entering San Pedro Harbor, Los Angeles Light has a personality all its own. Insert, upper left, displays a symphony of light by nightfall. U.S. Coast Guard photo.

landward. As a greeter light, it will remain a hallmark for greater Los Angeles for decades to come.

When the former diaphone foghorn sent out its roar some years ago, it set a world record. Though it may not be in the *Guiness Book of Records,* the United Fruit Company's steamer *Talamanca* picked up its signal a whopping 33 miles at sea.

Point Vicente Lighthouse is situated six miles northwest of Point Fermin and nine miles west of Los Angeles Light, displaying a group flashing light from the southwest end of the promontory. Its gentle lines which smack somewhat of Spanish architecture do justice to the 67 foot cylindrical tower which has frequently been used in movie and TV productions. In one play, the network was besieged with phone calls from irate watchers who weren't fooled by an attempt to pass the light off for one located in Hawaii, doubtless a move to hold down expenses. The producers should have known that such a prominent sea and landmark was one of a kind and could not be substituted.

Before the days of automation, Point Vicente was always a preferred duty station inasmuch as it was in the front yard of greater Los Angeles. There was a long waiting list, and keepers were always ready to make friends with the station ghost that appeared when the sharp beams of the beacon stabbed the night fog.

Several ships have been claimed by the rocky clutches below the lighthouse which unfortunately was not put into operation until 1926.

Anacapa Island, 11 miles southwest of Point Hueneme is the eastern-most of the northern Channel Islands group consisting of three islands separated by two very narrow openings, not sufficient for passage. The east opening is pockmarked with rocks and is bare. The west opening is only 50 feet wide and is blocked by sand, just the right size for a whale desiring a sunbath. Anacapa Island Lighthouse stands out in sharp contrast with the stark terrain at an elevation 277 feet above sea level on the eastern end of the island. Its strategic location at the east entrance to Santa Barbara Channel demands, in addition to the light, a fog signal and radio beacon. The lighthouse is automated but the Channel Islands, of which Anacapa is the most desired, is part of the Channel Islands National Monument. The only permanent residents are the park rangers who share their domain with scores of seals, sealions and pelicans.

There was agitation for a light at the location decades ago but the Lighthouse Board not wishing to pay the additional cost of an offshore beacon decided instead to build an economy lighthouse at Point Hueneme in 1874. Not until 1912 was a navigation light placed on Anacapa, that being an unmanned skeleton tower. With the increase of shipwreck and a commercial fishing boom in the area, a permanent lighthouse, of creative Spanish design with accompanying outbuildings was placed in operation in 1932, the last and one of the finest light stations constructed under the old Lighthouse Service.

Two years later, the wife of one of the assistant keepers, Mrs. Coursey, was critically injured in a fall. The principal keeper sent out radio message for assistance, and lo and behold, the call was answered by one of Uncle Sam's first-line battleships. It was a surprise to have the mammoth vessel anchor off the lighthouse and send in a boat for the injured woman. Due to prompt action by the crew of the dreadnaught, her life was saved.

The California Wreck Divers, an aquatic group, have made many dives on the wreck of the sidewheel steamer *Winfield Scott,* Captain Blunt, which crashed ashore off Anacapa in the fog on December 2, 1853. After all these years of languishing in the depths, the divers still bring up relics from the wreck which forced 250 passengers and crewmen to struggle for survival on Anacapa, living off fish and seabirds while awaiting rescue. Rumors claimed the vessel carried $150,000 in golddust, a tale never verified, but it is known that salvagers brought up a ship's chest in 1894, and never revealed its contents.

Anacapa Lighthouse, a gem in the rough on Anacapa Island, one of three islands in the Channel Islands National Monument. Built in 1932, and situated 277 feet above the sea, it continues its vigil, the former keepers dwelling now occupied by National Park rangers, the only inhabitants of the island. U.S. Coast Guard photo.

On the north side of the east entrance to Santa Barbara channel stands Point Hueneme Light, a white square tower on a rectangular building. The station was established in 1874. July through October keeps the station foghorn active when a frequent shroud hangs over the channel. There was excitement there in the spring of 1970 when the ex passenger liner *LaJanelle* lying at anchor awaiting plans for conversion to a floating restaurant was driven ashore and wrecked. The 465 foot vessel created a tourist attraction for several months.

Twenty-nine miles northwest of Point Hueneme is the resort city of Santa Barbara and two miles west of the harbor stands pint-sized Santa Barbara Light, a 24 foot tower, 142 feet above the ocean. It is a secondary light, but nearby is the location of the original Santa Barbara Light, built by George D. Nagle, which was one of California's pioneer watchtowers. It went into operation December 1, 1856, with Albert Johnson Williams as the initial guardian of the light. Nine years later, he turned the reins over to his wife Mrs. Julia F. Williams so he could pursue new avenues of employment. It was as though providence decreed it, for she not only excelled her husband at keeping a tidy lighthouse, but after the government made her position permanent on June 5, 1865, she was so dedicated to keeping the fourth order Fresnel spit and polished, and maintaining dust-free quarters that she gained the admiration of all who know her. For 40 years she minded the station, her faithful vigil receiving national

Point Conception Lighthouse, left center, shines seaward from a precipitous cliff at the north side of the west entrance to Santa Barbara Channel. The initial station built in 1856 was replaced by a new tower in 1882. This photo was taken in 1973. U.S. Coast Guard photo.

acclaim. She was still tending the light at 81, the year she fell and broke her hip, finally, but reluctantly resigning her position in 1905. She and her husband had originally come from Maine where lighthouses were a household word, and they continued a tradition.

There is never talk of the old lighthouse without the mention of "grandmother" Williams who not only was a good lighthouse keeper, but an excellent cook and one who kept a garden full of nasturtiums.

The Santa Barbara Light was severely shaken by an earthquake June 29, 1925, which rolled keeper Weeks out of his bed at 6:45 A.M. As the walls began to crumble he rescued his mother, sister and brother but the lighthouse was demolished and had to be replaced by a temporary light until a permanent structure could be installed.

An important landmark sought out by the Spanish galleons crossing the Pacific from the Indies was bold Point Conception, sometimes referred to as the "Cape Horn of the Pacific." Rough seas, swift currents and unpredictable winds are common occurrences often encouraged by strong gales. A marked change in climatic and meteorological conditions prevail in the vicinity of the 220 foot headland, rising rather ominously at the west end of Santa Barbara Channel.

The 52 foot pioneer lighthouse was located 133 feet above the water and the construction period was fraught with problems. Contracted out to Gibbons and Kelly, the work got underway in 1854-55, but as the station neared completion, lighthouse inspector Bache, cried, "inferior workmanship," and made the builders tear down the tower and rebuild it; no cure, no pay. Only after all requirements were satisfied did the schooner *General Pierce* deliver the lens and lighting apparatus. While landing the equipment through the surf, damage occurred which delayed a planned Christmas 1855 target date for commissioning. Because of missing parts the lamp was not lighted until February 1, 1856.

When George Parkinson, the assigned keeper arrived early to take his post, he found the lighthouse far from finished and curious Indians milling around inside. A few months later he complained to his superiors about spending much of his time having to nail on loose boards blown off by the incessant winds. He described his location as, "this dreadful promontory of desolation." He was still there in 1875 when large cracks developed in the lighthouse caused by the settling of the ground beneath the foundation. Parkinson, depressed with his situation, made minor repairs and when the inspector arrived he was horrified to see the deterioration, and recommended the authorities seek funds for a new lighthouse. Seven years were to pass before those appropriations were forthcoming, and none too soon. The new tower was constructed on the side of the primeval monolith, 100 feet lower than its predecessor permitting more freedom from the frequent

45

From 1901, an aid to navigation has marked Point Arguello, a dreaded sector of the California coast where many lives and ships have been lost. The inset shows the present Arguello sentinel, and the larger photo, one of the previous structures the Coast Guard utilized at the point.

prevailing high fog. At this writing, that tower, circa 1882, still stands in a nature-scarred sector of the California coast.

The shoreline between Point Conception and Point Arguello, 12 miles to the north, is riddled with flooded shelves of rock and hidden reefs where twisted steel, knarled timbers and bleached bones of wrecked ships lie. The graveyard of ships and men continues far north as Point Pedernales and the fearful Honda.

Due to a government oversight, Point Arguello waited a long time to receive a navigation light. Though pleas went back to the middle of the last century, funds were not appropriated until 1888. They, however, were inadequate and not until George Washington's birthday in 1901 was a lighthouse erected, the lighting fixture being only of the fourth order. A rectangular tower, not the original, stands there today utilizing an airway type beacon, the old structure having been replaced in 1934. The station also has a radio beacon and foghorn, to prevent the regrettable shipwrecks of the yesteryears.

At the Honda, it is undoubtedly true that 22 sailors and seven destroyers valued at $13 million, might have survived had the present day radio beacon system been operative. In a dense fog on September 8, 1923, a flotilla of 14 destroyers was en route from San Francisco to San Diego. Due to a mix-up in radio signals and confusion with a merchant ship in distress at nearby San Miquel Island, a terrible

tragedy was about to occur. George Olson, a lighthouse keeper at Point Arguello logged the following:

> At Point Pedernales of Point Honda on Pacific coast three miles north of Pt. Arguello on Saturday night Sept. 8, 1923, seven U. S. destroyers were wrecked by running on the rocks at 9:07 P.M., all running aground at intervals of two minutes. At 9:20 P.M. the last of the seven were on the rocks. High seas and a heavy fog. Twenty-two lives were lost. Seven hundred and seventy men including officers were on the ships.

Captain Edward Watson, Destroyer Squadron Commander, a Navy career man, had placed his judgement on dead reckoning to determine the position of the ships. As a result his command vessel, the *Delphy,* and six other counterparts, duck-trailing astern were ripped apart on the merciless devil rocks—the *Lee, Young, Woodbury, Chauncey, Nicholas* and *Fuller.* Imagine the horror that must have crossed Watson's mind? Not only was he responsible for the ships but more so for the lives of the men. He already knew beyond the shadow of a doubt that his brilliant Navy career had gone down the drain. Well of course, he honestly believed the squadron had passed the menacing clutches of rock along that dreaded sector of the California coast. As his command vessel turned sharply to port he was certain that deep water had been gained in Santa Barbara Channel.

As it turned out, the keepers from Point Arguello played a role in the aftermath of the disaster. Principal keeper G. T. Olsen, first assistant A. Settles and second assistant I. Mygrants saved five navy clad men who floated by on a raft about 10:30 P.M. The keeper on watch heard cries of distress. With difficulty, he and the others worked tenaciously in the dark to pull the survivors over the outlying rocks and up the precipitous cliffs, guided by hand lanterns. Suffering minor injuries and burns, the station attendants made the survivors as warm and comfortable as possible until aid arrived.

When the Naval Court heard the case, they placed the blame on Captain Watson and the other destroyer officers whose ships stranded while blindly following the *Delphy's* lead course. There was much confusion after the multi wrecks, and in some cases it was every man for himself as they struggled for survival on a pincushion of slippery, wave-swept rocks trying to reach the beach. It was nothing less than a miracle that the death toll wasn't far greater, and that may have been due to the calming affect of the fog on the water. Radio beacons at that period were in their infancy and mariners had not yet grown to place confidence in them.

Several years earlier the Arguello keepers were involved in another rescue. On July 7, 1911. W. A. Henderson, then principal keeper of the light, reported the following:

I was called up by one of the wireless boys and told that the steamer *Santa Rosa* was ashore somewhere above the Honda. We could not see her from the Point, and it was some time before we located her. The weather was clear; a very light breeze was blowing from the northwest; the ocean was very smooth. The *Santa Rosa* was lying broadside to the beach, resting easy. I did not think they would have any trouble in getting her off if they could get help before the tide got too low. A few minutes after I arrived there the steam schooner *Helen Drew* came and passed a line aboard the *Santa Rosa*; then shortly after that the steamer *Argyll* arrived and passed a line aboard, but it soon parted; then they made fast the wire cable. By that time the tide was ebbing, and they could not do much in the way of towing. About 12 o'clock a fresh breeze sprang up and the surf began to roll and break hard. There was nothing we could do on shore up to about 4 P.M. but stand and look on. By that time a great many of the people had left the beach and gone home. I asked friends to wait and see the steamer pulled off—that they would commence towing her off in a few minutes. They did not have to wait long before the steamer *Argyll* had a strain on her cable. The *Santa Rosa* began to move very slow to the north and her stern pointed to the west; but the strain was too great for the cable and it parted, and the *Santa Rosa* swung broadside to the beach again and soon after broke in two.

A few minutes later we saw a lifeboat come around the bow of the steamer on a big comber and capsize. One of the crew, a man by the name of Peterson, had jumped out of the boat as it passed the bow of the steamer and someone aboard threw him a lifepreserver which he caught and put on. But the mate and three sailors had nothing to help them keep afloat. The four without life preservers started to swim ashore but changed their minds when they saw how hard the surf was pounding the beach and swam toward the ship. We could hear them calling for help, but the four sank at the same time. A few minutes later we saw a man in the surf with a life preserver on, but he could not get out of the undertow. There was not a line we could throw to him. So we made a chain of ourselves by taking hold of hands and wading out, only to be knocked off our feet by the surf breaking the chain we had formed. At last a young man found a piece of window cord which he tied around himself and went out to the undertow and rescued the man.

Then a liferaft was thrown over the ship's side and a lifeboat lowered, which was soon filled with passengers and cut adrift. Both raft and boat drifted toward shore and were soon in the breakers. An extra large wave rolled in, and as the raft started to ride it, it broke under it, turning the raft upside down, throwing every one off. The liferaft rode the breaker all right. A few more heavy breakers came in and threw the boat up on the beach. Those that were able to jump and save themselves did so, while the others were dragged out by the rescue party on shore.

One lady passenger was caught under the boat and badly crushed. As she was being carried off by others I started to go up the beach, when I saw a woman in the surf not more than 30 feet from me. I started into the surf for her (a Japanese followed), but before I could get to her a big breaker rolled in and drove her under, and about the same time swept us off our feet. As soon as we could gather ourselves we rushed back into the surf. That time I managed to get hold of her and with the assistance of the Japanese, got her out of the undertow and away from the breakers.

Then they tried to shoot a line ashore from the ship, but something went wrong—the line parted. So they sent a boat inshore where they could throw a heaving line to us and returned to the ship and made fast a heavy line, which we hauled ashore. A few minutes later we saw four more men in the water come around the bow of the ship. Two swam for shore and two for the stern of the ship. By carrying our end of the line and dropping it in front of the two inshore they took hold of it and we pulled them ashore. The two that swam to the stern of the ship were hoisted aboard. As soon as they rigged up the breeches buoy on the ship we hauled the lifeboat ashore and the sailors made the end of the line fast to the railroad viaduct; then we commenced hauling the passengers ashore. First they used a distillate drum for a carrier, but it was so heavy that when it came halfway in, the rope sagged and the drum went into the water and filled.

There were but few of us on the beach, and I thought those in the drum would drown before we could haul it ashore. It was then that some of the women ran into the surf and took hold of the line with us men. The next time they used the cargo net for a buoy. It was much lighter and easier to haul in. In the meantime, they had thrown another raft from the ship and tied a rope to it and sent the other end ashore. Some of the people that came ashore were more drowned than alive when they got ashore. The women folks ashore took care of the women and babies as fast as they were landed. We were all about given out when the Honda railroad section gang arrived and gave us a hand in working the breeches buoy. Shortly after, a large gang of railroad men arrived and they got the liferaft to work. We could bring eight in on the raft at a time and few of them got wet. By 10:30 P.M. we had all of the passengers ashore. The last raft I helped haul ashore was loaded with ship's stores of some kind. Then I quit; thought I had done enough if the passengers were all landed. I was wet, cold and hungry; so I came home, arrived here 11:30 P.M.

Captain J. O. Faria master of the *Santa Rosa* had previously completed more than a thousand wreck-free coastwise voyages, but on that fateful occasion his record was shattered by the savage outcrops of Point Arguello.

In later years another favorite coastwise passenger liner, the 376 foot *Harvard* came to grief near Point Arguello. She was wrecked May 30, 1931, and though there was no loss of life, the rocky manacles sliced her hull open and ended the career of the prime mover of seagoing passengers between San Francisco and Los Angeles.

Vintage photo of the San Luis Obispo Lighthouse built in 1890, an ornate frame structure.

San Luis Obispo Light Station, shown just before automation came. Today the old lighthouse borders on the controversial Diablo Canyon nuclear power plant which is off limits to the public. The present beacon shines from a cylindrical structure east of the old lighthouse. U.S. Coast Guard photo.

A vintage photo of Mrs. M.E. "Emily" Fish who was keeper of the Point Pinos Lighthouse from 1893 till 1914. During her tenure she was known widely as a socialite keeper, heading many civic organizations and entertaining frequently at the lighthouse, activities that did not deter from running a spit and polish lighthouse and always keeping the third order Fresnel in tip-top condition. Photo courtesy Monterey Public Library.

48

Point Fermin Lighthouse pictured from a Coast Guard aircraft. The 1874 structure has been restored as a memorial to the past, while the present day light shines from a pole on the point. U.S. Coast Guard photo.

A California sea mist drifts over the little islet where stands historical Crescent City Lighthouse, now known as Battery Point Light. Photo by Andrew E. Cier.

Pigeon Point Lighthouse is one of California's tallest, rising 115 feet from its base to the focal plane. Photo by Andrew E. Cier.

Point Montara Lighthouse has become a host beacon to visitors in the popular Youth Hostel program, the station grounds and outbuildings now used for that purpose. Photo by Andrew E. Cier.

As if crowned by a halo, the Crescent City Lighthouse is cradled in a golden glow at the end of the day. Andrew E. Cier photo.

Smooth waters on San Francisco Bay featuring Alcatraz Island, its former prison and still active lighthouse. Photo by Andrew E. Cier.

Almost like a chapel dome of glass—the Fresnel lens at the Point Loma Lighthouse. Photo by Andrew E. Cier.

In an idyllic setting, Point Loma Lighthouse at the entrance to San Diego's Silver Gate. Photo by Andrew E. Cier.

Old Point Loma Lighthouse has become one of California's prime tourist attractions. Photo by Andrew E. Cier.

A Coast Guard helicopter hovers above prominent Los Angeles Lighthouse at the outer end of the San Pedro Breakwater. U.S. Coast Guard photo.

A lonely beacon guarding a rugged sector of the southern California coastline—Point Conception. U.S. Coast Guard photo.

Queen of the Channel Islands off the California coast is Anacapa Lighthouse. U.S. Coast Guard photo.

Sunset at Cleft of the Rock Lighthouse. Author photo.

Oregon's oldest lighthouse is Cape Blanco, dating from 1870, still in its original state, well preserved. U.S. Coast Guard photo.

Since 1894, Umpqua Lighthouse has graced the Oregon coast. Author photo.

Just horsin' around at Cape Blanco Lighthouse. A pastoral scene, horses graze in the green fields as a light fog drifts in from the Pacific. Photo by Andrew E. Cier.

Framed between the rotting piling of the old jetty rail trestle, Coquille River (Bandon) Lighthouse on the north side of the Coquille River entrance. Andrew E. Cier photo.

Scintillating beauty—the big first order lens of British manufacture, at Heceta Head Lighthouse. Photo by Andrew E. Cier.

Magnificant Yaquina Head Lighthouse. U.S. Coast Guard photo.

Like the gateway into Heaven—sunset at Heceta Head Lighthouse. Photo by Andrew E. Cier.

No lighthouse in all the world is in a more beautiful setting than Heceta Head Lighthouse on Oregon's central coast. Photo by Andrew E. Cier.

The fourth order revolving lens at Cape Arago floats in a bath of mercury. Author photo.

Inside the huge first order French made lens at Umpqua Lighthouse. Author photo.

Erosion slowly eats away the islet where Cape Arago Lighthouse stands, as can be seen in this Coast Guard aerial picture. At the bitter end of the peninsula is the remains of the first lighthouse, built there in 1866.

Yaquina Bay Lighthouse, circa 1871, only saw three years of active service, but lives on today as a monument of the past. Author photo.

Restored living room of the old Yaquina Bay Lighthouse—If only the walls could talk. Andrew E. Cier photo.

No longer an active light, Cape Meares Lighthouse has become a popular tourist attraction, viewed by scores of visitors annually. *Andrew E. Cier photo.*

Intricate design is formed by the spiral staircase as it winds up through the Yaquina Head tower. The lighthouse ghost has often been heard traversing the steps. *Photo by Andrew E. Cier.*

The rich, golden glow of the first order Parisian Fresnel shines forth from the Yaquina Head Lighthouse. *Photo by Andrew E. Cier.*

A mere speck in a great ocean, Tillamook Rock Lighthouse, without a light in its crown, is now a columbarium for the ashes of the dead. *Photo by Andrew E. Cier.*

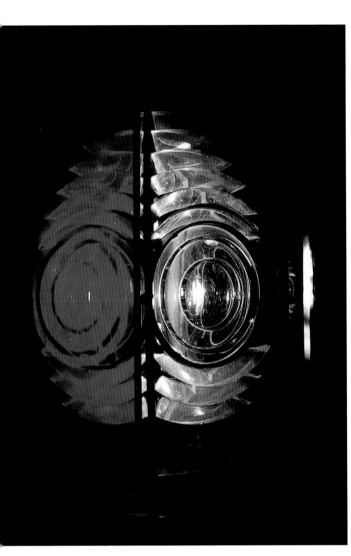

A precious gem of prismatic glass, the Cape Disappointment Lighthouse lens flashes alternating white and red beams through its bullseyes. Photo by Andrew E. Cier.

A picture that could not be duplicated by the painters' brush—sunset over the Pacific, silhouetting Tillamook Rock Lighthouse. Photo by Andrew E. Cier.

Night closes down on Cape Disappointment Lighthouse. M.W. Rodrigues photo U.S. Coast Guard.

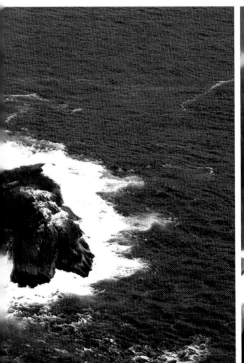

Winter wonderland at North Head Lighthouse, a beautiful covering of fresh snow as seen through the camera lens of Andrew E. Cier.

Set apart from the rest of the world, lonely Destruction Island Lighthouse. U.S. Coast Guard photo.

The stately tower, Grays Harbor Lighthouse. M.W. Rodrigues photo U.S. Coast Guard.

Lime Kiln Lighthouse in the San Juan Islands was one of the last American lighthouses to be electrified. M.W. Rodrigues photo U.S. Coast Guard.

The tower that diminished in height, New Dungeness Lighthouse on sandy Dungeness Spit in the Strait of Juan de Fuca. U.S. Coast Guard photo.

At the northwest tip of continental United States stands Cape Flattery Lighthouse on Tatoosh Island. M.W. Rodrigues photo U.S. Coast Guard.

Breakers roll in with clout below Cape Disappointment, an area where many ships have reached their port of no return. Photo by Andrew E. Cier.

Cattle Point Light on San Juan Island. M.W. Rodrigues photo U.S. Coast Guard.

Point Robinson Lighthouse, half way between Seattle and Tacoma, on Puget Sound. U.S. Coast Guard photo.

Alki Point Light at the southern entrance to Seattle's Elliott Bay. M.W. Rodrigues photo U.S. Coast Guard.

Point No Point Lighthouse is a little lighthouse with a big mission. U.S. Coast Guard photo.

CENTRAL CALIFORNIA LIGHTHOUSES

So tonight wandering sailors
pale with fears
Wide o're the watery waste a light appears.
—-Homer

Northward along the coast, old San Luis Obispo Lighthouse, 35 miles north of Arguello, has been terminated. In its place is a modern cylindrical light structure east of the former tower, 116 feet above the ocean. A foghorn and a radio beacon are also located there. The future of the old lighthouse at this juncture is in doubt for it rests in the shadow of the controversial Diablo Canyon Atomic Power Plant which is off limits to the public. Victorian in architecture, the colorful frame lighthouse was established in 1890, above an important searoad junction to San Luis Obispo Bay.

Piedras Blancas Light, 90 miles north of Point Conception, is shown from a 74 foot tower with an exposed beacon on top. Its lantern house, fitted in 1875 when the lighthouse was built, was severely damaged in a 1949 storm. The first order lens was removed, becoming a tourist attraction in the town of Cambria. A new lantern house has been considered but the present arrangement thus far has proven more economical for Coast Guard maintenance. The focal plane of the light is 142 feet above the Pacific and there is a radio beacon located there.

In recent years the lighthouse has become better known than in the past, partly due to the closeness of San Simeon, gateway to the world famous Hearst Castle, the estate of the former William Randolph Hearst.

When the wild flowers bloom around the lighthouse in the spring and summer it is a pretty sight, but most visitors ask, "What happened to the top of the lighthouse?" Along the area's shelving strands, tide pools hold a rich variety of sea life which attract countless gulls that gracefully soar above. Little heed is given to the obstructions that lie off the shore where tragedy has struck many who made their living from the sea.

Among the many wrecks along the ragged rock-bound coast was that of the British ship *Harlech Castle* in August 1869, the ship and cargo becoming a total loss. The rock which punctured the vessel's hull has since been known as Harlech Castle Rock, a half mile offshore, almost in the shadow of the Point. The wreck helped get appropriations for the Piedras Blancas Light, but at the subsequent hearing, the insurers claimed the wreck was a case of barratry, the stranding occurring in clear weather, mild seas and in board daylight. The captain and officers were accused of making false reports regarding the circumstances, and no insurance was paid.

When the Coast Survey party examined the locality several years later, some of the ship's masts were still protruding above the water.

In an area of haunting beauty sits Point Sur Lighthouse, south of Carmel. The beacon shines from a humpy islet connected to the mainland by a natural sandy causeway and is situated 250 feet above the Pacific, atop a gray stone tower on a fog signal structure. There is also a radio beacon there. The lighthouse dates from 1889 and the early keepers often complained about having to lug their supplies up the steep staircase to reach their abode. Later, a hoisting skidway was added and finally a crude road.

One of the shipwrecks responsible for the establishment of Point Sur Light was that of the steamer *Ventura*. She went down off the point April 20, 1879 with a variety of cargo including silks, linens, hardware, wagon parts and farm tools. The local folk had a field day recovering the spoils from the beaches, and for years, the farms in the area made good use of what providence had brought them.

The original first order Fresnel in the Point Sur tower is presently on loan and display at the Alan Knight Museum in Monterey.

The lighthouse has been off limits to the public but has been plagued by vandals. At this writing the Coast Guard was looking for a responsible group to use the grounds and building for recreation and historical purposes.

The Navy dirigible *Macon* crashed near Point Sur in 1935 because its main girders were incapable of standing the howling winds. The sky monster was lost but rescue efforts saved all but two of the airship's 81 man crew.

Point Sur is an area of rugged grandeur, a place where wildlife is abundant and where nature wears many faces.

On the point at the south side of the entrance to Monterey Bay stands Point Pinos Lighthouse, one of the original eight West Coast sentinels, and at this writing its original Fresnel is still in operation. It was General Persifor F. Smith of the Army's Pacific Division that first suggested a light at Point Pinos (Pine Point) in October 1849. For years, Spain used the portal for a settlement and a harbor of refuge, and when Richard Henry Dana came, he wrote of it while engaged in the hide trade in the 1830's. However, history tells of no light marking the entrance until Uncle Sam got on the bandwagon. Major Hartman Bache, the government supervisor, later lighthouse inspector, chose the site, and by the summer of 1853, a 20 x 30 foot stone and brick structure was under construction. A masonry addition was to be built to the back of the edifice but a shortage of funds necessitated frame construction of local lumber. Total cost of the station was $26,000, though only $15,000 had been appropriated. When the structure was completed in 1854, the intended lighting apparatus, a second order lens, proved too large for the tower, so the third order fixture purchased for the Fort Point Light was transferred to Point Pinos for placement. The station was the second California beacon to become operative on the coast, displaying its light on February 1, 1855. During that first year, principal keeper Charles Layton, moonlighting as a member of a local posse, was shot and wounded while attempting to capture the notorious bandito Anastacio Garcia. Having previously served in both the American and British armies he was appointed keeper at an annual stipend of $1,000 after earlier trying his hand at gold mining with little success. After his untimely passing a few months after the shooting, his widow who had assisted him from the inception, was officially appointed keeper on January 4, 1856. Four years later she remarried and turned the responsibilities over to her new husband, George C. Harris. The government made it official and he kept the post till 1863. Later, another member of the fairer sex, Mrs. M. E. Fish was keeper. In 1871, Captain Allen L. Luce was lighting the lucerne nightly. During his tenure eight years later, a tall, gaunt figure of a man with a Scotch accent, dressed Bohemian-style visited the lighthouse. Always a genial host, Luce gave the inquistitive stranger a tour of the lighthouse, entertained him on his piano and displayed his ship models. The questions asked of the keeper were many and varied, and as a result, the lighthouse was featured in a later essay entitled, *The Old Pacific Capitol*.

Ironically, the strange visitor was none other than famous author and poet Robert Louis Stevenson, who claimed the Monterey Peninsula to be the world's finest seascape.

Considerable damage occurred at Point Pinos Lighthouse in the same devastating California earthquake that leveled San Francisco in 1906. The entire building had to be reinforced. The station was electrified in 1915, earlier than most, but its beautiful Fresnel remained in place. Today the lighthouse stands as a monument but its one-time solitary location has been encroached upon by golf courses, houses and population. Thousands of visitors flock to the peninsula yearly. A museum showing the history of the light and local events are housed inside the former keepers' quarters, opened to the public by the city of Pacific Grove. The Coast Guard maintains the light, fog signal and nearby radio beacon.

PIEDRAS BLANCAS.

Artist's rendering of the Piedras Blancas Lighthouse on the California coast drawn in 1875, before the tower was completed.

Decapitated Piedras Blancas Lighthouse had its lantern house removed several years ago after it was damaged in a 1949 storm. An exposed aero marine type beacon was placed on its crown, destroying much of the beauty of the tower which was established in 1875.

The first order lens, revolving mechanism and pedestal formerly used at Piedras Blancas Lighthouse is displayed at Cambria, California on Highway 1. Unfortunately, the prisms have been exposed to the weather which has seriously discolored the glass and tarnished the metal. The lens dates from 1872. (Merle Porter photo.)

On the point at the west side of the entrance to Santa Cruz Harbor stands an active memorial lighthouse, constructed in 1967. The memorial lighthouse was funded by Mr. and Mrs. Charles Abbott, in remembrance of their son, Mark Abbott who drowned while surfing in the waters near the point where the structure was built. (The drowning occurred on February 28, 1965.) The Coast Guard accepted it as an official light. The original government lighthouse in the area was razed in 1948 after serving during World War 11 as a coastal lookout post for the military. It was replaced by a small wooden tower with a minor beacon which served nearby for two decades until the erection of the memorial lighthouse. The masonary building, a vintage replica, flashes its light every five seconds from the lantern house removed from the former Oakland Harbor Lighthouse on San Francisco Bay. The initial beacon marking the harbor, at

Lighthouse Point, was a frame structure with a square tower rising from the keeper's dwelling. It stood 35 feet high and featured a fifth order light with a fixed red characteristic. Established on New Year's Day 1870, it was later to become a victim of erosion by encroaching seas, as three dangerous sea caverns surrounded its position. Replacement was necessary and the building was moved to safer ground.

As early as 1849, when the steamer *California*, 20 weeks out of New York, steamed past Santa Cruz, the town elders laid plans for a lighthouse, but 20 years passed before it came to fruition.   Point Ano Nuevo, 18 miles northwest of Point Santa Cruz has nothing more than a whistle buoy as an active navigation aid today, and the 49 foot tower no longer stands on the small islet which is separated from the mainland by swirling tidal waters. Named for a Spanish New

Mukilteo Lighthouse, a frame structure, circa 1906, holds its dignity into the nuclear age. U.S. Coast Guard photo.

Little changed from its inception in 1881, West Point
Lighthouse has seen Seattle grow almost up to its doors.
M.W. Rodrigues photo U.S. Coast Guard.

Point Wilson Lighthouse commands an important position
at the entrance to Admiralty Inlet and Puget Sound.
M.W. Rodrigues photo U.S. Coast Guard.

Like a fly on the back of a beached whale, the Point Sur Lighthouse and radio beacon keep a vigil among the shadowed cliffs of the monolith on which they stand. The stone lighthouse has been operating since 1889. U.S. Coast Guard photo.

An aerial view of the Point Sur Station in the days when Coast Guard personnel were in attendance. Note the lighthouse below the crest of the land mass. U.S. Coast Guard photo.

Santa Cruz Memorial Lighthouse was erected in 1967, its lantern house being moved from the defunct Oakland Harbor Light Station on San Francisco Bay. The masonry structure, a replica of the past, is an active aid to navigation. A lighthouse was first placed at the harbor on New Years Day in 1870.

Year, the point was first lighted in 1872 by a lens-lantern, and utilized a 12 inch steam fog signal.

In a jolting earthquake on October 22, 1926, the lighting apparatus was shaken from its pedestal and fell through the hatch to the watchroom, shattering the glass. The keeper installed a standby lamp but a later tremor destroyed it as well. The quakes that followed did considerable damage to the tower and out buildings, but the attendants managed to get another oil flame burning in the lantern.

The islet is part of the Ano Nuevo State Reserve where screaming birds of many varieties, and hundreds of sea lions exist in a naturalists' paradise. One hour south of San Francisco on Highway 1, Ano Nuevo State Park is a beautiful, wind-swept area favored by abalone divers and surfers, by hikers and tourists. Beginning in mid-November elephant seals migrate to the rocky islet to mate and bear their pups.

The five miles of coastline between Point Ano Nuevo and Pigeon Point is low and rocky, definitely hostile to coastal shipping. Just off State Highway 1, halfway between Half Moon Bay and Santa Cruz stands imposing Pigeon Point Lighthouse, a 115 foot conical tower that lifts its massive masonry skyward in regal fashion. It was initially lighted on November 15, 1872 and at this writing its original first order Fresnel is still in the lantern house. The lens is composed of 1,008 prisms and was manufactured by Henry Lepaute, Paris, France. One account claims the fixture dates back to 1852. The keepers in recent years complained about the local brussel sprout and broccoli farmers plowing their fields. The clouds of dust dirtied the lantern panes and sifted into the lens and its carriage. To offset their extra cleaning chores they were often presented with gifts of vegetables by their farm neighbors.

The Coast Guard has been displaying a secondary modern light from the tower gallery, an economy move which takes away some of the charm of the historic tower. A radio beacon is also operated on the point and though a foghorn was installed there in 1872, none is presently listed in the Coast Guard *Light List.*

Another notorious graveyard of ships exists along that sector of the California coast. The point takes its name from an American Clipper named *Carrier Pigeon,* Captain Azariah Doane, which crashed on the rocks June 6, 1853, a considerable distance from the location of the lighthouse. A total loss, valued at $54,000, the vessel carried 1,300 tons of cargo. That wreck occurred two decades before the lighthouse was erected. It should have actually been named for the British ship *Sir John Franklin* which stranded near the lighthouse site January 17, 1865. Though part of her cargo was salvaged, the ship's master and 11 of his crew perished.

To add insult to injury, the steam schooner *Sea Bird* while salvaging the cargo of the *Carrier Pigeon* also ran aground.

Though wrecks in and around Pigeon Point were numerous in years past, modern technology has cut the toll considerably.

Since the automation of lighthouses, vandalism, deterioration and other problems have plagued the Coast Guard. One successful solution is utilization of premises by the American Youth Hostels. The Pigeon Point Lighthouse Hostel was developed in cooperation with the State of California Department of Parks & Recreation, and is now a sought out destination for bikers and hikers. The facilities include 30 beds in several bunkrooms, a dining room, commons room and kitchen; all are located in the outbuildings. Only the tower itself remains under Coast Guard supervision. Also serving in the hostel program are facilities at Point Montara and Point Arena. The San Francisco-based Golden Gate Council, affiliated with the International Youth Hostel Federation, features 5,000 such installations around the world, and thus far three are on the reservations of California coastal lighthouses.

The Montara Lighthouse Hostel is located on State Highway I between Montara and Moss Beach, 25 miles south of downtown San Francisco. Facilities there include 30 beds in five bunkrooms located on the ground surrounding the lighthouse.

Point Montara Lighthouse presently displays an airway type beacon which replaced its former Fresnel. Until the turn of the century there was no Montara lighthouse, only a fog signal (12 inch steam whistle) station established in 1872. A light was not put into operation until 1900. The existing 30 foot conical tower was built in 1928, at an elevation 70 feet above the Pacific. A lighted whistle buoy stands 1.5 miles west of the lighthouse warning vessels away from the covered rocks and ledges that have snagged several vessels.

When the fog-shrouded steamer *Colorado* stranded on an offshore ledge in November 1868, a public plea went out for a fog signal at Point Montara. The very year the fog signal was being installed, October 17, 1872, the sailing vessel *Acuelo,* Captain McKay, crashed into the rocks, laden with a $150,000 cargo of coal, iron and grain. Salvagers purchased the battered wreck for a mere $3,700.

In past decades, lighthouse keepers on the California coast spent considerable time watching sailing ships tacking back and forth offshore awaiting pilots or for the wind and sea conditions to moderate sufficiently for port entry. San Francisco Bay was the center of the shipping industry in the early years of coastal sail and steam. In the heyday of coastwise passenger liners, clocks could almost be set by precise scheduling. Ships of the Pacific Coast Steamship Company and the fast Admiral Liners operated between the Golden Gate and Portland or on the fast run from San Francisco to Seattle. Household words were the sleek liners *Harvard* and *Yale* on the San Francisco-Los Angeles run. A vast fleet of wooden and steel steam schooners and the transocean steamer arrivals and departures from the outset demanded a lighthouse be placed on the Farallons, lying 23 miles west of the entrance to San Francisco Bay.

Rocky islets, bare and rough, they extend for seven miles. Southeast Farallon, the largest of the group, is actually two islets separated by a narrow impassable gorge, the larger east islet being pyramidal in shape, over 300 feet high. Farallon Light is located 358

Lighthouse in Paradise, Diamond Head Lighthouse, near Honolulu, one of the nearly 48,000 aids to navigation in America maintained by the U.S. Coast Guard along 47,000 miles of coast, lakes and rivers—a length equal to nearly twice the circumference of the globe. If placed along the equator, there would be an aid every one half mile.

Kilauea Lighthouse at the northernmost protrusion of Kauai Island looks out over a vast blue Pacific guiding ships along a well traveled waterway. Courtesy U.S. Coast Guard, 14th District.

Pine Island Lighthouse is a quaint little station with a new look. Transport Canada photo.

Merry Island Lighthouse all dressed up for a Merry Christmas. Transport Canada photo.

Cape Beale Lighthouse on the rugged west coast of Vancouver Island is made to look larger by slatwork placed around the central column. Canadian Coast Guard photo.

Ano Neuvo aerial view showing the abandoned lighthouse, station buildings and thousands of California Sea Lions and Sea Elephants basking on the beach. U.S. Coast Guard photo.

Stately Pigeon Point Lighthouse, one of the tallest and most formidable on the California coast has raised its 115 foot frame skyward since 1872. The Coast Guard photo was taken before automation came to the station. The big first order lens in the lantern house has not been active in recent years, an auxiliary light being utilized from the tower's balcony.

feet above the water and is shown from a 41 foot conical tower on the highest peak, a commanding position for all corners of the compass, and a view that never stops. A radio beacon is 280 yards from the light.

Though the place abounds in history, the grim row menacing offshore reefs has taunted seafaring men since the 16th century. It has never been accertained just which Spaniard was the discoverer, but the name Los Farallones in Spanish means small, pointed isles. The credit for discovery generally goes to Cabrillo, though he left no such evidence in his log. Evidently Sir Francis Drake on viewing the ugly smattering of rocks in 1579 in the *Golden Hind,* wanted a piece of the action for he renamed them for Saint James, after his scurvy-ridden crew went ashore to gather seal meat and bird eggs to supplement their diet. The name Los Farallones was actually applied two decades later when Viscaino, the Spanish explorer, stood off the islets amused by the silhouettes of rock which he said jokingly reminded him of a group of hooded friars.

After the Spanish and the British, the Russians arrived about 1810 slaughtering great numbers of seals. In 1819, another ship of the Russian-American Company came, under direction of Zackhar Chichinoff leaving off a party of nine Aleut seal hunters who set up dwellings of planks and canvas, and then went about killing seals and sea lions for their skins, meat and oil. The effort by Chichinoff was to establish a commercial base to supply the needs of Fort Ross with salted sea lion meat. Scurvy broke out among the wretched Aleuts, who, as little better than slaves survived on bird eggs and fish.

In later years, after the Farallons became American territory, they were deemed essential for a lighthouse. In 1852, the southeast Farallon was chosen as the site. The famous "Egg War", which erupted when the construction crew arrived on the *Oriole* with their supplies, was later throttled by the government and work got underway. So demanding was the chore of hauling building supplies up the 300 foot crumbling slopes that the men went on a sit-down strike for a mule. Their pleas were answered, and the beast of burden was dispatched, but arrived desperately seasick. Stone (granite) for the base of the tower was quarried on the islet. Brick masonry formed the walls of the tower but when it was completed it stood empty awaiting the lens and lighting apparatus to arrive from France. Meanwhile the builders left the Farallons to build another lighthouse.

Point Montara Lighthouse was built in 1928, replacing earlier navigation aids at the location. A fog signal was placed there beginning in 1875. The beacon creates a unique pattern of light in this Coast Guard photograph.

The grounds of the Point Montara Light Station are utilized by the American Youth Hostel organization, and the Coast Guard maintains the light. U.S. Coast Guard photo.

The tidal currents sweep around the base of Chatham Point Lighthouse. Transport Canada photo.

Sisters Lighthouse, a prime example of a modern lighthouse on British Columbia's inside sea route. Transport Canada photo.

Active Pass Lighthouse at Georgina Point on Mayne Island on a rocky outcrop. Canadian Coast Guard photo.

Not all lighthouses look like lighthouses. This modern adaptation replaced a colorful frame lighthouse in recent years at Scarlett Point on Queen Charlotte Sound. Canadian Coast Guard photo.

Four Coast Guard aerial shots of Southeast Five Finger Island and its stately lighthouse taken in the 1980's. Note helicopter pad.

On December 12, 1854, the French ship *St. Joseph* arrived at San Francisco with the lighting equipment. As it turned out, the tower was too small to handle a first order apparatus. To the consternation of the contractors it had to be torn down and rebuilt. Thus it was not until January 1, 1856, seven years after the discovery of California gold, that the Farallon Light was first displayed.

Growing marine traffic also demanded a fog signal. Major Hartman Bache, in an economy move, suggested the use of a natural blowhole over which a brick chimney was built, topped by a whistle that was blasted by forced air created by ocean waves. Unfortunately, it was the most silent during foggy periods, and roared like a hyena in heavy surf. A fierce gale in 1871 created huge seas that demolished the brick chimney and shot the whistle skyward. It was later replaced by large steam powered sirens.

All the while, the Farallon Egg Company held their monopoly on gathering eggs for San Francisco gourmets. Even the blaring fog signal failed to move the birds from their roosts.

The keepers and their families lived in comfortable quarters on a plateau at the base of the steep cliff. The William Beemans and Cyrus O'Caines who tended the lighthouse from the 1880's until 1906 even convened a school to teach their children the ABC's.

"Boat day" was always a big occasion in the early years as all supplies and mail were eagerly awaited. A derrick at the old north landing was employed to lift food and fuel and to transfer personnel. The lighthouse tender *Madrono* was employed for such chores for many years.

While manning the light station, the O'Caines lost three children, two from diptheria and one who fell from the landing and drowned. The Beemans lost a son after a desperate attempt was made to row him in an open boat to San Francisco. It was a hard, demanding life for families.

Through the years, various methods of lifting personnel and supplies were tried at both the north and south landings. One of the derricks collapsed in 1905.

Ironically, the terrible San Francisco earthquake did only minimal damage on the Farallons, but the steamer *Mongolia* reported a "mountain of rock was lifted from the ocean 15 miles southwest of the Farallons and then disappeared."

A sketch made in 1856, which appeared in **Hutchings' California Magazine,** *depicting the Southeast Farallon with the just established lighthouse and the lesser Farallons strung out to the right. The artist was H. Eastman.*

With a never ending view, Farallon Lighthouse stands at the top of the heap, a fixture on the smattering of isles off the California coast since 1856. U.S. Coast Guard photo.

Standing through the ages marking a somewhat turbulent history, Farallon Light has been a symbol to mariners from the world over. U.S. Coast Guard photo.

Launched August 4, 1950, on the 160th anniversary of the Coast Guard, the **San Francisco Lightship WAL 612** *was on duty off the entrance to San Francisco Bay until replaced by an automatic buoy in April 1971. A lightship had served the post since 1898. U.S. Coast Guard photo.*

One of the many keepers who tended the light, George D. Cobb, put in four decades of service in California lighthouses during his career.

As early as 1908, the U. S. Lifesaving Service equipped the islet with lifesaving equipment and trained the keepers for emergencies.

When the Coast Guard took over the Lighthouse Service in 1939, the civilian family, long-term residencies began to wane. When the station was electrified and the first order lens replaced by an air-way type revolving beacon, the original lens was placed on display at a local museum.

In 1944, the liberty transport *Henry Bergh* rammed into the Southeast Farallon while carrying a thousand battle-weary veterans. The landing craft on board were lowered away and transported all hands safely to the islet, leaving the ship to its death agonies.

Coastguardsmen and their wives were at the station until December 1, 1972 when Brent Franze, the last keeper, was removed by the Coast Guard cutter *Resolute,* ending 117 years of manned service in favor of automation. The lighthouse and its radio beacon were thereafter monitored by a radio link with the Yerba Buena Coast Guard base.

Today, Coastguardsmen who service the lighthouse are either ferried to the islet by boat or come in by helicopter.

Wildlife is much happier with the present arrangement, since the Farallon Islands National Marine Sanctuary was established to protect and preserve the marine birds and mammals, their habitats and other natural resources on the islands. Of the many trees that attendants attempted to plant through the decades, only a couple have managed to eke out an existence.

Shackled to the ocean bottom, 15 miles from the Farallons in 108 feet of water, is the San Francisco Approach Lighted Horn Buoy SF (LNB). The huge conveyance is 42 feet high, displays a flashing light and utilizes foghorn, Racon and a radio beacon.

Located at 37 degrees 45.0′ N. 122 degrees 41.5′ W., it replaced the former San Francisco Lightship, a fixture off the entrance to San Francisco Bay from April 7, 1898 until the advent of the ocean buoy in 1971. Three different lightships and several relief vessels served the post during that period, the last being *San Francisco Lightship WAL 612.* The first was the steam powered *No. 70* which made a wee bit of history. On the eve of August 23, 1899 she dispatched the very first wireless message. It reached the Cliff House on San Francisco's ocean front, "Sherman is sighted! Sherman is sighted!"

According to the Lighthouse Bulletin:

"Ashore these words were hailed with loud acclaim. They meant that the Army Transport *Sherman,* with the California contingent in the Spanish-American War aboard, was near the end of its long journey from Manila; that it had been sighted from the San Francisco Lightship. This was the first wireless message to be sent, not only from a lightship in this country, but from any point in the United States."

When placed on station, *No. 70* was one of the most modern American lightships, equipped with electric generators. During the era of the San Francisco Lightship, many tempest-tossed souls were saved by its very presence in a vital navigation area. It was a nostalgic day when that era ended, but the economy measure by the Coast Guard has proved a success with the innovative unmanned buoy.

Nootka Lighthouse is in an historic location on Vancouver Island's west coast. Transport Canada photo.

Sand Heads Lighthouse at the mouth of the Fraser River, isn't pretty to look at, but renders yeoman service. Transport Canada photo.

A modern circular lighthouse now marks British Columbia's Lennard Island. Transport Canada photo.

Lightship **No. 83** which served off Blunts Reef from 1905 till the 1930s is seen here years later serving as the San Francisco Lightship. In 1916, 155 passengers and crew from the wreck of the SS **Bear** were housed aboard the little ship. U.S. Coast Guard photo.

In the spring of 1971, this large self-contained ocean buoy was towed to the position formerly kept by the San Francisco Lightship and has ably fulfilled the duties with its radar, light, fog signal and transmitter, all working in automated status. U.S. Coast Guard photo.

The crew of the San Francisco Lightship, in 1916, tolerated more than 2,221 hours of fog, 67 hours more than in the previous year, which had set a record. The mournful sound of a lightship foghorn for such an extended period was like being cooped up in a tin can with a hammer pounding on it..

Point Reyes lens and lamp (1927) manufactured in France in 1867 with 1,032 glass prisms. Courtesy Coastal Parks Association.

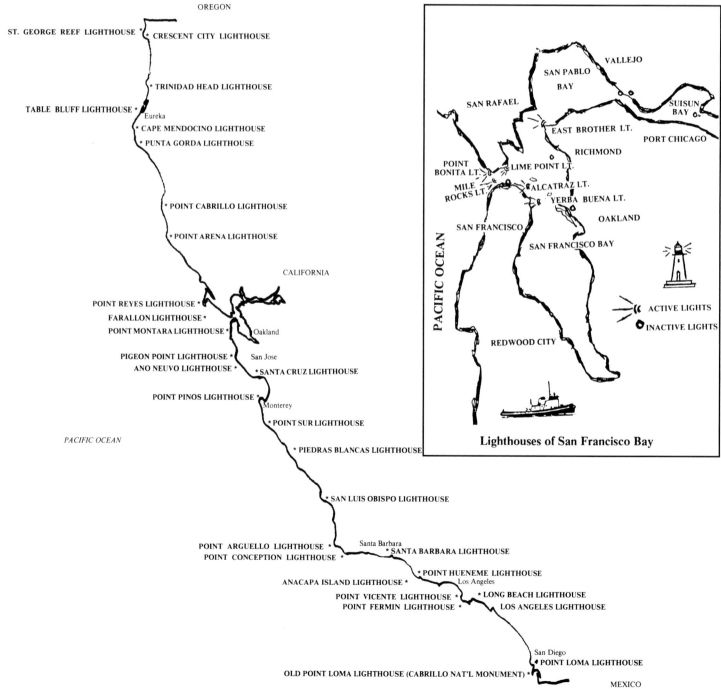

OREGON

ST. GEORGE REEF LIGHTHOUSE * * CRESCENT CITY LIGHTHOUSE

* TRINIDAD HEAD LIGHTHOUSE

TABLE BLUFF LIGHTHOUSE *
Eureka
* CAPE MENDOCINO LIGHTHOUSE
* PUNTA GORDA LIGHTHOUSE

* POINT CABRILLO LIGHTHOUSE

* POINT ARENA LIGHTHOUSE

CALIFORNIA

POINT REYES LIGHTHOUSE *
FARALLON LIGHTHOUSE *
POINT MONTARA LIGHTHOUSE *
Oakland
PIGEON POINT LIGHTHOUSE *
San Jose
ANO NEUVO LIGHTHOUSE * * SANTA CRUZ LIGHTHOUSE

POINT PINOS LIGHTHOUSE *
Monterey
* POINT SUR LIGHTHOUSE

PACIFIC OCEAN

* PIEDRAS BLANCAS LIGHTHOUSE

* SAN LUIS OBISPO LIGHTHOUSE

POINT ARGUELLO LIGHTHOUSE *
Santa Barbara
POINT CONCEPTION LIGHTHOUSE * * SANTA BARBARA LIGHTHOUSE

* POINT HUENEME LIGHTHOUSE
ANACAPA ISLAND LIGHTHOUSE *
Los Angeles
POINT VICENTE LIGHTHOUSE * * LONG BEACH LIGHTHOUSE
POINT FERMIN LIGHTHOUSE * LOS ANGELES LIGHTHOUSE

San Diego
* POINT LOMA LIGHTHOUSE
OLD POINT LOMA LIGHTHOUSE (CABRILLO NAT'L MONUMENT) *
MEXICO

VALLEJO
SAN PABLO BAY
SAN RAFAEL
SUISUN BAY
EAST BROTHER LT.
PORT CHICAGO
RICHMOND
POINT BONITA LT.
LIME POINT LT.
MILE ROCKS LT.
ALCATRAZ LT.
YERBA BUENA LT.
SAN FRANCISCO
OAKLAND
SAN FRANCISCO BAY
PACIFIC OCEAN
REDWOOD CITY
ACTIVE LIGHTS
INACTIVE LIGHTS

Lighthouses of San Francisco Bay

CHAPTER FIVE

Lighthouses of San Francisco Bay

Above our heads the sullen clouds
Scud black and swift across the sky;
Like silent ghosts in misty shrouds
Stand out the white lighthouses high.
...Celia Laighton

San Francisco Open Your Golden Gate, proclaims the popular song, and that's exactly what San Francisco did beginning with the California gold rush in 1849. Though it had always been a desired portal of entry, it reached its apex in that period in history. Thirteen years earlier, in December 1836, Richard Henry Dana, Jr. as a crew member of the Bryant & Sturgis hide brig *Alert* entered the harbor. In his *Two Years Before the Mast,* the young sailor told of the "magnificent harbor," and stated that, "If California ever becomes a prosperous country, this bay will be the center of its prosperity." How right he was. As the *Alert* came to anchor in the lee of Yerba Buena, Dana noted, "a shanty of rough boards put up by a man named Richardson who was doing a little trading."

The endless parade of ships has demanded safeguards, and lighthouses have played a big role in the harbor's history. It was the site of the first West Coast government lighthouse—Alcatraz.

At the north entrance to San Francisco Bay is Point Bonita, a sharp, black cliff 100 feet high, increasing to 300 feet on its seaward face. From northwestward it shows as three heads. The lighthouse is 124 feet above the water and displays its light from a 33 foot tower. It looks westward over the vast Pacific and southward toward the San Francisco bar, a semicircular shoal with depths less than 36 feet at low water. The bar extends from three miles south of Point Lobos to within a half mile of Point Bonita off the southern coast of Marin Peninsula.

As early as 1850 the Coast Survey recommended that a light be placed on the point. Appropriations were encouraged by the wreck of the Pacific Mail Steamship, *Tennessee* a big sidewheeler that went aground in the fog January 1, 1851. Though the passengers and mail were plucked from the splintered hulk there was no salvage, the loss being placed at $300,000. Had the vessel grounded anyplace else there would undoubtedly have been loss of life. Her resting place has since been known as Tennessee Cove.

Point Bonita Lighthouse was established on April 30, 1855. The original tower was separate from the residence unlike the other early California coast structures. The station was extremely lonely in the early years. The initial keeper wrote the lighthouse inspector claiming that, "there are no inhabitants within five miles from this point, from San Francisco to Point Bonita; there is no direct communication but by chance, a sail boat may be procured at an expense of $5, and from $2 to $5 for freight."

Seven keepers were to resign their positions in the first nine months.

The abundance of fog rolling in from the Pacific demanded concern so the very first fog signal on the coast was placed at Point Bonita, it being an Army surplus cannon.

The lighthouse inspector threatened dismissal of one Bonita keeper because glass chimneys controlling the flame inside the lens kept shattering. It was finally discovered that the lens had been installed off center in the lantern room providing insufficient ventilation. The man was exonerated.

Fog continued to be the bane of the lighthouse, 324 feet above sea level, and navigators entering the bay complained that the light was often shrouded by high fog when the lower slopes were fog-free. After considerable agitation it was deemed necessary to abandon the original light and build a new tower. The authorities chose "Land's End," the bitter end of Point Bonita, broken, unstable, narrow and steep.

It was extremely difficult and dangerous hacking out a pathway from basalt, crossing deep chasms and cliffs with loose rocks that tumbled to the ocean.

After months of arduous work and perplexing problems, the new lighthouse was completed, and on February 2, 1877, keeper John Brown trimmed the lamp's three circular wicks that lighted up the second order fixed Fresnel. A new fog signal building was erected in 1902, replacing the former facility and utilizing a first class steam siren.

The 1906 earthquake shook the station knocking down chimneys and cracking the 50 year old assistant keeper's home so badly that he had to take up quarters in the fog signal building.

Shipwrecks became so common that huge searchlights were installed in and around the point to aid rescuers at night.

Except by special permission the lighthouse today is off limits to the public due to the dangerous eroding cliffs, but it continues its vigil and still has its second order lens intact. Visitation is through arrangement with the National Park Service.

Some thrilling events took place at Point Bonita. In January of 1915 the steamer *Eureka* approaching the Golden Gate got her screw fouled in nearby Potato Patch Shoals, north of the light. Driven into the rock-bound shores as darkness approached the crew of the ship faced peril. With little regard for his own life, assistant lighthouse keeper Alex Martin who saw the distress flares made a line fast about his person and lowered himself down the perpendicular cliff in an attempt to reach the deck of the wreck, 150 feet below. His rope unfortunately was 50 feet short and he dangled between heaven and earth. Despite his sore muscles he somehow managed to struggle back up the cliff in the dark. Frustrated by his efforts and exhausted, he nevertheless took off on foot to alert the lifesaving crew and to offer his services. Surfmen launched their craft both at Point Bonita and Fort Point stations and were joined by a fleet of commericial fishboats. In a dramatic sea rescue all but one seaman were snatched from certain death. Ironically, the wreck did not explode in the breakers. Among the cargo were two tons of dynamite and a carload of gasoline.

The last keeper at Point Bonita Light before automation was Coastguardsman BM2 Vanbuskirk, although earlier that honor was to have gone to BMC Dusch. The light is now operated by remote control from the Coast Guard base.

Lighthouse buffs and mariners sent up a howl of protest when the Coast Guard decided in 1966 to level the Mile Rocks light tower and turn the facility into an ugly utilitarian aid to navigation. The Mile Rocks are situated 700 yards northwest of the sharp projecting point off Lands End on the north face of Point Lobos, and consists of two 20 foot high rocks about 100 feet apart. Mile Rocks Light, is 49 feet above the water and features orange and white horizontal bands rising like a drum from the rock. On top of the structure is a helicopter pad. The decapitation operation was completed at a cost of $110,000.

Standing guardian at the north portal to San Francisco Bay, Point Bonita Lighthouse has had a long and varied history. The present lighthouse has been standing since 1877, replacing the pioneer structure of 1855. It was the last of California's 59 lighthouse stations to be automated.

Built on a wave-washed rock where currents sweep by at the speed of a river, Mile Rocks Lighthouse was created in 1906 in a marvelous piece of engineering and perseverance by the builders. Note the Golden Gate Bridge.

There were a lot of unhappy San Franciscans when the Coast Guard, in an economy move, decided to dismantle the Mile Rocks Lighthouse in 1966 and leave only its base and first story intact. As ugly as it appears the structure still shows a light, sounds a foghorn and utilizes the upper platform as a helicopter pad. U.S. Coast Guard photo.

Restored Fort Point Lighthouse, dating from 1864, the third lighthouse erected at Fort Point, pops up above the walls of Fort Winfield Scott on San Francisco Bay. The initial lighthouse at the location had to be torn down in 1854 to make room for a fortification. The second was undermined by erosion. The existing tower's light was doomed by the erection of the Golden Gate Bridge. It closed down in 1934. Coast Guard photo, courtesy of Wayne Wheeler.

Mile Rocks, often inundated, have long been a menace to navigation. The Lighthouse Service, in November 1889 provided funds for a bell buoy just off the obstruction. One was set in place, but strong ebbs and severe winds set the buoy adrift. Every effort to anchor it ended in failure. There was even talk of dynamiting the rocks with undersea demolition.

When the fogbound SS *City of Rio de Janerio* went to her watery grave with 129 souls February 22, 1901, there remained no question of placing a major aid to navigation at Mile Rocks. Only 80 persons survived in one of the worst single ship tragedies on the California coast.

Congress appropriated necessary funds, and in early 1904 a contract was awarded to James A. McMahon. When his crew saw the perilous rocks they quit before they started. A new crew of men acquainted with the rigors of the sea was signed on. Work began in September 1904. The small motor schooner, the *Rio Rey,* was anchored just off the rocks as living quarters and supply vessel. First the rock was blasted for a foundation. Then there rose four foot thick steel reinforced walls. Work could only be accomplished when the seas were moderate. On occasion a worker fell into the water but none drowned. Built like a fortress, the tower's base was 35 feet high, containing cistern, fuel tanks and a staircase. From that level a tiered steel tower was fabricated. The first level contained oil engines to power the compressed air fog signal. The second level had an office, kitchen and day room, and on the second tier of that level were two bedrooms and a bathroom for the four man crew. The third level provided storage area topped by the lantern room, all of which

formed a unique piece of engineering. The 78 foot tower was fitted with a third order lens and lighting apparatus. On the exterior, a station skiff was cradled on the first level and booms and catwalks were mounted on opposite sides of the tower. Though it was in full view of San Francisco, the isolated duty was difficult, and several keepers referred to the place as "Devil's Island". While many asked for transfers, others liked the isolation such as Lyman Woodruff who served there for 18 years. The worst problem was the long periods when the fog signal was active, offering no escape. In protracted stormy periods more than one keeper was blown from the catwalks into the water. Most such accidents however, occurred when the tower was being painted or during exterior repairs. Jacob's ladders were used in various capacities and still are today.

Near the location of the rocks lies the 522 foot hull of the Navy hospital ship *Benevolence* which went to the bottom after a collision with the SS *Mary Luckenbach* August 25, 1950. Twenty-three persons perished out of the 405 souls aboard. Charges of dynamite leveled part of the hull in an effort to keep it from being a menace to navigation.

Theodore J. Sauer, years ago was presented with the Gallatin Award for his faithful years of service, some of which were spent at Mile Rocks. While there he narrowly escaped death when trying to repair a metal plate on the tower's exterior. It suddenly flew off, struck the staging and sent the helpless man down 25 feet. He struck his head on a bed of mussels, slipped off into the water and would have drowned had not the assistant keepers come quickly to his aid. He eventually recovered from the accident.

Engine generators operating 24 hours a day, unattended, keep the lighthouse in operation today, after a cable from the shoreside repeatedly failed.

Fort Point projects from the high cliffs on the south shores of San Francisco Bay, east of Mile Rocks. Long a city landmark, the red brick fort bordered by a stone seawall abuts 33 acres that are part of

Still intact, in the 20th century, historic Yerba Buena Lighthouse, showing the tower, circa 1875, the fog signal house and the keepers dwelling as seen from the air. The island has long been a nerve center for several Coast Guard activities, but its isolation from the mainland was greatly altered with the building of the San Francisco-Oakland Bridge which was linked by a tunnel under the island. Courtesy U.S. Coast Guard 12th District.

the Fort Point National Historical Site. Encompassed in the fort is an unusual abandoned lighthouse protruding above the fortress walls. Long neglected, in recent years it has been restored as an historic feature. The initial Fort Point Lighthouse had to be disassembled before being activated when the Army decided it needed the location for fortifications. Construction began on both Alcatraz and Fort Point lighthouses in 1852, and both sat idle on completion awaiting their lighting apparatus to arrive from France. Fort Point Lighthouse was only three months old when razed, and when its lens arrived in 1854, the authorities sent it to the new Point Pinos Lighthouse on Monterey Bay. As Fort Winfield Scott rose it was decided to build the second Fort Point beacon on a narrow ledge between the fort and the sea wall. It was a truncated frame tower with a fifth order lens.

The lighthouse was jinxed again, as erosion undermined the shoreline a few years later, and it too was removed. In 1864, work was underway on a third Fort Point Lighthouse, this, an iron skeleton tower atop the fort walls some 83 feet above the sea. A 70 pound weight revolved the lens on 24 ball bearings. The clockwork had to be re-wound every two and a half hours. A fogbell was part of the station equipment but dead spots often muffled the sound much to the consternation of mariners.

Several wrecks and collisions in the bay were blamed on the inadequacy of the station fog signal. The ill-fated *City of Rio de Janeiro* in 1901 allegedly scraped over the outlying ledge of rock in the fog off Fort Point before going to a watery grave. A compressed air fog signal blasting through a trumpet finally replaced the bell in 1904.

In an 1880 storm, considerable damage was inflicted on the keepers' dwellings on a bluff south of the fort; the light tower swayed violently but the keepers kept the beacon burning.

Principal keeper James Rankin resided 14 years at Fort Point after transferring from East Brother Light in 1878. During his tenure, he saved several people from drowning in San Francisco Bay.

Construction of the Golden Gate Bridge spelled the end of active service for Fort Point Light. The curtain came down September 1, 1934 when Keeper George Cobb put the padlock on the tower door and was transferred to Point Arena. The tower still stands six stories above the floor of the fort. Both the fort and the lighthouse are now open to the public as historic attractions.

Dwarfed by the Golden Gate Bridge, Lime Point Lighthouse sits on a small outcrop of rock against a steep cliff on the north side of the bay. It was a site chosen in 1883 for a fog signal station.

Frequent landslides of rock have rolled down the cliff from time to time doing damage at the station, the worst triggered by the 1906 earthquake. Added to the station's duplicate 12 inch steam whistles was a lens-lantern in 1900, but the fog whistles, the most important factor, consumed up to 150,000 pounds of coal per year, as the constant shrouds swept in from the Pacific.

Today the station is floodlighted by night. It displays a navigation light and blasts a foghorn from beneath the 740 foot high bridge supports.

Coast Guard personnel formerly stationed there were often dodging bottles thrown from the bridge. Once in 1959, a thug held up the two attendants and took their cash, one of the first recorded lighthouse stick-ups. The freighter *India Bear* tried to eradicate the station in June 1960 when the pilot, 200 yards off course, struck the outbuildings and severed air pipes connecting the fog signal with the air compressors. The ship received $60,000 in damage, the station $7,500. You can't fool with mother nature!

Automation came in 1961, when the dwelling was removed and the station made off-limits to the public.

Alcatraz Island, 2.5 miles east of the Golden Gate Bridge, is a small island bristling with buildings. It features a gray, octagonal, pyramidal light tower on the southeast sector, plus fog signals at the northwest and southeast ends of the island. Though the locale of the first government lighthouse on the west coast, the island is better known for the infamous prison that for many years housed some of America's most notorious criminals. Alcatraz is now part of the Golden Gate National Recreation Area, administered by the National Park Service.

The initial 1854 lighthouse on Alcatraz was a Cape Cod structure with the tower protruding from its center, in stark contrast to the present 84 foot reinforced concrete sentinel built in 1909. Gibbons & Kelly were the contractors for the first lighthouse, displaying a third order fixed light, initially shown on June 1, 1854. Two years after the light was established, a fogbell was added, but it had to be rung manually, a demanding task what with the frequent fogs. Totally frustrated, the keeper was fired when the inspector arrived one day and found him absent from his post. Even the inspector must have had some sympathy for the errant keeper, for shortly after, a clockwork mechanism was installed.

The 50 foot square domicile was enlarged through the efforts of principal keeper Leeds in the 1880's when he added new rooms and enlarged the existing ones.

A 3,000 pound fogbell struck mechanically was added in 1901. In 1902, the fixed lens was changed to a fourth order type with a flashing characteristic which better identified the station from the others on the bay.

The last keeper of the first lighthouse was George W. Young who had transferred to the "Rock" from the Farallons, rounding out 22 years of lighthouse service. In his 70's, and sporting a white beard, he figured it was time to put away the brass polish and cleaning rags.

For some time, Young and his associates had been sharing the island with a military penitentiary. As the walls got higher the lighthouse got smaller necessitating a loftier tower. The new 1909 station included sizable quarters to house three keepers and their families. The focal plane of the light was 200 feet above the water. It towered over the east side of the abandoned lighthouse which gave up its Fresnel for placement in the crown of its successor.

The 1906 earthquake three years earlier had done damage to the masonry work and the chimneys of the old lighthouse, but its demise as an aid to navigation was dictated by the enlarged prison. A changeover from a military to a civilian penal colony brought more notoriety to the island. There was virtually no chance of escape even if the walls were scaled. Swift currents and frigid waters surrounding the rocky islet would spell doom for the would-be escapees. The keepers were still allowed to have their families but were issued orders to keep all facilities tightly locked should the escape siren be sounded.

Prisoners sometimes did attempt an escape. The worst prison break occurred in 1946, a short distance from the light station. The Marines had to be called in after several prison guards were captured. Amid bullets, the Marines quelled the uprising and got the guards released.

During that occasion, Edward Schneider was in charge of the lighthouse, and he well remembered the incident as the bullets flew in all directions. The rotund individual put in a record 28 years on Alcatraz.

When the intolerable prison was finally terminated in 1963, the keepers for the first time had the place to themselves, but not for long. The lighthouse was automated in November of the same year and was serviced from the Yerba Buena Coast Guard base. The Fresnel was removed in favor of a double-drum revolving beacon, and automatic fog detectors were employed to control the fog signals.

Trouble of another kind erupted in 1970 when a latter day uprising occurred. A small band of armed American Indians claimed grandfather rights and took over the island. They insisted the prison rightfully belonged to them, and that excess lands could be reclaimed. Uncle Sam took a dim view of the proceedings and hoped the whole thing would just blow over. However, when the intruders utilized the

Graceful Alcatraz Lighthouse rising above the infamous Alcatraz Prison. The inset shows the lighthouse under construction in 1908-09 dwarfing the pioneer lighthouse of 1854, the first U.S. Government lighthouse on the Pacific Coast. The former lighthouse was too low to be seen above the rising walls of the prison. Coast Guard photo.

electric power which automated the lighthouse the complexion of things changed. In an attempt to force them out, the federal authorities cut the power supply and for the first time in well over a century there was no beacon shining on Alcatraz. Buoy tenders placed lighted buoys at each end of the island to take up the slack, but that failed to satisfy navigators.

The Indians attempted to relight the beacon as a symbol of their crusade, but later fire broke out damaging the lighthouse and burning down the duplex quarters which formerly housed Coast Guard attendants. A few months later the government lost its patience and federal agents landed on the island only to find some nearly starved stragglers of the original armed invaders.

At this writing the lighthouse is displaying its flashing light nightly; an authorized passenger ferry operates to the island and a museum features the former Fresnel. Empty prison cells are viewed by visitors to the famous island.

Yerba Buena Island, 345 feet high and located less than three miles southeast of Alcatraz, is covered with a scrubby growth of trees. It is the nerve center for several Coast Guard activities including the San Francisco Vessel Traffic Service Operation Center and a radar antenna site. It is also the locale of the Coast Guard Base where buoys are handled and service vessels are berthed and repaired.

Spaniards named the 140 acre island Yerba Buena, which means "good herb," for on its slopes grew an abundance of mint. Its climes were frequently visited by the early Costanoan Indians who gathered tule reeds, raised goats and cut oak trees. When the U. S. Army utilized the isle as a base in 1870, the poor Indians were driven off, but their goats remained. That was also the year the government set some of the land aside as a lighthouse reservation.

A large fogbell was delivered in 1874 while construction of the lighthouse was underway. The little Victorian tower and fog signal house became operative in 1875. A steam whistle was later installed and the bell used as backup, tule fogs being a constant concern for ship traffic.

Keepers who had children at the lighthouse sent them to the mainland by boat for their schooling.

A lighthouse depot was established on the island by the 12th District in 1873, catering to the needs of lighthouse tenders and buoys for the entire district.

With most of Yerba Buena's oak trees having been chopped down, California poet and naturalist Joaquin Miller started a replanting program there back in 1886, marking California's first Arbor Day.

In the 1930's when the World's Fair was staged on Treasure Island, just to the north of Yerba Buena, an entirely new era was begun. In 1936, the huge San Francisco-Oakland Bay Bridge became a reality and a tunnel was dug through the island as a mid-bay link. Gone were the grand fleet of San Francisco Bay ferryboats.

The Coast Guard automated the light in 1958 and it continues to shine today like a veteran soldier in the nuclear age. The original Fresnel is still in use after well over a century, and its maker Barbier & Frenestre, Paris, is still producing lenses under the name Barbier, Benard & Turenne.

The old Oakland Harbor Lighthouse, beloved by Oaklanders for many years, has been moved to a new location. It was abandoned in 1966, and eventually sold to a restaurant firm by the Coast Guard for $1. It cost $22,000 to have the Murphy-Pacific Corp. move it six miles down the Oakland Estuary where it was converted to Quinn's Lighthouse Restaurant.

Old Southampton Shoals Lighthouse, dating from 1905, was built on the ship channel between Berkeley and Marin County. Discontinued by the Coast Guard, it was moved in a novel manner in 1960 as two cranes lifted the entire structure and barged it up the San Joaquin River to become the summer clubhouse for St. Francis Yacht Club.

The first Oakland Lighthouse was built on wooden pilings and lighted January 27, 1890, displaying a fifth order light and 3,500 pound fogbell. Teredos and shipworms infested the piles after a decade, and though large rock was used to stabilize the foundation, by 1903 the damage threatened to topple the lighthouse. Appropriations were then made for a new Oakland Harbor Light. This time, concrete filled cylinders were used under the foundation. The new lighthouse was a two-story frame structure with short tower and iron lantern house at the peak of the hipped roof. It began operation July 11, 1903, as the old lighthouse was torn down and the wooden piling removed. As time went by, urban sprawl doomed the lighthouse. The Western Pacific Railroad Ferry slip surrounded the entire structure as ferryboats zoomed by on either side, day and night. Eventually the light became surplus to the needs of the Coast Guard.

San Francisco Bay's Angel Island was chosen in 1886 as a site for a fogbell. A lens-lantern was added to the station in 1900. Several wrecks and near wrecks occurred in and around the island, and keeper Juliet Nichols in 1906 had to toll the bell for more than 20 hours by hand when the clockwork mechanism failed. The first keeper was a Scotsman named John Ross. In 1872, while crossing the Columbia River bar on the lighthouse tender *Shubrick,* Ross was injured as a barge which was being towed got loose and the hawser recoiled across the vessel's deck striking him. It smashed his leg so seriously it had to be amputated. He later served in addition to Angel Island, at Fort Point and Yerba Buena Lights.

In 1952, radio beacon calibration facilities were transferred to Angel Island from Southampton Shoal Lighthouse. Angel Island has three aids to navigation—Angel Island (Point Knox), Point Blunt and Point Stuart.

Southampton Shoal Lighthouse was built in 1905 to warn shipping away from a two mile long shoal on the eastern side of the channel between Berkeley and Marin County. Constructed two miles offshore atop 11 steel cylinders, it was a handsome Victorian three-story affair. Its 3,500 pound fogbell clanged a double blow at alternating intervals.

The 1906 earthquake knocked the supporting caissons out of balance. In 1936, the station almost burned down when a blow torch being used by keeper Albert Joost to repair a radio antenna exploded, enveloping him in flames. His wife hurried to his aid and with her fire extinguisher dowsed the flames in the burning lighthouse. Afterward she bundled her husband in blankets and rowed him to Angel Island for first aid.

The Coast Guard replaced the fogbell with diaphone horns in 1939, but in 1960 decided the lighthouse was no longer needed, and that buoys would suffice. Giant cranes lifted the entire wooden structure onto a barge and moved it to Tinsley Island on the San Joaquin River where it serves as a clubhouse for the St. Francis Yacht Club.

East Brother Light, off Point San Pablo is of vintage redwood, Victorian in design, and was built in 1874. Today, mostly due to civic endeavors, the lighthouse has been completely restored and is serving as a bed and breakfast inn. All the original buildings remain and the Coast Guard has placed a fourth order Fresnel, similar to the original, in the tower.

The station first displayed its light March 1, 1874. The Lighthouse Service tried to close the station in 1934, but protests from the maritime world forced its reopening. Again in 1968, the Coast Guard came to the same decision, but Joseph Picotte, the officer-in-charge, mounted a campaign to save the island station. He looked up the

East Brother Island Light, saved from demolition by an aroused public. The classic harbor lighthouse erected in 1874 was completely restored in recent years and now serves as a bed and breakfast inn, although the Coast Guard maintains the light. The buff-colored edifice is one of the last of many San Francisco Harbor lighthouses that remains much the same as when it was commissioned. U.S. Coast Guard photo. Inset, sternwheeler **Gold** *passing East Brother in past decades. Courtesy Bob Parkinson.*

survivors of the light keepers, including J. O. Stenmark who put in many years as a devoted guardian of the light, and further enlisted the aid of the Contra Costa Shoreline Parks Committee and the Richmond Planning Commission to save one of the last remaining harbor family light stations. It was placed on the National Register. Restored and gleaming, the effort is a real tribute to those who want to save these colorful old lighthouses for posterity.

Another colorful family lighthouse that once marked the fringes of the bay was built at Mare Island in 1873. The gingerbread structure was bugled out of service in 1917. Nine days later, on July 10, the Navy's nearby ammunition depot exploded wrecking 13 buildings and shaking up the old lighthouse. Years later it was torn down.

Carquinez Strait Lighthouse built on the north side of the strait entrance near Vallejo in 1910 was located at the water end of a narrow pier extending almost a mile offshore. It was removed in 1951 in favor of a minor light. The lighthouse was offered for sale in 1955, but the purchaser, while trying to move the 150 ton building, almost lost his life in a fall. Finally in 1961, it was towed to Elliott Cove east

of Carquinez Bridge where it was to be converted to a marina, but still awaits its fate.

Then there was Roe Island Lighthouse built in 1891 at the east end of Suisun Bay, 33 miles inland from the ocean. It is best remembered because of a terrible explosion that occurred on the eve of July 17, 1944 when two merchant ships at the Port Chicago Ammunition Depot being loaded with thousands of tons of ammo, exploded. The horrifying blast was just across the Sacramento River from the Roe Island station. The sky was filled with smoke and flame. Clocks stopped at 10 P.M., and many residents nearby thought the world had come to an end. As ambulances, fire trucks and rescue teams rushed to the scene they were aghast. Two ocean cargo ships, the SS *Quinault Victory* and *E. A. Bryan,* a train, two Coast Guard vessels, numerous buildings and 300 men had been blown to kingdom come. The dead never knew what hit them.

Roe Island Light Station received major damage. It appeared like ten pins hit by a bowling ball. Less than a year later on May 5, 1945, the station was deleted from the Coast Guard *Light List.*

CHAPTER SIX

California Lighthouses, Northern Sector

Hope, like the gleaming taper's light,
Adorns and cheers our way;
And still, as darker grows the night,
Emits a brighter ray.
...Oliver Goldsmith

Point Reyes, 18 miles north of Farallon Light is a bold, pitted rocky headland that from the seaward side appears like a massive dried prune. It rises to 612 feet at the western extremity, running in an easterly direction for three miles. The place literally abounds in history, much of it tragic, for it was here that the first recorded shipwreck on the west coast occurred in 1595. The Spanish galleon *San Agustin* out of Manila, in charge of Sebastian Rodriguez Cermeno, trader, navigator and commander, with Francisco Chavez as master, reached her final port in Drakes Bay. The ship was driven up on the inhospitable shore after dragging her anchors. Two of her company allegedly drowned and the 130 ton cargo of silks, beeswax and general freight was mostly lost. In a subsequent dispute with the local Indians over the spoils salvaged from the wreck, a battle ensued and though the Indians were driven off, Cermeno lost food, supplies and 12 of his men. The survivers, about 70 in number, were packed like sardines in the ship's boat (vicoro) and miraculously reached Acapulco with only one of their number succumbing during the exhausting voyage.

In the year that followed scores of ships were to leave their bones bleaching on the rocks or in the swirling, crashing breakers that seemingly never take a holiday in that windy, fog-swept sector of the coast.

It was only natural that Point Reyes would be the site for a major aid to navigation, the only surprise being that is wasn't among the very first to be built by Uncle Sam. Stubborn landowners demanded $25,000 from Uncle Sam which at that time was considered highly excessive, plus it was the exact amount that had been authorized for both the land and the lighthouse. Uncle cried, "foul". In the interim, 14 shipwrecks occurred in the area. The bargaining got tougher; the government considered condemnation. An agreement was at last finalized in 1869 when 120 acres were obtained for $6,000. The following year, materials were landed in Drakes Bay and a wharf and storage shed were set up. Construction superintendent was New Englander Phineas F. Marston. He was just off a building job at Port Angeles where he constructed a frame lighthouse on Ediz Hook.

Preliminaries demanded blasting of rock and the hacking out of wagon roads over extremely rough terrain. Two terraces had to be carved out of solid rock, one at the 100 foot level for the fog signal building, and the other at 250 feet for the light tower. A combination coal shute and stairway from the plateau of the headland had to be constructed to reach the navigation aids, 300 steps down to the lighthouse, and 638 steps to the foghouse.

The lighthouse was bolted deep into solid rock to combat the strong winds. Encased in iron plate, it had two galleries and was sixteen-sided. The first order Fresnel installed was manufactured by Barbier & Fenestre of Paris and consisted of 24 flash panels and 1,032 glass prisms. A spacious frame dwelling, two stories high, was built at the top of the headland to house the four keepers and their families. Lighthouse authorities were so pleased with Marston's work that he was hired to build the Pigeon Point Lighthouse.

The lamp was lit on December 1, 1870, but two years later the station fog signal building burned to the ground. The replacement steam signal consumed 140 pounds of coal an hour. The needs

sometimes could not meet demands and the foghorn went silent at intervals.

Principal keeper John C. Bull, was an exceptional government employee. In 1875, when the lens rotation got out of balance he put his ingenuity to work, jacked up the multi-ton lens and discovered the wheels had worn badly. Using wedges to tilt the huge cage of glass, he inserted ten new bronze chariot wheels and got the apparatus working to perfection, proudly timing it with his service stop watch.

The year prior, one of his assistants, E. K. Lincoln had gone down to check on the wreck of the 988 ton British ship *Warrior Queen* which had stranded on the outcrops near the light station. Inbound from New Zealand for San Francisco the vessel came to grief July 20, 1874 amid suspicious circumstances. The crew allegedly had been

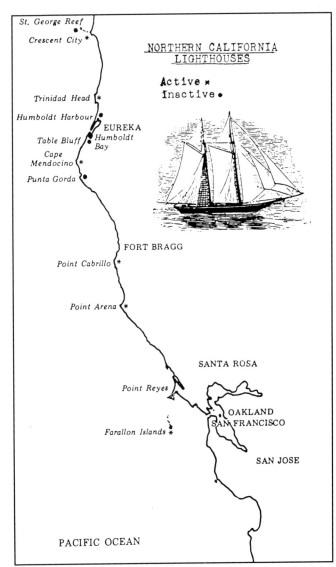

Point Reyes Lighthouse was built in 1870, and in its early years was a station with many difficulties. Wind, fog and shipwreck told the story of this weather-beaten sector of the California coast, Marin's treacherous shores. The scintillating first order Fresnel has been replaced by a utilitarian beacon near the old tower.

Coast Guardsman Gary Decker peers down the grueling 300 steps to the Point Reyes Lighthouse before the days of automation. The wind was sometimes so strong at Point Reyes that it blew the attendants over the railing. Photo courtesy International Harvester Company.

near mutiny and may have been involved in scuttling the vessel. Though most of the cargo was saved the ship was a total loss.

Adding further mystery, Lincoln never returned to the light station nor did he reappear any other place. He just disappeared, supposedly while surveying the wreck, but he left no clues to even verify that belief.

After Bull was transferred, growing dissension broke out among the keepers at the station, mostly over problems of keeping the fog signal operating properly during protracted periods of fog. Sleepless nights and extended working hours made nerves razor sharp. It all came to a boiling point when the hawser which pulled the handcart alongside the chute, snapped. Down plunged the metal car at uncontrollable speed crashing through the quarters used for housing the attendants on the lower level. Fortunately nobody was injured in the incident but the damage was considerable.

When Lighthouse Inspector S. Casey inspected the station on February 15, 1877, he claimed it to be "..in anything but a creditable condition showing in many cases want of care and attention."

And things failed to improve. A few years later when the government lighthouse tender *Shubrick* arrived with supplies, the inspector was appalled at the unacceptable performances as logged in the station journal, and he let his feelings be known. He did, however, better understand the difficult conditions involved. Though several transfers were made, the difficulties remained. All the while shipwrecks occurred with frequency, so much so that in 1881, the area's first U. S. Lifesaving Station was established at nearby Bolinas Bay. About the same time a telegraph wire was erected to connect the isolated post with San Francisco, greatly enhancing communications, especially during emergencies.

Unfortunately in 1885, the lifesaving station in an arson fire burned to the ground. Despite the rash of shipwrecks, shortage of government funds permitted four years to pass before a new lifeboat station was constructed, this time at Point Reyes Beach. During the same year of

the fire a pall of doom was cast over the lighthouse as expressed in the following poetic lines by keeper E. G. Chamberlain:

"Solitude, where are the charms that sages have seen in thy face Better dwell in the midst of alarms than reign in this horrible place."

Point Reyes' reputation was by now well established as the foggiest, windiest place on the entire California coast. The *San Francisco Chronicle* reported on September 25, 1887:

"The sirens had been in operation for 176 consecutive hours and jaded attendants looked as if they had been on a protracted spree."

When Principal Keeper John C. Ryan took over Point Reyes Lighthouse on January 21, 1888, he jotted in the station journal the following remark:

"In taking charge of this station I must say that it is broken, filthy and almost a total wreck from end to end."

He was just what the place needed, and under his leadership the assistant keepers began to pull their share of the load. The jinx, however, apparently continued, for the lighthouse journal several months later listed the dismissal of Ryan, he evidently having lost his cool.

Again we turn to the station journal and the report of January 30, 1889 in a continuing series of bizarre incidents:

"The second assistant (lighthouse keeper) went crazy and was handed over to the constable in Olema."

During the next two decades the conditions improved at the station but the inclement weather seldom took a holiday. On January 27, 1916, P. Nilsson, principal keeper reported winds of over 100 mph which did considerable damage. The tank house roof was ripped off, fences, chimneys, poles and wires knocked down. Winds in excess of 40 mph are often the norm for the weather-worn point, a fact to which residents of the Point Reyes area will attest to. Through the years the strong winds were always a dangerous deterrent to keepers who often traversed the 638 steps between the upper level of the station and the fog signal house on the lower level where the boilers had to be fed to sound the warning apparatus during the pea soup fogs. Given a choice, the oldtime keepers far preferred winding up the 180 pound weight that turned the three ton lens to keeping the old fog signal in operation.

One of the heralded heros of the Point Reyes station was Fred Kreth. After a fishing vessel was wrecked below the lighthouse, he went to the rescue of the marooned survivors by lowering himself down the steep cliff on a lengthy coil of rope. The castaways had clung to the slimey rocks for 13 hours and faced almost certain death. Winds of 80 mph were fanning the area. Kreth made one end of the rope fast and tied the other around his waist, then commenced lowering himself downward from rock to rock for nearly 200 feet. When he could go no further, he braced himself on a thin ledge of strata and uncoiled the rope until it reached the trembling hands of the trapped fisherman, 50 yards below. In a prodigious effort, he somehow managed to pull the trio of greatful men one by one to safety.

With time and progress, the hardships of Point Reyes improved and the keepers and their families got a much better deal. The old fog signal house was finally abandoned when endangered by falling rock. A new powerhouse with generators and air compressors was installed. When the lighthouse was taken over by the Coast Guard, the oil vapor lamp installed in 1911, was removed and the lens fitted with a 1,500 watt electric light.

Gustave Zetterquist who arrived at the lighthouse as an assistant keeper in 1930, remained there with his family until 1951. Unlike many of his predecessors he was pleased with the Point Reyes lighthouse life as was his family. After he left, the Coast Guard staffed

Point Arena Lighthouse, a 115 foot high tubular tower was established in 1908, replacing a lighthouse that dated from 1870, and which became the victim of an earthquake. The present lighthouse is still active, king of the jutting finger of land on which it stands. The lighthouse was specially engineered to resist earthquakes. U.S. Coast Guard photo.

Inset: Artist's drawing of the first Point Arena Lighthouse which was later destroyed by an earthquake.

the facility with various personnel until it was automated in 1975. The commodious two-story dwelling was raised in 1960.

Today, the old lighthouse has been retired. In its place, a flashing light of modern manufacture shines from the top of a square building. There is also a foghorn and radio beacon on the premises. The National Park Service has opened the old lighthouse for daily public inspection, weather permitting. The Point Reyes National Seashore has taken control, and park rangers tenant the former quarters of the light keepers.

Despite the lighthouse, fog signals, lifesaving stations and radio beacons, about 60 deep water ships have been wrecked around the ragged ramparts of Point Reyes, and scores of lives have been lost. The British Admiralty Charts showed a light on Point Reyes in 1865, five years before its actual establishment. In the interim the Russian corvette *Norvick* (Novick) stranded nearby, her master blaming the wreck on false charting.

Point Arena lies 68 miles northwest of Point Reyes and consists of a long, level plateau, the first prominent point north of Point Reyes. Point Arena Lighthouse, 155 feet above the water, is displayed from a unique 115 foot cylindrical tower with black lantern house and gallery. A radio beacon is nearby.

The grounds of Point Arena and its outbuildings are the site of another modern day hostel for hikers, bikers, and public transit, administered by the American Youth Hostels, Golden Gate Council.

The lighthouse shares honors with Pigeon Point as the tallest towers of their breed on the West Coast, (with the exception of St. George Reef) and guards an ocean stretch filled with rocks and reefs for 50 miles, offering no good harbors of refuge.

The point has been a victim of Mother Nature's wrath on several occasions. The initial masonry lighthouse, 100 feet tall, was erected 50 feet above the sea and displayed its light on May 1, 1870, a fixed first order Fresnel. It was similar in design to Pigeon Point Lighthouse. The narrow strand of land is treeless and cuts a swath into the Pacific, perhaps eons ago attached to Arena Rock, a huge offshore sea stack.

Family problems were evidently on the mind of first assistant keeper George Kooms, for a January 1880, journal entry read; "threatening weather and fighting children." On February 26, 1880, the weather must have won out, for the entry read the, "worst gale ever seen," and then he went on to list all the damage inflicted on the station, everything not bolted down being "hurled around like matchsticks."

A windmill had to be used to pump water from the cistern to the fog signal, lack of the liquid stuff sometimes a major problem at the station in the early years.

Unfortunately, the San Andreas fault runs immediately off Point Arena and the lighthouse has been frequently rocked by earthquakes. On April 18, 1906, the roof literally caved in. The great earthquake that destroyed San Francisco was to leave an idelible mark at Point Arena. The light tower suffered a fatal attack. Though it didn't collapse it was cracked throughout, gaping holes here and there and loose bricks laying on the ground. It was beyond repair, the lens was shattered and the keepers' dwelling a total loss. The families were without shelter and to make matters worse, a black bear terrified by the quake, ran amok around the premises and had to be shot.

A temporary lighthouse was immediately built and capped by the lantern house removed from the destroyed tower. A second order lens

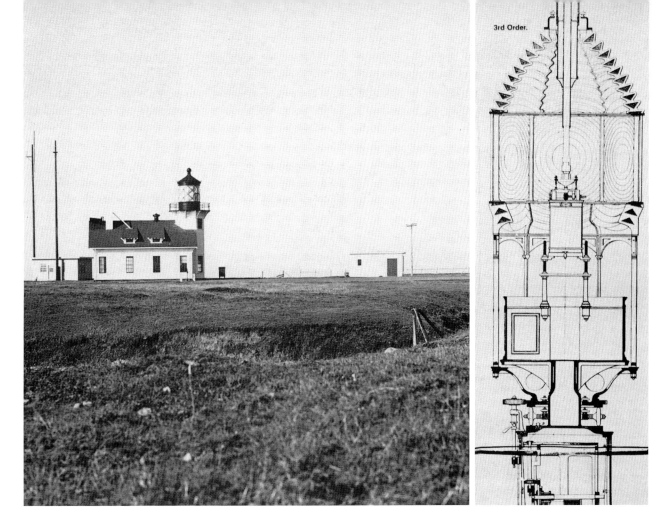

Point Cabrillo Lighthouse was often called the friend of the steam schooner navigators, lumber steamers that hugged the coast. The lightstation was established in 1909 and fitted with a third order lens and lighting apparatus. The structure is still in use, but in the early 1970s when the station was automated, a sizable reflecting beacon was mounted atop the roof, seaward of the tower.

was supplied by the Lighthouse Service and in operation by January 5, 1907. Fortunately the old fog signal building had survived the quake and continued to warn shipping during the emergency.

The remains of the former tower were dismantled, and lighthouse engineers were employed to produce a design that could survive the worst Mother Nature could dole out. A firm that specialized in constructing tall chimneys was hired. The result was the nation's first concrete reinforced lighthouse, strengthened by massive cement buttresses and featuring a protruding circular room around the base of the tower. It was designed to be earthquake proof and up to now has achieved its purpose.

The first order lens supplied for the tower, floated in a large tub of mercury which provided friction-free rotation, a system that had proven successful in other lighthouses. The lens rested on a vertical shaft that extended into a large container and turned when the weights dropped down through the trunk of the tower. (In later years small electric motors were employed in many lighthouses to turn the Fresnels.)

Four new cottages for the attendants of the Point Arena Light Station were built to replace the former residence following the big earthquake.

Shipwrecks along that iron-bound section of coast demanded a lifesaving station at Point Arena by 1900.

Wayne Piland and Bill Owens, traditional civil service light keepers were among the colorful personalities that formerly manned the station. Owens alerted the military authorities after Pearl Harbor that he had sighted a Japanese submarine surface off the lighthouse. The naval officer receiving his report told him to "go back to bed",

that no enemy submarines were in the area. A few days later the Standard tanker *Emidio* took a torpedo broadside off Blunts Reef and five of her crew perished.

On another occasion in World II, a Navy blimp having trouble controlling its flight pattern actually bumped into the light tower just below the lantern house and then continued its flight northward, seemingly without serious damage.

As of this writing, the station is operated by the "Point Arena Lighthouse Keepers," seven days a week. A $1 fee gains entrance to the old fog signal building and a tour of the tower, which is located less than two miles north from the town of Point Arena, via Lighthouse Road. The Coast Guard maintains the light.

It was a troublesome time in America in the 1920's during prohibition. The light keepers at Point Arena were on occasion intimidated among others, by a boyish looking figure of a man who with gun in hand warned them not to report unusual night activities along the coast. At the time, there was alot of illegal whiskey being run ashore in hidden coves and beaches. Pickup rumrunning craft were meeting foreign flag ships outside the three mile limit and making transfers in the dark of night. The boss figure was small of stature, with steel, cold eyes and went by the name of Lester J. Gillis, or just plain "Gill". His ready trigger-finger and deadly accuracy with a sawed-off machine gun was to later boost him up the ladder of criminal activity in Chicago's Alky syndicate.

Baby-Face Nelson became the country's most infamous criminal. When he was rubbed out in the 1930's, his picture and story appeared in newspapers across the land. It was then the light keepers at Point Arena recognized his picture as none other than the same Lester J.

Point Cabrillo Lighthouse before the days of automation was a favorite station for keepers and Coast Guardsmen as well. Photo courtesy Carl Christensen.

Gillis, the hood that prowled the Redwood coast making demands and threats. How Gillis came to be known as Baby-Face Nelson remained a mystery, but there was no doubt he was the boss gunner of a gang of rumrunners who had made a speciality of landing cases of illegal Canadian hootch, which in turn was trucked from Little River to a distribution center in San Francisco, protected by Nelson's henchmen.

What has long been known as the Redwood Coast of northern California is a unique stretch of coastline unlike that found anywhere else. It is a region of heavy breakers, strong winds, persistent fogs, big trees, and rocky bluffs. The shores are peppered with shipwrecks of coastal sailing schooners and steam schooners that in the flourishing era of coastwise shipping hauled the giant redwood logs and lumber out of the dangerous dogholes indenting the hostile coastline.

As a protective measure, a lighthouse was built on the Mendocino shores that was to be of great importance to the coasters. It was placed on Point Cabrillo, three miles from the town of Mendocino and 24 miles north of Point Arena. The light was illuminated for the first time on June 10, 1909, a 47 foot frame tower and fog signal house combined. The lens was of the third order of the system of Fresnel. Though the coastal redwood fleet is no more, the beacon remains a symbol of the past.

The 60 foot high bluff on which the lighthouses stands is riddled with wave tunnels hammered out by the pounding waves which sometimes send scud up to the plateau. In appearance, the octagonal tower and fog signal building from a distance resemble a country church, and it undoubtedly had an aura of the spiritual to tempest-tossed mariners who on stormy nights were warmed by the halo in its crown.

A German named Wihelm Baumgartner was the initial guardian of the light. As fog appeared that first night, he both trimmed the lamp and started up the air compressors that blasted the fog trumpets.

The unstable land on the point where livestock grazed presented problems on occasion. Sometimes the animals got too close to the edge and tumbled to the beach. It was a major job to haul them out. The station, however, was considered one of the more desired duty stations by lighthouse keepers. It was near town where their children could go to school, and where supplies were readily purchased. The station dwellings were roomy and comfortable.

A storm on February 8, 1960 struck with great force sending breakers thundering against the point and tearing out chunks of rock that were thrown great distances. The foghouse doors were ripped off and pieces of wooden siding peeled off. An air compressor and generator were shoved across the room, and debris was scattered all over. Keeper Bill Owens remembered the incident well, he being the last civilian keeper, spending 11 of his 33 lighthouse service years at Cabrillo. He was quoted as saying about automation, "Anything automatic always goes haywire just when you need it. We'll have a big shipwreck one of these days." Somehow time has a way of passing us all by, sort of like ships passing in the night, and new innovations are here to stay.

Coast Guard-manned till the 1970's, the change to automation saw an aero-marine type rotating beacon mounted on the roof, curtains put around the Fresnel, and the foghorns removed in favor of a buoy with sounding apparatus placed offshore.

Part of Cabrillo National Monument operated by the National Park Service, the lighthouse and park are presently open to the public from 9 A.M. to 5 P.M. daily and the third order lens is there for all to see.

Punta Gorda, is a high, bold, rounding cape, 83 miles northwest of Point Arena and 11 miles south of Cape Mendocino. The seaward face rises to about 900 feet, only 400 yards back from the beach and terminates in a spur, 140 feet high, almost overhanging the sea. In this bleak setting, bare of trees except in a series of frowning gulches, stands an abandoned gray, rectangular lighthouse, 25 feet high. Punta Gorda Lighthouse has a front yard where the wind, sea and currents are said to be as strong as any point on the California coast. Swift riptides confuse the seas which never seem to take a rest.

The lighthouse is a forlorn sight, far from any center of population and only visited occasionally by beachcombers who experience a long hike over rough terrain. The Spanish name means "massive point". The main reason for establishment of a lighthouse there was the number of ships that experienced disaster—eight, from 1899 to 1907. As early as 1890, Lighthouse authorities considered the place for a guiding beacon and fog signal, but it wasn't until the SS *Columbia* went to a watery grave in a fog-induced collision with the steam schooner *San Pedro* July 21, 1907, 16 miles south of Punta Gorda, that greater pressure was brought to bear. Newspapers across the land filled front pages with the story, 87 died, 150 survived.

The following year Congress appropriated funds for construction of the station. Surveyors chose a spot slightly less than a mile south of the point, near Fourmile Creek, desolate, lonely and difficult to reach. All materials had to be landed by small boat on the beach north of the site and delivered by horse drawn sleds.

The contract called for the construction of a small lighthouse which was overshadowed by three commodious dwellings, a fog signal building and several outbuildings for carpenter work, blacksmithing and storage. A water and sewage system was also provided. The lighthouse itself was only 23 feet long and 12 feet wide topped by an iron lantern featuring a fourth order flashing lens. The fog signal house went into operation before the light. Due to the difficulty of getting materials to the site and the inclement weather, the light wasn't illuminated until January 15, 1912, six months after the fog signal was activated.

From the inception, horses and mules were used to pull wagons along the beach between Punta Gorda and Petrolia when weather and tides permitted. It was an 11 mile trip but easier than the rugged overland route. Sometimes there were weeks when the beach was impassable.

During World War II, the Coast Guard sent several of its recruits to the area for beach patrol, increasing the population at the lonely outpost.

With improvements in aids to navigation, Punta Gorda Lighthouse after the war was placed on the endangered list as being too costly to maintain. Ships no longer hugged the coast as in earlier times. In February 1951, CBM Hank Mostovoy padlocked the door. Punta Gorda Lighthouse obituary read; "1912-1951, the light has been forever extinguished." The lens was removed, and a horse named "Old Bill," attached to the station for years, was sold for horse meat.

After abandonment, hippies found the old dwellings sufficient for their needs and moved in. Some tried to clean up the place but others turned it into a garbage dump. The government got involved from the liability standpoint and ordered them off the land, claiming the dwellings were fire hazards. Finally in 1970 the Bureau of Land Management ordered the buildings burned to the ground, only the concrete oil house and lighthouse remaining. There is a feeling of nostalgia there today. One can still see the steel remains of the SS *St. Paul* lying on the beach at low tide. She went aground October 5, 1905 a short distance south of where the lighthouse was built. Also the wooden planking of the steamer *Humboldt* wrecked a decade earlier shows on occasion, grim reminders of the past.

Should one visit the lighthouse today he must drive a mile south from Petrolia, turn west onto Lighthouse Road to a beach front parking area, then hike 3½ miles to the lighthouse. It is a rugged walk, not for everyone, but there are rewards for the hardy.

Cape Mendocino, 185 miles north of San Francisco is a mountainous headland, the favorite natural landmark of the old Spanish navigators returning from the Philippines. It is also a turning point for ships traveling north or south along the coast. Though it serves as a prominent land and seamark, it is also a dangerous place in thick weather, the sea bottom and currents being very irregular. It is an area of great climatic change. The face of the cape is precipitious and rock-bound, and the shoreline, long hammered by the Pacific breakers, is a contorted upheaval.

The presently abandoned pioneer Mendocino lighthouse, seemingly with tears in its crown, stands 70 yards from a double-drum airways beacon mounted atop a pole 515 feet above the water.

The cape was targeted for a lighthouse a century and a quarter ago. On September 14, 1867, the lighthouse tender *Shubrick* brought men and materials for the work, but 13 miles south of Punta Gorda she got off course and struck a giant rock that punctured her wooden hull. The skipper beached his command to avert sinking. Though eventually salvaged, all the ship's cargo was lost. New materials had to be landed through the surf at the base of the mighty monolith and transported up to the 422 foot level. The problems connected with the

Lonely outpost—Punta Gorda Light Station in a desolate sector of the northern California coast began operations in 1911 and was terminated and abandoned by the Coast Guard in 1951. Several years later all the dwellings and outbuildings were torn down to prevent squatters from living there, by order of the Bureau of Land Management. Only the abandoned lighthouse and one utility building remains. Lighthouse in photo is third from left.

Cape Mendocino Light Station established in 1868, 35 miles south of Eureka was one of the early victims of automation, it becoming an unattended station in December 1950. The loftiest in the 12th Coast Guard District at 422 feet, it no longer displays its light. As an economy measure in 1971, the Coast Guard replaced the beacon with a utilitarian light. Today it shines from a pole 515 feet above the Pacific. The old lighthouse sits in solitude at this writing. U.S. Coast Guard photo.

All that remains of the old Table Bluff Lighthouse, circa 1892, is the frame tower formerly attached to an ornate dwelling. The station was automated in 1953 and discontinued in 1972, and moves are afoot to take the tower to a new location in Eureka.

building of the station were legion, but the obstacles were overcome, and a 16-sided cast-iron, pyramidal lighthouse with double balconies was created.

The light went into operation December 1, 1868, but there was no fog signal due to possible confusion with menacing offshore Blunts Reef. Another prominent feature of the lighthouse was the close proximity of Sugar Loaf, a bold 326 foot sea stack connected with the cape at low tide by a narrow neck of rocks and shingle beach. The light was of the first order of Fresnel.

Consisting of 171 acres, the lighthouse reservation included accommodations for two keepers and their families, a barn, carpenter shop and several outbuildings. The light tower suffered a severe crack two years later, when the foundation settled. In an 1870 earthquake, the keepers' dwelling was so badly damaged it had to be torn down and rebuilt. The danger of getting to the tower to tend the light by night was often so dangerous, a special watch room was erected opposite the light tower in the late 1870's. Landslides also presented problems demanding laborious effort from time to time.

The keepers and their families frequently suffered from illness and poor living conditions to a much higher degree than comparable light stations. The 1906 earthquake knocked chimneys down and did other damage, the living quarters having deteriorated to such an extent that the 12th Lighthouse District ordered new dwellings built in 1908, 300 feet away from the lighthouse.

In 1881, tragedy struck when lighthouse inspector McDougal arrived on the tender *Manzanita*. While rowing to the beach by boat to inspect the lighthouse, breakers capsized the craft. He allegedly had strapped to his person a heavy bag of gold coins, pay for the keepers at the station. They may have been the cause of his drowning.

The lighthouse gained some offshore company in 1905 when the *Blunt Reef Lightship* was stationed offshore. The deadly barrier was about 3 miles in a westerly direction from Cape Mendocino. Mentioned earlier was the wreck of the SS *Bear* on the Mendocino Shores, but the most tragic shipwreck was when the SS *Alaska* rammed into fog-shrouded Blunts Reef at a high rate of speed. The vessel went down with the loss of 42 lives, including her master.

Aboard were 220 passengers. When the Humboldt Lifesaving crew arrived only the ship's foremast protruded from the water and scores of people were struggling in the ocean billows.

On another occasion, keeper M. M. Palmer was credited in October 1926 with getting out the word that saved the crew of the steam schooner *Everett* which was afire offshore. The newly installed telephone line allowed better communication, and rescue vessels came quickly to remove the vessel's passengers and crew.

Cape Mendocino Light was automated March 3, 1951, the lens removed to the information center at the county fair grounds in historic Ferndale. Twin rotating airway beacons were placed in the lantern house. By the 1970's, the Coast Guard decided it would be more economical to close the lighthouse and move the light to a steel pole. Since that time nearly all the station outbuildings have been razed to prevent further unauthorized use by squatters. Only the old lighthouse remains at this writing and its future is somewhat in doubt. A move is afoot to open it as an historical attraction or to dismantle the structure and move it to Ferndale for eventual remariage with its original lens. Insasmuch as the town is not on the ocean, if the plan is ever carried out, the vintage lighthouse, with its umbrella dome, would become landlocked.

Table Bluff Lighthouse, four miles south of Humboldt Bay, may not be there much longer. The tower is all that remains of the former station which formerly was attached to a dwelling. The frame Victorian structure was built in 1892 to replace the Humboldt Harbor Light Station. Plans are at this writing underway to move the aging tower to a specified location in the city of Eureka.

In the beginning, condemnation proceedings were threatened by the government before the reluctant owner finally sold six acres of his prime land for the aid to navigation. It was October 31, 1892 that Principal Keeper Tony Schmoll first lit the lucerne. For a short time the place was known as Humboldt Light Station in a gentle transition from the lighthouse it replaced, but because of the confusion the name Table Bluff Light Station was soon adopted and remained till the bitter end.

For several years, naval personnel were close neighbors to the Table Bluff keepers after a government radio sending and receiving station was erected nearby. In 1953, the light was automated, the fog signal discontinued and the dwelling razed. In later years a religous commune obtained rights to the station grounds naming it Lighthouse Ranch, but the Coast Guard kept the light tower in operation till 1972 when the beacon in its crown went dark. The residence was razed and the detached tower stood in solitude with its new neighbors. Finally the light became surplus to the needs of the Coast Guard with improved navigation aids at the harbor entrance.

The granddaddy lighthouse of the Redwood Coast is long gone, reduced to the realm of memory. A lighthouse at the Humboldt Harbor entrance was first suggested in the middle of the last century. A location was chosen on the north spit where its beacon could serve both as a seacoast and a harbor entrance light. Congress initially appropriated $15,000 for its construction. Designed by Ammi B. Young, the lighthouse was similar to the other pioneer coast lights in California, but differed in that its tower was higher.

The lamp was lit on December 20, 1856 by principal keeper J. Johnson. D. W. Pearce had been initially assigned but resigned before the lighting apparatus arrived. When Johnson died three years later, his wife Sarah became keeper of the light. She remained at her duties until 1863, surprisingly the longest any keeper of Humboldt Light remained at the post. Perhaps it was the constantly blowing sand and encroaching seas that discourged the other keepers.

With no fog signal at the station, an innovative bell boat was anchored in the waters off the lighthouse. The iron-hulled, unmanned contraption, about 30 feet long with a 300 pound bell mounted on a short mast, was rung by the motion of the sea. It however, proved unsuccessful and lasted less than two years when the government allocated funds for a steam fog whistle. There was a huge cost overrun on the boiler house when the builder decided on his own to make it earthquake proof.

In 1877, the light station was shaken by an earthquake cracking the walls of the structure and damaging the boat landing and boathouse. The builders had made a grave error. Had they read their Bibles they would have learned the folly of building one's house on sand.

Once in 1883, after 120 hours of continuous fog the old boiler petered out and no sound was emitted from the whistle. Shipwreck was narrowly averted before the signal was restored.

The lighthouse keepers had new neighbors with the establishment of the Humboldt Bay Lifesaving Station in 1878 to help alleviate the rash of mishaps and disasters on and around the fickle Humboldt Bay bar where lumber vessels were in abundance.

An almost unheard of event occurred in 1885 when a cyclone struck the station. Keeper William C. Price couldn't believe his eyes when he saw the roofs torn off the lighthouse dwelling and the foghouse. Unusually high seas driven by fierce gale winds slammed driftwood logs and debris into the lighthouse. Sand was eroded away from the foundation and seawater surrounded the edifice. Large cracks appeared and the cellar was filled with water.

The handwriting was on the wall. It was obvious the lighthouse had been built in the wrong place and was being undermined by constant erosion. It was decided to move the beacon four miles south to the safer climes of Table Bluff. Temporary lens-lanterns were set up at the harbor entrance until the new lighthouse was completed.

A contingent of War Department engineers lived in the former lighthouse dwelling temporarily while working on the Humboldt jetties. Though the damaged building was later ordered torn down, the order never came to fruition. Not to worry, Mother Nature would do the job for nothing. With each year the building crumbled away under nature's assault. Soon the dwelling fell apart. The badly cracked tower stood until the early 1930's, looking for all the world like a haunted tower of doom. One morning in 1933, as if a product of the

Trinidad Head Lighthouse as pictured about 1905. It was built in 1871 and has kept its perch since that date. One of the greatest waves ever recorded hit the structure in 1914, about 200 feet above normal water. Photo courtesy Carl Christensen.

Fred L. Harrington, keeper of Trinidad Head Lighthouse.

The folks of Trinidad liked their little lighthouse so much they decided to build a duplicate as a tourist attraction on the lee side of the head. The little memorial concrete sentinel provides housing for the former lens, and the original Trinidad fogbell is displayed nearby.

The pioneer Humboldt Bay Lighthouse after its abandonment. It was built in 1856, but was replaced in 1892 by a new lighthouse atop Table Bluff. Courtesy Carl Christensen.

nation's depression, the tower collapsed. Today, on occasion a piece of the brick masonry is seen here and there in the sands where the tower once stood.

Trinidad Head, 39 miles north northeast of Cape Mendocino and 17 miles north of the entrance to Humboldt Bay rises to a height of 380 feet. The sides are steep and covered with chaperal. From its slopes shines Trinidad Head Light, some 196 feet above the water. The mushroom-like 25 foot tower is situated on the southwest side of the head. A lighted whistle buoy is offshore and a radio beacon stands a considerable distance from the tower. This aged guardian of the sea front and Trinidad harbor once hosted numerous steam schooners and sailing vessels, but today is most important to the commercial fishing fleet that frequents the area.

In 1866, 42 acres were purchased by the government for the lighthouse on Trinidad Head. After considerable agitation for funds, $20,000 was appropriated and work started in 1871. The elevation was such that only a squat brick lighthouse was required. Keeper Jeremiah Kiler was the initial attendant, and on December 1, 1871 the lamp was lit. The keepers dwelling, 150 feet from the beacon, was far more gracious in architecture than the lighthouse. The fog signal equipment was slow in arriving, in fact, it was 1898 before a 4,000 pound fogbell was installed on a small shelf of rock 126 feet above the sea. The bell tower was battered down two years later and for a period manual ringing of the bell was required. The station was supplied for the most part by the Lighthouse tender *Madrono*.

After Kiler resigned in 1888, Fred L. Harrington was named keeper, and during his tenure a most unusual event occurred. He recorded the following account in the lighthouse journal.

The storm commenced on December 28, 1914, blowing a gale that night. The gale continued for a whole week and was accompanied by a very heavy sea from the southwest. On the 30 and 31st, the sea increased and at 3 p.m. on the 31st seemed to have reached its height, when it washed a number of times over Pilot Rock, a half mile south of the head. At 4:40 p.m., I was in the tower and had just set the lens in operation and turned to wipe the lantern room windows when I observed a sea of unusual height, then about 200 yards distant, approaching. I watched it as it came

in. When it struck the bluff, the jar was very heavy, and the sea shot up to the face of the bluff and over it, until the solid sea seemed to me to be on a level with where I stood in the lantern, (196 feet above sea level). Then it commenced to recede and the spray went 25 feet or more higher. The sea itself fell over onto the top of the bluff and struck the tower on about a level with the balcony, making a terrible jar. The whole point between the tower and the bluff was buried in water. The lens immediately stopped revolving and the tower was shivering from the impact for several seconds.

Whether the lens was thrown off level by the jar on thebluff, or the sea striking the tower, I could not say.Either one would have been enough. However, I had it leveled and running in half an hour. About an hour later another sea threw spray up on the level of the bluff, and the constant jars of the heavy sea was much over normal during the night and the whole of the next day. On the 3rd (January 1915), the sea moderated to some extent, but a strong southeast wind and high sea continued until the 5th. During the 26 years I have been stationed here there has at no time been a sea of any such size as that of the 31st experienced here; but once during that time have I known the spray to come onto the bluff in front of the tower, and but twice have I seen sea or spray go over Pilot Rock (93 feet high). During the prevalence of this storm about one third of the old wharf on the eastside of the reservation was washed away, the iron rails laid on the balance of it probably being all that kept the rest from going. The lower part of the division fence was also damaged to some extent, a number of lengths being washed out by the high sea.

That natural sea wave was probably one of the greatest ever recorded, climbing the precipitous headland and up to the lighthouse lantern, about 200 feet above the ocean.

Harrington retired from the service in 1916 and was succeeded by Edward Wilborg, but never since that time has anything like that monumental wave been recorded. The fourth order lighthouse lens was turned on ball bearings and displayed a fixed and flashing characteristic—a fixed white beam varied every minute by a red flash.

The last Blunts Reef Lightship tugs at her anchor off the dreaded reef. She was withdrawn from duty in 1971 in favor of a self-contained ocean buoy. Coast Guard photo. Insert shows the Blunts Lightship (523) that preceded the buoy on station, as the Coast Guard buoy tender **Balsam** *approaches with fuel and supplies in April 1956. Carl Christensen photo.*

A whaling station was established in Trinidad Harbor near the lighthouse landing in the early 1920's and the keepers often alerted crews when the big grays were blowing off the head.

The station was electrified in 1942, and compressed air horns replaced the bell, though the bell house remained in place. In 1947 the Fresnel was removed in favor of a 375 mm refracting beacon. Fifteen years later the keeper's dwelling was torn down. The little lighthouse lives on, still the hallmark for Trinidad Harbor.

The local citizenry thought so much of their lighthouse that they built a concrete life-sized replica in 1948 and created a little park around it. The old lens was positioned inside the lantern and the original fog bell mounted alongside the structure. The real lighthouse is only open to the public by special arrangement with the Coast Guard.

There have been changes in the area but Heceta and Bodega who discovered Trinidad Head, July 10, 1775, might still recognize the ageless headland could they see it today, as its appearance is little altered after 200 years.

Crescent City Harbor, protected by breakwaters, is midway between the Columbia River and San Francisco Bay and is the home of a large commercial and sports fishing fleet. Near the harbor entrance stands Battery Point, location of one of the original West Coast lighthouses, built there when Crescent City was in its infancy, sharing its limits with tall trees, Indians and wildlife. Crescent City lighthouse stands as a well preserved monument, little altered from its inception, December 10, 1856. After decommissioning by the Coast Guard a century later, it was leased to the Del Norte County Historical Society who maintained it as an historic attraction. In recent years the tenants were given permission to restore it as an active privately maintained lighthouse and it is now listed in the *Light List* as Battery Point Light.

In May 1855, Congress appropriated $15,000 for its construction on a rocky islet directly off Crescent City, connected with the mainland at low tide by a natural causeway.

The weathered stone and masonry sentinel had as its first keeper a Mr. Van Court, assigned temporarily by construction superintendent Potter until the assigned keeper arrived. Theophilis Magruder finally got there on Christmas, 15 days after the light was illuminated. He

was provided with two lantern curtains with 12 brass rings to protect the lens from sunlight; rouge and applicator brush for lens polishing; scissors to trim the wicks; wolfshead brush for cleaning; whiting for making putty; pencils, handlantern, sandpaper, scrub brushes, soldering iron, dust pan, brooms, turpentine, paper tripoli, buff skins, accounting books and triplicate forms to fill out, all standard equipment for light keepers. His salary started at $1,000 per year but before the year had ended, the Lighthouse Board, in an economy measure, informed him that his salary would be cut to $600. He resigned.

In 1874, the lighthouse was reported in a dilapidated condition and badly in need of interior repair. Mariners were complaining at the same time the harbor entrance was too dangerous for night-time transit, ships having to remain well at sea due to treacherous St. George Reef, six miles offshore. They pointed to the terrible tragedy of the SS *Brother Jonathan* wrecked on that reef at Northwest Seal Rock, on July 30, 1865 with the loss of 200 souls and only a handful of survivors.

It was reasoned that a beacon should be placed on the reef permitting the abandonment of Crescent City Light. Ultimately a beacon was erected on the reef, but mariners found they needed the harbor entrance light as well.

When keeper John H. Jeffrey came to the lighthouse in 1875, he and his wife Nellie took a genuine liking to the place and remained four decades, she also being in the employ of the Lighthouse Service part of that time, as her husband's first assistant. He almost lost his job once for dabbling heavily in to politics, for in those years keepers were often assigned or removed depending on their choice of parties. During their long tenure they were often repairing storm damage. From time to time there were salary cuts when times were bad, but they weathered both natural storms and economic storms until 1915. Their son followed the lighthouse tradition with assignment to the Oakland Harbor Light Station.

The Jeffrey's were replaced by John E. Lind who had put in five years of construction work on St. George Reef Lighthouse, and had then stayed on as an assistant keeper.

In 1907 the lighthouse received a new fourth order lens producing a flash every 15 seconds. It had also acquired a friendly ghost that

*Crescent City Lighthouse (Battery Point Light) is one of the finest examples of the original U.S. government lighthouses on the West Coast. Still intact, and still in good condition, it has crowned the little islet off Crescent City's Battery Point since 1856. When dropped from the Coast Guard **Light List,** it was turned over to the Del Norte County Historical Society who have used it as a lighthouse museum. In recent years, a light has been installed and permission granted to put it back in the **Light List** as Battery Point Light. At right, looking at the lamp inside the station's old Fresnel, part of the museum collection.*

*Several lighthouse keepers reported spotting an enemy submarine offshore following Pearl Harbor, but authorities ballyhooed their reports as imagination, until the tanker **Emidio** was torpedoed December 17, 1942 near Blunts Reef. Her forward section is shown here after drifting to the mainland.*

*Sketch of the steamer **Brother Jonathan,** the ill-fated sidewheeler that struck dreaded St. George Reef, July 30, 1865 and went to a watery grave claiming the lives of nearly 200 persons. It was her loss that started agitation for a lighthouse on the reef. Courtesy Del Norte County Historical Society.*

traversed the staircase of the tower on stormy nights. Those who encountered the wraith could not be shaken in their belief that it was for real, that is as real as ghosts can be.

A massive twisting waterspout skirted around the fringe of the lighthouse in 1925 and did considerable damage in Crescent City.

The lighthouse was automated in 1953, and last occupied by veteran keeper Wayne Piland and his family. The Fresnel was removed in favor of a 375 mm lens. When the structure was leased to the Del Norte County Historical Society, the museum curators took up residence there. On March 27, 1964 while Peggy and Roxy Coons were present, a seismic tidal wave inundated a section of the isle and cascaded with great force into the Crescent City waterfront and downtown streets claiming 11 lives. The lighthouse miracuously escaped damage.

The museum collection presently housed there includes maritime memorabilia of the lighthouse and relics from the area shipwrecks. Visits must be timed with the tide. One can't miss the lighthouse. Everybody in Crescent City knows its location.

The most expensive, and unusual lighthouse ever constructed in America stands on infamous St. George Reef, six and a half miles off the northern California coast. Its once powerful beacon has been discontinued and replaced by St. George Reef Lighted Horn Buoy, a big 42 foot self-contained navigation aid with radio beacon, anchored in 220 feet off the dreaded reef. The old lighthouse stands in dismal array awaiting its fate. St. George Reef is composed of nine visible rocks and covered ledges extending 6.5 miles northwest and west from Point St. George, each one a potential ship killer.

There had been agitation for a light on the reef ever since the *Brother Jonathan* tragedy in 1865. The Lighthouse Board requested the reef be reserved for a fog signal but a decade and a half slipped away till funds were allotted for a major aid to navigation. Northwest Seal Rock was the only place on the jagged reef where a lighthouse could be built and even then many claimed it would be an impossible undertaking.

Charles A. Ballantyne (A.Ballantyne) was chosen as the building superintendent, for he had gained world-wide renown for construction work on Tillamook Rock Lighthouse off the Oregon Coast. Survey

*Construction underway on St. George Reef Lighthouse in the 1880s, with the supply and barracks ship **Alliance** moored off the reef.*

*Getting the foundation laid at St. George Reef, the barracks schooner **La Ninfa**, is pictured shackled to the bottom with several large anchors. Note the line between the ship and the reef for transfer of workers and supplies.*

work at the reef began in 1882, but giant seas drove the surveyors off the rock. Landings were extremely difficult. In April 1883 Ballantyne came to the reef aboard the wrecking steamer *Whitelaw* which had the schooner *La Ninfa* in tow, a sealing schooner that had been temporarily used as a lightship off San Francisco Bay and was to serve as the barracks for the builders of the reef lighthouse. Stormy weather prevailed and a landing was thwarted. Thus the schooner was left at anchor unmanned and the crew returned to port on the *Whitelaw*. Then another storm struck, and by the time the men returned, the barracks schooner had disappeared, having slipped her mooring cables. A search ensued and the derelict was finally discovered drifting off Trinidad Head. Towed back once again she was tethered to the bottom with larger anchors and attached to four mooring buoys. The seas behaved just long enough for the construction crew to land, drive bolts into the rock, set up a donkey engine, and secure lines.

The steam schooner *Crescent City* was enlisted to bring supplies and mail every fortnight, relieving the *Whitelaw*. As the *La Ninfa* tugged at her moorings 350 feet off the reef, the crew chiseled out a foundation. The danger of waves sweeping over the rock without warning, demanded a quick escape route, and Ballantyne set up an aerial tramway with a circular cage whereby personnel could be transferred back and forth between the schooner and the rock. Blasting powder and other explosives, sent rock flying like missiles in all directions. One day in September 1883, when the excavation was nearly completed, huge seas combed the rock and knocked two quarrymen down the side into the water. Though bruised, battered and almost drowned, they were pulled to safety. After that, the workers were forced to quit for the winter.

Granite deposits on the Mad River were found to be of high quality and became the basic ingredient for the construction of the tower. A rail link was provided by which to haul stone to the cutters' shed on Humboldt Bay. Landslides at the quarry and piling work to bolster the worker's shack on Humboldt Bay's north spit further delayed progress. The steam schooners *Alliance* and *Santa Maria* were then chartered to carry supplies and rock to the reef, and the schooner *Sparrow* replaced the *La Ninfa* as the barracks ship. The summer of 1887 brought unseasonably bad weather and sea conditions. The derrick boom suffered damage and slowed the discharge of the cut rocks, which averaged 2½ tons each. One wave at the site moved a huge rock several feet. With all the setbacks, by the end of the working season in 1887, the base of the lighthouse had risen 22 feet, remarkable progress under the circumstances. The 1888 season saw the walls rise to 32 feet. During that year the *Whitelaw* and *Del Norte* delivered the building materials and supplies.

A temporary workman's quarters was then built, negating use of a barracks vessel, but inclement weather prevented any more work until the following spring when a rugged crew of 50 workers was transported to the reef aboard the steam schooner *Del Norte*. One night in May, a huge sea struck the worker's quarters washing the men from their bunks. Fortunately, nobody was seriously injured but for sure there was no more sleep that night. After repairing the damage, construction continued and eight more courses were completed by the end of the season. Within the core of the rising tower was the storage area, coal and boiler rooms.

Only minor progress was made the following year as the increasing cost of the project found funds lacking, but 1891 was a good year as the *Sunol* brought out a full load of cargo and machinery, plus 50

construction workers. Things looked rosey until they arrived and found the quarters badly damaged and the mooring buoys missing. Backtracking and repairing took time, but finally the elements cooperated and the latter half of the summer afforded a welcome respite as work progressed with a capital P. The carefully placed stones had been perfectly cut, and between each layer two-inch gun metal dowels secured the granite, even the smallest openings being filled, making it one of the strongest towers ever built. With the caission now 70 feet high, everything but the service rooms and cistern were filled with reinforced concrete. As the tower soared skyward, hoists and derricks lifted stone and cement to the various levels on the scaffolding. Then the first casualty occurred. A rigger fell to his death while letting go a tag line on the derrick boom.

When the tower was completed, it was a sight to behold and a great credit to Charles Ballantyne who had proven himself once again as champion of American lighthouse construction. After the lighting equipment arrived from France, three of the workman were assigned to remain on as keepers. The completed tower rose 134 feet, the tallest on the north Pacific rim. Total cost was a whopping $704,000, the most costly American lighthouse ever built, and perhaps for that period, the most expensive in the world. The price tag was five times that of Tillamook Rock, and twice that of Minot's Ledge. Within the building were 1,339 granite blocks, working out to 14,307 tons of granite. 1,439 tons of sand, 335 tons of brick and 272 tons of gravel, plus a generous amount of interior panneling—oak, redwood and Port Orford cedar. The total project had required 11 years to complete but was labled as one of the greatest engineering triumphs in maritime construction work. The light was a first order Fresnel, and the fog signals, dual steam whistles mounted atop of the light tower base. Square on three sides, the other side of the tower was semi-circular, encompassing a spiral staircase. The massive structure on different levels contained a boiler, coal and laundry room, galley, principal keeper and assistants quarters, watch room, (which in later years housed radio equipment) and the lantern room. The $15,000

Nearing completion in 1891, St. George Reef Lighthouse on the northern California coast was the costliest sentinel ever constructed by the American government. Old U.S. Lighthouse Service photo, courtesy U.S. Coast Guard.

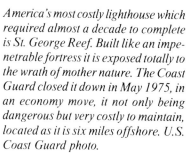

America's most costly lighthouse which required almost a decade to complete is St. George Reef. Built like an impenetrable fortress it is exposed totally to the wrath of mother nature. The Coast Guard closed it down in May 1975, in an economy move, it not only being dangerous but very costly to maintain, located as it is six miles offshore. U.S. Coast Guard photo.

Coast Guard cutter (buoy tender) **Blackhaw** *eases its bow toward St. George Reef lighthouse in the summer of 1983 with orders to remove the 24-panel first order lens, and deliver it to the Del Norte County Historical Society in Crescent City as a musuem piece. It was the first time the lighthouse had been entered since its abandonment in 1975. The crew faced a formidable task in removing the 6,000 pound apparatus, six feet in diameter, seven and a half feet high with 500 prisms. Rich Brandes commanded the* **Blackhaw**. *Coast Guard photo.*

lens was in place and operating on October 20, 1892. John Olsen was the head keeper and first assistant was John Lind, both of whom had been on the building crew. Three other assistants were also attached to the station.

The derrick boom was the means of transferring personnel and supplies to and from the lighthouse platform. Life was intolerably lonely, and launching a boat via the derrick boom was a dangerous occupation. On October 14, 1893, assistant keeper Bill Erickson tried to sail a small boat from the light to Crescent City and was drowned en route.

According to research by Ralph Shanks, Jr., in his excellent book. *Lighthouses and Lifeboats on the Redwood Coast*, from 1891 through

1930, of the 80 men that served at the station, 37 resigned, while 26 sought transfers to other stations. Several other keepers had to be taken ashore with illness, or mental breakdown. Another broke his leg during a boat launching. Two keepers were fired. It was demanding duty, but God made some men who could stand such rigors and like it. One such individual was John Olsen who put in 22 years at the station; another, George Roux an ex-French sailor spent two decades. Passing steamers often had pity on the lonely individuals and threw casks and barrels overboard filled with magazines and newspapers. Tremendous seas raised by gale force winds sometimes swept the base of the light 70 feet above the ocean and on more than one occasion leaped up the side of the tower and over the lantern house.

Only a handful of women ever visited the lighthouse, one of them being John Lind's wife. Counting inspectors and government officials, the total visitors seldom ever exceeded five per year.

When the Coast Guard took over the lighthouse the duty was of shorter duration but the problems persisted, especially in the landings. On April 5, 1951, the worst single accident at a California lighthouse occurred when five Coast Guardsmen were thrown into the rough seas while the station boat was being launched. Three perished.

On May 13, 1975, the cutter *Cape Carter* made the final run to the lighthouse to remove the last attendants. After the colors were lowered the derrick boom dropped two of them to the awaiting craft in the "Billy Pugh" net. Then, Chief Sebastian and petty officer Salter locked the massive door, climbed down to the rocks and rowed a rubber raft out to the cutter. Everything inside the lighthouse was left intact and was to remain that way for nearly a decade. There was no attempt at automation. A large, fully equipped ocean buoy was placed off the reef.

The darkened tower had no more visitors until 1983 when the Coast Guard donated the first order lens to the Del Norte County Historical Society for display at their museum in Crescent City. The Coast Guard buoy tender *Blackhaw* was ordered out in August 1983 to remove the 6,000 pound lens and lighting apparatus. Six feet in diameter, seven and a half feet high it consists of more than 500 ground glass prisms, set in brass frames mounted on a nine foot pedestal. To perform the task the crew was divided into four teams, a dismantling crew on the lantern gallery lowered the lens panels to a packing crew on the caisson, 70 feet below. They in turn wrapped the lens elements. A highline crew then lowered the pieces to the *Blackhaw*, moored 60 to 100 yards off the lighthouse. On board ship, the lens prisms were carefully stored for the trip to shore.

Before any work could proceed the Coastguardsmen had to clear a path through 500 disgruntled California sea lions that had taken up residence on the rocks below the tower. After climbing the ladder to the lighthouse entrance, the door was unlocked and the first one to enter nearly jumped out of his shoes. A human-like figure (manikin dangled from a noose inside the tower, a farewell gift from the last Coast Guard occupants eight years earlier. The operation was accomplished with only a few chips occurring in the prisms. It took about three days to complete the job including the usual horseplay as the team enjoyed starting and extinguishing little fires by letting the sun shine through the lens bullseyes. The usually restless seas cooperated, allowing the buoy tender to hold her position at anchor so as not to jerk the highline that ran between the rock and the ship.

Just what will be the future of the abandoned tower remains uncertain at this writing. Metal fittings turn red with rust but there is no way the great stone tower will collapse. It is as solid as the rock to which it is riveted. Of all the man-made structures in America, nothing has been put together like the St. George Reef tower and it is disheartening that it must be left to the whims of nature. Flash! At press time, St. George tower was placed on the block by the GSA, for sale to the highest bidder.

The most westerly point of Oregon is Cape Blanco, named by the old Spanish explorers. The entire cape is pictured here in this aerial Coast Guard photo taken in 1980, showing the lighthouse in the center.

A close up of the historic Cape Blanco Lighthouse, Oregon's oldest, built in 1870, little altered since its inception and still displaying its first order Fresnel shining seaward nightly. Eugene C. Hoff photo for Coast Guard.

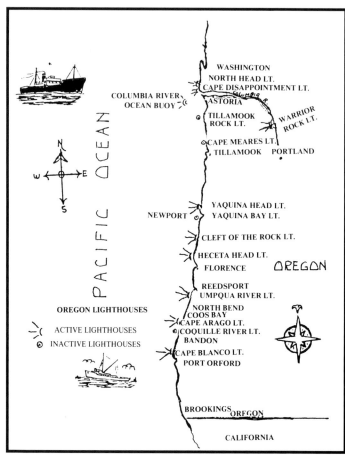

The Sentinels of Oregon

Roll on, thou deep and dark blue Ocean—roll!
Ten thousand fleets sweep over thee in vain;
Man marks the earth with ruin—his control
Stops with the shore.
....Lord Byron

In all the world there is no seacoast quite like that of Oregon. The moods, the splendor, the diversity of the sea and shore, are sights to behold. There, a natural battleground exists between the eternal restless breakers and the solid walls of basalt that are in constant combat. Great dunes pile up like pyramids created by the shifting sands. Pleasant beaches beckon young and old as winter storms cease and major battles of nature settle for minor skirmishes. Then there are the haunting fogs, the traditional Oregon mist, the tall brooding forests that come down to the shores.

The continental shelf is a marvelous caldron where an astounding spectrum of marine creatures of the deep and the shallow exist in great numbers. Deepsea ships cut a swath through coastal waters while commercial fishing vessels seek bountiful harvests for the hungry palate. Giant gray whales traverse an 11,000 mile trek between the Bering Sea and Mexico, hugging the Oregon coast en route, spouting, frolicking and lob-tailing. Aqua orbs, those treasured fish floats finalize their long drift from Oriental waters on Oregon beaches.

For nearly 400 miles, the Oregon coast is a delight for all who behold it. Fact and legend is part of the romanticism that dominates its history—tales of pre-discovery shipwrecks, buried treasure and Spanish galleons. European navigators were sailing within sight of the Oregon coast by the late 1500s in search of the fabled Northwest Passage. The chalky cliffs of Cape Blanco, Oregon's most westerly point, inspired explorers to penetrate farther north, but they were often beset by the contrary winds and seas.

Heceta Head, north of Florence, was named for the Spanish sea captain that discovered it in 1775, and one can motor over the great promontories named by the fabled Captain James Cook—Cape Perpetua, (just south of Yachats), and Cape Foulweather, (north of Newport), charted on his return from the Sandwich Islands in 1778. The marauder and fabulous searover, Sir Francis Drake, was also off the Oregon coast in the late 1500's, but though his name was applied to a bay in California, records are vague on his Oregon visit because of the "badde harbor," he allegedly anchored in south of Coos Bay. Nor did he apply a geographic name to anything along what he noted as a very hostile shore.

None could dispute that the ten lighthouses built along the Oregon coast between 1857 and 1900 were not urgently needed to mark bar entrances and to warn ships away from the scarred promontories and treacherous killer reefs along the coastline. In the day of sail the coastal waters were a mariners' nightmare; good harbors were at a premium and bar crossings were totally unpredictable. From the wreck of the first Spanish ship near the entrance to Nehalem River, below Mt. Neah-kah-nie in the 1600's to the Japanese freighter *Blue Magpie* in 1983, Oregon shores have been littered with shipwrecks, from Indian dugouts to ocean liners and everything in between.

Cape Blanco, Oregon's most westerly rampart and the first prominent chunk of land named by the early Spaniards, projects about 1.5 miles from the general trend of the coast. A bar table land terminating seaward in a cliff 203 feet high, it is located six miles west of Highway 101, north of the seacoast town of Port Orford. Atop the cape is historic Cape Blanco Lighthouse, built in 1870, the oldest active lighthouse in the state as well as the most westerly. The light,

still the original, a first order Fresnel, flashes around the clock from the 59 foot tower, 245 feet above the boisterous Pacific.

The *Pacific Coast Pilot,* shortly after the establishment of the light afforded the following description. (It must be born in mind, however, that during those early years Cape Blanco was known as Cape Orford. Geographers later changed it to Blanco to recognize its Spanish discovery.)

> This is a primary seacoast light, the lighthouse is situated on the highest part of Cape Orford from which heavy trees were cut when the buildings were erected. It is nearly 200 yards inside the western part of the cape. The tower is a frustrum of a cone, and is built of brick, painted white. The keepers dwelling is a two-story brick building painted white with green window blinds. It is situated about 35 yards southward of the tower. The light is a fixed white light of the First Order of the System of Fresnel. It was first exhibited on the 20th of December 1870, and shows every night from sunset to sunrise.

Today, the tower is little altered from it inception, but there have been several changes about the lighthouse reservation. The old keepers dwelling is gone as are many of the former outbuildings, but additional structures have been constructed through the years for various purposes including the radio beacon components. People flock to the area spring and summer, especially to the nearby Oregon State overnight park equipped with every facility for campers and RV's. At this writing, the lighthouse is off limits to the public. Visitation is by special arrangement with the Coast Guard.

In a move to update all the major lighthouses along the Washington and Oregon coasts, the 13th Coast Guard District has done a splendid job with Oregon's grandfather sentinel, which is the most southerly of the district's lighthouses and one of the finest. Could Martin d'Aguilar, credited with discovering the cape January 19, 1603, see the cape today he would be pleased with its appearance far more than he was when bucking contrary seas and peering through the Oregon murk at the ageless headland.

The town of Port Orford, only nine miles away, has adopted the light as its own, and in its dramatic setting it is easy to understand why. People first colonized old Port Orford in 1851, two decades before the lighthouse became a reality. That was back in the days when the proprietor of the town's Knapp Hotel, Louis Knapp, was so concerned for the seafarers fending for themselves along the unprotected southern Oregon coast that he personally kept a lantern aglow in a large hotel window that overlooked the ocean each nightfall. Many navigators were greatful for his humanitarian efforts.

What a contrast his little lantern was with the present second order Fresnel which has served the tower for many years, a revolving lens that remains in operation at this writing. Manufactured by Henry Lepaute of Paris, it has eight flash panels, is five feet in diameter and seven feet high. With a five wick oil lamp it produced 45,765 candlepower, but by using a 1,000 watt quartz-iodine bulb, it produces 320,000 candlepower, visible 22 miles at sea. The original lens and lighting apparatus cost $20,000, in those early years, very big bucks. Replacement cost today would be astronomical.

Overall view of Cape Blanco looking northward showing the Sixes River emptying into the Pacific. The lighthouse is at the left in front of the radio beacon. U.S. Coast Guard photo.

For decades, the slopes of Blanco have been a favorite place for sheep and horses to graze, wandering down from area ranches to munch in contentment in the ocean breeze. The surrounding shoreline below the steep cliffs is a beachcomber's paradise. When the lighthouse was built, several large trees had to be removed to prevent possible forest fires. It is said that the bricks in the walls of the tower were made from local clay deposits and that other materials had to be lightered in by water. Curious Indians would gather about during the construction period wondering what was happening to their happy hunting and fishing grounds.

Before the advent of Highway 101, the lighthouse was reached by a crude wagon road, and despite the hardship of reaching the place, there were 4,050 visitors logged in the station journal from 1896 till 1916. They were always cordially welcomed by the keepers and given a tour of the lighthouse and the grounds, usually camping overnight among the wildflowers before returning to their buckboards and buggies for the washboard trip back to Port Orford.

The one lighthouse keeper who became synonymous with Cape Blanco was James Langlois. He put in 42 years of service there and it is said he never set foot in any other lighthouse. His record tenure of duty began in 1875, when the tower was in its infancy. During his stay he saw many assistant keepers come and go, among them, two women. One of them was Mrs. Mabel E. Bretherton who probably was the first female assigned to a major Oregon seacoast lighthouse. In those days, that was considered a remarkable feat for one of the opposite sex. Her appointment came from the Light-House Establishment, Office of Inspector, 13th District, Portland, Oregon March 30, 1903. It read:

Madam:

Inclosed herewith is transmitted your appointment as Second Assistant Keeper of Cape Blanco Light Station, Oregon, for a probationary period of six months to date from 10 March, 1903, subject to taking the enclosed oath of office, and complying with the directions contained in the enclosed form 276, which papers you will fill out and forward to this office as early as practicable.

Very respectfully,
Commander, U.S.N.
Light-House Inspector

Mrs. Bretherton evidently proved herself worthy during the probationary period, for harmony continued at the station. She was later transferred to North Head Light Station and must have ended her lighthouse career there, for a letter from the Light-House Establishment office in Portland read:

Madam:

You are advised that your resignation as Second assistant keeper of the North Head Light Station, Washington, has been accepted effective close of October 31, 1907.

Respectfully,
Commander, U.S.N.
Light-House Inspector

Langlois from time to time lost some of his assistants due to financial cutbacks in the nation's capital which in turn tightened purse

Treasury Department,
OFFICE OF THE SECRETARY.

Washington, D. C., March 31, 1903.

Mrs. Mabel E. Bretherton,

Care of the Chairman

of the Light-House Board.

Madam:-

Having been certified as eligible by the United States Civil
Service Commission, you are hereby appointed Second Assistant
KEEPER of the   Cape Blanco   Light Station,
Oregon,   with compensation at the rate of
five hundred and fifty   dollars   ($550.00)   per
annum for a probationary period of six months, from March 30,
1903, subject to taking the required oath of office.

                                Respectfully,

Forwarded,

30 March, 1903,   H. A. Taylor
                                       Acting Secretary.

                   Commander, U. S. N.,
                   Light-House Inspector.

Lady keeper Mabel E. Bretherton, first woman assigned to an Oregon primary seacoast lighthouse is pictured here with her orders issued by the Treasury Department and signed by the inspector.

strings of the Lighthouse Service. Langlois, however, always maintained a spick-and-span station and during his long years of service made numerous friends who made repeated visits, often dining in the spacious and comfortable keeper's dwelling. He first came to Cape Blanco as assistant keeper under Captain C. H. Pierce, and shortly after took over as principal keeper. He was born in Silverton, Oregon in 1848. His family settled on Flores Creek in Curry County six years later, and his father, a former seafarer, engaged in the farming and mercantile business. In 1873, two years before being appointed to the light station, he married Elizabeth Rudolph, the couple raising five children while on the lighthouse reservation.

But lest anybody think that life was always a ball at Cape Blanco, think again. Storms often struck with great violence and did considerable damage. Strong winds are an accepted fact and the seas can be extremely rough off the point as evidenced by the many shipwrecks in the area. Two disasters stand out; the sidewheel steamer *Alaskan,* out of the Columbia River in Command of Captain R. E. Howes, foundered in May 1889. Of the 47 persons aboard, 31 perished, some in swamped lifeboats after the evacuation. Fortunately the ship was carrying a poor payload of passengers or the toll would have been far greater.

Within clear view of the lighthouse, the Associated Oil Company tanker *J. A. Chanslor* was driven into the scabrous rocks in foggy murk on December 18, 1919. Of her company of 39, only Captain A. A. Swayer and two seamen made it to shore on pieces of wreckage as voluminous seas continually swept over the wreck engulfing the helpless souls trapped within her confines.

Any seafaring man will tell you that the seas can be huge off Cape Blanco. On November 28, 1883, the steamer *Victoria* struck an offshore reef becoming a $120,000 total loss. In the late summer of 1930, the steam schooner *South Coast,* laden with 100,000 feet of cedar logs bound for Coos Bay from Crescent City vanished with her entire crew of 19, the only clue being part of her deckhouse and an empty lifeboat washed ashore southwest of the lighthouse.

Numerous other vessels, large and small, have fallen victim to the elements of nature in and around Cape Blanco, but the presence of the lighthouse down through the years has been a saving beacon to many men of the sea.

The Coast Guard has one man who watches over the lighthouse at this writing, while others service the important radio beacon station on the reservation. Some outbuildings on the grounds are being eyed by other government agencies for future purposes, but the veteran tower stands proud, one of the few that has kept most of its equipment intact placing it in the category of a "classic lighthouse."

In March 1976, the Hickey-Field Construction Company of Seattle was awarded a contract for $26,953 for the exterior rehabilitation of the abandoned Coquille River (Bandon) Lighthouse as an historic attraction. From the time the government decided in 1939 the beacon was no longer necessary as a navigation aid, it fell into a state of decrepitude. Vandals slopped streaks of red paint on its exterior and covered the walls with grafitti, bricks had been dug out of the walls, the roof leaked, all the metal was red with rust and corroding and the windows were shattered. Long before its demise the staircase and lighting apparatus had been removed. The year it was abandoned was the year the Coast Guard took over the Lighthouse Service and the graceful old lighthouse became an orphan without anyone to care for it. As it deteriorated through the years, local Bandonites had mixed emotions about its future—some thought it a dangerous hazard to the public, others figured it should be razed, and the third group wanted it restored and preserved for posterity. But who was going to put up the money? Finally after nearly 35 years of neglect, the Army Corps of Engineers and the Oregon State Department of Transportation agreed to share the cost of exterior rehabilitation. The building was listed in the National Park Service's Register of Historic Places.

It required four months to repair the roof, stairways, windows, concrete work, painting and minor landscaping. Once again the old tower came to life in its prominent location at the north entrance to the Coquille River. The interior is now open to the public and a minor light was dedicated for the lantern house by Oregon's governor to go along with the outlining of the tower in colored lights at Christmas time. There is free outside access where thousands of jetty fishermen, picnickers, beachcombers, artists or photographers appear every day. The lighthouse abuts Bullards Beach State Park, one of the Oregon Coast's finest, just a short distance north of the bustling seacoast town of Bandon.

Constructed in 1896, Coquille River Lighthouse was designed as both a harbor and a seacoast light. The treacherous Coquille River bar was considered by sailors of old to be one of the most dangerous to cross, especially in the heyday of the sailing vessel, and certainly there were numerous wrecks to prove the point. The 1900 *Light List* described the new station in the following manner:

> White, octagonal, pyramidal tower with black dome and lantern, attached to the easterly side of a white fog-signal building with black roof; white, one-and one-half story, double dwelling, with brown roof, on sand dunes about 650 feet (1/10th mile) northeasterly from the tower, and a white barn 150 feet to the northward of the dwelling. Fitted with a fourth order fixed light 28 seconds, eclipse two seconds. Height of light above mean water, 47 feet. Distance light

*Three-masted schooner **C.A. Klose** stranded right next to the Coquille River (Brandon) Lighthouse in a heavy fog, November 12, 1904. She was one of the fortunate vessels to be refloated, but less than two years later, was a total loss north of the Columbia River entrance.*

Construction of the Coquille River (Bandon) Lighthouse in 1895. Thirteen members of the work crew are pictured in this vintage photo. The station was commissioned in 1896 and served till 1939. Bandon Historical Society photo.

visible 12¼ nautical miles. Third class Daboll trumpet, blasts five seconds, silent intervals 25 seconds. To be changed to a first class siren. Height of tower above ground 40 feet.

The green years of the lighthouse were busy ones on the Coquille River as a large number of steam schooners and coastal sailing vessels crossed over the bar. There were great stands of timber, especially Port Orford cedar and coal deposits up river, wooden shipbuilding was established in Bandon, and lumber mills flourished.

On September 26, 1936, the lighthouse was engulfed in smoke and cinders as a disastrous forest fire swept into Bandon and virtually destroyed the town. By morning, only 16 of 500 buildings still stood and most of the townsfolk were homeless. There was no damage to the lighthouse as it was on the other side of the river, but the attendants had a big clean up job confronting them.

Though the lighthouse was the hallmark building of the area; it was also a place of considerable tragedy by shipwrecks both on the bar and around its entrance. At least two sailing vessels stranded right alongside the lighthouse. Within a few years of each other, around the turn of the century, the three-masted schooners' *Advance* and *C. A. Klose* almost shoved their bowsprits into the station fog signal house. They were luckier than most, being pulled free with repair bills that didn't totally bankrupt their owners.

One, if not the first recorded wreck at the Coquille entrance was that of the schooner *Commodore* which foundered October 22, 1870, 16 years before the lighthouse went into operation. Other well known wrecks in the area were the schooners *Western Home* and *Onward* in 1904; steamer *Del Norte* in 1905; the gas boat *Bessie K.* in 1907 with her entire crew of seven; gas schooner *Randolph* in 1915 with the loss of three crewmen; steam schooner *Fifeld* which left her bones on the beach on the outer fringe of the south jetty in 1916; steamer *Mary L. Moore* offshore in 1927 and the *E. L. Smith* in 1935. The gas schooner *Golden West* straddled the jetty in 1936; the SS *Cynthia Olson* in 1952, was one of the few to escape the clutches of the bar, which in turn claimed her running mate, the *Oliver Olson* the following year, (her hull later filled with rock as part of the jetty). Then there was the tug *L. H. Coolidge* which stranded in 1951; the tug *Elizabeth Olson* in 1960 and the tug *Rebel* went down with her skipper in 1960. In addition, several commercial fishing craft have been wrecked or sunk in and around the Coquille.

The station fog signal was in operation for 1,086 hours during the year 1929.

Coquille River Lighthouse as it appeared around the turn of the century showing the fog trumpet and the chimney of the boiler that powered the signal. Portland Post Card Company photo.

Minor lights and fog signals have been provided at the entrance to the Coquille since the abandonment of the old lighthouse. In its new coat of paint, even though a light no longer shines from its' empty lantern house, it makes a fine daymark for local fishboats, and the folks of the area continue to refer to it affectionately as "Bandon Light."

Cape Arago Lighthouse just south of Coos Bay bar 29 miles north, northeast of Cape Blanco, has long been the guardian of an important and dangerous segment of the coast. It shines 100 feet above the water from a 44 foot reinforced concrete, octagonal tower attached to a fog signal building. Situated on an unusual little islet, 2.5 miles north of Cape Arago, access with the mainland is by a footbridge.

It was as if an Indian curse had been placed on the Cape Arago Lighthouse Reservation. The nameless islet often referred to as "Lighthouse Island" is pockmarked with wave tunnels and is menaced by constant erosion around its sandstone cliffs. Presently on its third lighthouse due to encroachment, old Indians had a reason for the ensuing problems. On the land side of the footbridge is an ancient Indian burial ground which through the years has been somewhat desecrated by intruders. Though in recent years the Coast Guard has respected its existence, the descendants of the deceased Indians are still bothered by public disrespect. There are some recent Indian grave

*Drawn like a magnet, the three-masted schooner **Advance** pokes her bowsprit over the north jetty of the Coquille bar within a stone's throw of the lighthouse, December 29, 1905. She was refloated. Bandon Historical Society photo.*

Coquille Lighthouse as it appeared in 1985.

Vintage photo of the islet, location of Cape Arago Lighthouse. Both the first and second lighthouses built there can be seen. Due to erosion, the 1866 lighthouse was abandoned, visible center background, and replaced by the 1908 lighthouse at the center of the photo. The second lighthouse was later replaced by one built in 1934.

A Coast Guard aerial view of the present Cape Arago Lighthouse, circa 1934. Note the erosion in the sandstone cliffs surrounding the structure. Picture was taken in 1980.

markers along with those long forgotten. Instead of burying their dead and digging up the sod, Indians on occasion today bring the ashes of their dead and drop them from the cliff into the sea.

The initial lighthouse was placed on the islet November 1, 1866, displaying a fourth order Fresnel with a fixed white light varied by a white flash every two minutes. The tower, only 25 feet high, stood at the bitter end of the weather-beaten islet. It was an octagonal, wrought iron, truncated skelton structure with a masonry base. The keepers dwelling was a frame one-and-a-half story building on the wider portion of the isle. In the early years it was known as Cape Gregory Lighthouse as was the cape from which it took its name. Captain James Cook applied that title on his early observations of the coast. It was listed as Cape Redondo on the DeMofras chart of 1844.

In the 1880's, a U. S. Lifesaving Station was established on the eastern lee of the isle, closest to shore, and a volunteer crew responded when a ship was in peril. Ironically it was named the "Cape Arago" Lifesaving Station even before the lighthouse had its name changed. Several demanding rescues originated from the station, a difficult place from which to launch a surfboat.

Before the advent of jetties, transit over Coos Bay bar was dangerous, and only the most skilled of pilots risked crossing without the aid of a tug. Next to the Columbia River, no part of the coast of Oregon is more littered with shipwrecks than the Coos area. In the spring of 1868 the brig *Admiral* waited in the bay 31 days for an opportunity to cross the surging bar into the open Pacific. Other

Looking at Cape Arago Lighthouse toward the southwest. The hollow, center right, is the former location of the Cape Arago Lifesaving Station, where surfboats once put out on rescue missions. Photo by M.W. Rodrigues, U.S. Coast Guard.

vessels stood off the river entrance for weeks before conditions permitted a crossing. In 1861, a survey party could get but one day's work on the bar over a period of several months. The following year the Coast Survey brig *Fauntleroy,* drawing but ten feet, was unable to enter due to severe shoaling. Without warning the channels shifted at the whims of the currents and breakers.

The establishment of a lighthouse didn't solve the bar problems but it did give hope to mariners skirting the coast or waiting for an opportunity to enter the bay.

To stabilize the bar, the Army Engineers built the north jetty between 1890 and 1901 and the south jetty from 1924 to 1930, greatly assisting the growing marine traffic using the ports of North Bend and Coos Bay. The bay became the softwood lumber export capital of the world. Various wood products firms lined the banks of the bay, sloughs and rivers.

Meanwhile, back on Lighthouse Island, the pioneer lighthouse was threatened by erosion and funds were allotted for a new lighthouse. It replaced the grandfather light in 1908, a frame, octagonal tower with black lantern house attached to a one story fog signal building. The lens and lighting apparatus was moved from the old lighthouse and the new fog signal was a first class compressed air siren. Over a period of years, the former lighthouse gradually fell into ruin and today its foundation bricks are still scattered about on the ground at the extreme western end of the isle's narrow peninsula. The seas have continued to eat away at the cliffs, constantly changing the contour.

Continuing erosion and deterioration of the second lighthouse led to the construction of a third lighthouse in 1933-34. This time, it was a stoutly-built concrete reinforced 44 foot tower. The lens was shifted from the second lighthouse and is still in service, a fourth order Fresnel with five panels, three bullseyes and two drum panels floating in a bath of mecury. Manufactured by Barbier, Bernard & Turenne, Paris, it was electrified after placement in 1934.

On May 1, 1966 Cape Arago Light was converted to automatic operation. Though the tower badly deteriorated in the years following, the 13th Coast Guard District in the 1980's ordered all its

seacoast lighthouses restored to mint condition and Cape Arago accordingly got a new look.

The stately old keepers dwellings are no longer on the isle. Automation brought about changes and today a Coast Guard caretaker is housed on the mainland side, the lighthouse, presently closed to the public. Visitation is only by special permission of the Coast Guard Station at Charleston.

A half mile northwest of the lighthouse is Baltimore Rock. outermost rock of a menacing ledge. Five years before the erection of the lighthouse, the U. S. Coast Survey (in 1861) discovered the remains of the schooner *Baltimore* astride the barrier, its foremast protruding above the surface. It has since been known as Baltimore Rock.

Among the earliest wrecks in the area was the USRC *Lincoln,* in 1852. She stranded three miles north of Coos Bay leaving a contingent of military men castaway on the beach. On January 12, 1910, twenty-four crewmen died a terrible death clinging desperately to the rigging of the grounded wave-swept freighter *Czarina.* Sixteen others lost their lives when the steamer *Santa Clara* stranded on the bar November 2, 1915. The big freighter *Brush* ended her days on Simpson Reef, south of Cape Arago April 26, 1923, just west of the fabulous Shore Acres mansion of lumber baron and shipbuilder Louis Simpson. The Liberian freighter *Kalamas* hit the same reef in September 1960, but was later pulled free with $300,000 damage.

The light, foghorn and radio beacon at Cape Arago continue their warnings. Lighthouse Island gets smaller each year as seas continue their destruction and maybe the irate Indians of old will have the last laugh after all as nature gradually claims the sacred land taken from them long ago.

Erosion will never again claim the Umpqua River Lighthouse. Government surveyors and builders of old learned a hard lesson when they built the first Umpqua River light tower on a foundation of sand near the river entrance in 1855-57. Congress first appropriated funds for the lighthouse in 1851. Work commenced in 1855, but during construction the builders were constantly bothered by the local

Nearing completion in 1894, a vintage photo of the Umpqua River Lighthouse, with no plaster overlay or lens and lighting apparatus. Courtesy Douglas County Museum, Jena Mitchell, photo librarian.

marked on foreign charts for several years thereafter which may have directly or indirectly imperiled vessels hugging the coast.

Though some historians believe the Umpqua River to have been discovered by Viscaino in 1603, the claim is undoubtedly false for the Spaniard never reached that latitude. It was either the Umpqua or the Columbia hinted at as the fabled "River of the West", by Jonathan Carver in his narrative of 1766. He also used the name "Oregon", or "River of West". The Indian name below the rapids was Kah-la-wat-set, and the upper part, "Umptquah". On the De Mofras chart it is named Rio de Aguilar or R. Umpqua. Tebenkoff named the river entrance Umkwa and also marked an Indian village at its mouth in latitude 43 degrees 56'. In recent years, evidences of Indian habitation have been uncovered in the Umpqua area, the oldest yet discovered on the Oregon coast and perhaps in the Northwest, dating back, in all probability, to well before the life of Jesus Christ upon the earth.

The Coast Survey schooner *Ewing* anchored off the Umpqua entrance in 15 fathoms in 1850, but the first recorded deep water ship to successfully enter the river was the schooner *Sam. Roberts,* August 4, 1850, inbound from the Rogue River. The *Ewing* made a preliminary survey three years later, and in 1854, the first chart from the sea to five miles upriver was made by the U. S. Coast Survey.

Early pioneers who came seeking profits from the tall stands of timber believed the river would become the commercial center of the Oregon Territory, that river ports such as Gardiner would blossom into a great seaport. For several years it catered to numerous coastwise lumber vessels, but though it continued as an industrial area, the city of Reedsport across the river eventually became the business center and Winchester Bay, close to the river's mouth, the moorage site for a vast commercial and sports fishing fleet. Historic old Scottsburg, a few miles upriver, one of the earliest settlements, has remained stagnant, but maintains its historic flavor.

During the era without a lighthouse, the river bar became a portentous experience for mariners. Without jetties or dredging, the channels constantly changed without warning. Among the early wrecks on the Umpqua were the brig *Bostonian* in 1850; the schooner *Nassau,* and brigs *Almira* and *Roanoke* in 1852, the schooner *Loo Choo* in 1855. In the year 1873, another trio of vessels came to grief, the schooners *Meldon* and *Bobolink* and the steamer *Enterprise.* The schooner *Sparrow* left her bones to bleach on the sands in 1876 claiming three lives. As other vessels were wrecked or damaged in bar transit, persistent pleas were made for a new lighthouse and improved river buoyage.

Finally Congress acted in 1888 with $50,000 for a new seacoast beacon. To prevent the fate of the first lighthouse, the foundation was laid far back from the river entrance. The lighthouse tender *Manzanita* delivered most of the materials. Construction period was from 1891 to 1894 and the result was a splendid 65 foot lighthouse and station buildings, all quality. The reservation was described in the *Light List* as follows:

> White, octagonal pyramidal tower with black lantern; white workroom attached in rear; two galvanized iron oilhouses in rear of tower; two dwellings, 240 feet apart, about 120 feet, respectively, to the northward and southeastward of the tower; barn, 280 feet northward of tower; dwellings and barn white with brown roofs.

The two ton first order Fresnel with nearly 1,000 prisms, flashing white, showed a red flash every third time, from an elevation 165 feet above sea level, visible 19 nautical miles. Before the light became operative, a new pedestal to support the first order lens had to be ordered, as the existing one was 15 inches too short. The lens and lighting apparatus were supplied by Barbier & Cie, Paris.

Umpqua Light Station was always a favorite with Lighthouse Service keepers and Coast Guard personnel. Automated in the

Indians who insisted on purloining any tools they could get their hands on. So many were they in number that the workers refrained from starting a squabble. Likewise, the Indians were playing it crafty for they were apprised of the militia that had on other occasions put down uprisings. Still, the situation grew more tense. The guard was doubled at the supply house, for the workers knew if trouble did break out it might be days before help could come. It all came to a distressing climax one day when a construction worker passed an Indian hut and saw his sledge hammer propped against the outside wall. Infuriated, he grabbed the tool, but at the same time was jumped by two natives. A fracas broke out and amid the cries, Indians and whites came from all directions. Flying fists saw the outnumbered workers coming out on the short end. Fearing annihilation, the foreman made a dash for the supply house and hastily extracted sticks of dynamite. He lit the fuses and set off a tremendous blast frightening the Indians so badly that they hastily retreated. The whites returned to their quarters to dress their wounds.

An around-the-clock vigil was kept for fear of an Indian retaliation, but it never came, and both sides backed off as extra heavy winter rains pelted down from leaden skies for weeks thereafter. After less than four years of service, the river freshets and encroaching seas toppled the lighthouse on February 8, 1861, its third order lens forever darkened, leaving the Umpqua area without a major lighthouse for 37 years. Only a second class buoy marked the river entrance, and many ships were diverted to other portals of entry, fearing the river bar. Unfortunately, the missing lighthouse was

In 1980, the unmanned Umpqua station appeared slightly different with some of the outbuildings gone. The first lighthouse on the Umpqua (1857) was close to the beach and the river entrance. It was undermined and destroyed by encroaching waters after about three years of service. For more than three decades the Umpqua was without a lighthouse.

1960's, several of the former outbuildings were torn down. The Coast Guard operated the light on a 24-hour basis which eventually wore down the chariot wheels and gears, causing malfunctions in the timing. The Fresnel was terminated in 1983 in favor of a small revolving acryllic lens mounted on the tower balcony. Local citizens protested, gathering hundreds of names, even going to their congressmen to get the Coast Guard to restore the old Fresnel. They eventually won their battle despite the economy measures of the Coast Guard to utilize the auxiliary light or to eventually place an aero-marine type beacon in the lantern house. Costs for restoring the chariot wheels were far less than previously estimated and at this writing the grand old beacon is back in operating order.

The lighthouse is a prime attraction in the Umpqua Lighthouse State Park, just off Highway 101, south of Winchester Bay, the park offering overnight camping and picnic facilities. At present the lighthouse is not open to the public except by special arrangement with the Coast Guard. Renewed interest in the structure assures continued priority maintenance. It was placed on the National Register of Historic places in 1978. The light has been a faithful beacon with only temporary interuptions. On February 24, 1958, it was out for two hours when an overheated oil stove caused a fire at the installation.

A close sister lighthouse to Umpqua is the Heceta Head tower commissioned in the same year—1894. They are similar in appearance and design, the latter built between 1891 and 1894. It is highly doubtful, however, that any lighthouse in the world equals Heceta's scenic setting. Nary a visitors camera leaves the central coast without a photo of Heceta Head Lighthouse, so eye-catching that it seems God placed it there when time began. Heceta Head, named for Captain Bruno Heceta, has been a source of agitation for years, some pronouncing it "Hek'ehtuh" and others "He-see-tuh". Another group insists on the Spanish, "Aysay'tah". Brother Bruno would probably have preferred the latter but regardless of the pronunciation, his name is indelibly applied to the headland. In the service of Spain, he commanded an expedition that explored the Northwest coast, moving as far north as the 59th parallel in 1775, almost to the Russian capital at New Archangel (Sitka), Alaska.

The station formerly had two commodious dwellings, one for the principal keeper and the other for his two assistants. A total expenditure of $180,000 was necessary for the lighthouse and reser-

vation buildings, a large share of the materials shipped to the Siuslaw River and then barged to a cove just south of the proposed lighthouse site. Lumber came from local mills. Masonary and cement came by sailing vessel from San Francisco to Florence and was then reloaded onto a barge towed by the tug *Lillian* to the mouth of the Siuslaw. From there, team and wagon hauled the cargo along the beach to the foot of Heceta Head where it was stored until improved weather made it possible to put a wagon road to the site. The rock in the base of the tower was from Clackamas River near Oregon City, and was delivered by the Lighthouse tender *Columbine*.

All lighting equipment, including the first order lens and carriage was manufactured by Chance Brothers of England, marking a departure from total dependency on Parisian-made lenses. The lamp was a five-wick arrangement burning refined coal oil, and the lens rode on chariot wheels turned by geared clockwork weights. The weights had to be re-cranked every four hours, from an hour before sunset till an hour after sunrise. Focal plane of the light was 205 feet above sea level and the lens with its oil flame produced 80,000 candlepower, visible 20 miles at sea.

Principal keeper Frank DeRoy assists his lovely wife Jenny over a rut on the grounds of Heceta Head Light Station in the 1920s. They were little affected by the poltergeists that reputedly haunted the keeper's dwelling. Photo courtesy of Bob DeRoy, son of Frank, who spent some of his boyhood days growing up at Heceta Head.

In 1910, the light was changed to a gas type bunsen burner. In later years the tower was electrified. With a 500 watt or 1000 watt bulb the glass cage composed of 640 prisms, had an output of one million candlepower. The tower was converted to automatic operation on July 20, 1963, the last keeper being one of the grand old men of the former Lighthouse Service, Oswald Allik, who remained on with the Coast Guard after 1939. He also put in 20 years at Tillamook Rock and served on the Columbia River Lightship.

Allik and his wife Alice who lived in what is presently known as Heceta House gave hundreds of tourists tours of the lighthouse. During his tenure, on February 12, 1961, the light for the first time failed at Heceta Head due to a road slide caused by heavy rains. Electric wires were snapped and water lines broken. A portable generator failed, so Allik employed an Aladdin lamp, and he and two Coast Guard assistants turned the lens by hand, taking turns walking around the interior of the lamp room from midnight until 7:30 the next morning.

Principal keeper Frank DeRoy, who was at Heceta Head in the 1920's, often referred to the light as "old faithful." On miserable nights, he would say to his young son Bob, "The light's beam is like an auger boring through the storm to warn the ships at sea of the danger of the rocky shore."

DeRoy also put in several years at Warrior Rock and Lime Kiln Light stations, but always had a special place in his heart for Heceta Head, and as a former seafaring man, kept the place shipshape and Bristol fashion.

Another genial career keeper, Clifford B. Herman, also served at Heceta Head. Known to everyone as "Cap", he spent a half century in lighthouse service.

Abutting the lighthouse today is Devils Elbow State Park, popular at all times of the year. From the park, one can walk up to "Heceta House", the former keepers' dwelling, now listed in the National Register. It is presently under the jurisdiction of the U.S. Forest Service and leased to Lane Community College. The path continues up to the light tower which the Coast Guard maintains. Entrance to the lighthouse is only by special permission of the Coast Guard. At this writing, the revolving lens was having rotation problems from being overworked on a 24-hour basis. For a time the auxiliary light was displayed from the lighthouse balcony, but repairs got the classic light back in operation.

A mile south of the lighthouse is the famous Sea Lion Caves, the world's only mainland home of the steller sea lion, and one of the largest natural sea caves of its kind found along the Pacific rim. It provides a natural shelter for the wild mammals, some of which weigh over 2,000 pounds. Visitors are able to descend to the caves via a special elevator.

Ships have usually given Heceta Head a wide berth, perhaps because of the sea rocks that jut up directly off the head, namely Conical Rock and Cox Rock, the undisturbed home of numerous seabirds. There has never been a fog signal at the station what with ships remaining well offshore and the strange land mass formation that would probably cause inaudible dead spots at sea. In earlier times, navigators claimed the lighthouse should have been placed closer to the entrance of the Siuslaw River, gateway to Florence, ten miles southward. But though many shipwrecks occurred at the river entrance, the lofty promontory appeared a more logical site.

In the year 1976, on the north spur of Cape Perpetua a little sentinel, privately-owned, attached to a chalet type home was built. Named Cleft of the Rock Lighthouse, the tower was designed from plans of the 1898 Fiddle Reef Lighthouse near Victoria B.C. It was the first time the historic cape ever had an aid to navigation, although its hulking mass has the steepest rise directly from the ocean of any Oregon coast headland, 800 feet less than a quarter mile from the beach, and 1,000 feet at a distance of 0.8 miles. The 31 foot driftwood gray, pyramidal tower is situated 100 feet above the sea and displays a flashing light, five white flashes followed by one red, every minute. The lighting apparatus was formerly used at sea-girt Solander Island, a small, totally exposed insular dot off the west coast of Vancouver

Two faithful wardens of the Heceta station, Frank DeRoy and Harry Waters take time out from their duties to smile for the cameraman. Courtesy of Bob DeRoy. Snapshot taken about 1925.

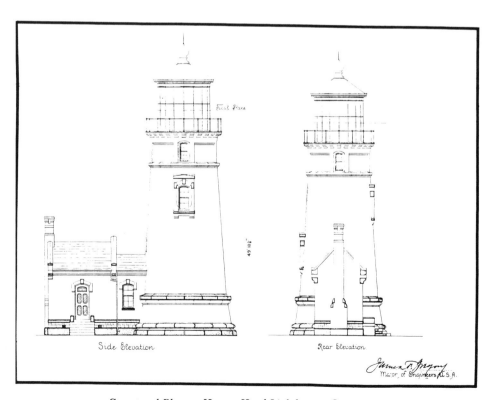

Structural Plans—Heceta Head Lighthouse, Oregon.

Heceta Head Lighthouse appeared to be immune to ghosts, leaving the wraiths to remain implanted in the keeper's dwelling. In this Coast Guard aerial photo, taken in recent years, the lower windows in the tower and rotunda have been cemented over to prevent vandalism.

Island. It was manufactured by Stone Chance Ltd., of Sussex England, successors to the Chance Brothers Ltd., which supplied the first order lens and lighting apparatus at Heceta Head nearly a century ago.

Cleft of the Rock Lighthouse is ten miles north of Heceta Head, at milepost 166. It is not open to the public but is easily viewed from Highway 101, a mile south of Yachats. Built by Hoen & Hamilton, it was accepted as an official beacon, and placed in the *Light List* on the 200th anniversary of the discovery of Cape Perpetua by Captain James Cook R. N., master of the HMS *Resolution*. He named the cape in March 1778, and Captain George Vancouver verified the location when he sailed by in April 1792. Tebenkoff on his survey retained the name, as did the U. S. Coast Survey reconnaissance of 1850. It was carried on all navigation charts from the time of Cook's discovery, but until recently was never marked by a light because shipping remains well offshore from the bold promontory. The bountiful outlying waters attract commercial fishing vessels in large numbers. The cape's slopes were a favorite camping grounds for the Yahutes Indians in ages past and shell mounds are found in abundance. The face of the cliff appeared so red in color that the U. S. Coast Survey of 1869, applied the second name of "Red Bluff".

Cape Perpetua was reputedly named for St. Perpetua's day, honoring a Greek woman who was martyred at Carthage in 203 A.D., in the cause of Christianity.

Yaquina Bay Lighthouse, still standing as a relic of the past, holds two records for Oregon—one; it is the oldest frame lighthouse in the state, and two; it had the shortest period of active duty of any lighthouse in Oregon. Restored as an historical museum, it is maintained by the Friends of Yoquina Bay Lighthouse and the U.S.

Forest Service. It resides in a setting of shore pines above the entrance to Yaquina Bay and an ocean seascape supreme.

The colorful lighthouse was built by Ben Simpson of Oneatta, Oregon, and fitted with lantern and iron work by Joseph Bien of San Francisco. Total cost of the station was $20,000. Supplies were landed by ship and brought to the site by ox team.

The lighthouse went into operation in 1871 with Charles H. Pierce, as keeper, he having earlier distinguished himself as a Civil War captain. The light was a fifth order lens, the lamp burning whale oil. The entire lighthouse reservation consisted of 36 acres, formerly homesteaded by Lester and Sophronia Baldwin, the area's first permanent white settlers who gained title to their land from the government in 1868. Their property was then sold back to Uncle Sam less than three years later for $500 in gold coin. Construction began May 1, 1871 and was completed November 3, of the same year. With the establishment of a primary coast lighthouse four miles to the north, at Yaquina Head, the Yaquina Bay light was deemed no longer essential and was terminated October 1, 1874, slightly over three years from its inception.

In 1877, the abandoned station was placed on the auction block by the government, but the offers were so meager the sale was withdrawn. Deterioration continued, but there was renewed hope of relighting the tower when the Oregon Pacific Railroad was completed from Corvallis to Yaquina City in 1885, completing a planned link with coastwise passenger liners. Unfortunately, the SS *Yaquina City* was wrecked while entering Yaquina Bay on December 4, 1887 after her rudder cable parted. Then, barely a year later her sister ship, the SS *Yaquina Bay* parted her hawser while being towed across the bar and she too went aground and became a total loss. A cry of sabotage went out loud and clear. Though accusers claimed Columbia River interests fearing direct competition had engineered the double tragedy, the charges could not be proven, and the bay lighthouse remained dark without hope of resurrection.

In 1888, the War Department gave permission to the U. S. Engineers to utilize the keepers quarters (attached to the tower) as a barracks for construction workers on the bar jetty. A decade later the U. S. Lifesaving Service, (established at South Beach in 1896) occupied the edifice for crew quarters and maintained surveillance for distressed vessels.

Abandoned once again, the place was claimed to be haunted, a tale that didn't bother a park caretaker who took up residence there in 1934. He did, however, complain loudly about the place being exposed to weather, claiming it to be extremely uncomfortable. In 1946, the Oregon State Highway Commission insisted the place be either torn down or moved. Demolition was delayed until 1948 when the Lincoln County Historical Society came to the rescue. After a struggle for finances, government aid came with placement in the National Register. Following a major overhaul, the Yaquina Bay Lighthouse lives on.

It shouldn't have happened but it did. Yaquina Head Lighthouse should have been Cape Foulweather Lighthouse, but due to a geographical error, the materials were taken to the wrong location, and it was there that one of the cardinal lighthouses on the Pacific Coast was commissioned in 1873. The land was surveyed by U. S. Army engineer J. S. Polhemus, and included 19.35 acres set aside by President Andrew Johnson's order, June 8, 1866.

The 93 foot masonry tower, a creation of beauty topped by a black lantern and parapet stands proud after well over a century, 162 feet above the Pacific.

Construction was difficult as most of the supplies came by lighter into a small cove in the lee of the headland where disturbed waters were totally unpredictable. A staircase was hammered out of the solid rock with handholds and footholds. A windlass and derrick were set up to handle materials and supplies and mules were harnassed for hauling. Several accidents were narrowly averted, and on occasion immersions in the cold sea water occurred.

The lighting apparatus at Yaquina Head was a fixed first order lens, manufactured by Barbier & Fenestre of Paris, in 1868. Two and a half panels have brass reflectors while six are full prismatic glass panels. There are 114 steps in the tower's spiral staircase winding upward from a marble floored rotunda. For many years, guests were asked to remove their shoes when visiting the tower, it being one of the best maintained on the west coast. The lamp was illuminated on August 20, 1873 and has continued to shine since that date, its original fixture still in service utilizing a flashing quartz-iodine globe, in place of the oil light of the early years. A radio beacon was installed at the lighthouse in later years.

Not all of the civilian lighthouse keepers were thrilled with their lot in life. Take the case of John Zenor, late of Otter Rock, who put in 22 years at Yaquina Head Lighthouse. He emphatically stated that he "doesn't care if he ever sees the inside of another one as long as he lives."

He began his lighthouse career at the Umpqua River Lighthouse in 1928 when the coal oil lamp was still in use. Later he was transferred to Ediz Hook Lighthouse at Port Angeles. "I was there 30 days before I saw anything, the area was socked in with fog," he recalled, "and the foghorn drove me nuts!"

After a short stay at Grays Harbor Light where he was trained in electronics (then being placed in coastal stations) the service transferred him to Yaquina Head where he spent more than two decades. It was then a three man station, one single dwelling and a duplex. When the lighthouse was electrified in 1935, including installation of a radio beacon, the crew was cut to two.

It was the constant winds that bothered Zenor the most and he said many of his visitors were literally blown about the grounds. At times he had up to 600 in a day, so popular was the lighthouse. In 1931, 14, 196 visitors came to Yaquina Head.

Zenor claimed that the lighthouse lens, made in France, was cut five degrees off center. The light was set for a distance of 18 miles and

Yaquina Bay Lighthouse above the Yaquina River bar entrance, and abutting the city of Newport, sits at the center of Yaquina Bay State Park. The photos show a front and rear view of the frame structure which has stood since 1871, but only saw three years of service as an active lighthouse. A lookout tower manned by the Coast Guard is still in use next to the lighthouse.

Lifting its massive masonry, Yaquina Head Lighthouse displays its original first order French made lens which shines seaward as it has for well over a century. The Coast Guard dwellings in the foreground, (not the original dwellings) were about to be torn down when this Coast Guard photo was taken.

hit about ten feet above the water on the bridge of a ship.

From the son of an engineer involved with the original construction of the station, Zenor learned that it was too difficult without a road to transport the materials to Cape Foulweather, so they were offloaded at the wrong site. The man said he kept this secret until his father's death. It was a number of years before the government learned that Cape Foulweather Lighthouse was really on Yaquina Head. By then it was too late to rectify.

Remaining on after takeover by the Coast Guard, Zenor remembered considerable action around the lighthouse during World War II. Among other activities there was a 24-hour weather station, and the overall crew at the reservation increased to 16.

Zenor was well acquainted with the lighthouse ghost. He said he just accepted it, as did others. At times he recalled "someone unseen would come in and go up the spiral stairs. After the war we never heard him again."

Glad for his days of retirement, the octogenarian, stated, "I never could understand people's interest in lighthouses." That was a strange statement from a man who spent the greater part of his life keeping the lamps aglow.

The classic old lighthouse dwelling was torn down years ago when it demanded a major overhaul, being so drafty that some claimed "a catalog could be lifted right off the floor." The Coast Guard built new dwellings after it took over the Lighthouse Service. Those too were removed in 1984, when the Field family, Larry, Alice and Helen tore them down and utilized the components to build a new house up the Yachats River.

In remarkably good condition despite its years (commissioned in 1873) Yaquina Head Lighthouse is a great credit to its builders. U.S. Coast Guard photo.

To reach the lighthouse from Newport, one turns left on Lighthouse Road four miles north of town, then west a mile passing the old quarry site which until 1983 supplied most of the rock for Lincoln County roads. The government has purchased the quarry property and will convert the land into a state park right up to and including the lighthouse grounds. The tower will remain under the jurisdiction of the Coast Guard displaying its big Fresnel. Considering its age, the Lighthouse is in remarkable condition despite the harsh elements of nature that buffet the bluff. The surrounding seascape is rich in marine life and many come to study the tidepool creatures. Seabirds, which are in abundance, are protected in their natural habitat. On Yaquina Reef, near the north jetty and south of the lighthouse, the wreck of the concrete ship *John Aspin* rests just under the surface, and the remains of the Japanese freighter *Blue Magpie* are in disarray against the jetty.

Forty-eight miles north of Yaquina Head is Cape Meares, marked by a lighthouse since 1890. Its story might better be described as "the misplaced lighthouse." The confusion perhaps goes back to July 6, 1788, when Captain John Meares, master of the *Felice Adventurer,* was sailing southward along the coast of present day Tillamook County. He sighted a prominent landmark which he logged as Cape Lookout, and accordingly gave a description and illustration.

Though in later years a lighthouse reservation was set aside for a beacon at Cape Lookout, ten miles south of its present location, it was due to an error on the coast navigation charts of 1850 and 1853, that Cape Meares was somehow labled as Cape Lookout. In 1857, the error was discovered but instead of shifting the names on the charts it appeared more simple to exchange the names of the promontories. Not even the local Indians had a name for that one, and the, "rather switch than fight attitude" later caused a migraine sized headache that required the President's signature to rectify. In 1889 bids were let by the U. S. Lighthouse Establishment for the construction of a lighthouse where the charts listed Cape Lookout. When the construction workers arrived, the pelting Tillamook rains had turned everything into a quagmire and it took the better part of a day for the ox and horse teams to gain the summit. The sticky mud made transport so difficult that it was determined to set up a blacksmith shop and brick making kiln at the site. Bricks were made from the clay deposits and the outbuildings were constructed of wood cut from the tall stands of timber. As construction continued, it was discovered that the place was not really Cape Lookout, but Cape Meares. It was too late to cease operations. With the small coastal population and the limited funds granted the Lighthouse Establishment by Congress there was no way that another lighthouse could or would be built elsewhere. As several officials scratched their heads and the usual red tape ensued, President Benjamin Harrison finally signed a bill that solved the problem.

The stubby 38 foot masonry tower, encased in iron, stood on the side of the precipitous cape, 232 feet above the Pacific and was fitted with a first order lens, gears, chariot wheels, weights and pedestal, manufactured by Henry Lepaute of Paris. The eight flash panel fixture with red and white sectors was lighted by a five wick, coal oil lamp. It was replaced by an IOV (incandescent oil vapor) lamp in 1910, and in 1934, electricity was provided by twin Kohler generators.

The proud little lighthouse, the pride of Tillamook County, seven miles west of the city of Tillamook, and five miles south of the entrance to Tillamook Bay, is a destination for numerous visitors. In 1963, the lighthouse was replaced by an ugly 17 foot utilitarian concrete structure with an exposed airway type beacon, and resident personnel were no longer retained at the station. Oregon has built a state park in and around the lighthouse reservation. The tower was an attraction until vandals broke in and knocked the bullseyes out of the old lens. A large fence was then placed around the empty lighthouse, and neglected, the iron plates soon turned red with rust. Volunteers eventually came to the rescue and funds were forthcoming to spruce

up the sentinel and open it to the public as an historic attraction. Today, scores of visitors tour its rotunda and climb the staircase to the lantern room to view the slightly desecrated lens. Some of the missing lens prisms were eventually recovered.

To reach the lighthouse, travel on the Three Capes Loop road northwest of Tillamook. The route takes one to Cape Meares, then onto the Netarts-Oceanside recreation area, past Cape Lookout, (the intended site for the lighthouse) and on to Cape Kiwanda.

Moves made by the Coast Guard to eliminate the present beacon at Cape Meares were fought by commercial fishermen, based on Tillamook Bay. They were heeded for several months but in the spring of 1985, the last act was performed, and the beacon dropped from the *Light List.* The heavy coastal traffic of bygone years is no more and deepsea ships on Loran (long range aid to navigation) and satellite navigation keep well offshore. Tillamook Bay today is for commercial and sports fishermen only, where once coastal schooners and small steamers crossed the hazardous bar.

Numerous vessels were wrecked around the Tillamook entrance in early times, and today the Coast Guard station at Garibaldi stands ever vigilant to aid vessels in trouble.

Tillamook Rock Lighthouse is famous or infamous, take your choice. It is one the world's best known sentinels, at least it was until it became obsolete to the Coast Guard in 1957 after 77 turbulent years of service. The lighthouse was built in 1879-80, a mile and a quarter offshore on an exposed mass of basalt rising sheer from the menacing Pacific. Located due west of Tillamook Head between Cannon Beach and Seaside, it was considered an isolated lighthouse, and though viewed by legions of people from the shoreside it was tantamount to an unclean leper of old—see me, but don't touch.

When the government, by auction, disposed of the lighthouse after its abandonment, numerous bidders responded, none of which had any inclination of the problems connected with a sea-girt upheaval. Passing from one owner to the next, the lighthouse fell into a sad state

Pictured here is the utilitarian beacon that replaced Cape Meares Lighthouse in 1963. After much agitation, the Coast Guard decided to continue the above light in the spring of 1985, on demand of the local commercial fishermen who did not want to have the cape unlighted on approach to Tillamook Bay. Photo by M.W. Rodrigues for Coast Guard.

of neglect. The Nevada group that first purchased it, sight unseen, were rumored to be planning the making of nuclear components there, or perhaps to set up an offshore gambling casino. Another owner, a New Yorker of substance, had plans for a summer home and was wealthy enough to hire a repair crew who went back and forth by helicopter on occasional days when the weather cooperated. He found the problems compound. Another owner borrowed money, put on a publicity campaign and planned to restore the place. He almost drowned trying to reach the rock in a small boat. Then the lender foreclosed on him. Still another owner proposed dismantling the structure stone by stone and re-erecting it in California as a restaurant, a plan totally incredible, virtually impossible and absurd. Finally, an attractive young real estate woman from Portland came up with what appeared the only practical plan for the disheveled sentinel—conversion to the world's first lighthouse columbarium, permanent storage for cremated remains. The idea would have made the old lightkeepers turn over in their graves, but the difficulties of maintaining an unmanned lighthouse open to the fusillades of the sea and weather demanded it being sealed like a tomb, all windows and portholes cemented over and steel plates welded over the lantern panes.

The lady's name is Mimi Morissette, and her dream was named Eternity At Sea Columbarium. In her mind it was the only way to retain the image of Tillamook Lighthouse for its second hundred years. She was joined by partners Joseph VanHaverbeke, Cathy Riley, Marshall Morissette and Richard Bartlett, who purchased the rock for $50,000, the first private owners having paid less then $6,000. It took an investment of nearly $100,000 to gut the entire interior down to the bare rock leaving it one large empty cavern, (except for the spiral staircase), filling it with urn racks and rehabilitating the exterior.

Mimi and her crew put on a big celebration after the lighthouse conversion. Celebrities and friends from all over Oregon came to celebrate "Terrible Tilly's" 100th anniversary. Helicopters ferried a few at a time out to the small landing below the lighthouse, and at no time during the history of the Rock were there that many visitors. During the time the lighthouse was active, only a handful of women ever set foot on its climes. Of course, no helicopters were then available, all landings being by derrick and hoist from a boat's deck, which often was prevented by heavy seas and adverse weather.

Four years after the creation of the mausoleum, only seven persons had their ashes entombed in the lighthouse, but 100 other niches had been sold. There are, however, 100,000 receptacles available, and at this writing, Mimi as director and Rudi Milpacher as president of Eternity at Sea, launched a nationwide campaign to sell the niches. They are among those who plan to have their ashes placed there and reason that thousands of other seafaring and martime-oriented people will do the same. As the only columbarium in the world offering "true burial" at sea, the service includes a ride to the Rock for the bereaved by helicopter, along with the ashes of the deceased, weather permitting. The owners are banking on a study done in 1980, that by the year 2000, 50 percent of Americans will choose cremation as opposed to only seven percent desiring cremation in 1980—rather "grave predictions."

Prices for the service range from $1,000 in the old derrick house graduating up to more than $5,000 if the ashes are placed in the "Celebrity Room." The latter designation is the inside of the iron lantern house from which the lighting apparatus was removed in 1957 when the Coast Guard abandoned the station.

From a distance the lighthouse looks authentic today. Sea birds, for the most part, have reclaimed the Rock and often turn it white with their droppings, but that just goes with the territory. After all, they were there first. The seas that breach the Rock during storms help sweep the residue away. The fear of flying rocks breaking the panes in the lantern house is no longer a problem because everything breakable has been sealed over with cement or iron plate.

R.M. Tabor sketched this drawing of the proposed Tillamook Rock Lighthouse about 1878, and it was signed by Colonel G.L. Gillespie, of the Army Engineers, who was responsible for the construction of the station. The inset shows the colonel, who was not only responsible for the lighthouse but several of the Oregon Coast bar jetties and other projects as well.

At one minute past the hour of midnight, September 1, 1957, keeper Oswald Allik tripped the switch that cut off the probing shaft of Tillamook Rock's light that had moved across the dark, boundless ocean for nearly eight decades, and by deed restriction no light was to ever again be displayed there. Allik, a highly dependable civil service keeper and his assistants, left on the buoy tender, and for the first time in 77 years the rock was without human life. This writer who put in time with Allik in 1945-46, was honored when asked to help him pen the final entry in the station log, now preserved at the Columbia River Maritime Museum in Astoria. It read:

Farewell, Tillamook Rock Light Station. An era has ended. With this final entry, and not without sentiment, I return thee to the elements. You, one of the most notorious and yet fascinating of the sea-swept sentinels in the world; long the friend of the tempest-tossed mariner. Through howling gale, thick fog and driving rain your beacon has been a star of hope and your foghorn a voice of encouragement. May the elements of nature be kind to you. For 77 years you have beamed your light across desolate acres of ocean. Keepers have come and gone; men lived and died; but you were faithful to the end. May your sunset years be good years. Your purpose is now only a symbol, but the lives you have saved and the service you have rendered are worthy of the highest respect. A protector of life and property to all, may old-timers, newcomers and travelers along the way pause from the shore in memory of your humanitarian role.

O. Allik
September 1, 1957

For a time, a radar-equipped ocean buoy was anchored off the Rock as a warning to ships, but after several years, it too was removed.

Tillamook Rock Lighthouse was considered an engineering triumph by its very creation. During the initial landing the surveyor was drowned trying to gain a foothold, and the word went out that the hoodoo pinnacle rock was totally unsuitable for a lighthouse. Local workers shunned offers of jobs, and the construction engineer, Charles A. Ballantyne, was forced to round up a new crew unfamiliar with the problems. To keep them separated from the local folk, he housed them out of Astoria until the USRC *Thomas Corwin* was available to transport them to the site. To gain the Rock, they had to fight off hundreds of angry sea lions coddling their young on the lower slopes. During the landing, some of the quarrymen nearly drowned, only four reaching the Rock, the others having to stay aboard the anchored cutter until the seas moderated several days later. The workers endured untold hardships and privation in their efforts to blast more than 20 feet off the leaning pinnacle at the summit in order to forge a foundation. They clung like barnacles to the side of the Rock using footholds and handholds deeply imbedded to protect them from flying rock during the blasting. That first winter, seas swept clear over the Rock, the storehouse was knocked into the sea; tools and supplies carried away; the shelter holed by flying debris and filled with sea water. Food nearly ran out and clothing never dried. Life was miserable with a capital M, and no relief ship could approach the Rock for days. The cookstove was the only means of heat but it too was often flooded with sea water.

With intrepid leadership the undaunted Ballantyne kept his miserable crew from total despair. Finally a relief vessel was able to get reasonably near the Rock, but the only way to get a line to the men was to rig up a kite with a rope attached, and let it soar toward them with the wind. It was successful and a lifeline was rigged to bring in desperately needed food, clothing and supplies.

The cornerstone of the lighthouse was laid in 1880, but even as the tower began to rise, the seas continued their unrelenting onslaught. It took 525 days and $125,000 to finish the job, the hardest part, landing the huge blocks of stone. A derrick house with a steam donkey was installed to operate a long boom that reached out over the water to lift personnel and supplies from surface craft. Sometimes a breeches buoy from ship to Rock had to be employed.

*Earliest known photo of Tillamook Rock Lighthouse, taken about 1895, when the Pacific had one of its few mill-pond days. The lighthouse tender **Columbine** is shown anchored off the rock transferring supplies via the station derrick boom.*

Shortly before the big Fresnel went into operation, the British ship *Lupatia*, 1,300 tons, in command of R. H. Raven, nearly struck the Rock in the fog. The workers could hear commands being shouted and lit fires to warn the ship away. The vessel veered off but later crashed into Tillamook Head drowning her entire crew of 16, the only survivor being a young dog. The suffering animal found whining on the beach after its harrowing experience soon found a new home.

First principal keeper of the lighthouse was Albert Roeder, who with four assistants operated the light and fog signal. Leave was on a rotating basis. The light was lit on January 21, 1881. Year after year the seas swept the Rock inflicting great damage. Eventually the metal roof of the fog signal house and quarters holed continually by flying rock had to be replaced with reinforced concrete and at the same time the building raised a half story. The fog trumpets were frequently clogged with debris thrown up by seas stampeding through the fissure splitting the southwest corner of the Rock. Railings were often flattened or tanks knocked from their blocks. Eventually all windows on the south and west sides had to be either replaced with deep set ship's portholes, or cemented over. Storm seas at times inundated the entire building, throwing green water over top of the lantern, 134 feet above sea level. The derrick boom was frequently sheered off and the derrick house flooded. Numerous times the panes were knocked out of the lantern house tossing rocks, seaweed and fish into the lantern room. The 1934 storm which inflicted thousands of dollars in damage, knocked the panes out of the lantern and battered the Fresnel beyond repair. At the same time the interior of the lighthouse was flooded. On that occasion the keepers worked up to their necks in water in order to install an auxiliary light. All communication with the shore had been lost, the telephone cable snapped. One of the keepers had to rig up a radio sending device to make contact with a ham operator who in turn contacted the lighthouse inspector to tell of the Tillamook dilemma.

It was an oft-repeated story. In 1886, a half ton mass of concrete filling was sheered off and thrown over the railing 90 feet above the sea. In 1912, driving seas ripped off the overhanging west end of the Rock diminishing the basaltic mass by several feet and leaving a scar that remains to this day. The noise was so deafening that the keepers thought the lighthouse would be thrown into the vortex.

The cost of maintaining the Rock was substantial, all fuel, water, food, mail and supplies having to come out by lighthouse tender, motor lifeboat or cutter. It was a welcome day when the original steam siren was replaced by a first class automatic compressed air siren and an even better day when the station was electrified and indoor plumbing installed. The fog signal house contained generators, compressors, and a huge bank of dry cell batteries for reserve. The water and oil tanks for the most part were mounted outside the building.

In all 77 years of service the guest register showed about 300 persons had visited the Rock, including lighthouse inspectors and repairmen. Women were almost unseen by the keepers and wives or families were forbidden, due to the isolation.

Now the light is gone; Oswald Allik has passed to his reward as have all the other civilian keepers once attached to the Rock, but the shell of the old structure is alive and well, even though its mission is to hold the ashes of the dead.

Antedating Tillamook Rock Lighthouse by six years was the erstwhile Point Adams Lighthouse, built in 1875, on the fringes of Fort Stevens at the south entrance to the Columbia River. Unlike the other seacoast lights it stood on the southwest 40 acres of a military reservation. The 50 foot tower with attached keeper's dwelling housed a fourth order Fresnel with fixed red characteristic produced by a colored glass chimney placed over the flame. Originally the light had a red flashing characteristic which was changed after the establishment of Tillamook Rock Light. The beacon was visible 11¾

miles from an elevation 99 feet above the sea and the white building stood out in sharp contrast with the green forests.

The initial keeper of the light was H. C. Tracy who lived there with his family. Captain J. W. "Joel" Munson was appointed keeper in 1881, perhaps the most revered light keeper in northern Oregon. In addition to being a steamboat captain he was a civic-minded humanitarian gentleman who entertained with his fiddle at every special local event. As former keeper at Cape Disappointment Lighthouse, on his own, he started the first lifesaving service by commandeering a lifeboat from a wrecked ship in 1885 and making it available to rescue shipwrecked sailors. His wife Clara later became mayor of Warrenton, the first woman mayor west of the Rockies.

The lighthouse was bugled out of service before the turn of the century, its demise being two fold: First, the extension of the Columbia River south jetty; and second, by the placement of the Columbia River Lightship off the river entrance in 1892. No longer considered helpful to navigation, the curtain came down on January 31, 1899 ending a short but colorful existence. The reservation that was once alive with the laughter of children and a host of visitors who wiled away happy hours with the sociable Munson family, was no more. Unfortunately no attempt was made to maintain the structure and it soon fell into disrepair at the mercy of trespassers and the elements of harsh weather. Finally, in 1912, the U. S. Secretary of War, aware of potential fire danger, ordered it demolished, and soon it was only a memory.

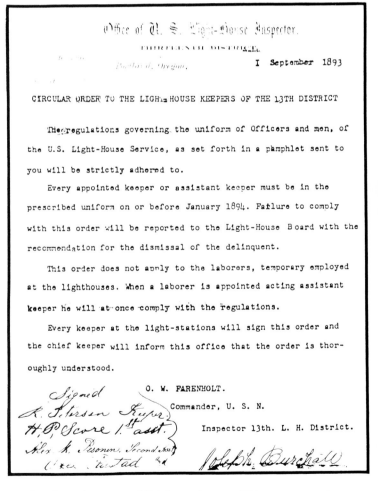

Circular order sent to all lighthouse keepers. This copy was sent from the office of the U.S. Light-House Inspector, 13th District, Portland, Oregon to Tillamook Rock Light Station. By order, the keepers each had to sign their signatures. The date, September 1, 1893.

After a savage sea knocked out the derrick boom in the 1930's a breeches buoy was rigged to transfer personnel and supplies at Tillamook Rock. From old Lighthouse Service files.

Returning to Tillamook Rock in 1957 for a final adieu before Coast Guard abandonment, the author is seen ensconced in the breeches buoy at the end of the derrick boom. Oswald Allik was the last keeper of the light before its demise.

New life for an old rock— Abandoned Tillamook Rock Lighthouse is converted to a lighthouse columbarium (Eternity at Sea Columbarium). Its windows and portholes were cemented over; its lantern panes welded in steel plates; the entire interior gutted down to the bare rock and filled with racks for the urns that hold dead people's ashes. The conversion was spearheaded by Mimi Morissette, Portland real estate broker seen at the right in the inset picture. At left is Cathy Riley, one of the original partners, and in the center, Sam Foster, Seaside photographer and correspondent.

Historic return to Tillamook Rock in the summer of 1969, 12 years after the abandonment of the lighthouse by the Coast Guard. On the right is "Ossie" Allik who put in 20 years on the Rock and who then became the last civilian keeper of Heceta Head. He and his wife Alice lived in Heceta House, and she firmly denied it was haunted. Ossie, who was acquainted with the ghosts at both stations had little comment. At left is Sam Foster, elite photographer and news media reporter of Seaside.

Assistant keeper Bob Gerloff at Tillamook Rock Lighthouse. This old salt was so attached to the "Rock" that he refused to go ashore when his time for leave came. When forced to retire he petitioned the government to let him stay on without pay in the 1930s.

CENTENNIAL CELEBRATION

To "Tilly" on her 100th Birthday

In honor of Charles A. Ballantyne and the brave men that helped him build her.

In honor of all the construction crews who have kept her restored over her 100 years.

In honor of Oswald Allik, the last, longest, most famous keeper, and all her other keepers.

In honor of the U.S. Coast Guard who manned her and kept her supplied.

We at Eternity at Sea Columbarium pledge our allegiance to you and promise to preserve your beauty, stature and dignity to the best of our ability from this day forward.

"TILLAMOOK ROCK LIGHTHOUSE"

Originated June 24, 1880
Celebrating 100 years of History June 24, 1980

Sponsored by Eternity at Sea Columbarium, Tillamook Rock, sometimes referred to as "Terrible Tilly," marked its centennial celebration on June 24, 1980, numerous friends and celebrities airlifted to the Rock by helicopter. When the Coast Guard abandoned the site in 1957, the deed restriction forbade a light to ever again shine from its climes.

Keeper Ossie Allik put in 20 years on Tillamook Rock and was its potentate when the Coast Guard closed the facility as an aid to navigation in 1957. He is pictured standing by the upper tier of the revolving lens at Tillamook, the one that replaced the first order Fresnel destroyed by the devastating 1934 storm.

Two Gallatin award winners for meritorious service with the Lighthouse Service and U.S. Coast Guard, C.B. "Cap" Herman, right, who put in four decades of service and Roy Dibb who is remembered as a prominent golfer who practiced in foul weather and calm by tethering a golf ball to a stanchion of the railing on restricted Tillamook Rock.

At Ecola Park on the northern Oregon Coast, with Tillamook Rock Lighthouse in the background, a scene for the recently filmed movie "The Goonies" was taken, an adventure production featuring secret caves, the mock-up of an old lighthouse (pictured in the scene), a lost map, treacherous traps, and hidden treasure. Courtesy Sam Foster.

Point Adams Lighthouse commissioned in 1875 at the south entrance to the Columbia River was a unique frame structure. Its active life however, was relatively short, brought to a halt by the extension of the Columbia River south jetty and the presence of the Columbia River Lightship. It ceased operations in 1899 and was razed in 1912, near the present site of Battery Russell at Fort Stevens. Photo from a Buchtel & Stolte stereograph, courtesy of the Columbia River Maritime Museum, Astoria.

For a time the station also had a steam foghorn but that was discontinued in 1881, the year the Munson's arrived, mostly because the roar of the breakers made it inaudible.

Point Adams was named by Captain Robert Gray, who discovered the Columbia River in 1792. The Indians referred to it as "Klaat-sop." It is located near the site of some of the earliest Indian habitation around the Columbia River, where castaways from shipwreck were taken as slaves by the natives years before the river was discovered.

On October 29, 1979, a revolutionary new aid to navigation, the Columbia River Approach Lighted Horn Buoy CR (LNB), was placed in operation. It was the replacement for the Columbia River Lightship *No. 604* which was retired after 29 years of service off the river entrance. The buoy, equipped with radio beacon, racon and foghorn could operate at a fraction of the cost of a manned lightship. The 42 foot high apparatus was towed to her post by the Coast Guard buoy tender *Iris* and positioned seven miles off the river entrance. When the changeover occurred the lightship was at Tongue Point Coast Guard Station awaiting replacement of an anchor lost in a storm. Deployment of the buoy had been delayed three days by rough bar conditions. Since its placement, the buoy has proven highly successful, continually identifying itself by an electronic radio devise that transmits the letters CR in Morse code, and containing radar that renders a clear picture on the scopes of approaching vessels.

The demise of the lightship spelled the end to an era. Since 1892, a lightship had been on station at the river entrance, the first and last lightship station on the Pacific Coast. Congress appropriated $60,000 for a lightship on March 23, 1889, and when the bids were let, Union Iron Works of San Francisco won the contract. In April of 1892, the Columbia River Lightship *No. 50* was launched. Towed north, the vessel had no engine, her steam plant used only for heat, electricity and power to raise the lanterns by nightfall. For emergencies, she was schooner-rigged.

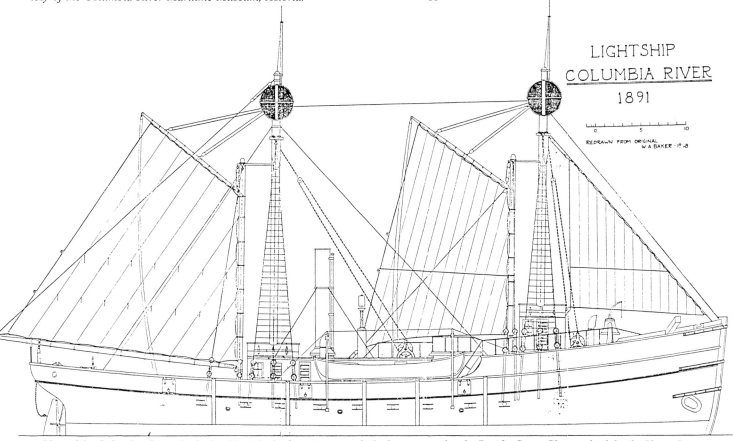

LIGHTSHIP
COLUMBIA RIVER
1891

*Plan of the Columbia River Lightship **No. 50**, the first American lightship assigned to the Pacific Coast. She was built by the Union Iron Works of San Francisco in 1891. Credit W.A. Baker, in American Neptune.*

After seven years of service, the wooden-hulled vessel fell victim to a severe gale that raged at the river entrance November 28-29, 1899. The voluminous seas caused her to part her heavy anchor cables and go adrift. Her sail power proved useless and she was swept hard aground on the beach below McKenzie Head. Following several unsuccessful attempts to refloat the vessel, a house moving firm was hired to jack her up, place her on skids, and by using teams of horses and machinery move her overland. The unusual salvage endeavor which gained international attention hauled the 296 ton vessel over the sands, up a hill and through the woods for nearly a mile, and then readied her for relaunching into Bakers Bay on the river side. The project required the work of 40 men, several teams of horses and $12,000 worth of equipment. The relaunching took place on June 2, 1901, after the vessel had been landlocked for a year and a half. After repairs, *No. 50* was towed back to her post off the river.

It was a case of poor food in 1907, so bad that the crew, all but the cook, resigned their jobs. The lightship continued on station until 1909 when it was replaced by a new lightship, the *No. 88* which had steamed around the toe of South America from the east coast with a fleet of other Lighthouse Service vessels. After her retirement, *No. 50* was sold to the highest bidder in 1914 for $2,600. She served as the Mexican steamer *San Cosme,* and then came back under the American flag as Red Salmon Canning Company's *Margaret* in 1920. In 1935, she was junked at Antioch, ending the career of the coast's first lightship.

In 1898, lightships were placed off the entrance to San Francisco Bay *(No. 70)* and at Umatilla Reef off the northwest coast of Washington *(No. 67).*

After the turn of the century lightships were placed at Blunts Reef off the northern California coast and at Swiftsure Bank outside the Strait of Juan de Fuca. Today, not a single lightship remains on the U.S. Pacific Coast or in British Columbia. Several of the veteran vessels have been relegated to museum groups, and one is even serving as a floating restaurant, the old *Swiftsure* at Neuport, Oregon.

The last to be removed from service, *Columbia River Lightship No. 604* is on display and open to the public at the Columbia River Maritime Museum in Astoria, a popular attraction visited by scores annually.

Desdemona Sands Lighthouse for years was a popular attraction at the mouth of the Columbia River, adjacent to the city of Astoria. Built atop a wooden platform supported by piling sunk deep in the river sands, the lighthouse marked a portion of Desdemona Sands, a shoal area that extended from just inside the entrance of the river for about eight miles southeastward, dividing the river into the main channel to the south and a secondary channel to the north.

It was named for the wreck of the bark *Desdemona,* which under Captain Francis Williams entered the river without a pilot January 1, 1857. Bound for Astoria, heavily laden with cargo, she sailed in under a fair breeze on a flood tide and ran hard aground on the shoal. She became a total loss including a large portion of her cargo.

Captain Williams cried foul, that the stranding was caused by the lower river buoy being adrift, but his pleas fell on deaf ears.

Not until 1902 was a lighthouse placed at the obstruction. The fixed fourth order Fresnel was displayed 46 feet above the water, and a third class Daboll fog trumpet was activated during thick weather. The octagonal tower rose from a one and a half story dwelling and was a pleasant sight to the parade of ships and smaller craft constantly passing its door.

In 1916, one of the keepers accidentally knocked over a container of alcohol which exploded and set the wooden building on fire. As

*Birdseye view of the **Columbia River Lightship No. 93**, taken from a Coast Guard aircraft in the late 1940s. A lightship was on duty off the entrance to the Columbia beginning in 1892 with the **No. 50**, and continuing till November 1979, when the **No. 604** was withdrawn as the last lightship on the Pacific Coast.*

Desdemona Sands Lighthouse, built in 1902, sat on piling in the center of the Columbia River off Astoria for a half century, and then like so many of the fine old lighthouses was cancelled out and dismantled. Its fourth order light and fog signal were well known to mariners plying the Columbia, and to a steady parade of deepsea ships. Photo, courtesy of the Columbia River Maritime Museum (Woodfield photo).

flames shot skyward, several boats rushed to the scene to help fight the blaze, but the keepers, trained for such eventualities, managed to get the flames under control with their fire fighting equipment.

As more lighted buoys were placed at the river mouth it became necessary to change the fixed characteristic of the beacon by installing a triple flashing Fresnel to better facilitate navigators.

Like so many of the classic frame lighthouses, Desdemona Sands in later years was flanked by minor lights negating a manned facility, and was accordingly dismantled after World War II, eliminating a colorful seamark for Astorians. Its replacement was a small pyramidal tower on a pile structure, succeeded by a small white house on the same platform in 1955, and finally a minor light on a dolphin. They call it lighthouse evolution in reverse. Had it remained it would have been dwarfed by the Astoria (trans-Columbia River) Bridge between Astoria and Megler, the last link in Coast Highway 101, connecting the states of Washington and Oregon, a 4.3 mile long bridge, containing one of the nation's longest continuous spans. The height of the bridge allows the tallest ships to pass beneath with room to spare.

Warrior Rock Light is the only aid to navigation on the Columbia River that still qualifies as a lighthouse. Every Columbia River pilot is totally familiar with its presence. Though the channel turn off the light is slight for passing ships, pilots are always wary, for beneath the river lurks a basalt ledge that has played havoc with its victims. In 1984, the tanker *Mobiloil* tore a big hole in her side which spewed oil into the river that flowed all the way to the sea. The stranding was caused when a broken cotter pin fouled up the steering mechanism. When the ship was finally freed a few days later the damage was such that repairs were not justified.

Four years earlier, in 1980, a nearby buoy was moved closer to the edge of the channel without proper notification in the *Notice to Mariners,* and as a result the Greek bulker *Ypatia Halcoussi,* with pilot aboard, turned short and struck the reef inflicting costly damage. The owners sued the Coast Guard for moving the buoy; the federal government sued the pilots against any judgement, and the pilots sued the owners to hold them harmless. In September 1984, the government was found at fault, both pilot and ship's crew being freed of blame.

The original Warrior Rock Lighthouse on Sauvie Island built in 1888-89; it was replaced by a cement tower in the 1930s. The cable at the center of the photo was used by keeper Frank DeRoy as sort of an aerial tram when water covered the rock. Courtesy Bob DeRoy. Photo taken in the 1920s.

The keepers quarters at Warrior Rock Light Station in the 1920s. Courtesy Bob DeRoy.

Like a glorious halo the beams from the Fresnel lens set the night sky aglow.

*Insert shows the lighthouse tender **Manzanita** which replaced the **Shubrick** in catering to the needs of Northwest lighthouses. Built in 1879, she was wrecked in the fog in 1905 off Warrior Rock, abandoned as a total loss, later salvaged, and rebuilt as the tug **Daniel Kern.** She operated until 1936.*

Warrior Rock Lighthouse after being rammed by a runaway barge in the Columbia River on May 27, 1969. Much of the stone foundation was knocked out. The Coast Guard debated for a long time whether or not to restore the structure. Finally it did. Lawrence Barber photo.

Located on Sauvie Island just above St. Helens, Warrior Rock Lighthouse was established in 1888, a small frame structure placed atop a sandstone foundation right on the edge of the Columbia. It consisted of a single service room with quarters for the keeper on one floor and on the next, a sheltered half deck housing a lens-lantern and fogbell. Later, a dwelling and barn were added, separate from the lighthouse. When the river was high the lighthouse foundation was virtually in the water. During the river freshets logs and debris would sometimes be thrown against the dwelling, barn and carpenter shop.

Bob DeRoy, son of the late keeper Frank DeRoy, remembers growing up there as a young lad in the 1920's and how the river steamers like the *T.J. Potter* and *Georgiana* would pass within a stone's throw and sometimes thoughtlessly cut the commercial fishermen's nets, or send in huge waves that slopped over onto the lighthouse property. On occasion irate fisherman would fire their rifles at the pilot houses of passing steamers in protest of the violations.

His father often had trouble with the lighthouse fogbell. He named it the "Black Moria," for frequently the striking mechanism and weights malfunctioned and the bell had to be rung manually for long periods of time. It, however, was a historic bell, in fact the oldest fogbell in the Pacific Northwest. It was cast of bronze in Philadelphia by B. J. Bernhard & Co. in 1855 for the Cape Disappointment

Lighthouse. The roar of the surf often made it inaudible there, and the 1,600 pound apparatus was moved to Puget Sound before being transferred to Warrior Rock in 1889.

Back in the early years the tender *Manzanta* supplied the station having earlier delivered the building materials for its construction. Ironically, the same vessel ran afoul of the reef just off the lighthouse in 1905 and was abandoned as a total loss. Months later the firm of Kern & Kern purchased salvage rights, refloated and rebuilt her as the tug *Daniel Kern*.

In the 1930's, the little frame lighthouse was replaced by a concrete pyramidal tower atop the same sandstone foundation. On May 27, 1969 a runaway barge slammed into the base of the lighthouse and sent the sandstone tumbling in a heap, disabling the light and fogbell. A buoy was temporarily placed offshore while the Coast Guard decided whether the damaged lighthouse should be rebuilt. While the historic bell was being removed, the supporting ropes parted and it fell into the river, badly damaged. Later salvaged, but cracked, it was presented to the Columbia County Historical Society at St. Helens where since it has been on display. Unfortunately, the "Black Moria" will never toll again.

The Coast Guard, however, did restore the foundation and the tower, and that light and fog signal continue to guide river traffic.

Historic fog bell, cast in 1855 in Philadelphia was first placed in service at Cape Disappointment, but was claimed to be inaudible. It was then used on Puget Sound and finally finished its service at Warrior Rock. After the latter station was damaged, while removing the bell, the Coast Guard handlers allowed it to fall into the river and severely cracked the apparatus. It is now on display at the Columbia County Museum in St. Helens. Lawrence Barber photo.

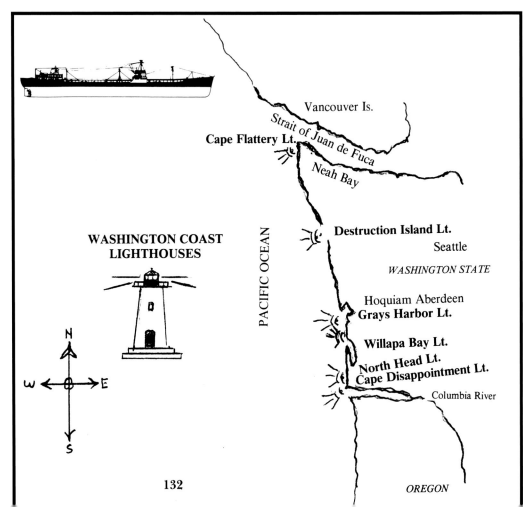

WASHINGTON COAST LIGHTHOUSES

Vancouver Is.

Strait of Juan de Fuca

Cape Flattery Lt.

Neah Bay

Destruction Island Lt.

Seattle

WASHINGTON STATE

Hoquiam Aberdeen
Grays Harbor Lt.

Willapa Bay Lt.

North Head Lt.
Cape Disappointment Lt.

Columbia River

PACIFIC OCEAN

OREGON

CHAPTER EIGHT

Washington Coastal Lighthouses

Trim your feeble lamp, my brother;
Some poor sailor tempest tossed,
Trying now to make the harbor,
In the darkness may be lost.
....Philip P. Bliss

When one stands atop the fabulous cape with its breathtaking view he would never in the world understand why it was named Disappointment. God spared nothing in creating one of the western world's most beautiful maritime panoramic vistas. Doubtless it was such a view that inspired popular songs like, *"On a Clear Day You Can See Forever."*

The history of the cape, however, has had its disappointments. It began back in the days of the Spanish explorers who were searching for the fabled "River of the West." Always the cape would loom up, but white-lipped breakers from shore to shore continued to hide the entrance to the river. Other than Indian eyes, nobody knows who first saw the bold headland but for some reason it kept its secret about the greatest river in western America. The mighty Columbia was to become the last great plum of discovery in the Pacific Northwest. The cape is the north point of the entrance to the river, and is the only headland that breaks the low line of sandy shore which stretches from Tillamook Head to Point Grenville. South of the cape the low land from Tillamook Head to Point Adams recedes from the general direction of the coast which tends to give prominence to Cape Disappointment. The cape presents a rather unusual formation composed of irregular columnar basalt rising to an elevation 287 feet, broken by rounded hills.

On August 17, 1775, Don Bruno de Heceta, commanding the frigate *Santiago* logged what he titled "Una boca que se Ilamo de la Asuncion , o entrada de Heceta." He failed to enter it on account of great conflicting currents which caused him to believe that it was the broad mouth of some large river, or strait which gave it passage through to the sea. He placed himself in 24 fathoms of water between the two capes, which he named San Roque and Frondosa. Cape Disappointment he called Cabo San Roque, and Tillamook Head, Cabo Frondoso.

It was on July 6, 1778 that John Meares in the ship *Nootka* arrived off the cape and found that a "Prodigious easterly swell rolled on the shore," and he had soundings of 15 fathoms over a hard, sandy bottom. "After we had rounded the promontory, a large bay, as we had imagined opened to our view that bore a very promising appearance, and into which we steered with every encouraging expectation." As he entered the bay he wrote, "The water shoaled to nine, eight and seven fathoms, when breakers were seen right ahead, and, from the masthead, they were observed to extend across the bay. We therefore hauled out.....The name Cape Disappointment was given to the promontory, and the bay obtained the title Deception Bay."

Captain George Vancouver, navigating in the area, a few years later, not desiring to give the Spaniards credit, retained the name Disappointment. It was called Cape Hancock or Disappointment by the U. S. Coast Survey on examination of the river entrance in 1850. The name Hancock was for a time used by the government on the Lighthouse List, but Disappointment finally won out. But be that as it may, the real name of the cape should be "Kah'eese," for that was the age-old title given to the great monolith by the local Indians who had frequented its climes for centuries before the age of exploration.

To Yankee trader Captain Robert Gray fell the honor of being the actual discoverer of the Columbia River. The intrepid seafarer, more concerned with finding a good supply of furs for the China market than with the honor of discoverer, was the first to enter both the Columbia River and Grays Harbor. Ironically, on April 30, 1792, Captain Vancouver had logged the following remarks:

"It must be considered a very singular circumstance that, in so great an extent of sea coast, we should not until now have seen the appearance of any opening in its shores which presented any prospect of affording a shelter, the whole coast forming one compact and nearly straight barrier against the sea."

His face was perhaps slightly red when on May 11, 1792 Gray entered the river in the 230 ton ship *Columbia Rediviva* and opened the gate to one of the world's greatest rivers, which he affectionately named for his ship.

Initial consideration for a Pacific Coast lighthouse was at the entrance to the Columbia River, which well before the middle of the last century had proven itself an extremely dangerous bar portal. There, shoals shifted constantly, influenced by the strong confrontation between the relentless ocean swells and the residue swept seaward from the river which had its source in the high country of British Columbia, flowing 1,214 miles to the Pacific Ocean. It was to become a portal of world commerce, and initially, the bane of mariners.

The U. S. Coast Survey recommended a lighthouse on Cape Disappointment as early as 1848, and the newly formed Lighthouse Board, gave it priority over all other sentinels scheduled for the Pacific Coast. Initially only $15,000 was alotted for lights at Disappointment, Tatoosh Island, New Dungeness and for the Columbia River buoyage. A total expenditure by Congress for all the initial West Coast lights was $143,000. As was earlier mentioned, Gibbons & Kelly who won the contract for the first coast lights dispatched the bark *Oriole* to the river with construction supplies for the lighthouse, but the vessel came to grief directly below the southwest spur of the cape where the beacon was to be built. As a result, the materials for Cape Disappointment Lighthouse and cargo for others as well, was a total loss. In command of Captain Lewis H. Lentz, the vessel was off the river entrance September 10, 1853 after a 13 day voyage from San Francisco. The irascible bar was such that the ship had to wait off the entrance for eight days, before the skipper was willing to risk a crossing. On September 18, a pilot schooner rendezvoued with the *Oriole*, but the pilot refused to guide the bark in until the following day when the bar swells moderated. When the vessel got under way the tide was ebbing but a fair breeze moved her along at a fair gait. The heavily laden vessel then experienced what every sailing ship master feared. On the bar the breeze suddenly ceased leaving the vessel at the mercy of the confused seas and currents.

More canvas proved to no avail and soon the *Oriole* was thumping against the shoals. Frantic efforts were made to get deeper water beneath her keel, but swells kept banging her against the obstruction, weakening her timbers. The pumps were constantly manned, but water poured in. For a moment the vessel was free, but mounting

Cape Disappointment Lighthouse, guardian at the mouth of the Columbia River has sent its warnings to sea since 1856. U.S. Coast Guard photo.

Cape Disappointment Light shines out over a vast graveyard of ships. In agonizing disarray lies the wreck of the tuna seiner **Bettie M.,** *wrecked with a load of 900 tons of fish in her holds, March 20, 1976. Seaside photo by Sam Foster.*

North Head Lighthouse, companion to Cape Disappointment Light was commissioned in 1898. U.S. Coast Guard photo.

Life Boat Drill
Klipsan Beach Life 9...

breakers shoved her even harder against the reef splitting her timbers. As the wind began to blow again the ship was already down by the stern and the lives of 32 crewmen and construction workers hung in the balance. With the ebbing tide the ship's situation was hopeless, so the captain and pilot ordered a small lighter carried on deck put over the side in an effort to save some of the valuable cargo. When it became apparent the *Oriole* was nearing her final plunge, Lentz ordered abandonment and all hands took to the boats. Shortly after, the bark rolled over on her beam ends and sank.

The captains's boat attempted to take the lighter in tow and was later joined by a second lifeboat in charge of the pilot. As night came on with mounting seas, the lighter had to be cast adrift only to vanish in the dark. The survivors spent a horrendous night trying to gain safe harbor by using both sail and oar. By morning, frozen to the marrow and pale as ghosts, the occupants of the boats were still being tossed about like corks. At last their plight was discovered and local craft came to their aid.

The loss of the *Oriole* set back the construction of the lighthouse several months. In the interim, forests were cleared, wagon trails built and a site cleared. Indians who had long utilized the headland continued to do so, but fortunately remained friendly, and except for being bothersome, caused no trouble.

The 53 foot lighthouse and reservation buildings were built at a cost of $38,500, but with the long wait for the lighting apparatus to arrive, it was October 15, 1856 before the first order fixed Fresnel was displayed, almost six years from the time of the initial planning. A 1,600 pound fogbell was placed at the station but proved to be a dud because its sound was inaudible due to wind, land contour and roaring seas. It was suspended in 1881, and as previously mentioned, eventually ended up at Warrior Rock Light. The lens is believed to have been used at an East Coast lighthouse before coming to Cape Disappointment, and was one of the earlier units ordered by the government from French makers. It is on display today at the interpretive center on Cape Disappointment. Even as the lighthouse came into being, to the delight of the maritime industry of the Oregon Territory, Portland was only a fledgling town on the Willamette, and Astoria, the first white settlement west of the Rockies was a struggling little seaport. Astoria had been founded as a fur trading post in 1811 by the Astor party. It would be yet three years before Oregon would become a state.

Less than a decade had passed before the keepers at Cape Disappointment got neighbors, not necessarily to their liking. Giant batteries of Fort Canby were placed around the plateau on which the lighthouse stood. In an attempt to guard the Columbia River entrance during the Civil War, the armament along with other fort facilities sprang up in 1864. When the big guns were fired the explosion shook the lighthouse severely and on occasion cracked panes of glass.

Today the old fort is part of a Washington State Park and a favorite camping and picnic grounds for thousands of tourists. Though huge empty concrete batteries are hidden about the cape, in all probability the military will never again utilize the area for war purposes. The guns were never fired in anger from the inception of the fort, which included several major wars. The closest the fort came to being fired on was when a Japanese submarine surfaced off Fort Stevens on the south side of the river entrance during World War II and lobbed in several shells. No damage occurred and no guns returned the fire from either Fort Stevens or Fort Canby.

Before the advent of the lighthouse, ships entering the Columbia had to depend on makeshift navigation aids, bonfires by night or by day, notched trees, stumps or white rags. When a ship was sighted, Indians often carried the news to Astoria via their dugout canoes to alert the settlement. Volunteers would travel 12 miles in all, crossing the river by boat and hiking up a switchback trail to rig up a marker.

The choice of the southwest spur of the cape for the lighthouse was wisely made by William P. McArthur who led the survey party on the U. S. Coast Survey schooner *Ewing*, and a proper choice it was, for the sentinel is the oldest active lighthouse in the Pacific Northwest and has endured all the punishment that could be expected of any highly exposed masonry lighthouse—severe winds, pelting rains and sleet, the blasting of big guns etc. The beacon has been the star of hope to many seafarers for nearly a century and a half.

McArthur made the following recommendation in his survey of the Columbia River entrance sent to his superiors in Washington D. C. September 25, 1850:

> There is now a good pilot at the mouth of the Columbia and I have recommended a lighthouse on Cape Diasppointment and five buoys to be placed under the jurisdiction of the pilot who will always know when any change in the channel has taken place and he can move the buoys to such positions as he might think best. By such means the dangers and delays attending the navigation of the Columbia would be mostly eliminated. The greatly increasing commerce of Oregon demands these improvements be made immediately. I have examined all the charts that have been made of the Columbia River from the time of its discovery to the present, and find that there has been continual changes going on, but that all times there has been a good deep channel at the mouth of the river. To these

changes in the channel is to be attributed the great dread which navigators had of the Columbia.

The original contractor of the lighthouse recovered $10,558 from the government for the loss of lighthouse materials that sank with the *Oriole*. The second shipment of materials didn't arrive until 1854. After the installation of the big 12 foot high Fresnel, the oil light was provided with five oil wicks, 18 inches across, set in a base atop an eight foot high pedestal. Consumption was 170 gallons of oil a month, which figured out to almost five gallons a night.

Though government archive records are incomplete, it appears that the initial keeper at the Disappointment station was John Boyd. Pacific County records list him and his family dwelling there in the 1860 census.

Perhaps the most prominent of the station's early light keepers was the previously mentioned Captain Joel Munson. He and his family had homesteaded at a little settlement named Lexington on the Skipanon River, also known as Upper Landing, in 1854, where the stage coaches met the river boats coming in from Portland and upriver ports. A humanitarian at heart, while he was keeper at Cape Disappointment, he became alarmed by the increasing shipwrecks occurring at the river entrance. It was in 1865 that the bark *Industry* was wrecked with the loss of 17 lives and nobody was able to go to the rescue. When the wreckage was washed up on the beach he recovered a boat containing metal airtanks and conceived the idea of converting it into a rescue craft. To get the necessary gear, he arranged for several dances to be held in Astoria and charged $2.50 per person to raise money. An expert on the fiddle he played for all the square dances. He not only was able to equip the boat but further interested the Lighthouse Service in providing a temporary shelter. His superiors also said that the craft could be used if volunteers could be found during any emergency.

At Fort Canby, just a year later, an official U. S. Lifesaving Station was established, and Munson's boat became part of its equipment. During that first year, with light keeper Munson as a volunteer, surfmen went to the aid of the bark *W. B. Scranton* and rescued 13 survivors. Again in 1875, the boat picked up ten survivors of the bark *Architect,* wrecked at the entrance to the Columbia.

Third assistant keeper George Esterbrook had a rare experience at the lighthouse. After cranking up the weights and checking the timing, the 17 year old went out on the balcony on a stormy night to clean the glass panes in the lantern. The wind was so strong that he could hardly keep his balance. It was the midnight hour and the rain was coming down in sheets. Suddenly the upper balcony metal storm door blew shut behind him, locked itself from the inside and left him stranded. His calls for help were carried off into nothingness and the dwelling was at the base of the cape a quarter mile away. All he could hear was the howling wind and the trees on the cape being snapped off like pipe stems. In his miserable situation, he, out of desperation decided to lower himself down to the second balcony by clinging to the copper lightning rod that ran down the side of the tower. With gusts threatening to tear him lose from his white knuckle grip, he clung tenaciously, inching himself downward, finally landing in a heap on the iron decking, drenched to the skin. As luck would have it he found the lower storm door had not been bolted from the inside and he said a little prayer as he stumbled inside. Finishing out his watch in misery he was thankful to have survived his trapeze act, and was a much wiser lad for his harrowing experience.

Originally, the Cape Disappointment Light was equipped with a first order fixed Fresnel. When that lens was transferred to North Head Lighthouse, a six panel fourth order lens and lighting apparatus, manufactured by Barbier and Benard in 1896, was installed displaying an alternating red and white characteristic. The maker of the original lens was L. Sautter & Cie., Paris.

In the 1980's the 13th Coast Guard District gave a face lift to the lighthouses under its jurisdiction. Cape Disappointment received metal component repairs including some welding work on the umbrella roof top of the lantern house and a paint job on the interior and exterior of the tower. The present color scheme on the exterior, to better distinguish it from its neighbor at North Head, is white horizontal bands at the top and bottom with a black horizontal band in the middle, and a gray-green lantern house. The tower was formerly white with a black lantern house.

An important radio beacon is attached to the station and is picked up by ships several miles at sea. In the lee of the cape, the Coast Guard maintains a lifeboat station, and a school, the only one of its kind on the West Coast, to train recruits for motor lifeboat duty. On-the-scene exercises in the roughest surf conditions are part of the demanding course.

Shipwreck in and around the Columbia River entrance is without precedent on the Pacific Coast. More than 200 deepsea vessels and countless commercial and sports fishing craft have been victims of the vagaries of the bar and the shoals spreading out to the north and south. Nor have the Coast Guard rescue craft been without accident. Several service men have been drowned when swamped by "sneaker waves" both in the act of rescue and on training missions.

Through it all the sentinel atop Cape Disappointment has continued to shine. Though the tower is not presently open to the public, the grounds attract scores of visitors who are rewarded by ascending the steep incline to the lighthouse from the Coast Guard station.

To reach Cape Disappointment, the road starts at Ilwaco and winds up the cape, numerous signs pointing the way to the many attractions on the historic bastion.

Though subject to change from month to month, the Coast Guard's 13th District operates 23 manned units, and 700 Coast Guardsmen take part in the maintenance of 1,900 aids to navigation along the district's countless miles of shoreline. There are 28 lighthouses under their jurisdiction and with the public the sentinels receive the most interest, mostly because of their beauty, history and purpose. Automation provides better use of manpower and is far more economical, for according to the service branch a manned lighthouse costs $130 a day to operate, an unmanned unit, $12 a day. Although much of the old equipment in the lighthouses has worn out from 24 hour a day usage, the Coast Guard asserts it is cheaper to keep lights on all the time at an average cost of 25 cents a day. Duplicate systems are installed to cut the time utilized by maintenance crews.

North Head which is actually the extreme western knob of Cape Disappointment is the site of another prominent lighthouse. North Head Lighthouse, just a hop, skip and a jump from Cape Disappointment Light was commissioned in 1898, a regal 65 foot masonry tower standing 174 feet above the ocean. Its placement so close to its companion light is somewhat perplexing to the viewer, but the contour of the land necessitates the presence of both beacons. The establishment of North Head came about partially because of the growing number of shipwrecks along the North Beach (Long Beach) Peninsula.

C. W. Leick, was the architect and engineer in the creation of the lighthouse which has a sandstone base tapering upward with several courses of brick masonry and a cement plaster overlay. Initially, the tower was equipped with the hand-me-down Fresnel from Cape Disappointment. When the Coast Guard took over the Lighthouse Service in 1939, a fourth order, American-made, McBeth-Evans, double-bullseye, prismatic lens was placed in the lantern. (American manufacturers made classic lenses for a brief period well after the turn of the century). That lens was replaced by a Crous-Hinds beacon in 1961. That was the year automation came to the station, and on July 1, the attendants were removed for other duty. Though maintenance

Imperiled by erosion, the pioneer Willapa Bay Lighthouse, built in 1858, is seen about to tumble into the sea in 1940. It was a total loss as have been scores of other structures at the north portal to Willapa Bay.

crews made periodic checks on the lighting apparatus thereafter, the physical condition of the tower began to deteriorate. In 1984, however, it was restored to mint condition. Most of the outbuildings have been torn down and the former keeper's dwelling is rented out for other purposes.

North Head in the early 1900's had its one and only woman keeper, second assistant Mabel E. Bretherton, who formerly served at Cape Blanco.

Winds are often extreme at North Head and for several years a weather station located there frequently clocked winds of over 100 mph. On occasion, trees were flattened and chimneys and fences were knocked down. The gloom of winter once overcame the wife of a lighthouse keeper there, and she committed suicide by hurling herself off the precipitous cliff near the tower.

The principal keeper reported in the station journal on April 19, 1932 that a wild duck, in dive bomber fashion, crashed through the plate glass of the lantern house and took a small chip out of the lens. The wardens of the light allegedly had a duck dinner that night.

Northward from North Head is finger-like North Beach Peninsula, an unusual barrier of sand bordered on one side by the Pacific and on the other by Willapa Bay. From Cape Disappointment to Willapa Bay is a straight 22 mile stretch of beach, one of the longest of its kind on the Pacific Coast. Its fringes and outer shoals are littered with the bones of wrecked ships, some of which appear and again disappear at the whims of the shifting sands and tidal action. North Head Light seemingly stands like a monument over the graveyard of ships that

Willapa ocean erosion has prompted the continual moving of aids to navigation. Pictured here are the second and third light structures. The original lighthouse is under fathoms of water and even today there is no guarantee that the present light tower is safe.

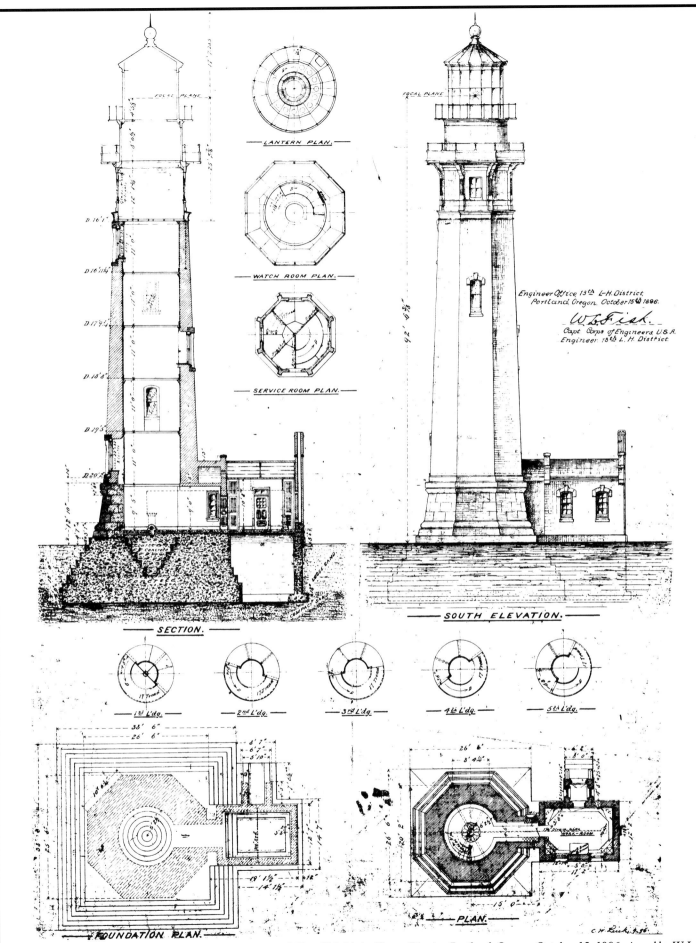

Structural plans of Grays Harbor Lighthouse, Engineer Office 13th Light-House District, Portland, Oregon October 15, 1896, signed by W.L. Fisk, Captain, Corps of Engineers, U.S.A.

spreads out below its lofty perch, its powerful flashing revolving beacon warning of the existing danger zone.

Willapa Bay is a lamentable reality and a continuing tragedy. The pioneer lighthouse, circa 1858, lies under several fathoms of water as do numerous other buildings and houses of the area where encroachment by the sea continues a devastating role, swallowing land masses like a hungry dragon. Several light towers have marked the north entrance to the bay, the existing 64 foot tower of skeleton design capped by a small white house with an exposed navigation light on its roof, 113 feet above the ever charging breakers.

Willapa Bay's entrance is 24 miles north of the Columbia bar. The bay with its several tributaries provides an outlet to an extensive area of timber. Oyster beds cover much of the muddy shoalwater, pleasant to look on at high tide and equally as ugly on the ebb. Until the bar entrance silted over in recent years, deep-sea ships formerly entered to load logs and lumber at Raymond, but perhaps never again will the bay host vessels other than commercial fishing craft and pleasure boats, because the cost of erecting jetties to control bar depths is considered prohibitive. Thus the ocean continues to have its way. In the past four decades, erosion has claimed the Willapa Lighthouse, the Coast Guard station, North Willapa Grange Hall, dozens of homes and small farms plus the undermining of the highway numerous times, necessitating an alternate route temporarily protected by the dumping of thousands of tons of heavy rock. Landowners have tried to thwart the devastation with various means of riprapping, but the onslaught continues, and real estate in many places is no longer worth the paper it is written on.

To add insult to injury, the Willapa Channel encroachment in 1977 threatened the pioneer graveyard with headstones dating from 1889 to 1956. North Cove pioneers and Pacific County received permission to undertake the grizzly job of moving the coffins to new and safer ground which was donated by a veteran citizen of the area. Among the dead were the remains of six unidentified persons whose bodies washed up on the beach at diferent times during the 60 year span of the cemetery.

The Willapa Bay Coast Guard Station, last located in Tokeland where it was moved after the abandonment of the former facility, was likewise abandoned in recent years. Assistance for fishing vessels now must come from the Grays Harbor Coast Guard Station, or by helicopter from Astoria.

The casual visitor to the North Cove-Tokeland area is unaware that there were once tree-covered lands, dunes, homes, schools and highways extending for miles where now only watery acres ebb and flow. The sea gives no indication of retreating, and as Bryron once said, "Man's control stops with the shore."

The original Willapa Bay Light Station for many years was known as Shoalwater Bay Lighthouse. It was similar in design to the initial lighthouses built in California, and a near sister to the Smith Island Lighthouse, commissioned likewise in 1858 at the eastern end of the Strait of Juan de Fuca. The name of the initial keeper of the Willapa station is missing from the national archives. The first name recorded is that of an assistant keeper named Daniel Wilson who served from February 1, 1859 to February 21, 1859 at a annual salary of $600. His duty was brief evidently stemming from problems at the lighthouse. According to a report in the archives:

> This lighthouse was established on October 1, 1858 in position 46 degrees 43' N. 124 degrees 04'25 W. and was temporarily discontinued on September 1, 1859 due to problems caused by isolation when adequate oil could not be supplied for the operation of the light. The station was officially in operation again by July 1861. This station consists of a dwelling with a tower rising through the center of the roof. The tower is conical in shape and has a focal plane of 32 feet. The light is 81 feet above sea level.

During the time the lighthouse was in limbo, James G. Swan, government agent and historian of merit, who had lived among the coastal Indians for many months studying their lifestyle, visited Keeper Wilson and dined with him at the station dwelling. In his writings he told of the problems commensurate with the lighthouse.

On August 16, 1861, local settler Robert H. Espy, was named keeper of the light at a stipened of $800 a year. Apparently he wasn't too happy with his position for he only remained until June 27, 1862. Evidently supplies and food were a nagging issue for it was said the keepers were forced to buy their provisions from the Indians, and were additionally expected to wait extended periods for their pay. As time progressed the supply line improved and the station began to operate normally.

Rated as a secondary seacoast light, the sentinel was situated two-thirds of a mile inside the ocean beach at the commencement of firm land, at the highest part of the dunes. The illuminating apparatus of the fourth order was a fixed white light varied by a white flash every two minutes. It illuminated the entire sea and bay horizon, but there were no catadioptric rings toward the forest, calculated to keep the forest fires from starting when the sun reflected through the lens. The course of steamers between San Francisco and the Strait of Juan de Fuca was about 30 miles outside Cape Shoalwater and the light therefore was not visible at that distance, although ship lookouts from that far were able to see the higher mountains on the far eastern side of the lighthouse. Taking away some of the lonely aspects of the early station, the U. S. Lifesaving Service set up a facility near Cape Shoalwater on the north shore of Lighthouse Cove to aid the coastal ships negotiating the bar and surrounding area. It was operated on a volunteer basis.

The name change from Shoalwater to Willapa (Whil-a-pah) rightfully honored the tribe of Indians that had inhabited the lands for centuries. Some translators spelled the name A-whil-a-pah or Ah-whil-lapsh, and inasmuch as the tribe had no written language it appeared a matter of the easiest pronunciation. John Meares used the name Shoalwater in 1788. Lewis and Clark called it Point Lewis; the U. S. Survey of 1852 named the point Toke, for an old Indian chief, although the ancestral Indian name was Quahpt-sum. Twenty years before the turn of the century it made little difference to the Indians what names were used because by that date most of them were gone, victims of reservations, migration, white man's diseases or alchohol.

Keeper H. Peterson kept the lamp burning at the Willapa station longer than any other attendant, from 1895 until his death in 1913. He was formerly at Tillamook Rock for a hitch after coming around the Horn on the lighthouse tender *Manzanita,* in 1885.

The demise of the lighthouse started on December 22, 1940 when serious erosion knocked at the door. The sands were eaten away foot by foot until the structure tumbled down the bank and was swallowed by the persistent watery ramparts that for so long had been cutting the cape to ribbons. Just eight days after the abandonment, the Coast Guard reported that the lighthouse had collapsed and was totally destroyed.

A new light was placed atop a skeleton steel tower, 380 yards east northeast of the former lighthouse, but 12 years later it too faced the same fate. On January 1, 1952, the second light tower was moved to another location and in the interim was replaced by a temporary wooden structure, 14 yards northeast of the charted position. On February 15, 1952, the light was shifted to a new permanent location on higher, safer ground, 148 feet above the water. On December 18, 1958 it was moving time once again to a position 15 yards northwest from the charted position. On March 12, 1959 the light structure was placed at a new permanent post at Latitude 46 degrees 44' 03 N. Longitude 124 degrees '04' 37", 1,100 yards, 345 degrees from the former charted position. And there it has remained, but there is no guarantee of its permanency.

The original Grays Harbor Light Station showing the majestic tower and the fog house where steam was generated to blast the trumpets. The latter burned to the ground in 1919, five years after this photo was taken. The lighthouse was built in 1898.

In a new coat of paint, Grays Harbor displays its third order light above the coastal evergreens in 1984.

One of the finest towers on the Pacific Northwest coast, Grays Harbor Lighthouse appears virtually brand new despite its years of service. U.S. Coast Guard photo.

With the continuing destruction by the hostile acts of nature, plus the wrecks of several ships on its sandy claws, it might be well for the geographers to rename the place "Tragedy Bay" and the old sentinel, "Hide-and-Seek Lighthouse." To say the least, the Willapa Bay Lighthouse has had a "moving experience."

The existing light structure is anything but a tourist attraction, lacking any of the flavor of the pioneer lighthouse which over the past years has perhaps become a habitat for denizens of the deep. There is also a radio beacon at the station today.

Most of the Willapa Bay oyster fleet remains inside the protected shoalwaters of the estuary, operating out of South Bend, Bayocean and Nahcotta. At the west side of the bay is historic Oysterville, which back in the early history of the area shipped oysters to San Francisco gourmet restaurants by sailing schooner. The town lost the status of county seat to South Bend many decades back, but remains a breath of the past with its row of vintage houses restored and placed in the National Register of Historic places, some dating back to the 1860's when the pioneer lighthouse commenced its role.

Grays Harbor Lighthouse near Westport, Washington, just south of the entrance to Grays Harbor, is the tallest sentinel in the state, and one of the most impressive on the Pacific Coast. Noble in appearance, it stands 107 feet tall, and is located 123 feet above sea level. At this writing the original third order Fresnel, manufactured in 1895 by Henry Lepaute of Paris, is still in use, the light source a 1,000 watt quartz-iodine bulb. When the light hits the bullseyes it renders a flash of 1.5 million candlepower, visible 23 miles at sea. The characteristic is alternating white and red. The lens assembly turns in a drum containing 20 gallons of mercury, providing a near frictionless movement, requiring a motor of only one-sixth horsepower.

The tower, designed and engineered by C. W. Leick became his greatest achievement—a masterpiece in every respect. It contains an iron spiral staircase with 135 steps. Set on a sandstone base the four foot thick lower section tapers gently to the top of the tower. For many years it was the tallest building of any kind in the county, the destination point for landrovers and a sought-out landfall beacon for mariners. It has stood the test of time well and remains a monument to its creator.

A powerful radio beacon and fog signal are located nearly a half mile from the lighthouse. The Coast Guard operates a busy motor lifeboat station in Westport, home of a huge fishing fleet. Visitation to the lighthouse is only by special permission of the duty officer at the base.

Unlike most lighthouses, the Grays Harbor sentinel has been relatively free of mishaps or major problems, with one exception. In 1916, an engulfing fire destroyed the original fog signal building which was located immediately west of the tower. It housed the boilers and equipment for sounding the steam powered fog trumpets. It took considerable fuel to fire up the boilers, and the keepers labored much harder at that task than at keeping the lens and lighting equipment cleaned and polished. The mournful sound was via a Brown's automatic siren. Probably the attendants were happy when the building burned down, for replacement equipment placed at a different location, was powered by compressors and generators.

Perhaps the good life of the lighthouse stemmed from early civic pride, as the townsfolk from Aberdeen, Hoquiam, Westport and all the little settlements in between, came en masse to dedicate the tower in 1898. The Reverend J. R. Thompson of Aberdeen presided over the ceremonies and great fanfare followed. The lighthouse improved the lot of seafaring folk and prevented several shipwrecks.

As at other bar entrances along the coast, a large number of vessels have been wrecked in the area, both before and after the beacon was installed, but the toll would have been far greater without its presence, especially during the latter day of commercial sailing vessels and during the heyday of the steam schooner.

Metal-plated, Destruction Island light tower crowns the lonely island off the northwest Washington coast where it has been a major factor in safe navigation since 1891. U.S. Coast Guard photo.

Low tide at Destruction Island reveals a mishmash of rocks of all formations teaming with various aquatic creatures. The lighthouse keeps its lonely vigil in seclusion since automation came. Coast Guard photo.

For decades Aberdeen, Hoquiam and Cosmopolis have attracted deep-sea ships which have loaded logs, lumber and lumber by-products, and the harbor continues today as an important shipping portal. The lighthouse in the interim continues its faithful vigil south of the entrance, and the local folk have adopted it as their special beacon, referring to it as "Westport Light" rather than Grays Harbor Light.

An extremely lonely 30 acre patch of land off the northwestern Washington coast is Destruction Island where a graceful lighthouse stands in solitude. Located three miles off the mainland amid a smattering of rocks and reefs, the island is 90 feet high, a half mile long and 300 yards wide. Its tower is 94 feet high and 147 feet above the sea with a commanding view at all points of the compass. Its light and fog signal are monitored from the Quillayute Coast Guard station at La Push, 20 miles away, and maintenance crews periodically check the navigation equipment.

The Spaniard Heceta is alleged to have discovered the island in 1775, applying the name La Isla de los Delores, or Isle of Sorrows, but the position and description he gave were not totally applicable. Its adopted name was rendered by Captain Charles Barkley, master of the *Imperial Eagle,* who sent a long boat from King George's Sound to explore as far south as latitude 47 degrees. The officers and crew of the small craft entered a shallow river, either the Hoh or Quillayute, and rowed up some distance, where they were attacked and murdered by hostile Indians. Ironically, some of Heceta's men had suffered the same fate when they came ashore for water in the same vicinity.

Before the lighthouse was built, local Indians occasionally utilized the island to grow potatoes. Sometimes they would reside there for a short time but generally returned to the mainland during the winter months.

Destruction Island Lighthouse was built between 1889-91, all building materials brought in by lighthouse tenders, lightered into the rough landing area and hauled up to the isle's plateau. It was a laborious undertaking and the builders did a splendid job on the 94 foot masonry tower, which, because of its isolated location, was encased in iron plates. The Army Corps of Engineers supervised the building of the station for the Lighthouse Service, and when one considers the difficulty of water transport and the landing of materials in a spot tantamount to an obstacle course of riven rocks, the accomplishment is more readily appreciated.

The completed tower was fitted with a first order Fresnel measuring 8.9 feet in height, 6.2 feet in diameter, composed of 24 bullseyes and a total of 1,176 prisms. One writer described the scintillating beauty of the lens as a "fairy tale greenhouse." All the components were landed in crates and assembled in the lantern house. By the time the light was put in operation in 1891, nearly three years had passed, including the erection of derricks and hoists to lift the materials up to the island plateau. The tower sat on a sandstone base with massive masonry walls four feet thick on the lower levels tapering to 18 inches beneath the lantern house. The spiral staircase circled artistically upward 115 steps. On completion, the *Light List* described the station in the following terms:

> White conical tower; black lantern and parapet; two oilhouses, 75 feet; two dwellings, 550 feet, a barn 650 feet, ENE, and a fog-signal building 130 feet northwesterly of the tower; buildings white with brown roofs.

The boiler-fed first class steam siren in later years was replaced by a diaphragm horn which caused the station bull to go on a rampage thinking he had a rival for the cows grazing in the pasture. He knocked down several fences and dug up mounds of sod before he could be controlled.

Visitors were almost nonexistent during the years the station was manned except for those on special missions. Some families dwelled on the island and made the best of their lot despite the isolation, separated by a 20 mile trip by water from LaPush. It was a hard but rewarding life for those who lived there, and it was a naturalist's paradise with an abundance of sea creatures and birds. The elements of weather were extremely harsh at times. According to a report in the 1930's, a fierce gale sent seas crashing up to the plateau of the island, doing some damage to the station outbuildings, and cracking some of the windows in the tower.

Though there exists a rugged switchback trail from the landing, when the station was manned a derrick and boom with an attached box-like conveyance were employed for raising and lowering personnel and supplies. Today, in an emergency, if something goes wrong at the lighthouse, maintenance crews can be flown in by helicopter, though occasionally Coast Guard motor lifeboats from the Quillayute station are used for the purpose. Automation came to the station in 1968, which left the place void of life for the first time in seven decades. Four keepers were originally attached but when the Coast Guard manned the facility there was frequent rotation; some personnel had their wives reside on the island. The station mascot for several years was a small deer named Bambi. The early keepers raised much of their food on the island and kept cows, pigs and chickens. The soil was sufficient for raising vegatables.

Before the lighthouse was constructed, by executive order of June 8, 1866, Captain James S. Lawson went to the island in the U. S. Coast Survey ship *Fauntleroy* and officially reserved it for lighthouse purposes. No bids were let however, for 22 years thereafter. The initial outlay for the station, monetarily speaking, was $45,000, but the difficulties incurred demanded almost twice that amount before the station was completed. The work was so tedious the first winter that by the end of the year only one house was completed, part of the second dwelling, a barn and cistern. Some initial work had also been accomplished on the water catchment basin and a landing area, but bitter weather soon put the damper on progress and considerable time elapsed before work was resumed.

Just what the future of the lighthouse and the island are, only time can tell. As of now the lighthouse continues to function much as it did from its inception, the big Fresnel still doing its job. The Coast Guard has dismantled many of the former buildings that comprised the station, and visitors to the island are extremely few. It is generally considered off limits to the public unless one is escorted by Coast Guard personnel, but it is readily viewed from a section of Coast Highway 101, or from the commercial fishing craft that work the bountiful waters lying off the island. The Coast Guard has from time to time given serious consideration to closing down the facility as an economy measure. In 1963, it was proceeding with plans to do just that, but the maritime industry strenuously objected and the agency relented.

When the light was first illuminated on December 31, 1891 it was a Happy New Year for mariners. Principal keeper was Christian Zauner, and he and his assistants put in considerable time supplying fuel to the boilers to get up a head of steam for the fog signal. Four keepers were usually in attendance, some of whom had their wives and children present. Sometimes their offspring had to get room and board on the mainland during their school years, and on other occasions the wives became the schoolmistresses on the island. Frequently, when the sea had a calm spell, off-duty keepers would use the station dory to go out fishing for additional morsels for the lighthouse menu.

When Destruction Island was automated in 1968, the radio beacon and Loran station there were moved to Point Grenville, ten

Replaced by buoys, Umatilla Reef Lightship **WAL-196,** *was the last lightship to serve the post. She was withdrawn in 1971.*

miles north of Copalis Head. Today the local radio beacon is at James Island, 15 miles north northwest of Destruction Island on the north side of the Quillayute River. James Island Light, established in 1924, is displayed from a small white house on the south part of the island, 150 feet above the water.

With the exception of the lighthouse, Destruction Island since resident personnel departed, has become somewhat like a ghostly plot in the ocean. The lawn is no longer mowed and weeds have grown up along all the cement walkways. The buildings not torn down are boarded up and the tramway rails are red with rust. The horn-billed auklets are back in large numbers living in harmony with the gulls, and the bracken and salmon berries are growing. Except for the buildings, it is almost like it was when the natives paddled out in ancient times to plant potatoes, gather berries, collect bird eggs and feast on mussels—almost as though time has stood still.

The lighthouse chores of scraping metal, applying red lead and white paint, cleaning glass prisms, polishing brass, handwiping the five-wick lamp or packing coal oil up the spiral staircase to the watchroom are only fragile memories of the past. The tenantless sentinel struggles on toward the century mark, its light and foghorn operating automatically, almost as if ghostly hands were in control.

Northward up the Washington Coast is Cape Alava, the most westerly point of Continental United States. The land protrusion has never been marked by a light but is located in one of the most primitive sections of the country, little changed since the days the first Indians frequented its beaches. Located 13 miles south of Cape Flattery, it is now part of the Olympic National Park area. The Ozette Archaeological Expedition was established in 1970 to unearth the site of an ancient Indian village covered eons ago by mudslides. Outcrops off the cape are a pincushion of small islets, sea stacks and rounded rocks. Two miles from the cape in a northwesterly direction, the Umatilla Reef Lightship guarded a dreaded reef from 1898 until 1971, when buoys were placed at either end of the obstruction. A distant neighbor was the Swiftsure Lightship positioned off the entrance to the Strait of Juan de Fuca from 1909 until July 1, 1961 when era navigation innovations no longer required its presence. The colorful manned lightships of yesteryear have all vanished from the scene.

"A Lighthouse, is much needed also at Cape Flattery and I would recommend that it be situated on Tatoochi Island, a small island, almost touching the Northwest extremity of Cape Flattery, "stated Wm. P. McArthur on his survey of the area in 1849-50. He went on to say, "to vessels bound from seaward a lighthouse on this island would be of much assistance. It would enable them to enter the Straits, when the absence of a light, would frequently compel them to remain at sea till daylight. Once inside the Straits vessels are comparatively secure. The advantage of having the lighthouse situated on the island instead of on the extremity of the cape is that being so situated, it would serve as a guide to vessels seeking Neah or Scarborough harbor, a small but secure harbor of refuge four miles inside the straits. Strong contrary currents will cause navigators to seek the little harbor quite frequently," McArthur concluded.

The writer was in charge of the expedition surveying for lighthouse sites, aboard the U.S. Survey schooner *Ewing,* and his findings concerning a lighthouse on Tatoosh Island were sent to Professor A. D. Bache, superintendant of the U. S. Coast Survey in Washington D. C. On McArthur's recommendation, plans for a lighthouse at the northwest tip of continental America took root. Prior to McArthur's report, a joint Army and Navy commission that visited the strait in 1849 on the steamer *Massachusetts* came to a similar conclusion, that the little island was the logical location for a navigation beacon. Nobody bothered to ask the natives for their permission despite the fact that they had used it for a fishing and whaling locale for perhaps centuries.

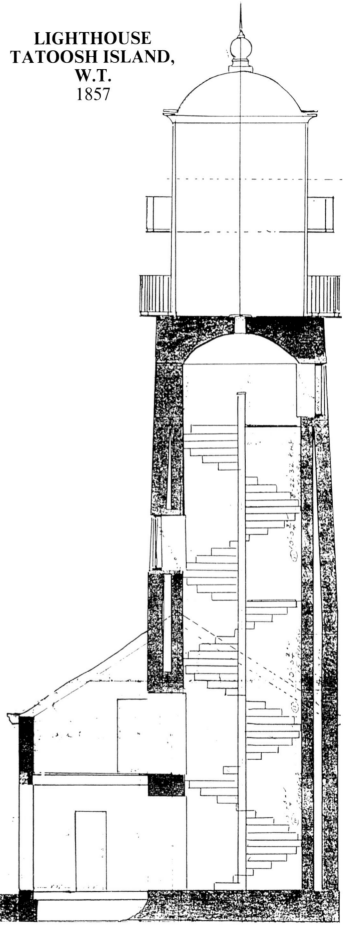

LIGHTHOUSE TATOOSH ISLAND, W.T.
1857

Structural plans of Cape Flattery Lighthouse in 1857, when Washington State was a territory.

Cape Flattery Lighthouse about 1898, showing the keepers, workers and weather personnel in front of the famous lighthouse, built in 1857. Several large vessels disappeared after signaling the keepers and heading out to sea. In the lower photo, the old steam fog signal lets out a plume of white as it blasts its warning. Note the tall chimney protruding from the fog house, and the water storage tank. Thomas photos.

Based on McArthur's advise, Congress agreed to alot funds for beacons at both Cape Flattery and New Dungeness, but construction was not authorized until $39,000 was made available in August 1854. Once given the green light, a Coast Survey crew under George Davidson landed on the little island and chose and suitable spot for the lighthouse at the highest elevation, 100 feet above the Pacific. He noted the place had neither a source of wood or water and that the Makah Indians frequented the island in large numbers especially during the summer to catch salmon and to spear whales. Additionally they planted potatoes on the 20 acre plateau. Only one landing site was available.

Without thought of compensation to the Indians, plans proceeded for this their favorite summer retreat.

With the arrival of the construction crew there were fears of an Indian uprising. George Davidson who had headed an earlier survey party reported that his mission "has been executed at the risk of the life of everyone at work on it. The only means of conveyance I could furnish was two small canoes which were forced to land on the rocks and at rocky points... I consider the station to have been occupied at very great risk from the hostility of the Indians; but a knowledge that we were always prepared for an attack, without doubt, prevented one. We built a breastwork and could fire 60 rounds without reloading. Guard was kept six hours every night."

At the time of his report, 150 Indians were on the island and there was tension and agitation among the tribesmen over the unwarranted invasion. Davidson's findings were backed by the further reconnaissance with the arrival of the survey steamer *Active* in 1853. The Makahs were bitterly disturbed during that summer after a widespread smallpox epidemic broke out claiming the lives of nearly half of the 1,000 members of the tribe. They blamed the "Bostons" for the dreaded disease and were in a mood for revenge, prompted even more by the takeover of Tatoosh.

To add to the friction, the warlike Haidas arrived in the area in 40 of their big canoes, disguised as traders. They, like the Noresmen, were hit-and-run warriors. With the presence of the well-armed *Active* however, things remained under control. The loud reports of the ship's cannon in gunnery practice put a damper on the hostile plans of the Indian tribes.

Superintending the construction of both Cape Flattery and New Dungeness Lighthouses, was Isaac Smith. Among the building materials he acquired were huge blocks of dressed sandstone from the Bellingham area, blocks measuring two feet in thickness. By 1855, construction work was well underway, but with the difficulties encountered, it required a year and a half to complete the station. Curious and often abusive Indians milled about, occasionally stealing tools and being generally obnoxious which necessitated the erection of a blockhouse in which 20 muskets were stored for protection should a sudden uprising occur. The construction schedule was lagging due to delays caused by inclement weather and the slow arrival of materials.

Collector of Customs Morris H. Frost who was in charge of aids to navigation, asked for assistance from the lighthouse authorities in protecting the building materials during the winter because of the bitter attitude of the natives. Smith meanwhile rallied his laborers to speed up the work and cited competition with the construction crew at New Dungeness Lighthouse, virtually pitting the respective teams against one another to see which lighthouse would be the first to be lighted. The challenge spurred the men to a greater effort. The light was commissioned December 28, 1857, just 14 days later than New Dungeness, yet considering the fact that the beacon was on an island and that the transport of building materials and personnel was more difficult than at the other station, it was a moral victory worthy of merit.

Originally referred to as Tatoosh Island Lighthouse, it wasn't until later that the official name Cape Flattery Lighthouse was adopted. The name Tatoosh perhaps was more difficult for navigators to understand than the mainland cape which was given the name Flattery by Captain James Cook in 1778.

Frost's nominee for principal keeper of the new station was George H. Gerrish of Port Townsend. He accepted the post and, in turn, chose James Barry, William Webster and George Fitzgerald as his assistants. Their stay was short, however. After three months, all but Barry handed in their resignations on the same day, March 23, 1858, citing their isolation, difficulty of obtaining provisions which demanded half their salary, problems with troublesome Indians and inferior lard oil which clogged the lamp wicks as their reasons. They further complained that the total pay for one month for Gerrish and his assistants was only $220.83. Additionally, they were required to purchase food from the Indians who they found to be shrewd traders.

From the initial lighting of the lamp on December 28, the keepers had experienced problems in keeping a proper flame burning. The smoking lamp smutted up the big first order fixed Fresnel and demanded extra hours in cleaning the prisms and polishing the metal. Fortunately their quarters were in the same structure to which the sentinel was attached. It was a gray sandstone edifice and the masonry tower of whitewashed brick was surmounted by a black balustrade and lantern.

The replacement for Gerrish was Franklin Tucker who was shifted to Tatoosh from temporary duty at New Dungeness. His assistants were John Thompson and James Mutch, but the second crew also threw in the towel after less than three months, claiming poor pay and the fear of annihilation by the increasing number of Indians who were at times seemingly in control of the lighthouse.

The frustrated Frost then appointed F. W. James as principal keeper, but he was dismissed when masters of passing vessels claimed the low burning beacon was not properly maintained. He lasted only a month. On dismissal, he appealed his case and was rehired, but when the collector of customs refused to supply a boat for the station, (he having wrecked the previous craft) James tendered his resignation.

At that juncture, the Fraser River goldrush was in full swing and the shortage of manpower was such that Frost had to plead with the Revenue Cutter Service for assistance. Lieutenant W. L. Hyde, commander of the USRC *Jefferson Davis* loaned two crewmen to aid in the maintenance of the lighthouse. At the same time, Hyde let it be known among the abusive Indians that if they molested or mistreated his crewmen he would return and fire the ship's "boom boom" at them. The threat was effective.

Captain William W. Winsor of Port Angeles was named principal keeper in the winter of 1860. That same year hurricane winds on November 9, blew the top off the old blockhouse, and did considerable damage to station property.

Renowned historian and government official James G. Swan visited the lighthouse in July 1861, following a similar visit to Willapa Bay Lighthouse. Though impressed with the place, he called attention to the weather damage, water having seeped under the roof shingles causing moss to grow on the interior walls. He further noted down drafts which constantly sent smoke down the chimney flues filling the dwelling with nauseous smoke. He further expressed a deep feeling for the keepers in their isolated role often spending weeks and months without relief, the difficulty of securing supplies, the consumption of a quart of oil an hour for the lamp and the chore of lugging large amounts of oil up the winding staircase. He reasoned that the outside world little appreciated the difficulties suffered by the little band of keepers.

Winsor, however, was not one for feeling sorry for himself. He moonlighted, picking up extra pay by trading with the Indians for

Vintage photo of Tatoosh Island showing the lighthouse and the wireless poles strung about 1920; one of the first wireless stations on the coast. Note the eroded cliffs of the island. Courtesy Bob DeRoy.

cranberries and oil, plus selling parts from wrecked ships. Swan said of him:

"This man, like an old fish hawk or carrion crow perches himself in his eyrie on Tatoosh Island, watching every opportunity to make a descent on the adjacent coast, either trading with the natives old copper and sailors' clothes for fish, cranberries and oil or picking up old anchors and junk."

Winsor owned a schooner with his partners Rufus Holmes and Captain Alexander Sampson, and when something promising surfaced, he would get word out via Indian messengers for his partners to respond. At Port Gamble, berries sold for 40 cents a gallon and fish oil brought 55 cents. Recovering salvage from wrecked ships in the area and along the west coast of Vancouver Island also fetched a good price.

As the years progressed, the problems of the station got ironed out and the white keepers and the Indians lived in relative harmony, the latter coming to their summer retreat in large numbers, scores of canoes lining the singular beach pursuing their fishing and whaling activities. As late as the turn of the century they held potlatch celebrations there.

An appropriation of $10,000 was made for the erection of a steam fog signal facility on Tatoosh and it was placed in operation on

The derrick boom lifting the "basket" used for transporting personnel up from the landing and for handling supplies at Cape Flattery Light Station on Tatoosh Island. U.S. Coast Guard photo.

When all was alive and well on Tatoosh Island, the lighthouse and weather station manned by personnel, it looked like a real going enterprise off the tip of continental United States' northwest coast, but automation put an end to an era. Coast Guard photo.

November 1, 1872 blasting a 12 inch steam whistle. In 1913 an air siren was installed, and in later years a big diaphone horn. A weather station was also located on the island in 1883, and became one of the major reporting stations of the U. S. Weather Bureau.

Improvements were also made in the illuminants for the oil lamps through the years. Coal oil (kerosene) was substituted for lard oil in 1885, and in 1896, an IOV lamp was installed. The original station lens, of the first order, was manufactured in Paris by Louis Sautter & Co., in 1854 and shipped around the Horn by sailing vessel. In later years it was replaced by a smaller Fresnel. The first lens was stored in a waterfront warehouse in Seattle and later acquired by a local glass company that allowed it to go to pieces. The writer rescued one small panel which is now in the possession of the Puget Sound Maritime Historical Society.

Around the turn of the century a disconsolate keeper at the station attempted suicide. Despondent over his isolated lifestyle, he hurled himself from a cliff into the sea, and was later found on the rocks unconscious. Revived, he was sent ashore never to return.

For many years between infrequent visits by lighthouse tenders, the only communication with the mainland was via Indian canoe, and for a small fee faithful Indian paddlers would deliver supplies, mail and personnel, seas permitting. The best known messenger was a Makah known as "Old Doctor." During the years of operating his canoe taxi between Neah Bay and the island he had three of his dugouts smashed to kindling on the rocks when coming into the beach landing. Tenacious in his endeavor, he always secured another canoe and fearlessly continued challenging the surf, and none could deny his skill at handling his craft in the most contrary seas.

Telephone cables from the shore in later years were often severed in heavy seas, and speaking of storms, Tatoosh has had its share. Sometimes it was as if the entire island was shaken by an earthquake, sea caves running long distances under the island. In gale conditions breakers and swells rumble through them like a stampede of wild horses.

Though there is a rough trail of sorts from the beach landing to the plateau of the island, a derrick and hoist utilizing a "canvas box" was the most frequently used conveyance for transferring supplies and personnel during the manned days of the station.

From time to time, keepers' families dwelled on Tatoosh, raised livestock and grew vegetables. There was even a school there at one time to teach the ABC's to the children of the keepers and the weather station attendants. School was closed in 1908 when a diptheria epidemic broke out isolating the islanders for weeks. Fortunately the victims all recovered. Good fortune was not always the case, for during the decades, 14 government employees succumbed on Tatoosh, along with numerous Indians. One Weather Bureau employee was killed when the catwalk between Tatoosh and lesser North Island collapsed. The island was also found to be sacred to the ancient Makahs, for when digging up the sod some years back for the placement of a radio beacon, the workers unearthed a burial ground containing the bones of several Indians. Its discovery only added to the numerous tales of the ghostly intervention about the station.

South of the island, is Fuca Pillar, named for the reputed discoverer of the Strait of Juan de Fuca, the Greek mariner with the Spanish name Juan de Fuca. Rising in sea stack fashion, almost obelisk in shape, 140 feet high, it has long been considered virtually unscalable, but the Makahs claimed that in olden times a young brave reached the summit in search of duck eggs. He was filled with fear when trying to make his descent, and rather than risk death on the jagged rocks below, he remained atop his perch and died of starvation. For decades, Indians were firm in the belief that his spirit stood guard over the pillar, making it prohibitory to the tribe.

There are many rocks and reefs around Tatoosh Island, some marked by buoys warning ships of the notorious maritime cemetary. A buoy that marks Duntze Rock set a record of sorts by having the longest anchor chain in the 13th District, some 810 feet in length.

The colorful island of Tatoosh lies 0.4 miles northwest of Cape Flattery, and probably in the ageless past was connected with the

Today, many of the buildings on Tatoosh have been demolished, but through it all, from the days when the Indians resorted on the beaches fishing and whaling, till the days of automation the light tower lives on atop a knarled island. M.W. Rodrigues photo for Coast Guard.

mainland. On heaving to off the island on June 29, 1788, Captain John Meares, the renowned British navigator and explorer had the following words for Tatoosh:

"....the island itself appeared to be a barren rock, almost inaccessible, and of no great extent; but the surface of it, as far as we could see, was covered with inhabitants, who were gazing at the ship... The chief of this spot, whose name is Tatooche, did us a favor of a visit, and so surly and forbidding a character we had not yet seen."

Meares noted both Duncan and Duntze rocks near Tatoosh and was impressed by the columnar leaning pinnacle known as Fuca Pillar to which he applied the name Pinnacle Rock. As far as the early Caucasians who came to the area could ascertain, the original Makah Indians came from Nootka on Vancouver Island in the ageless past. The origin of the name Tatoosh has also taken several avenues. Most historians believe it originated from the Nootka name for thunderbird, which is too-too-tche.

For over a decade the lighthouse has been automated. The outbuildings that have not been torn down are brooding in loneliness. The light, fog signal and radio beacon are all monitored by remote control and when repairs are necessary the Coast Guard either takes personnel out by boat or lands them on the plateau of the island by helicopter.

Inhabited by Indians on and off for perhaps 1,500 years, and by whites from the mid 1850's, the isle sits abandoned, a place that literally overflows with history and drama with the distinction of being the extreme tip of northwest mainland America. As tidal streams from the strait swirl past its fringes the lighthouse keeps automated guard. Sea stacks and forested cliffs check the white surge at Cape Flattery, lying 1,300 miles north of the Mexican border. The timeless island lives on but it has never been quite the same since its inhabitants departed.

Vintage photo of the first lightship to serve Swiftsure Bank, northwest of the entrance of the Strait of Juan de Fuca. She took up her position in 1909. The steam powered No. 93 was equipped with sail for emergencies. With new aids to navigation coming into vogue, the lightship was withdrawn July 1, 1961.

Slip Point Lighthouse at Clallam Bay on the Strait of Juan de Fuca was established in 1905, and was replaced by an unmanned navigation aid in 1951. Inset, the clamshell lens and oil vapor light that served the Slip Point Lighthouse.

Compressors for blasting the fog signals at Slip Point Lighthouse in its early years.

CHAPTER NINE

Lights of the Strait of Juan de Fuca and the San Juan Islands

*There is nothing that moves the imagination
like a lighthouse.
.....Samuel Adams Drake*

Childhood memories sometimes are immutable on the mind. As a lad, this writer recalls his first full tour of a lighthouse more than a half century ago, and it left such an impression that it seems like only yesterday. It was the kind of lighthouse with a friendly, uniformed keeper and rustic marine setting that should have remained forever. Today, that lighthouse is gone, the keeper is dead, the area has changed, but the memory lives on.

The lighthouse in question was at Slip Point on Callam Bay, the eastern point of the bight, high, wooded with a light colored streak, like a landslip down its face. The light and fog signal station were located on a low, narrow shelf on the western extremity of the point. A reef extending westward for a quarter mile was marked by a buoy.

Slip Point was the last major light established on the American side of the Strait of Juan de Fuca, and it had an inauspicious beginning. Congress set aside $12,500 for its construction on June 6, 1900, but the landowners were reticent to depart with the property and balked against the government, holding out for an exorbitant price. Following was a battle of words, Uncle Sam prevailing by threatening condemnation proceedings. The problem was solved on June 5, 1902 when the owners reluctantly accepted $2,562 for the tract.

Even at that late date, the area was considered isolated and pristine, with many Indians living about, and few permanent white residents. Neah Bay, the largest Indian settlement, was only 15 miles westward of the lighthouse, and as part of the Makah Indian Reservation it was the nearest trading center of importance, the tiny fishing villages of East and West Callam boasting only post offices and a telegraph station as their principal connection with the outside world.

Bids for the construction of the lighthouse brought excitement to the area but they were so excessive that the government decided to hire workers by the hour, skilled labor being difficult to come by. It was not until April 1, 1905 that the lighthouse was completed, consisting of a single story frame fog signal building with a third class Daboll fog trumpet, a lens-lantern and a keeper's residence. Way behind schedule, the rising costs were such that short cuts were necessary. Thus the planned tower was not erected. In fact, it wasn't until 11 years later that the originally intended frame tower was added, capped by a cylindrical lantern house. At that juncture, the exposed lens-lantern was replaced by a powerful fourth order, double-bullseye clamshell prismatic lens which afforded a light powerful enough to not only scan the strait but to bathe the shores on the Canadian side. With its IOV flame, it produced 130,000 candlepower which in those years was a formidable light for a fourth order apparatus.

To service the beacon, keepers walked a fifth of a mile, skirting the unusual contour of wrinkled terra firma, and across little wooden foot bridges. Nestled as neat as a bug in the rug against a green hillside, passing ships noted the large letters USLHE (United States Lighthouse Establishment) mounted above the fog signal house trumpet.

Memory fails the writer as to the name of the keeper on his visit in 1928, but he was everything one would expect of a lighthouse keeper, and he took great pride in the station, each item in perfect order; even his U. S. Lighthouse Service uniform was freshly pressed.

It was distressing in later years to learn of the Coast Guard's decision to close down the lighthouse. It came in 1951, after which the structure was dismantled and replaced by an unattended square tower on a pile structure utilizing a Crous-Hinds beacon and a diaphone fog signal. The old lighthouse was one of the early victims of the Coast Guard's sweeping demolition program eliminating manned stations in favor of unmanned navigation facilities. The clamshell lens was taken elsewhere and local citizens hauled away much of the lumber of which the former lighthouse was built.

Most of the shipwrecks in and around Slip Point occurred before the lighthouse was built, which said a lot for its presence. The five-masted schooner *Bianca* was wrecked in a blinding snowstorm, five miles west of Clallam Bay on December 15, 1924 with a full cargo of Alaska canned salmon, despite the fact that the station fog signal was blaring and the light filtering through the murk.

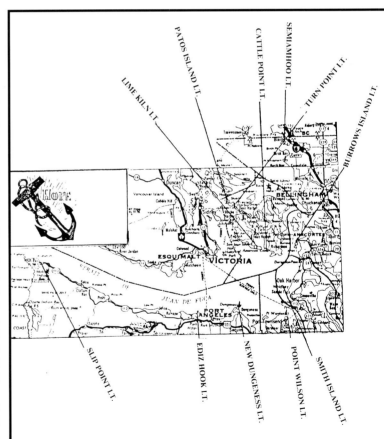

**American lighthouses on the Strait
of Juan de Fuca and San Juan Islands**

*Slip Point Lighthouse foghorn was blaring in a driving snow storm on Christmas eve in 1924 when the five-masted sailing vessel **Bianca** was wrecked between Clallam Bay and Neah Bay (left photo). She was a total loss. Right, the U.S. Lifesaving crew of surfmen go out on a practice run in the 1920s from the Waadah Island (Neah Bay) station.*

The present aid to navigation at Slip Point is a light and fog signal on a skeleton structure, at left. The old keepers' dwelling is center right. U.S. Coast Guard photo.

154

The original Ediz Hook Lighthouse, circa 1865, on the finger of land protecting Port Angeles Harbor. Also shown is the bell tower and its 3,150 pound fog bell. The lighthouse was replaced by another in the same location in 1908. Thomas photos, courtesy of Tom Reed.

*The lighthouse tender **Heather** at the U.S. Lighthouse Service repair and buoy yard at Port Angeles about 1905. Thomas photo, courtesy Tom Reed.*

The present Slip Point navigation aid was victim of an accidental shelling in January 1962 when Canadian Naval vessels practicing anti-aircraft gunnery in the strait inadvertently lobbed some shells into Callam Bay, nicking the light structure. No serious damage occurred, but there were some naval officers who got a dressing down over the incident.

At Ediz Hook, Port Angeles, another colorful light station of yesteryear has given way to a modern navigation light, this one atop the control tower at the Port Angeles Air Station. It serves both as a marine and an air beacon. Mounted 78 feet above the water, it has a green and white characteristic and a nominal range of 23 miles. At the station there is also a radio beacon and fog signal plus a radio station that keeps the Coast Guard aircraft and cutters based nearby on alert.

But with all the modern innovations, much of the color of the historic former lighthouses that once marked the location is gone. Ediz Hook, a low, narrow sandspit, three miles long is a natural protection for Port Angeles Harbor (56 miles east of Cape Flattery) and has been marked by beacons since 1865. Even before the first official lighthouse, local citizens maintained crude fire signals on the spit to guide ships. In 1863, $5,000 was granted for a government lighthouse at the site. The signature of President Abraham Lincoln appeared on the papers of the land purchase, and with the limited funds, a 35 foot frame lighthouse protruding from the keepers dwelling was erected. A fifth order Fresnel with a fixed characteristic was visible for 12 miles and was illuminated on April 2, 1865 by keeper George K. Smith. Practical but inexpensive, the lighthouse was surrounded by a white picket fence, and close enough to town that visitors were numerous. Keeper Smith proved a popular personality and kept his light in apple-pie condition for the ships passing through the Strait of Juan de Fuca or entering the harbor at Port Angeles.

Frequent fogs were a source of continued concern by seafarers, and finally in 1885 the station was fitted with a large fogbell mounted in a pyramid shaped bell tower, with clockwork machinery that gonged it every 15 seconds.

Perhaps the most celebrated keeper of the original station was Captain Franklin Tucker who kept the lamp burning and the bell tolling in the 1880's and 1890's. The gentle, bewiskered old salt had made a name for himself in the early west. Born in Maine, he had been the world over in sailing vessels, once being a castaway from a brig wrecked in the Bahamas when five of the nine man crew was drowned. He later became master of the first mail packet on Puget Sound—the schooner *R. B. Potter*.

By 1908, the pioneer lighthouse had succumbed to erosion and deterioration. It was replaced by a larger frame lighthouse designed by Carl Leick. It was fitted with the former tower's lens and lighting apparatus but the lamp was changed from coal oil to IOV. Within the structure was housing for a first class compressed air siren to warn of the persistent fogs. The life of the second lighthouse was also relatively short, for in 1945, the Coast Guard decided that it too must go, partly due to the unstable land beneath its foundation, and partly as an economy measure by placing the beacon atop the air station control tower. Automation was also a contributing factor. Since 1946, the present arrangement has proved both satisfactory and economical. The color is gone but the purpose remains fulfilled.

New Dungeness Lighthouse was built under the supervision of Isaac Smith who at the same time was overseeing the building of the sentinel on Tatoosh Island off Cape Flattery. There was some friendly competition between the construction crews at each project to see which would be the first station officially commissioned. As it turned out, the Dungeness crew came out the winner by a scant 14 days. The light was the first major navigation light on the Strait of Juan de Fuca and the second in the waters of what later became Washington State. In those early years it was still a territory, and very primitive.

It was on the fog-filled night of September 21, 1868 that a party of 18 Tsimshian Indians, men, women and children were paddling their canoe back to Fort Simpson in British Columbia. Plagued by the gray shroud, they came ashore on Dungeness Spit for the night. The braves had been picking hops for wages near Puyallup and had earned about $500 in gold among them which they were proudly taking back to their homeland. All the while their actions had been observed by a group of Clallam Indians who for many years had been arch enemies of the Tsimshians. Just after midnight while the campers were asleep, 26 Clallams made a sneak attack on the party, first cutting the tent

156

New Dungeness Light Station as it appeared originally, inset. Structural weakness cut the tower's height almost in half in 1927 when the lighthouse engineer ordered its reconstruction to make it more stable. The lighthouse was commissioned in 1857 and is still in operation at the bitter end of a long sand spit.

*Black Ball steamer **Sioux** hard aground on Dungeness Spit in October 1914, despite warnings from the New Dungeness fog signal. It was a costly salvage job, but the vessel was finally freed.*

ropes then pouncing on them with clubs and salmon spears. It was a bloody assault which continued until all were massacred, the sands running red with blood. All were dead except one, a pregnant Indian squaw who feigned death despite the agony of 20 stab wounds. While she lay still she was divested of her bracelets and the rings on her hands and ears. When the marauders departed, the badly wounded woman managed to get into the water, and by crawling and struggling with painful resolve somehow managed to reach the New Dungeness lighthouse where the station keeper Henry Blake took her in and summoned his compassionate wife to tend to her wounds. The victim tightly clung to a five dollar gold piece the attackers had overlooked. She was the sole survivor of the vengeful act.

A few hours later, some angry Clallams, apprised of her escape, banged on the door of the lighthouse demanding her life. They had counted the dead corpses on the beach and found one missing. Tracing her path in the sand marked by a trail of blood, they were led to the lighthouse. Blake stood his ground and refused to relinquish the suffering woman. The masonry dwelling he felt was safe from being torched. It was a stand off for awhile but finally the Indians withdrew fearing reprisal by military forces should they vent their wrath on the keeper of the light.

When the word of the massacre got out the next day, local white settlers were incensed by the brutality They saw to it that the butchered bodies were given proper burials on what became known as "Graveyard Spit." James G. Swan, the U. S. commissioner, with the help of law enforcement volunteers and Indian agent Charles King, rounded up ten of the culprits. Still later, 11 others were apprehended in the Dungeness area and delivered to King. Finally, the other five were rounded up and all 26 were placed in irons on the reservation and kept at hard labor.

The pregnant Tsimshian woman finally recovered enough to be sent back to her people at Fort Simpson aboard the Hudson's Bay steamer *Otter*. With her went most of the property stolen during the massacre. The vessel also carried gifts from the Bureau of Indian Affairs to hopefully mend the long lasting rift between the Tsimshians and the Clallams. For years there had been incursions between the tribes, many pitched battles having been fought on the beaches along the strait.

With the aid of the Indian agents and missionary to the Tsimshians, the Reverend Mr. Hall, acts of reprisal were quelled. Although the keepers witnessed other disputes and fightings among the Indians in the Dungeness Bay area, the white settlers kept law and order whenever possible.

When E. A. Brooks was keeper of the lighthouse just after World War I, an Indian came ashore on the spit one day in his canoe. When the keeper went down to engage him in conversation, the visitor referred to the massacre that had occurred a half century earlier, and of the pregnant woman who was the only survivor. Amazingly, the visitor claimed the woman was his mother and that he was the child she delivered after her recovery. Brooks' ears perked up and a smile came across his face as he informed the Indian that the son of the former keeper still lived in Dungeness Town and would be overjoyed to meet him. Though the Tsimshian said he would go to see Richard Blake, he changed his mind and paddled back to the Canadian side of the strait.

From Port Angeles the coast trends east for 13 miles to the end of Dungeness Spit which encloses picturesque Dungeness Bay. The bay offers shelter in the west winds but is open to the east, a dangerous place in winter gales. The bay is formed by a sandpit extending northeast four miles and forming, in addition to Dungeness Bay, a small lagoon at the head of the harbor for light-draft vessels only. New Dungeness Light marks the area at the outer end of the spit shining seaward from a 63 foot tower. A foghorn and radio beacon are also at the site.

The station has a rather unusual story. Though most of the 1857 building remains, the tower has been reduced in size from 100 feet in height down to 63 feet, probably one of the only times in history that a major lighthouse was shortened rather than raised. In happened in 1927, when Clarence Sherman was the chief lighthouse engineer in the district. Vibration from rumbling guns at Canadian fortifications on the other side of the strait was given as one reason for the deterioration of the mortar in the masonry at the top of the lofty tower. That and other contributing factors had structurally weakened the tower and it was in urgent need of repair. Under Sherman's direction the iron lantern house was unbolted and dismantled piece by piece, after which a shute was rigged to send the upper four courses of masonry to the ground, brick by brick. The double walls were tapered on the exterior and veritcal on the interior with an air space in between providing very limited work spaces for the laborers.

In the interim, an auxiliary light was kept burning, and after the tower was lowered to the recommended height, a new gallery (balcony) and deck railing was installed. The larger diameter at the top of the masonry demanded a different style lantern house, so to conserve funds, Sherman removed the unit from the abandoned Admiralty Head Lighthouse tower on Whidbey Island and reassembled it atop the Dungeness tower, and there it has remained since.

An 1857 description of the New Dungeness Light Station read:

> It consists of a keeper's dwelling of stone of a grayish-yellow color, with a tower of brick 89 feet high and rising 65 feet therefrom. It is the frustrum of a cone, of which the upper half is painted black and the lower half white. But when seen from the northward at some miles the dark-gray dwelling makes the tower appear to have a lower dark band. The tower is surmounted by an iron lantern, painted red;the height of the focal plane is one hundred feet above the sea. The light, burning lard oil, was first exhibited, December 1, 1857, and shows every night from sunset to sunrise, a fixed white light of the third order of Fresnel, illuminating the entire horizon.

A steam fog signal was established at the station February 1, 1874, 150 yards northeast of the tower and was evidently very effective, for the officers on the surveying brig *Fauntleroy* reported while at anchor in Port Townsend Bay, a considerable distance away, the sound came through loud and clear.

George Davidson, author of the *Pacific Coast Pilot,* noted in his early surveys that Dungeness Spit was so low that vessels bound in or out of the strait, before erection of the lighthouse, were upon it before they were aware of the danger. Several ships had run ashore on the outside beach, and in 1855, while anchored close under the point with the weather thick and hazy, Davidson noted that a vessel from Admiralty Inlet had been set out of her course by the currents, and came driving in with studding sails set. Her skipper only saw his mistake when the black hull of the survey brig loomed up, else the spit might well have claimed another victim.

In December 1871, the spit was literally sliced in two by raging seas during a northwest gale, leaving a 50 foot wide breach. It cut the lighthouse off from the mainland leaving it temporarily on an island. The seas also sheered over 100 feet off the spit northeast of the lighthouse and reduced the distance the sentinel was from the water by that amount. At times during that same December 2, gale, clouds of sand arose and completely enveloped the tower infiltrating everything at the station. Despite the changeable spit, it usually mends itself and the lighthouse has remained bolted to its same foundation, now well into its second century of service.

During the winter, Dungeness spit is almost like a no man's land, a domain of sand and driftwood. Clouds shift from dove gray to almost black, their profiles changing constantly as they hump and peak across lonely strips of land. Surf often mounts and spray flies. The spit serves as one of five wildlife refuges in the greater Puget Sound area. Free from predators, birds feed and rest, thousands of black brant, sandpipers, dowitchers, black turnstones and an estimated 30,000 ducks of many varieties, not to mention the ever soaring gulls. Harbor seals find the beaches an excellent place for basking, especially at the end of the spit near the lighthouse, or off Graveyard Spit, where lie the remains of the massacred Indians.

The area is not without touches of the human element. Oysters are harvested commercially inside the bay and the famous Dungeness crabs are trapped in pots. (crab rings) Even octopus has been caught and sold to Oriental fish markets.

Historically speaking, the Spanish explorer Quimper discovered the bay in 1790, naming it for himself, and the long spit, Point Santa Cruz. George Vancouver had other ideas a few years later. He said, "The low sandy point of land, which from its great resemblance to Dungeness in the British Channel, I called it Dungeness..."

With the commissioning of the New Dungeness Lighthouse, Franklin Tucker and John Tibbals of Port Townsend, were named temporary keepers having been appointed to fill the void until the arrival of Captain Thomas Boyling and H. H. Blake, on February 11, 1858. Boyling, a seasoned seadog, formerly master of the schooner *Willimantic,* was named as principal keeper with Blake his assistant. Later, the latter took over the head keepers job and in turn was succeeded by Jacob J. Rogers, following the Indian massacre of 1868. Several other well known keepers also held posts at the station— Charles Blake, Franklin Tucker, Amos Morgan, Oscar Brown and Joseph Dunn. The usual problems commensurate with the early stations were present at Dungeness. The big fogbell in 1867, for instance, became inoperative and keeper Blake and his assitant had to strike it by hand 24 hours around the clock and well into the following day—five strokes at intervals of ten seconds.

There were continuing shipwrecks along the spit, usually when fog or murky weather blotted out the light or deadened the sound of the fog signal, but probably none caused more excitement than did the bark *Ocean,* inbound from San Francisco in October 1868. She stranded amidst overpowering smoke from a devastating forest fire sweeping the Olympic Peninsula foothills. Coughing and gagging, the keepers hastened to the scene and aided in the rescue of the crew. The fire raged on for days, the ship quickly went to pieces, and the survivors were temporary guests at the lighthouse.

So many strandings occurred along the narrow, sandy finger of land that it was sometimes referred to as "Shipwreck Spit," and many claimed the formation of the obstruction was in the shape of a finger beckoning ships to their doom.

There were Indian troubles of another kind at Smith Island Lighthouse in the early years. When the lamp was lit on October 18, 1858 at the eastern terminus of the Strait of Juan de Fuca, John Vail was keeper, aided by his wife Jane. Keeper Applegate was assigned as assistant, and it was that gentleman who stood ready to take on the northern Indians in battle. It all started after Vail was given permission by the lighthouse inspector to hire two laborers to help cultivate the soil on the 15 acre island so that the attendants could raise their own vegetables. The isle's population was then five, but when the laborers completed their task two weeks later it was back to three and was destined to go down to one.

Over on the Canadian side of the strait there was great concern about rumors of a large number of often hostile Haida Indians gathering enmass, 5,000 strong not far from Victoria B. C. They were coming down in their big canoes from the Queen Charlottes and other sectors of northern British Columbia with intent to trade with the American settlers. The alert went out that their true mission was not to trade but to attack. Tensions mounted.

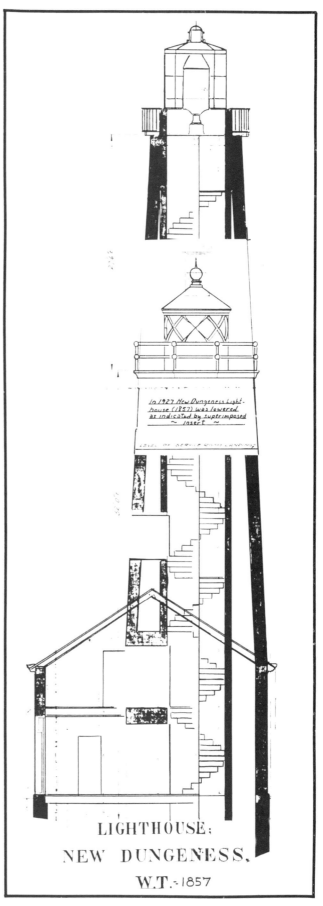

LIGHTHOUSE:
NEW DUNGENESS,
W.T.-1857

The original structural plans of New Dungeness Lighthouse, and the superimposed lowering of the tower which took place in 1927, reduced from 100 feet down to 63 feet.

SMITH
ISLAND
LIGHT

B.B. MEAGHER,
KEEPER.

BUILT - 1857.

Smith Island Lighthouse at the eastern end of the Strait of Juan de Fuca was commissioned in 1858, and was almost the scene of an Indian war a few months thereafter. Its longtime keeper B.B. Meagher is pictured in his uniform along with pictures taken of the island including the natural causeway (upper right) that connects Smith Island with Minor Island at extreme low tide.

All that remained of the old Smith Island Lighthouse in 1984 is one section of the building, the rest of it having tumbled over the cliff, victim of continuing erosion. Several years earlier a utilitarian navigation aid was established in the center of the island. Photo courtesy John W. Adams, Seattle architect.

Turn Point Light, on the very end of the northwest point of Stuart Island in the San Juans shines from a stubby concrete tower built in 1936. A light and fog signal were placed there in 1893. U.S. Coast Guard photo.

On a spring morning in 1859, a Haida war canoe was reported near Port Townsend Bay, and news came that one of the local Indians had already been killed. The white residents in alliance with the local Indians, knowing the warlike ways of the Haidas, worked themselves into a lather, joined forces and rushed to the beach to intercept the canoe. It was carrying 21 women, three boys, one blind old chief and another lesser chieftain with a missing hand. Brandishing guns, knives and clubs, the attackers stormed the craft and rudely yanked from its confines the unsuspecting occupants, who in turn were muscled to the local jailhouse.

Coming to their rescue was Indian agent Robert C. Fay who freed the terrified squaws and restored the goods purloined from the canoe. Amidst the confusion, the local Indian reported to have been murdered showed up in town knowing nothing about an attempt on his life.

Fearing a genuine reprisal from having abused a Haida Indian chief the local Clallams and Chemakum tribesmen tried to befriend the mistreated victims, but the fat was already in the fire. They departed in their canoe bitter over the harassment.

Shortly after, three Haida war canoes were reported off Point Wilson. The schooner *Carolina,* with Captain J. Jones as master, sighted five large war canoes standing off Smith Island. He hove to inquiring about their mission and was informed that they planned to hunt ducks on the island. Jones was skeptical, and put a boat ashore to warn the Vails of the dangerous situation. As a result, Applegate agreed to remain to tend the light while the Vails were transported back to Port Townsend until things cooled down. After delivering his passengers, Jones and his crew returned to the waters off Smith Island to keep an eye on the war canoes.

Applegate signaled the schooner that some of the Indians were already on the island but as of that moment had caused no trouble. When the Haidas saw the *Carolina,* they returned to their canoes and

*The Canadian Pacific liner **Empress of Asia** passing Turn Point Light Station in the 1920s. Borchers photo.*

Patos Island Lighthouse on scenic Patos Island near the Canadian border in the sunny San Juans. Photo taken in the 1920s. Borchers photo.

Back in the days when Patos Island Lighthouse was under the U.S. Lighthouse Establishment. The lighthouse was built in 1908, successor to an earlier structure established there in 1893. Borchers photo.

in warlike manner dared the "Bostons" to fight. Both Captain Jones and the local sheriff who was aboard, tried diplomacy before turning loose some angry volunteers hidden down the hatch standing ready with their guns. The Haidas were warned to stay off the island or face trouble, and fortunately they backed water. The schooner stood by until the canoes were out of sight.

The following day a skiff bearing two Kanakas arrived at Port Townsend with urgent news from Applegate. The Haidas had returned and fired several shots at the keeper while he was performing his duties. Fleeing up the spiral staircase to the lantern room, musket in hand, he had returned the fire. With an eagle-eye view of the island from his 40 foot loft, he wounded one of the Indians, who was dragged off by the others, leaving a trail of blood.

The situation reached a climax. Fearing an all-out confrontation, the bark *Mary F. Slade* was enlisted to carry militia and volunteers in charge of Major Haller, in what was being termed the "Battle of Smith Island." The vessel dropped her anchor off the isle and the troops stormed ashore and took over an old blockhouse that had been erected when the lighthouse was under construction for just such an eventuality. The quiet island was immediately converted to a temporary arsenal with sentries on duty day and night. As the weeks went by there was no further action, not a sign of a war canoe. At last, word came that the 5,000 Haidas had weighed the odds and decided to return to their northerly haunts. The undeclared battle ended with only one wounded Indian.

John Vail, his wife and grandson returned to the lighthouse, and kudos went to Keeper Applegate for his brave stand. And certainly, the lighthouse was a fine fortress, a staunchly constructed stone block dwelling with masonry tower.

Smith Island was discovered by the Spaniard Eliza in 1791 and named Isla de Bonilla. The U. S. Exploring Expedition in 1841 attached the name of Blunt's Island which was applied to the lighthouse when it was first built. An English Admiralty chart of 1847 attached the name Smith's Island and in time that name was officially adopted.

Albert Milton replaced the Vails as keeper in 1860 and served till 1864 when James Bartlett became potentate for a decade. Outside of Applegate, perhaps the best remembered warden of the light was Bernard Meagher. He was credited with going to the aid of the steamer *Samson* in the station skiff in 1917, after the vessel had become disabled by a broken steam pipe and was dragging its anchors toward the island outcrops. Meagher picked up the steamer's first mate, rowed him to the nearest telephone 11 miles away where he could call for assistance, then rowed 11 miles back in time to put the light in operation just as darkness dropped its veil over the island. The *Samson* was towed to safety, much to the delight of the diligent keeper.

The original lens and lighting apparatus at Smith Island was a fixed fourth order light. In 1885, another lens was installed with six flash panels, producing 24,000 candlepower. It was manufactured by Barbier and Fenestre of Paris, and is on display today in a Seattle museum.

Smith Island through the years has had relatively few visitors. Today vessels are warned away due to a restricted area of an air-to-surface weapons range west of the island utilized by the military. Additionally, there are massive beds of kelp circling the fringes of the isle, and waters around its girth are shallow. Presently a light and radio beacon are located there.

In April 1957, long feared erosion caught up with the lighthouse and it became apparent it was short for this world. The west side of the island had been breaking down for years while the easterly side was building up. The replacement light was an airway type beacon mounted atop a skeleton tower. In 1949, the old lighthouse was only 40 feet from the sluffing cliff. By 1960, it was only ten feet from the edge and in 1969 it began to tumble down the cliff in a mass of stone blocks, brick and mortar, until only one corner of the building remained at the top of the bluff.

In 1964, before the end came, this writer received permission of the Coast Guard to remove all or any part of the doomed structure. An engineer estimated the total weight at 300 tons which precluded any chance of moving the entire structure to another location. Instead, the Leiter Hockett Salvage team was engaged to dismantle the 1858 iron lantern house and transport it to Skunk Bay where it was re-assembled and placed atop a newly constructed vintage light tower. When the plates of the lantern house were removed at Smith Island the bolts came out as bright and shiny as the day they were placed a century and a quarter earlier, for each had been packed in white lead, which showed the skill and care used by the artisans of old.

The watermelon seed shaped island is connected at extreme low tide by a narrow, sandy causeway which leads to tiny Minor Islet where a minor navigation light has been displayed since 1907.

For several years, beginning in 1950, the Coast Guard maintained an important radio station on Smith Island which was responsible for assisting many vessels. Two bungalow dwellings were provided for the Coast Guard crew. The island has a brackish well and cistern but it never provided sufficient water for those who dwelled there in the past. Most drinking water was brought from the mainland by boat. The problem was solved with the automation of the navigation aid.

There were several trees on the island at the time of the construction of the lighthouse in the 1850's, but most were cut down so as not to restrict the light or be the cause of fires. Today, only a low grove of bushy trees and bracken grows. Wild rabbits and seabirds are the only regular residents since the full-time human element departed. Fog is also familiar to the islet which has less than ten miles visibility for a sixth part of the year.

Among the shipwrecks that occurred around the island, none was as unusual as the episode of the four-masted schooner *Minnie A Caine*. As she was being towed to sea by the tug *Magic* in December 1901, a furious Christmas storm was spawned. In turbulent seas the towing cable snapped and the schooner went adrift. The tug made a dash for shelter in Port Townsend Bay, and the *Caine* crashed aground on the shallows off Smith Island, only to become a constant companion of the lighthouse for months thereafter. In fact, she held so fast that it took a salvage crew of 40 six months to get her seaborne again. During that period, three times the schooner was raised from her shackles onto temporary ways but each time storm waves thwarted the effort to relaunch her. Finally in May of 1902, on a flood tide, the vessel was nudged from the ways into deep water and towed away by the tug *Tyee* for repairs at the Moran Shipyard in Seattle where she had been built several months earlier.

Another unusual stranding occurred off Smith Island on May 29, 1961, when the C-2 motorship *Island Mail* of the American Mail Line struck a submerged rock off the island. With Pilot Dewey Soriano aboard, and Captain H. D. Smith as master, the vessel got off course and tore a gaping 134 foot gash, ten feet wide in her hull on the starboard side. To keep her from going down in deep water, the freighter had to be beached in 25 feet of water off Fidalgo Island. With a temporary patch placed over the hole, the ship was eventually pulled free and towed to Seattle for costly repairs and a lengthy litigation.

It was a sad obituary for old Smith Island Lighthouse when it slid off the cliff, and few were anywhere near to shed a tear over its demise.

There is probably no more beautiful scattering of islands to be found anyplace in the world than the American and Canadian San Juans. It is as if legions of emeralds once fell from the heavens and planted themselves in all shapes and forms about an aquamarine sea. The American San Juans alone are comprised of 172 islands and

C.B. "Cap" Herman and Frank DeRoy were the first keepers of the Lime Kiln Lighthouse established in 1914 and updated in 1919. These Borcher photos show the lighthouse under construction as well as the keepers' dwellings. Lime Kiln was one of the last lighthouses in America to be electrified. Courtesy Bob DeRoy.

islets plus a myriad of smaller unnamed rocks, crags and reefs. Only the major islands of the archipelago are inhabited, and the primitive and often pristine nature of the area remains even today.

The waters of the San Juan Islands embrace the passages and bays north of the east end of the Strait of Juan de Fuca. The passages are used extensively by pleasure craft during the summer months. Tugs and barges and automobile ferries frequent the waterways the year around, the latter, operated by the Washington State Ferry System out of Anacortes through Thatcher Pass, Harney Channel, Wasp Passage, San Juan Channel, Spieden Channel and across Haro Strait to Sidney B. C. Ferry landings are at Lopez, Shaw, Orcas and San Juan islands. Ocean vessels normally use Haro and Rosario Straits and do not as a rule run the channels and passes in the San Juan Islands.

To mark the intricate waterways, the Coast Guard employs numerous and varied aids to navigation in waters where tidal currents sometimes race at river speeds. There are also some lighthouses maintained in the islands that have aided shipping for several decades.

Turn Point Lighthouse was established in 1893, at an important turning point for ships, on the northwest tip of Stuart Island. The original station displayed a lens-lantern and a Daboll steam fog signal. A small concrete tower with exposed 300 millimeter light and diaphragm foghorn updated the station in 1936. The keepers dwelling

Gracefully situated on the fringes of San Juan Island, Lime Kiln Lighthouse was fenced in after the beacon was automated. U.S. Coast Guard photo.

and outbuildings were considerably larger than the light tower. Before automation, the place was considered a highly desirable family station.

Turn Point's most revered keeper was Edward Durgan who raised a sizable family at San Juan light stations. While at Turn Point he earned a certificate of merit along with his assistant Peter Christiansen for an act of bravery on the night of February 16, 1897 after the tug *Enterprise* with a crew of intoxicated drifters ran aground near the station. The skipper of the tug was the only sober man aboard. The barge the vessel was towing had gone adrift with men still on its deck.

To make matters worse one of the inebriated crew of the tug went amok brandishing a knife. He had to be forcibly subdued. The keepers helped get the tug to a temporary sheltered anchorage and then took out in the station skiff to rescue those on the runaway barge. Finally all the survivors were bedded down in the keeper's dwelling and the knife wielder chained in the hen house. The guests remained for three days.

Patos Island Lighthouse, erected the same year as Turn Point (1893) is on a 260 acre isle, the northernmost of the American San Juans. It was named Patos, which in Spanish means "ducks," by explorers Galliano and Valdez in 1792. The existing frame lighthouse, circa 1908, replaced the original facility which consisted of a lens-lantern and a third class Daboll trumpet. The old keepers dwelling was torn down in 1958 and a two-story duplex built for Coast Guard attendants where during the Lighthouse Service years a lush vegetable garden had flourished.

From its inception, Patos was a favored station and most of the past wardens of the light and their families enjoyed their tours of duty there until the day of automation. The mild climate and relatively light rainfall made it an ideal location. Alden Point, on which the lighthouse stands, was named for Lieutenant James Alden, commander of the government survey and reconnaissance steamer *Active*. In the 1850's, the ship brought James S. Lawson to Patos to set up a temporary survey station. Hydrographic studies included disputed territory at Canada's Saturna Island a short distance from Patos. The same vessel made surveys of Shoalwater Bay, Puget Sound and Grays Harbor, and further landed troops on San Juan Island during the boundry dispute that almost started a war between England and the United States.

When the visitors register was first kept at Patos, beginning in 1895, the most frequent entry was that of the lighthouse keeper from Saturna. His light was located at East Point just five miles from Patos. That Canadian lighthouse was established in 1888, five years before Patos, and the keeper was glad to have Yankee company. Very few visitors came to either lighthouse outside of the inspectors, and it remained pretty much that way until more recent times.

A water problem has always existed at Patos. There was never an abundant source and many times it had to be shipped in by tender. During the Coast Guard era, the cistern was contaminated when tanks on the reservation leaked diesel oil into its contents.

Patos Island was immortalized in literature when Helene Glidden, wrote her book, *The Light on the Island*. Her father was Edward Durgan, keeper of the light who moved to Patos with his wife and 13 children in 1905, after previous service at Turn Point. Due to the isolation and privation, three Durgan children died because they could not get prompt medical attention.

In the period after the Coast Guard took over the station, the attendants were not versed in the care of Fresnel lenses and the fourth order lens at Patos was so mistreated that it had to be replaced with another lighting fixture. With automation at the station, the radio beacon formerly located there was removed.

In the rumrunning days, boats freighting illegal whiskey into the United States from British Columbia made good use of the Patos beacon and further, allegedly utilized certain island caves to stash hot

Cattle Point Lighthouse is a concrete structure built in 1935, although the point was first marked by an aid to navigation in 1888, a place where livestock from Victoria was landed in the early days.

Fourth order lens manufactured by Barbier, Bernard and Turenne for the Semiamhoo Lighthouse. It is shown here on a brief stint at Skunk Bay Lighthouse, inside the old Smith Island lantern house.

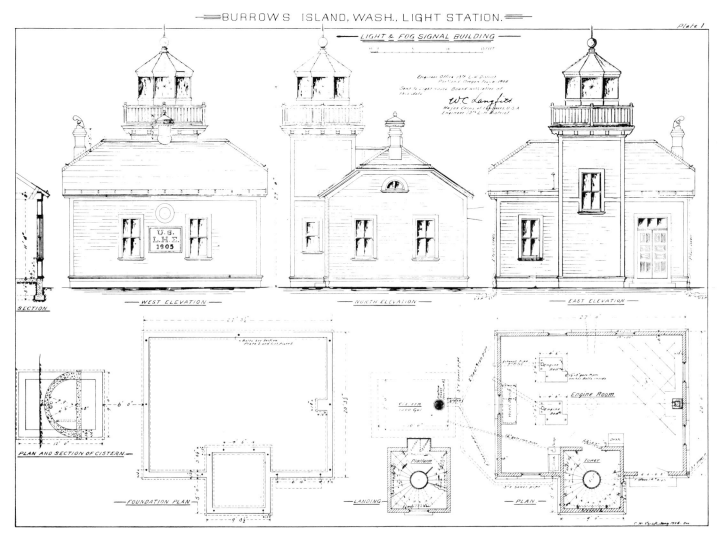

─ LIGHT & FOG SIGNAL BUILDING ─

─ SECTION ─

─ WEST ELEVATION ─   ─ NORTH ELEVATION ─   ─ EAST ELEVATION ─

─ PLAN AND SECTION OF CISTERN ─

─ FOUNDATION PLAN ─   ─ LANDING ─   ─ PLAN ─

Structural plans of Burrows Island Light Station, Engineer office 13th Lighthouse District, Portland, Oregon, February 6, 1905, signed by W.C. Langfitt, Major, Corps of Engineers, U.S.A. Courtesy U.S. Coast Guard, 13th District.

liquor. In similar fashion, before the lighthouse was established "Smugglers Cove" at the south end of the island was used to bring illegal Chinese laborers across the border from Canada.

Patos is a lovely isle with a pleasing growth of madrona, salal, conifer, mosses and fern, and hopefully the old lighthouse will continue to grace its gentle slopes for many more years. Nearby Active Cove is the destination of hundreds of pleasure craft that visit the island during the summer months.

There are two lighthouses on San Juan Island, the largest piece of land in the archipelago. Thirteen miles long, rugged and partly wooded, the isle's highest elevation is atop Mount Dallas, 1,036 feet. The two lighthouses are Lime Kiln and Cattle Point.

Lime Kiln Light, 55 feet above the water is shown from a 38 foot concrete tower, one of the last lighthouses placed in the San Juans. Established in 1914, and updated five years later, it was also one of the last on the Pacific Coast to be electrified. It wasn't until after World War II that a cable to that sector of the island allowed the IOV lamp to be replaced by an electric bulb.

The lighthouse derived its name from the surrounding limerock cliffs where limerock was mined commercially for many years. There are still the remains of several kilns about the area.

Located in a strategic shipping lane with a delightful marine vista of both American and Canadian waterways, it was always a waiting list station for those aspiring to maintain its light and fog signal. Resident personnel departed the premises August 1, 1962 when the station was automated. On that date the light was changed in intensity to 11,000 candlepower, and an electric fogbell was sounded continuously. Later it was changed to an automatic foghorn.

On the southeast point of San Juan Island stands an attractive little tower known as Cattle Point Light. A navigation aid has been located there since 1888, but the present concrete structure was built in 1935.

The point was named when a vessel stranded nearby in 1857 forcing the cargo of cattle to swim to shore. The area, from the days of the early settlers was used as a landing for livestock freighted in from Vancouver Island. It was one of the first choices for an aid to navigation in the San Juans.

The lighthouse went Hollywood in 1984. It became the backdrop for an Exxon television commercial. The producers searched all over the country for a lighthouse that was "just right" for its purpose. Not one was found with the desired characteristics. Cattle Point came close, but demanded make-up and mock-up work. The weather-beaten tower, marred by graffiti at the hands of thoughtless visitors,

An aèrial overall view of Burrows Island Light Station, an enjoyable family station until automation came along. U.S. Coast Guard photo.

was fitted with a temporary new look. A hipped roof and lantern house was added, which from a distance appeared like the real thing, especially under a fresh coat of paint. Permission for the filming had been previously granted by the 13th Coast Guard District Head-quarters in Seattle. Two radio tower beacons were cemented together to form a high powered lens, providing the finishing touches.

One would never have known from a distance that the mock-up wasn't genuine. The lighthouse was now ready for the camera crews. When it appeared on television many lighthouse buffs unaware of the facade were unable to guess the name or location of the sentinel, and that's just the way the producers wanted it.

After the filming was completed, Cattle Point was restored to its original appearance, a small low range light atop a staunch concrete octagonal tower. With the excitement over, the disturbed sea birds returned to their haunts on the rocky shores below the lighthouse.

Nestled below a tall stand of trees on a gentle plateau, Burrows Island Lighthouse is a storybook sentinel in a storybook setting. Designed by C. W. Leick, and built in 1906, the station appears more like a resort than a lighthouse reservation, at least it did before automation came. The 34 foot wooden tower attached to a fog signal building is seen by pleasure craft, commercial fishermen and deep-sea

vessels bound to or from points in the San Juan Islands or from Bellingham Bay. Fitted with a gem-like fifth order Fresnel, the fixed lens with flashing light of 25,000 candlepower has a red sector warning of a danger area over Dennis Shoal and Lawson Reef.

Currents sweep with rapidity around the fringes of the island and when the station was manned a landing dock and derrick were an integral part of the station equipment. Three Coast Guardsmen lived on the island and were permitted to have their families during a two year tour of duty. The grounds were almost park-like with play-ground facilities for the kids. The station had its own power plant, and the buoy tender *Fir* delivered fuel oil for the generators and other uses every eight months. Life there for servicemen was almost like owning one's own island. The spacious keepers dwelling plus a modern bungalow afforded comfortable quarters and the attendants actually lamented the closure of the station to resident personnel. The unit remains functional.

An unusual Victorian-style lighthouse was established in Semiah-moo Harbor, near Blaine in 1905. A near sister to the Desdemona Sands Lighthouse near Astoria, it stood on a platform supported by treated piling driven deep into the harbor bottom. The self-contained lighthouse was a one and a half story building with a cylindrical

Semiahmoo Lighthouse built on a platform supported by wooden piling in Semiahmoo Harbor near Blaine in 1905. A self-contained unit, the colorful edifice stood till 1944, when replaced by an automated structure.

lantern house and balcony at the center of the peaked roof. The light was a fourth order fixed lens with a dark sector between west and north and was manufactured in Paris by Barbier, Benard & Turenne. According to Lighthouse Board correspondence, 1901-1910, the Semiahmoo lens and lighting apparatus was purchased from the French maker through the lighthouse district engineer, expressly for the station in 1904, at a mere $370, a bargain to say the least.

The fog signal at the station was a third class Daboll trumpet which along with the light served as a navigation aid for Drayton and Blaine Harbors, a short distance south of the Canadian border.

The aforementioned Edward Durgan, who put in three decades as a light keeper, suffered a fatal heart attack at Semiahmoo in March 1920 when engaged in hoisting the station skiff up in the davits. His wife Estelle, who had been given the status of an assistant keeper, one of three woman serving on the coast at the time, took over her husband's duties.

The unique lighthouse was one of the early victims of the Coast Guard austerity program. It ceased to be a manned station in 1944, and was shortly afterwards torn down and replaced by an unmanned structure. Today, the light and horn are on a skeleton tower with a diamond shaped daymark, a marked departure from the classic lighthouse of yesteryear.

Established in 1895, Willamette River Lighthouse was positioned at the confluence of the Columbia and Williamette rivers, off the northerly end of what was once known as Nigger Tom Island. On a platform of piling, the structure consisted of a white one and a half story frame dwelling with lead colored trimming and a red roof. Shown nightly was a lens lantern displaying a fixed red light. A huge fog bell, operated by machine, gonged every ten seconds. When the machinery failed, the bell had to be rung manually. In later years the structure was demolished and the keeper transferred.

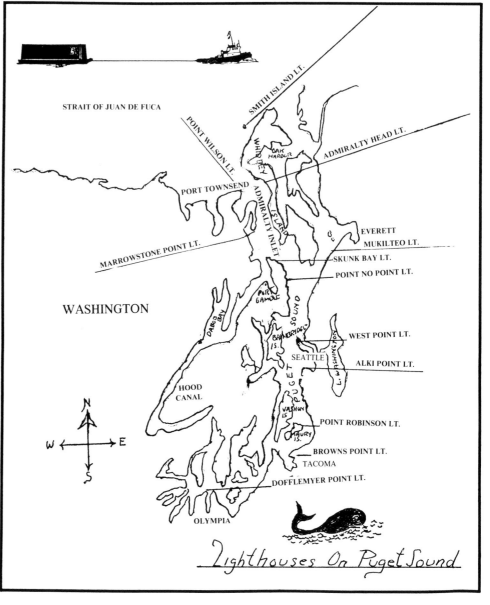

Puget Sound and Admiralty Inlet Lights

Wrapped in a mantle of darkness,
lashed by the wind and the wave
Swaying beneath their encounters,
Often their furies I brave.
...Alexander Corkum

There was much fanfare when Point Wilson Lighthouse was established at the west side entrance to Admiralty Inlet and Puget Sound in 1879. Its strategic location was near the bustling seaport town of Port Townsend, which was in those years targeted for the major shipping center for that corner of the world. Sailing vessels and steamers ran in and out of the port with regularity, and next to San Francisco no port had a more boisterous and sinful waterfront than did old Port Townsend. Houses of ill repute were numerous and the shanghaiing of sailors and drifters was a day to day occupation for both runners and grog shop owners.

Every navigator entering or departing Puget Sound had to take Point Wilson into his reckoning if he didn't want to strike an obstruction lurking under the salty brine. When the weather was clear one could properly give the point a wide berth, but the culprit was fog, and when it settled over the local waters, sailor beware. Unfortunately, for three decades after settlement of the area, mariners rounded Point Wilson without the assistance of either a guiding light or fog signal, rather incredulous when one considers the importance of the major turning point from the Strait of Juan de Fuca into Admiralty Inlet.

Pressure of the most determined variety finally got action from the Lighthouse Board to press Congress for funds, and on December 15, 1879 the beacon became a reality. It was a light of the fourth order, and to alert ships in foggy periods, a 12 inch steam whistle was installed.

David M. Littlefield, a veteran of the Civil War and a highly respected citizen of the community was the unanimous choice of the lighthouse inspector to serve as the guardian of the light.

Captain George Vancouver, the renowned British navigator probably rested easier in his grave knowing that the spike of land which he named Point Wilson was finally marked by a navigation aid. He rounded the tip of the sandy promontory in a heavy fog and was unable to judge the extent of the body of water into which he had entered. With some of his men charting the shore and others sounding in the boats, he continued sailing along the beach until another projection, now known as Point Hudson, was sighted. There as if by magic, the sun broke through revealing perhaps the most beautiful scenery ever seen by the eyes of the sea-weary Britishers. Admiralty Inlet and Puget Sound were gazed upon in rapture. To the northeast, a white-domed mountain towered above the tree-covered foothills, reflecting the glow of the noonday sun. The Utopian site was the same mountain sighted earlier from the Strait of Juan de Fuca to which Vancouver applied the name Baker. Against the western horizon were the snow-capped peaks of the Olympics with their dynamic, sawtooth character, and above the skyline to the south, the greatest surprise of all—king over all it surveyed, the lofty 14,000 foot majestic, snow-covered mountain to which the explorer bestowed the name Rainier, after Rear Admiral Rainier of the British Navy. Unfortunately, little regard was given to the ageless name applied by the native Indians—Tahoma. Beneath that marvelous ring of mountain ranges spread a series of deep, intricate waterways, the fabulous inland sea which was named for another British man of the sea—Peter Puget. Puget Sound was to become a place set apart.

Point Wilson, once the haunt of Indians who brought their canoes to rest on its shores, and fished its bountiful waters for centuries, was now the site of a lighthouse. It was a 46 foot frame tower rising from the keeper's dwelling, with a fog signal unit attached. To differentiate the sentinel from the one on Admiralty Head, the fixed white light in the lantern was varied by a red flash every 20 seconds.

With each passing year Point Wilson Lighthouse became more important to commerce. In 1913, funds were granted for an improved facility, a formidable concrete structure with an octagonal tower rising 51 feet above the water. The fog signal was upgraded to a chime diaphragm status. The new station became operational in 1914. Still in mint condition, the lighthouse continues its vigil, and at this writing it was one of the last in the greater Puget Sound area that still maintained Coast Guard personnel on the premises. An important radio beacon is also at the site.

It was Point Wilson light keeper William J. Thomas who dispatched word of the tragic collision between the coastwise passenger liner *Governor* and the freighter *West Hartland* in a thick fog off the point on April 1, 1921. The keeper heard the grinding crash even though he was unable to see what had occurred. He was to learn later that the liner went down in deep water, claiming eight lives. The large number of passengers aboard were safely evacuated in the few minutes before the *Governor* took her final plunge. The badly damaged *West Hartland* remained afloat, her bow crumpled clear back to No. 1 hold. Hasty rescue operations picked up several survivors from the lifeboats.

In recent years divers have managed to reach the liner in 240 feet of water and bring up a few relics, with the hope they could recover the vessel's safe.

A share of vessels have met with mishap near Point Wilson, but the lighthouse has been a welcome sight to mariners ever since its inception. Though Port Townsend was destined to lose out to other Puget Sound ports as the hub of shipping, specifically after the rail links remained on the eastern shores of the Sound, it nevertheless played a key role in maritime history. The lighthouse became the greeter light for the entire Puget Sound area and continues that important role today.

Along the western shores of Admiralty Inlet, Point Hudson was marked with a light and fog signal in 1887, only 1.7 miles south southeast of Point Wilson. Marrowstone Point, the eastern point of the entrance to Port Townsend Bay, received a light and fog signal in 1888. The latter fixture was four miles south of Point Wilson, near old Fort Worden, one of three forts (including Flagler and Casey) built by the government at a cost of $10 million to protect the waters of Admiralty Inlet and Puget Sound before the turn of the century. Part of the defense unit was located at Point Wilson where Battery Kinzie was situated in the dunes back from the beach. Not far from that spot, Captain Alfred A. Plummer began the erection of a primitive fort in 1855, designed to protect the early settlers against incursions by hostile northern Indians from British Columbia, famous for their hit-and-run attacks.

At Marrowstone Point, the initially placed fogbell was often the complaint of mariners who claimed it was inaudible, due to dead spots. Lighthouse authorities than authorized the use of an experimental Scotch fog gun, but that too was dismissed as unsatisfactory. During World War I when traffic was heavy on the waterways, the government built a fog signal house at the site and equipped it with three large trumpets in as many different directions. That innovation solved the vexing sound problem. Wilson, Marrowstone and Hudson all continue as active aids to navigation.

Point No Point is a low sandspit projecting over one quarter of a mile from the high land and has been marked by a lighthouse since January 1, 1880. Located on the west shore of the sound about three miles southeast of Foulweather Bluff, it is near the town of Hansville. In 1878, a 40 acre tract was purchased for $1,800 by the government as a lighthouse reservation following tough negotiations with the landowners who were reluctant to give up the land. The structure was erected the following year, a short 27 foot masonry tower. A foghorn house was not attached until 1900 at which time the original fog bell was retired.

The lamp was lit for the first time on New Years Day 1880 by keeper John Maggs, although neither the glass for the lantern house nor the lens had been delivered. According to Maggs' station journal report, those first few days were hectic for he had to, by order, hang a common household kerosene lantern from the dome of the lantern house without protection from the weather, and to make matters worse it was mid-winter with two feet of snow on the ground and a persistent wind blowing.

Carpenters were still working on the station dwelling and Maggs' was trying to get things ready for the arrival of this family coming by boat from Seattle. The lens finally arrived on January 10, but there

Point Wilson Lighthouse shortly after its completion in 1914, replacing the 1879 sentinel.

*The Indian freighter **State of Punjab** passes close to the Point Wilson Lighthouse in 1972. Photo by E.A. Delanty.*

Marrowstone Point Lighthouse, southeast of Port Townsend on the main shipping channel (Marrowstone Island) has been a familiar site since 1888. The present structure was built in 1918. Note the old fog trumpets compared with the newer models in the insert photo.

*The Coast Guard cutter (buoy tender) **Fir** served Puget Sound buoys and lighthouses for nearly a half century. She has, for the most part, operated out of the Coast Guard repair yard and buoy tender station on the Lake Washington Ship Canal, Seattle.*

Point No Point Lighthouse on the west side of Puget Sound is the original structure dating from 1879. Its fog bell was replaced by a fog signal building in 1900. U.S. Coast Guard aerial photo.

Close up of the snug little Point No Point Lighthouse. U.S. Coast Guard photo.

A page from the Point No Point lighthouse station journal in January 1880.

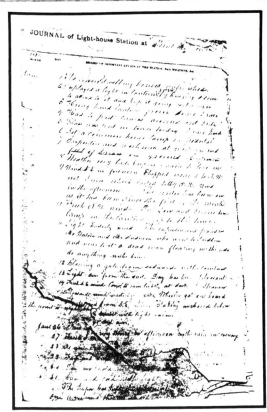

was still no plate glass for the lantern house. The source of light continued to be the kerosene lantern. Not until February 1, were the plate glass panes delivered. Only after their installation did the frustrated station keeper and his assistant, Henry H. Edwards settle down to the normal duties of lighthouse keepers.

On April 14, according to the station journal, the lighthouse tender *Shubrick* arrived with inspector Captain George C. Reiter accompanied by his assistant H. S. Wheeler. The two made a day long inspection of the station before finally giving it a passing mark.

Six days later, the schooner *Granger* anchored off the lighthouse to offload a cow, which was to supply milk for the anticipated child of the pregnant Mrs. Maggs. She had a baby girl on July 21, the first child born at the lighthouse.

In October of the same year Maggs was chosen as a member of an elite group that was to go to Seattle to meet the President of the United States, Rutherford B. Hayes. It was considered one of the highlights of his career.

The highlight of his life, however, was eroded by trouble at the station after his return. His assistant, Edwards was transferred to another station and replaced by N. S. Rogers whose stay for reasons unexplained was extremely short. Then replacing him came an assistant named Manning, and almost from the outset he and Maggs

Skunk Bay (memorial) Lighthouse built in 1965 crowned by the old Smith Island lantern house. Insert, after remodeling in the early 1980s, expanding the dwelling.

were at loggerheads. It all started in an argument over the improper ringing of the fog bell. Maggs insisted Manning had put the bell unnecessarily in operation for three hours when the weather did not merit its usage. Words flew hot and heavy.

Maggs in turn got a letter off to his superiors telling of the incident. The situation worsened after Maggs accused his assistant of "keeping the lamp in a sloppy manner." Manning flew into a rage, following Maggs out of the tower uttering threats and flashing an open pocket knife. Later, according to the journal report, he went to his quarters, took a pistol and left for a nearby logging camp. Bringing another man back with him, the two immediately went to the light tower, locked the door and refused entry to the principal keeper. Maggs insisted but was told he would enter at his own risk.

When the head keeper returned to the tower at 1 p.m. he found it empty and the lamp unattended. He immediately took off for Port Gamble and telegraphed the collector of customs to send a revenue cutter and to inform Inspector Reiter of the problem.

On June 27, at 12:10 p.m. the cutter arrived, and at the request of Maggs, Lieutenant Willey and two armed men were sent ashore to enforce order at the station. Manning was accordingly told he was to be submissive to the principal keeper, to clean the glass and handle the lamp properly, to inform Maggs on change of the watch and to obey all rules and regulations in accordance with the issued code of the U. S. Lighthouse Service. The reluctant assistant had no recourse.

Two days later, on June 29, inspector Reiter arrived aboard the *Shubrick* to investigate the charges. He gave both parties a chance to air their differences. His conclusion was that Manning and his family were to pack up, lock, stock and barrel and go back to Seattle aboard the awaiting lighthouse tender. Whether or not he ever got another post with the agency is not recorded, but at any rate, peace and tranquility returned to Point No Point.

Maggs got a new assistant named Neil Henley, and station operations thereafter worked smoothly. When inspector Reiter returned to inspect the station on January 24, 1882, he gave the facility an A-OK rating. Four months later, however, on May 1, a minor earthquake shook the station and did some damage.

In 1888, the Maggs family departed Point No Point, and a newly assigned keeper named Scannel took over as principal keeper. He found the station to this liking and remained at this post for 26 years. His assistant, Carey shared those feelings by outdoing him one year,

Point Robinson when it was still a manned station, its octagonal tower gleaming with a fresh coat of paint.

his term ending in 1937 after 27 years. Since 1939, several Coast Guard personnel and their families have lived on the reservation, and today the beacon and fog signal continue to function. One could never say that there was "no point" in having a lighthouse at Point No Point.

Skunk Bay Lighthouse, a small memorial sentinel which became active somewhat by accident, shines a mile west of Hansville, and about three miles northwest of Point No Point. Its iron lantern house is from the old Smith Island Lighthouse, circa 1858, and the tower was built in 1965 from structural plans of the Mukilteo tower, circa 1906. For a time, the fogbell from the Columbia River Lightship *No. 88* was atop the dwelling, but on request of the late Rolf Klep, it was transferred to the Columbia River Maritime Museum at Astoria and re-installed on *No. 88* when it was part of the museum display. When the museum sold *No. 88* to private interests and replaced it with lightship *No. 604,* the old bell was retained.

An oversight by this writer led to the Skunk Bay Lighthouse becoming a navigation aid by accident. With a Fresnel mounted in the lantern house, it was a practice to sometimes blink the light momentarily at ships being piloted into Puget Sound. One night the light was left on by accident, and the following morning the Coast Guard was barraged with calls complaining that an unauthorized beacon was shining over the shipping lanes, and toward the Whidbey Island Naval Air Station.

Point Robinson Lighthouse on Maury Island, halfway between Seattle and Tacoma was always a favorite with its attendants. The existing buildings were constructed in 1915, although a light and fog signal had marked the point since 1885.

Browns Point, near Tacoma has been lighted since 1887. The insert shows the original structure which housed a lens-lantern and fog bell. The new tower was built of concrete in 1933 and is still in use today.

The only lighthouse at the far southern end of Puget Sound is Dofflemyer, on the east side entrance to Budd Inlet, near Olympia. the present tower was built in 1936 replacing an aid to navigation established there in 1887.

"What latter day "moon cusser" is attempting to run ships aground for their loot," quipped a local news sheet. That was a misdemeanor. The next day, a Coast Guard officer, with considerable goldbraid, arrived on the scene demanding an explanation. After an inspection of the lighthouse, he said, "It looks about as good as anything in the district." He paused a minute, "Either turn it off permanently or operate it continuously in accordance with the rules and regulations of the U. S. Coast Guard for private aids to navigation," he warned.

So from that day, Skunk Bay Lighthouse became operative, but with a much reduced fixed red light. In 1971, the structure was sold to a group of 20 professional men which formed the Skunk Bay Lighthouse Association. A decade later the owners updated the living quarters and at the same time placed a vintage 1939 fogbell on display.

Following along the western shores of Puget Sound is an important lighthouse marking the midway point between the ports of Seattle and Tacoma—Point Robinson Lighthouse. The station became a reality on July 1, 1885, but at that date it was only a fog signal facility, blasting a 12 inch brass whistle. It became apparent that a light was essential, and on December 12, 1887, a lens-lantern with a fixed red characteristic was added. Like a growing child, the lighthouse continued gaining importance with the increase in marine traffic. In 1894 the light was raised to a height of 40 feet, but full maturity was not reached until 1915, when a handsome new lighthouse with concrete octagonal tower and fog signal building was erected. The lighting apparatus was of the fifth order of Fresnel, manufactured by L. Sautter, Lemonnier Cie, of Paris.

Located on Maury Island, connected to Vashon Island, Point Robinson is an ideal location and a picturesque setting for a lighthouse, just far enough off the beaten path and yet within a near

Alki Point Lighthouse at the south entrance to Seattle's Elliott Bay has been operating since 1918, although the point has had an aid to navigation since 1887. The concrete structure is near the place where Seattle's first settlers landed in 1851. Insert, shows Albert Anderson, who was at Alki for several years as well as other lighthouses, including Tillamook. He was a Gallatin Award winner for his many years of faithful service. The commandant of the 13th Coast Guard District Headquarters in Seattle now resides in one of the keepers' dwellings on the station grounds.

radius of land and sea activity. Its keepers in the past preferred the station to any others in which they had served, as did their families. The aid to navigation continues as vital to the marine traffic between Puget Sound's two largest seaports.

At the far end of Puget Sound, near Olympia, is Dofflemyer Point Light. Generally not considered in the category of its more prominent sister lights, the sentinel marks the east side entrance to Budd Inlet, 29 miles by water from Tacoma. The channel opening runs between Cooper and Dofflemyer points, the latter, first marked by a lens-lantern on a 12 foot stake back in December 1887. Not until 1936 did the point rate a lighthouse, a 30 foot pyramidal tower which displayed an 1,800 candlepower 300 millimeter light and fog signal.

Amid the numerous aids to navigation in the Tacoma area, the only one that classifies as a lighthouse is Browns Point. Its light shines from a 31 foot concrete tower with exposed beacon, and a fog signal which gets considerable usage. The tower was built in 1933, but the point has been marked by a beacon since December 12, 1887, the same year that a large number of minor lights were placed at strategic points on Puget Sound waters. The original lens-lantern was upgraded in 1893 when a tubular lantern and light of greater intensity proved more effective in marking the north point to Commencement Bay.

In 1981, West Point Lighthouse marked a century of service, the same tower and the same fourth order Fresnel still in operation. Rocks have to be constantly dumped around the structure to protect it from driftwood. The lighthouse marks the north entrance to Seattle's Elliott Bay and the south entrance to Shilshole Bay. Port of Seattle photo by Harry Gilmore.

The station was described as a two-story frame tower, the lantern projecting from its westerly side, and a fogbell suspended under the gable above the lantern. It was an arrangement similar to the station at Warrior Rock on the Columbia River and the erstwhile Willamette River Light established in 1895. The keeper and his family lived in a one and a half story frame dwelling, 300 yards from the lighthouse. The station was automated on May 1, 1963.

Marking the entrance to Seattle's harbor, Elliott Bay, are two prominent lighthouses, one at Alki Point and the other at West Point. Alki at the south entrance is shown from a 37 foot concrete octoganal tower attached to a fog signal building. Connected with the station is a special radio direction finder calibration facility.

The beacon is near the spot where Seattle's first white settlers landed aboard the schooner *Exact* in 1851 on a rainy fall day. As the city grew up around the lighthouse, neighbors frequently complained about the mournful groan of the fog signal, but after all, the lighthouse had priority, and ear plugs were suggested for those suffering from disturbed sleep. An official navigation aid has been at the point since 1887.

The land, originally part of the C. C. Terry donation claim, was later under the ownership of David S. Maynard who sold it in 1868 to Hans Martin Hanson and his brother-in-law Knud Olson, 320 acres for $450. The value of the land today would be in the multi-millions of dollars. The two families lived there from 1869 to 1880 and kept an unofficial oil lamp burning for passing mariners, as a humanitarian act.

Finally the Lighthouse district inspector realizing the importance of the point, authorized an official light there as of 1887 and named Hanson as the keeper at a salary of $15 a month. A lens-lantern was placed on a wooden scaffold and directions were issued for the light to be lit each evening and extinguished each morning the year round. Every six months several barrels of coal oil were lightered in from a

Coastguardsman Kinkade dusts red panel in the fourth order lens at Seattle's West Point Lighthouse. Harry Gilmore photo.

178

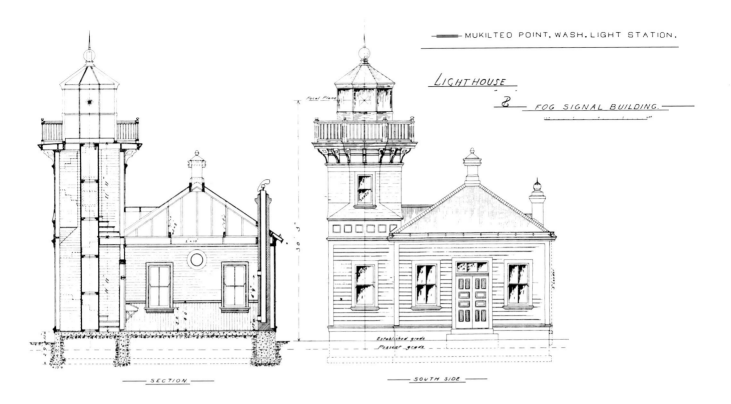

Structural plans for Mukilteo Lighthouse, drawn and engineered by C.W. Leick, in 1905. Courtesy U.S. Coast Guard, 13th District.

lighthouse tender and the drums were rolled along the beach to the desired area.

As the years progressed, Hanson's son Edmund, the only boy among six girls was given the responsibility for tending the light. He in turn often conned his sisters into trimming the wicks. When the father died in 1900, much of the 320 acre tract was divided among his offspring. Though for many years he had been listed as the official keeper, he was often more interested in entertaining with his guitar, singing yarns and jingles dressed in fancy suits, derby hat, spats and cane. He was the colorful character of the area, known for his wit and good humor.

By 1910, the government realized that Alki Point deserved more than a minor navigation aid, and elected to purchase a pie-shaped acre and a half parcel right at the very point of the land for $9,000. Through government insistence, the Hanson clan reluctantly relinquished the property. Still it was eight more years before the new lighthouse was finally commissioned.

Lighthouse Service veteran Albert Anderson put in two decades of service at Alki before he retired in 1970. Forty-three years total, he served with the Lighthouse Service and the Coast Guard beginning as a fireman aboard the Columbia River Lightship. Later he transferred to the lighthouse tender *Rose* after which he put in duty at Tillamook Rock and Cape Blanco.

After the lighthouse was automated, one of the two keepers' dwellings became the residence of the Commandant of the 13th Coast Guard District. In fact, several Commandants in turn have dwelled at the fine old edifice and all have been impressed with the prime marine seascape and the pleasant surroundings. Many social events have been held there. Perhaps the greatest booster was Katherine Larkin, wife of Rear Admiral Charles E. Larkin who raised her two children there in the late 1970's, and was hostess to numerous parties involving military personnel.

In November 1981, West Point Lighthouse, at the north entrance to Elliott Bay celebrated its 100th anniversary. The trim, little structure has endeared itself to Seattleites for many years and except for a few additions it is little altered from its inception. Eight years before Washington became a state, the tower was sending out its friendly beams with the same fourth order Fresnel, the illuminent going through the evolution from oil to electricity. A 1,000 watt quartz iodine bulb presently lights the lens and gives a sharp flash through the bullseyes with its white and red alternating characteristic. The apparatus makes one revolution per minute.

The first fog signal, a steam whistle was installed at West Point on February 7, 1887, and at the turn of the century a new fog signal building provided equipment to blast second class Daboll trumpets which served many years till the advent of more modern foghorns.

Two spacious residences were provided for the keepers which helped make the station a pleasing place to live and raise a family. There has only been one drawback down through the years. Often times during the winter months logs and debris have been cast up on the station grounds, sometimes against the stout masonry tower. Heavy rocks and riprap have frequently been collocated to protect the lighthouse which is located precariously near the water.

The beacon has been placed in the National Register of Historic Places which assures its preservation. From its seaward side opens one of the more scenic vistas of Puget Sound, both Mount Rainier and Mount Baker standing out in all their glory on a clear day. Marine traffic passes close to shore, affording a continuous parade.

A former warden of the light adept at figures calculated in the late fall of 1981, that after a century of service the French made L. Sautter, Lemonnier & Cie, Paris, Fresnel with its 12 bullseyes had given out better than 35,000 nights or about 395,000 hours of light over those decades. The fog signal has logged an annual average of 344 hours.

179

A prime example of the splendid frame lighthouses built on the fringes of Puget Sound by the old Lighthouse Service in the early part of the century, is Mukilteo Lighthouse. It was built in 1906 and is pictured as it looks today in the photo. The insert, was taken in 1908 showing the old keeper dwellings. The main picture is a Coast Guard photo and the insert is from the Pete Hurd collection.

Situated below Fort Lawton, its compatible neighbor for years, the lighthouse was joined by a new neighbor in recent times, somewhat on the debit side—a massive metro sewage treatment plant.

A guest register was kept at the station from 1895, and many prominent personalities were listed among the visitors. Found taped to one of the pages was an old directive issued to the station keeper, dated November 17, 1887. It read:

Mr. George F. Fonda
Keeper, West Point Light Station
Sir:

Enclosed is a recipe for mixing white wash which you will post in the "Instructions to Light Keepers" and will use instead of the old recipe given in the instructions. After giving this recipe a trial, you will report to me the result.

Respectfully,
U. Sebree
Inspector, 13th Light-House
District

The formula read: "To ten parts of the best freshly-slacked lime add one part of best hydraulic cement. Mix well with salt water and apply quite thin."

Progress was bound to make its mark on the lighthouse. Whitewash used on early station buildings almost exclusively was long ago replaced by paint, a much better way to maintain a bright, more durable appearance.

One of the latter day attendants at West Point was officer-in-charge Ron W. Kinkade, Boatswain's Mate first class. He shared the station residence with his wife and nine children, four dogs and a cat named Fred.

Prior to his coming, Chief Boatswain's Mate Christian Fritz was officer-in-charge. His wife was blind and was led about the premises by a well trained seeing eye dog, a boxer named Cookie.

Mukilteo Light abreast the town of Mukilteo, has been in existence since 1906, marking the waterway at Point Elliot on the east side of Possession Sound along the searoad to Everett.

Designed by C. W. Leick, the frame lighthouse is located on an historic tract of land where Governor Isaac Stevens of Washington Territory signed an important peace treaty with the Indians in 1855. A similar treaty was signed in the same year at Point No Point. Involved were 1,000 Indians from the Chimacum, Skokomish and Clallam tribes who agreed to end hostilities.

A familiar scene to countless persons, Mukilteo Lighthouse shares its historic corner with sports fishermen and ferryboat users. The Washington State Ferry System operates units of its fleet on the busy Mukilteo-Whidbey (Columbia Beach) Island route, the ferry dock within a stone's throw of the watch tower.

For a time the Coast Guard planned to demolish the classic lighthouse and replace it with a navigation light on a pole. Civic intervention put the economy move on the skids and the lighthouse will continue to stand just where it has always been even if it is eventually deactivated. Originally there were two keepers dwellings on the tract, but both have been removed. There was also a former windmill for pumping water, but it too has disappeared.

One of the longer tours of duty at Mukilteo was put in by Coast Guardsmen Vivian R. Corrie, who tended the light from 1946-1960. The station has been automated for the past several years, maintenance crews being dispatched on demand.

The shift in marine traffic caused a short life for this beautiful lighthouse—Admiralty Head Lighthouse, built in 1903, was out of service by the mid 1920s. In 1927, its lantern house was removed and placed atop the tower at New Dungeness. This vintage photo was taken during the prime career of the Whidbey Island sentinel.

Though for six decades no light has been shown in the crown of the Admiralty Head Lighthouse, the restored structure has become one of the most popular tourist attractions on Whidbey Island. Positioned at the east entrance to Admiralty Inlet and Puget Sound, the lighthouse has been restored and opened to the public under the auspices of the Washington State Parks and the Island County Historical Society.

In the 1920's when maritime traffic tended toward the Point Wilson side of the channel, the importance of Admiralty Head waned, unlike the era of the sailing vessel when its presence was extremely important. In fact, it was chosen as a site for a lighthouse before Point Wilson, on a section of the head known as Red Bluff, where construction began on August 1, 1860. The light was first exhibited on January 20, 1861, from a frame tower attached to a dwelling, affording the appearance of a little country church from the waterside. The lantern was 41 feet above the ground, and the basic structure measured 29 by 30 feet, containing the living quarters. The light was a fourth order Fresnel with a focal plane 108 feet above the water.

As mentioned, early surveys for lighthouse sites had given Admiralty Head priority over Point Wilson, and in 1858 a reserve was set aside. The land was purchased from John and Caroline Kellogg, who had homesteaded the acreage just five years earlier.

William Robertson was assigned as keeper after the lighthouse was completed. He was given the assignment because he was a Democrat and lost it with the next Republican administration. They played politics in the early days of the lighthouses. He was succeeded by a Mr. Pearson, whose health was so poor that his two daughters, Flora and Georgia performed most of the lighthouse chores.

When Uncle Sam decided to fortify the entrance to Admiralty Inlet in 1897, the lighthouse was in the way. Two years later the government brought about a switch in properties, whereby the lighthouse would be relocated to higher ground a half mile to the north. Carl Leick was ordered by the U. S. Engineers Office, 13th Lighthouse District, to design and supervise the construction of a new lighthouse with his usual prowess, his standard motto being, "Build 'em big for stout." His 1903 creation was just that, a splendid masonry lighthouse, the tower connected to an attractive two-story edifice, claimed to be the most comfortable dwelling on the coast. Focal plane of the light was 127 feet above the sea and the fourth order lens provided a beam visible for 17 miles.

Unfortunately the life of the lighthouse was relatively brief. By the mid 1920's, the maritime traffic pattern had changed and the Bureau of Lighthouses put the aristocratic sentinel out of business. Then in 1927, with the reconstruction of New Dungeness Lighthouse, they decapitated the tower by removing the lantern house to the other facility leaving the structure looking like a small castle with a medieval turret.

This is how Admiralty Head Lighthouse looked in 1950, abandoned after World War II, having been previously used for an officers residence at Fort Casey. It has since been completely restored as a tourist attraction by the Washington State Parks, and appears very much as it did when it was an active aid to navigation. The initial Admiralty Head Lighthouse was at a more southerly location, commissioned January 1861 (at Red Bluff).

During World War II Fort Casey was activated to full strength and the dwelling converted for the quarters of a high ranking officer. It was painted olive drab and almost lost its identification as a former lighthouse. After the war when the fort property became surplus to military needs, Seattle Pacific College acquired 87 acres and the State Parks and Recreation Commission successfully applied for transfer of 100 acres of the battery area, including the lighthouse structure, for an historical site. They revamped the sentinel and restored it to its original appearance, even installing a new lantern house atop the tower. There is no light in the lantern, but the former lens used at the Alki Lighthouse is on public display in the lighthouse rotunda.

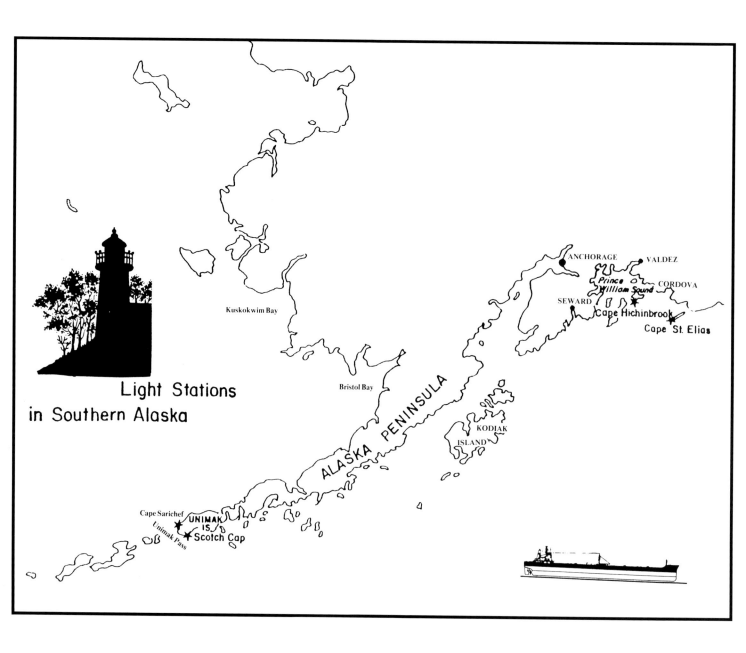

Light Stations
in Southern Alaska

Kuskokwim Bay

Bristol Bay

ALASKA PENINSULA

KODIAK
ISLAND

Cape Sarichef
UNIMAK
IS.
Unimak Pass
Scotch Cap

ANCHORAGE   VALDEZ
Prince
William Sound   CORDOVA
SEWARD
Cape Hichinbrook
Cape St. Elias

CHAPTER ELEVEN

Lighthouses of Alaska

Men of the High North, the wild sky is blazing,
Islands of opal float on silver seas;
Swift splendors kindle, barbaric, amazing;
Pale ports of amber, golden argosies.
....Robert W. Service

Alaska, the Great Land, has 33,000 miles of coastline, three million lakes larger than 20 acres and ten of its rivers are longer than 300 miles. The Yukon River wanders 1,979 miles from Canada to the Bering Sea.

Many Alaskans rely upon the sea for their livelihood, the fishing industry alone, employing multi-thousands annually. Despite increased safety precautious approximately 1,300 lives are lost each year in the state of Alaska, many due to maritime related accidents. Is it any wonder that aids to navigation in Alaskan waters are important? Mile for mile, Alaska probably has fewer navigation aids than anyplace in the world, due mostly to its sparce population and seemingly endless expanse.

The two greatest incentives for spurring trade and commerce in Alaska have come three-quarters of a century apart. In 1897 it was the discovery of gold, and in the 1970's it was black gold (oil) that brought great wealth to the state. During the goldrush, following the arrival of the steamer *Portland* at Seattle with the famous "ton of gold" from the Alaskan diggings, a huge armada of ships moved northward packed to the gunwales with gold-thirsty persons. Steamship inspection laws were lax and frequently inexperienced navigators commanded unseaworthy wooden and steel floating coffins. During those years and in the decade to follow the complex and difficult Alaska waterways were to claim scores of ships and men. Dots on the charts denoting shipwrecks were numerous, names like the passenger liners *Princess Sophia, Islander, Mexico, Corona, Laurada, Ohio, Valdez, State of California* and on and on, vessels whose final ports were the reefs and rocks of both the Inside and Outside passages. The most tragic was the loss of the SS *Princess Sophia* that foundered with her entire complement of 343 persons after slipping off Vanderbilt Reef in a 1918 blizzard.

To thwart the rash of marine disasters, the government attempted to establish navigation aids at the most perilous points, but the effort in many cases was too little and too late.

Alaska is wrapped in maritime history, and it is the Russians who get the kudos for establishing the first official lighthouse north of Mexico. Though the Spaniards made some feeble attempts at guarding their "New Spain" waterways, it was the Russians in 1837, that first employed a light enclosed in a lantern, atop the old administration building, frequently referred to as "Baranof's Castle," at the port of New Archangel, (Sitka). That was 30 years before Uncle Sam purchased the territory for $7.2 million. (See Chapter 2).

The toll of lost ships and men on the northerly route from Siberia was costly, the Aleutian chain claiming many Czarist vessels, mostly of the Russian American Company. There was little succor for the unfortunate castaways. The Russians based most of their activity at Sitka and at Kodiak and saw no feasibility for placing lighthouses at intervals along the onerous sea route.

Two and one fifth times larger than the state of Texas, Alaska's general coastline runs nearly 6,700 miles compared with only 4,800 for the East, Gulf and Pacific Coasts of continental United States. Alaska's discovery, as white man counts discovery, must be credited to a Dane, Vitus Bering, (Behring) employed in the service of Russia. He discovered Bering Strait, separating Asia and North America in

1728 in the ship *St. Gabriel,* but may not have found the true Alaska until his second voyage in 1741, when he explored the coastline in the ship *St. Peter,* accompanied by the *St. Paul* in command of Chirikof.

On March 30, 1867, William H. Seward, as secretary of state under President Andrew Johnson, purchased Alaska, a transaction labled as "Seward's Folly." The official turnover took place on October 18, at which time Alaska became a district of the United States until 1912, a territory until 1969 and finally the 49th state.

With the annexation of Alaska, the government was extremely slow in reacting to the desperate need for navigation aids, perhaps due to the apathy of many solons who considered Alaska a royal white elephant. Under the Czarist regime the situation was somewhat similar. In 1799, Fort Archangel Gabriel, both a fortress and trading post, was constructed on the shores of Sitka Bay. It was ruled by the sword and knout and its principals practiced the old Russian proverb, "God is high above and the Czar far away." Demanding and ruthless in their treatment of the native Aleuts and Thlingits, there was considerable agitation between the two factors.

In 1802, the natives attacked the Russian fortress and nearly wiped out the garrison. Revenge was swift. The Aleuts succumbed to the superior Russian weapons, but the more determined Thlingits continued their opposition, claiming their grandfather rights to the land. The showdown came two years later when Baranof led a reprisal attack with sophisticated weapons that annihilated scores of natives in the worst kind of brutality. Resistance waned and eventually died. Baranof set himself up as the so-called "Lord of Alaska" and exerted autonomous authority. The fortresses in the area were made stronger and the ships of the Russian American Company arrived in increasing numbers bringing supplies and often returning to the mother country with cargoes of furs.

What was erroneously named Baranof's Castle was actually the Russian governor's mansion and administration building, and was completed in 1837. When Sir Edward Belcher, R. N. visited Sitka in September of that year he described the log structure as being "140 feet in length, by 70 feet wide, two stories high and capped by a lighthouse in the center of the roof. Some of the building logs measure 76 by 80 feet in length, and squaring one foot. They half dovetail over each other at the angles, and are treenailed together vertically. The roof is pitched, and covered with sheet iron."

Belcher further told of the fortifications containing 40 cannon, mostly old ships guns, 12 to 24 pounders. The arensal on low ground at the foot of the building was well stocked. He noted the craftsmen at work at the sawmill cutting fine-grained yellow cypress of which they built boats and exported plank to the Sandwich Islands. The settlement's lone shipyard was a busy place.

The 'castle' was never lived in by Baranof. It served as the official residence of the chief managers of the Russian American Company and was the fourth such structure at the settlement. As earlier mentioned the first was built by Baranof in 1804-05. Kuskov built the second and Murayev the third in 1823. The 1837 building was erected under the direction of Kupreanov.

The lighthouse atop the latter structure was a cupola or tubular lantern house containing a beacon, which though feeble, was like a

One of the earliest sketches of the Administrator's Building, commonly known as Baranof's Castle, is depicted at the center of the upper drawing. The artist was Voznesenskii, about 1849. The building housing Alaska's first lighthouse in the roof cupola was built in 1837. The lighthouse beacon in the Russian's description was 34 meters above the sea. I.G. Voznesenskii was on a voyage with the Russian American Company. Lower photo, is one of the last pictures taken of the old lighthouse building before it burned down in 1894. The W.H. Case photo shows an overall view of Sitka's colorful harbor with the "castle" at the center left, the lighthouse cupola still intact.

*Ill-fated Canadian Pacific steamer **Islander** that struck an iceberg and foundered off Douglas Island with the loss of 42 lives and a reputed treasure in gold in 1901. When salvaged three decades later only a fraction of the gold was recovered.*

*The original Sentinel Island Lighthouse commissioned March 1, 1902, along with Five Finger Light, is seen at the right in this Winter and Pond photo. The SS **Princess May** is seen stranded on Sentinel Reef August 5, 1910. Passengers were evacuated and the vessel was eventually refloated. In the lower photo, the SS **Princess Sophia** is seen astride Vanderbilt Reef in much the same situation in 1918. She slipped off the reef during a nighttime gale and went down with her entire complement of 343 persons, Alaska's worst ship tragedy. Both ships were owned by the same company—Canadian Pacific.*

heavenly star when spotted after the rigorous voyage from Siberia. The light was produced by four small, square copper cup-like containers in front of a reflector, each fitted with a wick, the burners fed by either seal or whale oil, acquired locally. Situated 110 feet above the water, the light was visible for approximately five miles.

Prior to the lighthouse, members of the Russian garrison often utilized ships lanterns attached to the fortress walls to guide vessels safely into the harbor. When the lighthouse came to fruition, the attendant was kept busy carrying containers of oil up the stairs to feed the lamps. He was commanded "to keep the copper and brass equipment polished and the glass smudge-free at all times."

When the 'castle' became United States property in 1867, it was used by the commanding officer and his staff. The lighthouse at that period was reported in bad need of repair, though the oil lamp and large reflector were still in place and usable. The Collector of Customs requested an allowance to maintain the light and was in turn appointed superintendant of lights for the territory, there being only one. Army Ordinance Sergeant George Golkell was then appointed keeper for a stipend of 40 cents a day.

In 1877, just a decade later, the Army regiment was removed and the lighthouse attendant along with it. From then on the light was improperly cared for and fell into serious disrepair.

Congress remained indifferent to pleas by the Lighthouse Board for navigation aids in Alaska, and few tears were shed when the historic old Russian building burned to the ground in 1894 destroying what remained of the pioneer rooftop lighthouse.

Records in Alaskan archives list thousands of vessels lost in the inland waters of Alaska, in the sea adjacent to it, on the east coast of Kamchatka and along the northern and western coasts of Siberia between 1740 and the present time. When one considers the physical and meteorological conditions and the fact that virtually no navigation aids nor reliable charts existed until after the purchase of the territory, the perils faced by the old Russian seafarers are readily understood. Several of their ships were lost without trace. Disasters are on record as far back as 1745, when the Russian ship *Eudokia* was wrecked on Kanaga Island. Other early Russian ships that met with disaster were the *Trinity* on Umnak Island in 1764; the ship *John the Forerunner* on St. Paul Island in 1791; the ship *Northern Eagle* on Montague Island in 1799; tender *Avos* and the brigs *Sitka* and *Otkrytie in 1801;* the schooner *Chirikof* lost in 1809, and the *Neva* wrecked off Cape Edgecomb in 1813.

In 1835, the whaler *Ganges* out of Nantucket, took the first right whale off Kodiak Island, and started the American whaling industry in the North Pacific. Between that year and 1869 whaling operations extended well into the Arctic, but lack of charts and restricted ice-free periods took a heavy toll of ships. During the Civil War the Confederate privateer *Shenandoah* captured and burned several vessels in Bering Strait. One incident involved the ship *Brunswick* which was caught in the icefloes. The nearby whaling ships that went to her aid were spotted by the raider and destroyed.

In the fall of 1871 a terrible disaster struck the whaling fleet. Off Point Belcher, 34 whaling ships were brutally crushed after their respective masters had refused to heed the warnings of the Eskimos to get out before the freeze. A change of wind from the southwest on September 2 trapped the bark *Comet* in the ice. Five days later the *Rowan* and the *Awashonka* were imperiled. By September 14, the entire fleet was endangered. In all, 1,219 whalermen, along with some women and children had to abandon their respective ships, and make their way over the ice-choked seas pushing and shoving the whale-boats when the ice was solid and rowing when they reached open waters. Under the direction of Captain D. E. Frazier of the whaler *Florida,* they made their way southward to Blossom Shoal where seven whaling ships, all that remained of the fleet lay at anchor.

The survivors were divided among the ships and transported to Honolulu to await passage back to New England.

That tragedy triggered the decline in the armada of Yankee whalers working the waters of the Far North. The northern ice jams crushed the barks *Eliza* in 1874 and the *Clara Belle* in 1876. The last disaster was in 1897-98 when four whaleships and a trading schooner were crushed in the Arctic ice, their stranded crews being rescued weeks later by the Revenue Cutter *Bear*.

During all that period there was not a single navigation aid of any kind to assist the victims.

Alaska shipwrecks that resulted in heavy loss of life in addition to the earlier mentioned *Princess Sophia* (343 lives), were the cannery sailing ship *Star of Bengal* wrecked off Coronation Island, September 20, 1908 with the loss of 111, mostly cannery workers; SS *Clara Nevada* which vanished off Eldred Rock claming 100 persons; the barkentine *Oneida* on Sanak Reef with 77 victims, plus numerous others with lesser losses of life.

Commercial codfishing, utilizing sizable schooners once flourished in Alaskan waters. Inasmuch as the Czar had previously discouraged American ships from such operations, the fleet consisted of only three in 1867, but with purchase of the territory, 14 entered the cod fishery the following year. Between 1877 and 1927, 29 codfish schooners were wrecked in Alaskan waters.

The advent of modern lighthouses, and later radar, radio beacons, Loran and depth finders somewhat abolished the heavy toll in ships, but annually, numerous smaller craft meet their Waterloo, mostly commercial fishing vessels. Among the more recent ship losses was that of the passenger steamer *Yukon* of the Alaska Steamship Company. She struck the rocks off Johnston Bay, 40 miles from Seward on February 3, 1946 claiming 11 lives. The vessel broke in two and there were some harrowing moments before the remainder of the passengers and crew could be rescued. On September 7, 1952, the $4 million Canadian Pacific passenger liner *Princess Kathleen* went to her grave after slipping off the reef at Lena Point. Excellent evacuation procedures saved the lives of the 400 passengers. The luxury Dutch cruise liner *Prinsendam* sank in deep water in the Gulf of Alaska in October 1980 after her capacity load of passengers were rescued.

With the exception of a few strandings, the Alaska State Ferry System has established an enviable record, and almost any officer in the fleet of blue-hulled vessels will give much credit to the splendid system of modern navigation aids both on ship and ashore that guide the sleek vessels through the intricate channels of the northern state.

The United States State Department in 1867 requested the Treasury Department to send the Revenue Cutter *Lincoln* into Alaskan waters to make a preliminary survey of the possession. George Davidson of the Coast Survey and eight aides were detailed to assist in determining the most valuable channels for commerce, to make a reconnaissance of the coast, and to inquire into the geographical and physical characteristics of the country. The results of the survey were evidently placed on the back burner for it was not till the spring of 1884, that the government finally appropriated funds for 14 unlighted iron buoys all of which were placed along the Inside Passage in southeastern Alaska. Nor did the gold rush really awaken Uncle Sam to the urgent need for navigation aids in the intricate waterway systems. Those struck by gold fever were little concerned about a crusade for legislation to safeguard Alaska's waterways, despite the heavy losses inflicted on commerce at that point in history.

During the excitement, Seattle and other Northwest ports turned into boom towns, vessels or every size and description sailing northward overloaded with passengers and cargo. Once they passed out of British Columbia waters there was nothing to guide them through the tortuous inside channels and offshore waterways but a few inferior unlighted buoys, and a single minor lighthouse, established in 1895,

*Wreck of the Alaska cruise liner **Princess Kathleen**, at Lena Point, Alaska, September 7, 1952. The more than 400 passengers were evacuated before the ship slipped off the reef and went down in deep water. A heavy rainfall and strong currents in Lynn Canal caused the vessel to get off course. She was one of the last three-stackers.*

*Another tragedy of the sea. The Alaska Steamship Company's 47 year old SS **Yukon** struck the jagged rocks off Johnston Bay, February 3, 1946, claiming the lives of 11 persons. The wreck was 40 miles southeast of Seward. There were 371 passengers aboard, some of which can be seen in lifejackets on the boat and promenade decks.*

The existing Five Finger Lighthouse built in 1935, replaced the pioneer structure. With Sentinel Island, it was the first lighthouse in Southeast Alaska, commissioned March 1, 1902. The station was the last to be be automated, the logo over the front door depicted in the inset. U.S. Coast Guard photo.

near the site of the old Russian sentinel at Sitka. It stood on a post at the top of Castle Hill with William Marrett appointed as its overseer. No other navigation lights were installed till after the turn of the century.

Not until 1900, did Congress appropriate $100,000 for lighthouses in Alaska, 11 of which were for the Inside Passage route and four for Southwestern Alaska, including one on the Bering Sea. In June 1901, the Lighthouse Board let a contract to build the first lighthouses, at Southeast Five Finger Islands and at Sentinel Island. It has always been debated which of the two was lighted first, but it would appear that the accepted light-up day for each was on March 1, 1902.

Southeast Five Finger Light Station was located in the northerly part of Frederick Sound. It was contracted for in July 1901 and completed late in January 1902, at a total cost of $22,500. The 49 foot frame tower rose from the southerly end of a two-story dwelling with a fog signal facility attached. The light was of the fourth order with a fixed white characteristic, and the fog warning device was a Daboll trumpet. A landing platform nearby accommodated tenders bringing in supplies and personnel.

In 1931, the station was fitted with a radio beacon, the sixth one to be erected in Alaska. Two years later, on December 8, 1933, while the lighthouse tender *Cedar* was landing supplies, the lighthouse and fog signal building suddenly burst into flames threatening everything on the reservation. Joined by the tender's crew, the keepers fought the

blaze, but all that could be saved was the boathouse and carpenter shop.

At a cost of $92,267, a new station constructed on 2.9 acres was commissioned on a nearby island in December 1935. Fire was the first thing in the minds of the lighthouse authorities, and to negate a recurrence of the earlier tragedy, the new structure was built of reinforced concrete and located on a concrete pier. The one-story building contained a square 68 foot tower displaying a fourth order electric light 81 feet above the water, and provided quarters for three keepers.

The station was the first in Alaska manned, and the last to be automated, personnel not leaving the premises until 1983, ending a colorful bit of Alaskan maritime history. The lighthouse gets serviced periodically by Coast Guard maintenance crews.

Sentinel Island Lighthouse marks the northerly end of Favorite Channel into Lynn Canal. Its builder was George James of Juneau who constructed the station on a bid of $21,267. The light was illuminated on March 1, 1902, the same time as its companion at Southeast Five Finger. The frame lighthouse and outbuildings had yet to be completed even after the light was officially illuminated, which is probably why Southeast Five Finger has always been claimed as Alaska's pioneer. Sentinel's beacon was a fourth order fixed white light displayed from a square 42 foot tower 82 feet above the water and was attached to a two-story dwelling with hipped cross gables.

Sentinel Island Lighthouse as pictured here was built and commissioned in 1935, replacing the 1902 structure. U.S. Coast Guard photo.

The fog signal building housed a third class Daboll trumpet.

In 1926, a new illuminating apparatus was installed upping the candlepower, and again, three years later, the illuminant was changed from acetylene to electricity. A radio beacon was installed at the same time.

Between 1933-35, a new reinforced concrete lighthouse replaced the former structure at a cost of $35,310. It consisted of a square tower rising above the roof of a two-story fog signal building. Automation came in 1966. The keeper's dwelling remained till 1971 and was then ordered burned down by the Coast Guard, leaving only the tower and fog signal building on the 6.55 acre reservation.

In 1910, Alaska was made a separate lighthouse district under a local inspector and a depot was constructed at Ketchikan. For the first time, a supply tender was not required to travel 1,000 miles from Puget Sound to service Southeastern Alaska lights. From 160 aids to navigation in 1910, Alaska boasted 329 five years later, all of which were lighted, due much in part to the usage of unattended acetylene gas beacons.

When the *Princes Sophia* foundered in 1918 at Vanderbilt Reef, the lighted buoy which was to have marked that reef was aboard the lighthouse tender *Cedar* en route to the area. Had the buoy been in place and operating, Alaska's worst marine calamity might have been averted.

On May 20, 1912, one of the largest and finest floating units of the U. S. Lighthouse Service, the lighthouse tender *Armeria* was wrecked while bringing coal and supplies to the newly established Cape Hinchinbrook Light Station. The vessel struck an uncharted rock and ripped open her hull a few miles from the lighthouse. Replacement cost of the tender was placed at $450,000.

Scotch Cap Lighthouse, the third sentinel lighted in Alaska, became a reality on June 18, 1903; it was also the first major lighthouse on the outside coast of the Great Land. Situated on the southwest end of Unimak Island it was considered one of the most isolated of American lighthouses. The winters were intolerable and the hardships legion, the initial keepers were soon to learn. But misery loves company and a year later, Cape Sarichef Light was established at the west end of the island, 17 miles from Scotch Cap. Those were the only two habitations on the lonely Aleutian Island, and the journey between the two installations was an adventure once undertaken, never forgotten. One keeper froze both his hands while traversing the rugged trail. He got lost in a snowstorm and had to be guided to his destination by a dog. Duty was so difficult that the early keepers were given a years vacation for every three years of duty.

Bids for the construction of the Scotch Cap station were opened on March 22, 1902, but all were rejected as excessive. As a result, the Lighthouse Board was compelled to purchase most of the construction materials and to hire day labor. On June 23, 1902, the steam

*The U.S. Lighthouse tender **Armeria** sliced her hull open on an uncharted rock near Cape Hinchinbrook while delivering coal and supplies to the station May 20, 1912. She became a total loss, the station keepers aiding in the rescue of the crew. The replacement value of the vessel was set at $450,000. Note the inverted ensign and distress signals flying.*

Two proud keepers of the Scotch Cap Lighthouse on desolate Unimak Island. The pioneer structure pictured at the far left was commissioned in the summer of 1903.

schooner *Homer* departed Seattle with 30 workers and a doctor. The construction period was restricted to the good weather months. Many difficulties ensued and the soaring costs undermined the budgeted funds.

The lighthouse was commissioned on July 18, 1903 at a total cost of $75,571. The lantern was fitted with a third order Fresnel, and the fog signal was a ten inch air whistle. Octagonal in shape, the tower rose from a one-story frame fog signal building with pyramidal roof. Focal plane of the beacon was 90 feet above the ocean and 35 feet above the ground. Southwestward of the tower were three keepers dwellings, a boat house and utility buildings.

At the entrance to Unimak Pass in the Aleutian chain, the strategically placed beacon was like an oasis in the desert to castaways from shipwrecks. Take the case of the cannery supply ship *Columbia,* wrecked on Unimak Island May 28, 1909. The survivors managed to

get to the rugged shoreline and then set out for the lighthouse. When the lighthouse keepers saw a string of 194 cannery workers and crew members descending on the station they wondered if the place was being turned into a hotel. Before they could be relieved of their guests, food supplies dwindled down to nothing and extra clothing had all been doled out. Finally a relief vessel arrived.

During World War II, the Russian freighter *Turksib* ran aground off Seal Cape after Captain Mashnikov made a navigation error. Outbound from Portland for Vladivostok, she carried 35 crewmen, including five women, none of whom spoke English. The lighthouse was nine miles away from the wreck. The USS *Rescuer,* a salvage vessel, was diverted to the scene in an effort to free the stricken vessel. Shortly after her arrival, a mighty 80 mile blizzard vented its wrath and the salvage vessel was shoved aground in the same watery plot as the Russian freighter. The hours that followed pitted men and women against the sea in an awesome battle for survival. Those who were on the beach or who managed to escape from the two wrecked ships began the nine mile journey to Scotch Cap. Among the casualties in the survival effort were Captain Mashnikof and a Russian seaman. Several others received injuries. With only the clothing on their backs, and many without shoes, they traversed the rugged terrain—60 survivors from the two ships, a blending of Russians and Americans. As a result of the stormy days that followed and rough sea conditions, the guests stayed on at the lighthouse for several weeks, and once again supplies ran extremely short, before a rescue ship arrived. Perhaps it was best that the Russian shipmaster perished with his ship, as in those Stalin years, a captain responsible for losing his command often faced the death penalty on return to the homeland.

The Japanese freighter *Koshun Maru* was wrecked in a snowstorm in 1930, directly below the lighthouse, as one writer put it, "with the Scotch Cap siren blowing in her ear." Its remains were demolished by the terrible seismic wave that wiped out the beacon on April 1, 1946.

Several improvements were made at the station during its active years, including the installation of radiotelephone facilities in 1923, and seven years later a radio beacon was erected. Between 1938-40, at a cost of $150,000 Scotch Cap got a whole new look with the

Tragedy personified, occurred when the Scotch Cap Lighthouse was completely demolished by a devil seismic tidal wave on April Fools Day in 1946, killing all five of the Coast Guard attendants. The rugged, concrete reinforced structure, only six years old, was located about 70 feet above normal water and was struck with such force as to literally pulverize the building and all its contents. It was Alaska's worst lighthouse tragedy. U.S. Coast Guard photo.

construction of a reinforced concrete lighthouse and fog signal building plus a concrete sea wall. unfortunately, it was that formidable structure that was violently torn from its foundation by the giant wave that claimed the lives of the five Coast Guardsmen, Colvin, Dykstra, Petit, Pickering and Ness in that regrettable tragedy on April Fool's day in 1946.

Following the disaster, a temporary unwatched light was displayed from a small white house, and a radio beacon installed. A new lighthouse and fog signal installation was completed in 1950 at a higher elevation than that of the ill-fated sentinel. The one-story concrete structure displayed a revolving electric light of 240,000 candlepower, 116 feet above the water.

In 1971, lighthouse personnel were removed and the station automated. Seven years later, the Scotch Cap beacon was reduced to a light atop a skeleton tower with a diamond shaped daymark, and the fog signal discontinued. The original lighthouse reservation in the early 1900's consisted of 8,852 acres, probably the largest tract of land ever set aside for an aid to navigation in North America.

Mary Island Light Station became the fourth major lighthouse commissioned in Alaska. Located north of Revillagigedo Channel, south of Ketchikan, it was the earlier site of a customs house in 1892.

Because of the customs installations, funds of $80,000 were requested for a lighthouse on the island in 1894 with the hope that it could be watched over by the Customs employees for an annual stipend of $800 per annum. Congress however, refused to recommend the funding, and the plan fell flat.

After gold was discovered, the government reconsidered Mary Island for a lighthouse and authorized the station. Further delays put back the awarding of the contract till April 11, 1902. The builders did not complete the project until July 31, 1903, although the light was first displayed on July 15. The station consisted of a one-story octagonal fog signal building with a pyramidal roof surmounted by a 45 foot octagonal tower and lantern house. A fourth order Fresnel was displayed 67 feet above the water and a third class Daboll was the noise maker. Spacious dwellings, a boathouse, carhouse and derrick were also provided. A radio beacon was installed in 1931.

Because most of the early Alaska lighthouses were of frame construction their years of service were relatively short. Severe weather, isolation and the threat of fire were three reasons why most were replaced in later years. The Mary Island Lighthouse succumbed to a concrete reinforced successor built between 1936 and 1938 at a cost of $54,792. It was an impressive tower, 61 feet high, atop a building

The third Scotch Cap lighthouse was built in 1950 at a higher location. Coast Guard photo.

Mary Island Lighthouse is another of the stout concrete structures on Alaska's inside route. It was commissioned in 1938 replacing the 1903 lighthouse. U.S. Coast Guard photo.

Lincoln Rocks Light Station had a turbulent history, the original contractor having lost his barge filled with materials to build the lighthouse. Its services were discontinued in 1968. U.S. Coast Guard photo.

that housed all the machinery for the station needs including air compressors, electric generators and radio beacon transmitters. Other features were a boathouse, tramway, cisterns and three smaller utility structures, all of which were connected by cement walks.

Located on 198 acres of land, the station, bowing to progress, was automated in 1968.

Lincoln Rocks Light Station, at the west end of Clarence Strait was activated December 1, 1903, but it got started on a bad note. The lone bidder was awarded the job, but while en route to the site in rough waters lost both the barge laden with lumber and the small steamer towing it. Down but not out he reconnoitered and landed with his materials in the spring of 1902. Unusual summer storms hampered progress and then making matters worse, the lighthouse inspector accused the builder of using substandard materials which resulted in cancellation of the contract. The Lighthouse District was forced to hire day labor and it was the end of 1903 before the project was completed.

The station included a two-story dwelling on a concrete pier with a 41 foot tower at the southerly corner, housing a fourth order Fresnel with a fixed white characteristic. A Daboll trumpet was provided as a fog signal. With the rock on which the beacon stood virtually submerged at high water, a cutwater was erected on the south side of the pier to break up high waves and keep them from striking the lighthouse. Its purpose was negated, however, for several months after the station was commissioned breaking seas carried away the landing platform and derrick. The precarious position of the lighthouse permitted major damage by the seas on November 28, 1909 and again on April 14, 1910. The latter storm almost destroyed the lighthouse necessitating the setting up of an auxiliary light, and the evacuation of the keepers on the U. S. Army vessel *Peterson*. The station was damaged to such an extent that it had to be rebuilt and

relocated in March 1911. Congress authorized funds not to exceed $25,000, which meant the installation would be reduced in status. A fog signal was erected on a small offshore rock 440 yards from the lighthouse. The new light was a secondary acetylene fixture. The project was completed on October 10, 1911 and the builder was credited with some sharp figuring, the total cost amounting to $24,774.

In 1968, the curtain closed with removal of personnel and the closure of the station. Lincoln Rock West Light was established in 1961 and was considered sufficiently effective to eliminate the former navigation aid. It shines from a skeleton tower on a concrete base 58 feet above the water.

Early in 1970, Coast Guardsman Jake Boggis cleaned, polished and oiled the Tree Point fourth order eight bullseye Fresnel and lighting apparatus so that Captain Richard Hagadorn could officially present it to the Ketchikan Museum. It had served Tree Point Lighthouse from its inception April 30, 1904 until decommissioning on January 30, 1970. On that date the station was automated and reduced to a secondary aid to navigation.

Located at the south entrance to Revillagigedo Channel, (Alaska's most southerly lighthouse) Tree Point Lighthouse construction was begun with hired labor April 24, 1903 and was not completed until April 30, 1904. Two weeks after commissioning, the station suffered a flash fire which demanded several repairs before normal operations could continue. More and more it was realized the mistake of building the early Alaska lighthouses of wood instead of masonry.

Situated on a 1,207 acre reservation, the Tree Point station was considered vital to the increasing marine traffic traversing the Inside Passage and was accordingly equipped with a third order lens displaying a fixed white light with a red sector covering jagged Lord Rocks. The fog signal was a first class air siren. Designed similar to

Tree Point Lighthouse was first lighted April 30, 1904 and was replaced by this concrete structure in 1935. The station was reduced to a minor light in 1969. U.S. Coast Guard photo.

Isolated Cape Sarichef Light Station as it appeared in 1948 on the rock slopes of western Unimak Island. The station was established in July 1904 and was so isolated the lighthouse inspector refused to let families live there, two of the dwellings going unused.

other early Alaska lighthouses, it was a one-story wooden octagonal building with pyramidal roof and a 56 foot octagonal tower displaying its light 86 feet above the water.

Modernization of Alaskan navigation aids by the Bureau of Lighthouses reached Tree Point in 1933, the old structure being replaced by a reinforced 58 foot concrete tower and one-story fog signal building with space for all the station equipment, including a 5,000 gallon fuel oil tank, coal bin and battery storage. The lighthouse is still vital as the first seen by ships sailing northward and the last seen by those going southward on Alaska's Inside Passage.

The Russians called Unimak Island "The Roof of Hell," for around it they witnessed smoking volcanic peaks and felt the ground tremble in the early occupation years. Cape Sarichef lighthouse was the seventh to be erected in Alaska and was lighted on July 1, 1904. Considered one of the most desolate spots in the world, and the nation's most westerly sentinel, it was the only major American lighthouse situated on the Bering Sea. When ice choked the seas during the winter, the light was extinguished, for no traffic could move through the offshore waters. Supplies of food, mail and fuel were sometimes months in coming in the early years, and keepers were subjected to total separation from the outside world. There was one period when no boat arrived for ten months. Even when vessels did arrive, landing conditions were often perilous. Supply tenders came only once or twice a year in the early part of the century.

When the station was constructed it included three spacious dwellings, but two stood vacant after the government inspector decided the place was so isolated that neither wives nor children would be permitted.

Many years ago, 27 year old third assistant keeper Ted Pedersen became woman struck. He had not seen one of the opposite sex for

many long, weary months. One morning, a passing steamer anchored off the station during the summer and a boat was lowered and rowed to the landing carrying a young, attractive lady passenger. The keeper was so taken by her presence that he just stood gaping at her while she did all the talking. He wanted to beg her to stay, but no words came forth from his mouth. After a few minutes of one-sided conversation she shoved a piece of paper in his hand and was rowed back to the steamer. When Pedersen finally came to his senses he discovered the slip of paper was a receipt. The lady, a magazine sales agent, had sold him a dozen different subscriptions.

The same old faces and the same old climes often got to the keepers. The lighthouse was on a reservation of 1,845 acres, but they were barren, rugged and often raked by freezing winds. The only other habitation on the island was Scotch Cap Lighthouse, and once in a great while a keeper would risk the 17 mile trek over the brutish land mass for a visit. One assistant keeper, Lee Harpole, by name, overcome by loneliness was driven to make a visit to the companion lighthouse just to see a few different faces. He attempted the hike in late spring with the snows still on much of the ground. After nine bitter miles, he came to a swollen stream, fringed with ice. The temptation was to turn back, but being about half-way to his destination he decided he would press on. But how to cross the stream? Hands and feet already numbed by the sub-Arctic cold, he quickly peeled off his clothes down to his long Johns, rolled them in a bundle and then tied them together. He intended to throw them across the 20 foot stream, traverse the chilling water, dry off on the other side and then put the dry clothes back on.

With a mighty heave he threw the parcel toward the opposite shore but it fell short, dropped into the icy waters and was carried away by the swift current. Knowing that he could freeze to death without

Cape Sarichef Lighthouse in a land the Russians labled as, "the roof of hell,," in bygone ages lives on in solitude, its navigtion light today shining from a pole.

protection, he quickly dived into the stream and swam after the bundle. The blood seemed to freeze in his veins as he watched the apparel vanish from sight. Struggling up on the other side, blue with cold, he was yet several miles from Scotch Cap and an almost equal number of miles from Cape Sarichef. Clad only in his dripping underwear and a cap that had managed to stay on his head, he had no choice but to start running barefooted over the tortuous trail all the way to Scotch Cap. An eternity later, his underwear half ripped off and feet cut and bleeding, he reached his destination. When the attendants got the man inside the dwelling he could hardly speak, so they wrapped him in blankets and poured hot coffee down his gullet. It took hours to get Harpole back to his normal composure.

Behind the old Sarichef station is "Graveyard Hill." Buried there is a keeper who died in 1918. A storm came up the day the tender arrived to transport him to a hospital. When a boat was sent ashore to pick him up, it was swamped in tempestuous seas near the landing and all nine of its occupants were drowned. Later, the ailing keeper died without ever having left the island.

On another occasion an attendant had to be removed from the station in a deep mental depression. Cowering and gibbering about ghosts of Aleuts slain by Russian hunters, he never again returned to the lonely outpost.

Of the many gales and blizzards that struck the station, none was more severe than that of Christmas Eve, December 24, 1914. William J. Parson, first assistant keeper afforded the following report:

> On the 24th of December we had a very heavy southeast gale with a terrific sea running on the beach. It continued running heavy and kept increasing in fury until 10 minutes to 7 in the morning of the 25th a tremendous sea swept up past the houses up onto the cement sidewalk and smashed the outer storm door and the inner glass door all to splinters, and flooded the storeroom, cellar, dining room, kitchen and pantry, the water being waist deep in the house (126 feet above the sea). I am glad to report that there is no loss to the rations, as I had made a table and put up a set of shelves in the storeroom, so the rations were out of the way of the water, with the exception of 200 pounds of half-ground salt. The biggest part of the salt is gone and a dead loss, as sand, rocks, grass and moss were strewn so thick we had to scoop it out of the rooms.

Two survivors from the wreck of the schooner *Gladiator* once walked 18 miles to reach the lighthouse, first going one way and then the other in an attempt to find the station. They left their ailing skipper on the wreck as he was too weak to make the trek. The keepers then radioed the Coast Guard to send a rescue craft to pick up the castaway. Responding, the cutter *Chelan* arrived a considerable time later, but the surf was so high that the boat sent in to pick up the

individual capsized throwing its 11 volunteers into the breakers. All struggled up on the beach but the craft was beyond repair and there was no way of returning to the cutter. Instead of one, there were now 12 disheveled men waiting rescue. By wigwag signals from the beach and radio contact between the ship and the lighthouse, it was determined their only hope of survival was an old trappers cabin a few miles away. Supporting the *Gladiator's* suffering skipper, a few hours later the Coast Guardsmen located the battered shack which afforded temporary shelter but produced no food or fuel. Attempting to keep warm they mixed rain water with the alcohol from the wreck's salvaged compass, and distributed the vile tasting liquid among them. After a miserable night they set out for the lighthouse, and though bruised and battered all made it and recovered from the ordeal.

For several days the *Chelan* stood off the lighthouse waiting for the seas to moderate sufficiently to send in a boat for the 14 men.

After nearly ten days, the light keepers decided to use the station dory to run the survivors out to the cutter. Only a couple could be accomodated at a time, and it took several trips back and forth, but the lighthouse personnel proved adept at handling the boat in difficult sea conditions and finally succeeded in delivering all 14 without a mishap.

When the proposed lighthouse at Sarichef was ripe for construction in March of 1902, the bids were all so high that it was decided to hire labor. The station was completed on October 1, 1903, but the lighting apparatus had not yet arrived so the workers departed and returned again in May 1904 to install the light and put the finishing touches on the station buildings. The light was illuminated on July 1, 1904, a third order fixed Fresnel. The overall cost of the a station was $80,000 including the first class automatic fog siren. During the first year of operation, the boathouse, engine house and derrick, located on a reef southwest of the tower were so badly damaged by encroaching seas they had to be replaced. The lighthouse was located 126 feet above the water, well out of the reach of the rampaging seas.

Ironically, the station was not a victim of the devastating 1946 seismic waves that destroyed Scotch Cap Lighthouse, but only by a fluke of nature. Still the government wanted to take no chances and relocated the station at an elevation of 177 feet above the unpredictable sea, replacing the aging wooden sentinel with a reinforced concrete tower, fog signal building and a modern radio beacon. The new light was illuminated in 1950. However, time changes things and today the station buildings are utilized during the favorable months by the other government agencies and the navigation light is perched atop a skeleton tower installed in 1979, 170 feet above the water.

Under the 13th Lighthouse District, a light station was recommended on 298 acres of land at Fairway Island, just inside the easterly entrance to Peril Strait in 1900. It was lighted on September 1, 1904 displaying a lens-lantern from a wooden hexagonal tower, one of Alaska's early minor lights. The tower, if it could be referred to as such, was only six feet high, but stood 41 feet above the water. A one and a half story dwelling was provided for the keeper.

The history of the station is rather sketchy as it dropped out of the *Light List* between 1917 and 1925, during a period when effective unmanned stake lights were established in Peril Strait.

In 1943, Fairway Island Light 32, was placed on an abandoned dwelling at the north end of the island showing a flashing red light, but the original station seemed to have gradually faded away.

Would you believe that the gripe of Coast Guardsmen attending Guard Islands Light Station in the mid-1960's was that they were fed up with juicy T-bone steaks? Said one of the attendants, "They've fixed 'em broiled, grilled, simmered, planked, fried, in sandwiches, boiled in butter sauce, swissed, gay with garlic, dressed up with dressing, for breakfast with eggs, sided with onions, lavished with mushrooms—in fact, about every way except smothered with pork chops."

Guard Islands Lighthouse established in late summer 1904 was replaced by this unique little lighthouse and fog signal building in 1924. Today only a low blockhouse-like navigation aid remains on the reservation. U.S. Coast Guard photo.

Some kind of mistake was made in the ordering of food for the station and when the supplies arrived by boat it was heavily imbalanced with top grade steer meat. Instead of living high on the hog all they did was "beef," when in the beginning they would have gladly accepted a good ol' American hamburger.

Their grievous problem was solved a few years later when the station was automated.

Located far from the lights of Ketchikan, Guard Islands Light Station had the reputation of one of the wettest spots on the west coast, in fact, rain supplied nearly all of the 21 million gallons required during the station's residency years.

One of the island's well-known mascots was "Wickie," better known as "Wacky Wickie," a small deer. As a fawn in 1966, she was found wandering in the Alaska wilderness by a hunter who presented her to the lonely station attendants. Wickie's best friend and protector was fireman Daniel Young of Anchorage. The two dogs at the station were slow to accept the intruder and when they finally did, the doe had no compulsions about giving them a swift kick if they played too rough. The curious animal often found herself in precarious situations such as standing next to the men during rifle practice or getting in front of the tramway cart that carried supplies up from the landing.

The name Wickie was a natural. Lighthouse keepers from olden times have been labeled as lamp lighters or wick tenders, and from the latter evolved the name "Wickie." The deer slept at the foot of Young's bunk and romped with him wherever he went. There was only one protester, the officer-in-charge, Boatswain's Mate Donald Webb who complained, "I wish someone would tell us how to housebreak an Alaska deer."

Located on the largest of two islands, Guard Islands Light Station marked the easterly entrance to Tongass Narrows. Hired labor constructed the station in the summer of 1903, but adverse winter weather put a halt to operations and it was not until June of the following year that work was resumed. The light was not officially commissioned until September 15, 1904, a lens-lantern atop a square frame tower 34 feet above the ground and 79 feet above the water. It was one of the few Alaska stations fitted with a fogbell which was activated by machinery at the northern face of the light tower.

In 1923-24, a reinforced concrete tower and fog signal building replaced the former facility, and a second keeper's dwelling was installed. Total cost of the new station was $46,586. In 1938-39, a radio beacon and radio-telephones were added to the equipment, and in 1956 the radio beacon was modified to accommodate both marine and air traffic. A decade later the station was automated. Today a flashing white light installed above the rectangular building, along with a radio beacon and a special direction finder calibration facility, gives the station an important role in Alaska marine navigation.

Point Retreat Lighthouse on the northerly point of Mansfield Peninsula, Admiralty Island, was the tenth major light station constructed by the government in Alaska. It was established on a 1,505 acre reservation on September 15, 1904, displaying a lens-lantern from a black, hexagonal lantern house set on a six foot hexagonal tower. Two dwellings were constructed for the keepers, but one burned down shortly after the station was activated.

Before America's entry into World War I, Point Retreat was divested of personnel and downgraded to a minor facility. However, a

*The U.S. Lighthouse tender **Rose** saw considerable service in Alaskan waters as well as along the coasts of Washington and Oregon. Borchers photo.*

Point Retreat is shown here with a revolving reflecting beacon atop the tower. A light first marked the point in the summer of 1904, and the station was updated with new buildings in 1924. U.S. Coast Guard photo.

need for more reliable safeguards brought about the rejuvenation of the station in 1923-24 with the construction of a reinforced concrete light tower and fog signal building, located 63 feet above the water. All the outbuildings, dwellings for two families, a landing wharf, derrick, hoist, cisterns, (chiseled out of solid rock) and boathouse were all included in the contract and the total price was $58,242. Later, a radio beacon was added to the station.

Resident personnel remained until 1973 when automation came, which reduced the aid to a minor light with a battery operated fog signal.

One of the last of the watched minor light installations in southeastern Alaska was established at Point Sherman on October 18, 1904, a short hexagonal tower with lens-lantern. The dwelling was a frame building, the station surrounded by 600 feet of fencing. Though records are vague, the original station was abandoned in 1932, but most of the buildings remained. The point today is marked by a light atop a skeleton tower established in 1981 to facilitate marine traffic in Lynn Canal.

"Cheaper by the dozen," goes the old saying. Number twelve beacon erected in Alaska by the old Lighthouse Service was at Eldred Rock, an islet at the northern portion of Lynn Canal. Nearly all marine traffic traveling the Inside Passage is familiar with the lighthouse. Melancholy in appearance since automation in 1973, it sits like a pauper's castle awaiting the return of the human element.

Eldred Rock was the last of a series of lighthouses constructed in Alaska between the years 1902-06. Built with hired labor, the construction period was often hampered by adverse weather conditions and was not completed until June 1, 1906, seven months behind schedule. Fitted with a fourth order lens, the oil flame producing 2,100 candlepower, the light was displayed from an octagonal tower atop a two-story fog signal building which additionally included the keepers quarters. Unlike its sister lighthouses, Eldred Rock was built of concrete on its lower half and wood on the upper, an unusual

departure from the established practice. It paid off, for Eldred Rock was one of the only original stations that did not have to be replaced. The tower was 56 feet high, and the focal plane 91 feet above the water. The fog signal was a first class automatic siren. Other station facilities included a boathouse, tramway and derrick, plus a boat landing.

Frequently the subject of cameras among cruise ship passengers, the structure appears to be an empty relic of the past, but its beacon is still performing, the present light showing a higher intensity beam up Chilkoot Inlet and down Lynn Canal.

The real estate on which the lighthouse stands is 2.4 acres of rocky terrain with bits of grass and bracken. From a distance it appears cradled below the tall coastal range of mountains, but is a unique little islet that is an entity unto itself. Automation came in 1973 when Coast Guard personnel lowered the colors and waved farewell.

Lighthouse keepers at Cape Hinchinbrook were often referred to as "Cliff Dwellers," their edifice located high above the sea, featuring a beacon visible 22 miles with a power of 200,000 candles. The station was, and remains the highest major marine navigation light in Alaska. Nearby rises basaltic hills reaching 1,400 feet. The focal plane of the light is 235 feet above the water on the southwest point at the eastern side of Hinchinbrook at the entrance to Prince William Sound. In the days before automation all supplies and transfer of personnel was by derrick boom 150 feet above the rock-littered beach.

Some years back when Coast Guardsmen were still resident at the lighthouse, the icebreaker *Northwind* hove to en route the Arctic to drop off supplies for the attendants. Twenty-two officers and men came ashore by boat to visit the lighthouse and its keepers. Before they could return to their ship, the seas got so rough that they were forced to remain at the lighthouse for two days.

It was a hard station, lonely, isolated and demanding. Sometimes the confinement got to the men, especially during the reign of the Lighthouse Service when tours of duty were far longer than under the

Eldred Rock Light was illuminated in 1906, and is one of the few early Alaska lighthouses that did not have to be replaced. With an octagonal tower and main building it smacks of early Russian architecture. U.S. Coast Guard photo.

Cape Hinchinbrook light keepers were referred to as cliff dwellers, due to the high location of the lighthouse. The inset shows the first light on Hinchinbrook, a lens-lantern predating the inauguration of the first lighthouse in the fall of 1910. The large Coast Guard photo is the existing lighthouse built in 1934, an ornate reinforced concrete structure. The previous tower, considered one of the finest in Alaska, was threatened with erosion.

Coast Guard. An example of what can happen under trying conditions was revealed by a lighthouse inspector several years ago. When he paid his annual visit to the station he found that the three keepers were all refusing to converse with one another. In fact, they hadn't spoken to each other for months, performing their duties in total silence.

It all started when one of them desired his potatoes fried and the other insisted they be mashed. When the third, the pincipal keeper attempted to settle the squabble and bring about a culinary truce, a second argument erupted over a missing ring. Again the peacemaker stepped in, but his time got overly involved, and, as a result all three were estranged, for six long months, each performing his duties and his turn at cooking in solitary. The only sounds at the dinner table were the crunching of food and the slurping of coffee.

Such unfortunate incidents frequently led to requests for transfer, vented anger, vengeful acts and in some cases mental instability.

As the only major beacon in south central Alaska, situated at a pivotal point for shipping, Hinchinbrook was first recommended for a navigation aid in 1900, spurred on by the wreck of the SS *Oregon*. Although $125,000 was appropriated in 1906, a stubborn Congress did not release the full amount, but doled it out in segments, $25,000 in 1906 and $50,000 the following year. The remainder was not released until 1908. A. B. Lewis, a Seattle contractor was the successful bidder and commenced work in the spring of 1909. A crew of 40 men were employed to build what residents of Cordova claimed would be the finest and most expensive lighthouse in Alaska. The weather, however, failed to cooperate and a scow filled with lumber and building materials was swept away in heavy seas. It came ashore on the beach at Montague Island where it was discovered by two Indians, Willie Johnson and Johnny Paul. Most of the material was recovered.

In September 1909, work was halted for the year as the howling northerlies set in. Only the tramway from the wharf and the concrete walls of the main buildings to the first story had been completed. A keeper and his wife were assigned to remain on the scene to operate a temporary fixed light on the unfinished structure until work could be resumed.

By June of 1910, 30 laborers were back on the job, and C. W. Leick, a name with which we are already familiar, then chief draftsman for Alaska, was called in as an overseer. He gave the project an excellent report. By November 15, 1910, the station was completed and the permanent beacon, a third order lens and lighting apparatus were put into service, producing 20,000 candlepower with an oil flame.

The octagonal tower of concrete rose above the center of the main building and supported a cast iron deck and first order vertical bar lantern house, 12 feet in diameter and 18 feet high with large panes of plate glass. The tower was 47 feet from ground level and the light 235 feet above sea level. The fog signal unit was attached to one side of the main building, the air sirens powered by two coal oil engines and an air compressor. The self-contained station house additionally contained comfortable quarters for four keepers, sitting room, dining room, kitchen and pantry. Hot water heat was provided and there was a 15,000 gallon cistern. The total package including utility out-buildings cost $100,323, well under the estimated cost, and was one of Alaska's prime lighthouses. Station equipment included a large derrick for hoisting boats and personnel up the steep cliff and a tramway from the mouth of Lennon Creek to the lighthouse. Later, the Forest Service hacked out a six mile trail between the sentinel and the protected waters of English Bay at Port Etches, where emergency landings were possible.

As mentioned earlier, the lighthouse tender *Armeria* while delivering coal and supplies to the station struck an uncharted rock off the cape in 1912 and had to be abandoned as a total loss. The Hinchinbrook keepers aided in the rescue of the vessel's crew.

The derrick and derrick house above the beach at Cape Hinchinbrook with scores of fuel-laden drums brought into the station by the ice-breaker **Northwind** *in 1950. When sudden high winds arose, the visitors from the cutter were forced to remain at the station overnight. Coast Guard photo.*

In the beginning, the light and fog signal were invaluable to ships carrying ore from the copper mines at Kennecott; to tugs and barges and to commercial fishing craft that frequented the surrounding bountiful waters during the summer and fall.

In 1922, the station was provided with a powerful diaphone fog signal.

On the debit side of the register, the so-called indestructible, self-contained Alaska lighthouse, became a victim of earthquake action in 1927-28, which proved once again that nothing made at the hands of man can stand against the acts of God. The 180 foot cliff on which the lighthouse stood began to cave in bit by bit endangering the building. It was thus decided by the authorities that a new lighthouse would have to be built at a safer location. Though threatened, the old tower remained in operation until its successor was completed in 1934 at a cost of $91,793. It was located 130 feet from the former site and everything was of reinforced concrete, featuring a square tower projecting upward 67 feet, displaying the former third order lens with a new electric lighting system. The base of the main building was 44 by 54 feet and the structure was finished in weather resistant Medusa paint. Beautifully designed, the structure had a regal appearance and was bolted solidly into the natural rock formation.

Automation came in 1974, and the 5,000 acre reservation became a quiet, lonely place as it was before the era of the lighthouse. A light, foghorn and radio beacon are still functioning at the unmanned station.

After considerable agitation, a light station was finally approved for Cape St. Elias. A sum of $115,000 was set aside for the project on October 22, 1913. In a backwater out of the world place, it took its name from Mt. St. Elias named by Vitus Bering in July 1714. The cape was considered one of the most dangerous coastlines in Alaska. Earlier plans for a lightship were rejected in favor of a beacon, and the location chosen was at the south end of Kayak Island, a mutilated tract of rock off the mainland. A temporary gas lighted buoy marked the site in 1914, and as survey work got underway that year, an acetylene blinker light was established. Lighthouse construction commenced in the spring of 1915 and after arduous months of work disturbed by frequent delays, the lamp was lit for the first time on September 16, 1916. At the same time, a 13 ton buoy with acetylene blinker, whistle and submarine bell was anchored off Southeast Rock.

The 55 foot high 12 by 12 foot tower and accompanying fog signal building were the pride of the service. The Fresnel and fog apparatus, prior to installation at the lighthouse, were put on exhibit at the Panama Pacific International Exposition at San Francisco. Adding prestige to the station, the U. S. Signal Corps placed wireless equipment there and trained the keepers in its usage.

In 1927, Alaska's second radio beacon was installed there, and for an outpost lighthouse, it was well endowed with everything then available to safeguard the waterways.

Automation came in the summer of 1974, but the spledid structure remains in tact with its light, foghorn and radio beacon.

In 1964, Frank Reed, a homesick Coast Guardsman stationed at the Cape St. Elias "hermitage," wrote a letter to the Armed Forces Radio Station requesting a record dedication to his three associates, two mascot dogs and himself. He asked them to play, *I Want To Go Home—Detroit City.* Unfortunately he never got to hear the disc spun, nor did he ever get to go back home to Detroit City. The letter was written March 26, and slightly over 24 hours later, Reed was carried to his death by a giant seismic tidal wave that swept the lower portion of the lighthouse reservation, spawned by the Good Friday Alaska earthquake.

After learning of the tragedy, Sergeant Ervin C. Elswick, MC of the country music program at the Armed Forces station at Elmendorff Air Force Base, played the request for Reed posthumously, for his lamenting buddies and dogs, Wolf and Midnight.

"We hope somehow, somewhere, Frank is listening," said Elswick and then he spun the record.

Earthquakes and giant waves are common occurrences in southwestern Alaska, such deep—rooted upheavals often shaking and shifting the land and sometimes exacting heavy tolls in lives and property. Though struck by tremors many times, Cape St. Elias holds firm, continuing its vigil in seclusion.

Former keepers and attendants of the outside Alaska light stations each claimed to have the most forlorn and forgotten edifices, but Rear Admiral C. C. Knapp, former commander of the Coast Guard's Western Area, nominated Cape Spencer Light for that claim. On his visit there in 1964 he insisted that it was the most isolated station in Alaska. To get to the lighthouse he had to board a plane at a small landing strip in Gustavus, population 75, counting pets. Next he boarded a Coast Guard cutter, the *Sweetbriar* for a three-hour run to the cape. The cutter anchored in the lee of awesome offshore rocks after which the admiral boarded a 25 foot supply boat to run the surf. While the craft pitched and rolled beneath him, he clambered into a basket at the end of a hoist and was lifted 70 feet to a platform from whence he walked the remainder of the way to the lighthouse.

Despite his rank, the officer thereafter showed a much greater respect and appreciation for the four lonely men who tended the light. No television reception was then available, nor had the station ever been visited by a woman or child. During the Admiral's visit, the skipper of the *Sweetbriar,* quipped, "If any man figures how to get his wife or girlfriend to this rock he ought to be promoted and given a transfer." The Admiral agreed.

In 1968, Coast Guard 17th District Headquarters at Juneau proposed that all Alaska light stations be converted to automatic operation, and not suprisingly, Cape Spencer was first on the list.

At the entrance to Cross Sound, the cape was first lighted in 1913 with a small unwatched acetylene beacon, 90 feet above the water. Though there had been recommendations and outright demands for a lighthouse in the remote spot since 1906, funds were not authorized for the lighthouse until 1923. Construction began in May 1924 and was completed December 11, 1925 as bitter winds howled over the outpost, leaving no tears in the eyes of the departing construction crew. Total cost of the lighthouse was $174,881. The beacon was situated on the outermost large islet south of the cape, the tower rising 25 feet above the main building all of which was built of concrete heavily reinforced. Everything was housed within the one structure with the exception of the two hoist houses, a blacksmith shop, derrick, tramway and landing platform. The flashing light sent out 110,000 candles of power. A radio beacon was added in 1926 with a range of 200 miles.

Though automated in 1974, the lighthouse is still very important to commerce, the light, foghorn and radio beacon in full operation. Probably none of its former attendants had serious regrets over their excommunication from the 3,840 acre reservation, nor life within the concrete walls of the domicile.

Cape Decision Light on the extreme southern tip of Kuiu Island mid-way along the Alaska panhandle, was officially commissioned March 15, 1932, although a temporary light was on the cape two years earlier and during the period of construction. The lighthouse was the last built in Alaska under the old Lighthouse Service.

When the Coast Guard assumed responsibility for the beacon it assigned men to the station who soon found their life was one of isolation, hostile shores, jagged mountains and unpredictable weather. There were only two ways to gain access to Cape Decision Light. The usual method was by sea, landing by derrick and hoist and ascending a ladder at the opposite end of a horseshoe-shaped causeway. The other, when the weather behaved, was a very difficult 31 mile hike from the small village of Port McArthur. Not much of a choice.

Before automation came to the friendless station in 1974, off duty hours found the attendants pursuing such hobbies as painting, guitar strumming, fishing, hunting, cribbage or rough-housing with the station's mascot Bourbon—a frisky 95 pound Boxer. Each tour of duty was 12 months, and there was no television.

Cape Decision's 40 foot reinforced concrete tower rises from a flat-roofed building which housed the keepers of the light. Focal plane of the beacon was 96 feet above the sea. When a mechanical malfunction occurred at a station such as Decision, and the attendants were unable to make repairs, maintenance experts stoodby at the base in Ketchikan on 24 hour alert to move to the trouble spot by ship or by plane.

Situated on a lighthouse reservation encompassing 216 acres set aside for the sentinel in July 1929, Cape Decision Lighthouse played a special role in serving shipping catering to salmon canneries, herring salteries and reduction plants on the shores of Chatham Strait, Sumner Strait and Prince of Wales Island in the 1930's. Congress appropriated $59,400 for the project in 1929, but that was far short of the money needed. Thus much of the work was delayed and additionally, the weather was uncorporative. As a result it wasn't until March 15, 1932 that the lighthouse was commissioned at a total cost of $158,000. A flashing electric light of 350,000 candlepower and a first class fog signal featuring two Tyfon horns plus a Class A radio beacon, equipped the station with the latest technology in pharology.

Cape Decision became the last of Alaska's 16 major lighthouses constructed between 1902 and 1932, an era of great activity and changes in safeguarding the intricate waterways of the Great Land.

One might properly ask why a state the size of Alaska has so few major lighthouses. Early in the century, Dr. Henry S. Pritchett, a Lighthouse Board member encouraged his associates as well as the

Cape St. Elias Lighthouse in a pictu-resque setting opposite mammoth Pinnacle Rock, 1,800 feet high. Eagles nest at its peak, sea lions frolick around its base and at low tide one can walk there from the lighthouse. This lighthouse was established in 1916 along what was considered one of the most dangerous sections of the Alaska coastline. The station was automated in 1974. U.S. Coast Guard photo.

*Cape St. Elias lighthouse just after completion. Note the unusual temporarily mounted fog trumpets. A lighted buoy was to have been placed off the station before the construction period but it was lost with the wreck of the **Armeria** at Cape Hinchinbrook.*

This Coast Guard aerial view of the Cape Spencer station tells the story of its isolated role, set apart from the world.

Cape Spencer Lighthouse, in a very isolated sector of Alaska was commissioned in December 1925 and automated in 1974. The original buildings still stand in the rock-strewn setting. U.S. Coast Guard photo.

Cape Decision Lighthouse, the last major sentinel erected in Alaska was not completed until 1932, after several protracted delays. It was manned until 1974 and was then automated, its buildings remained at this writing. U.S. Coast Guard photo.

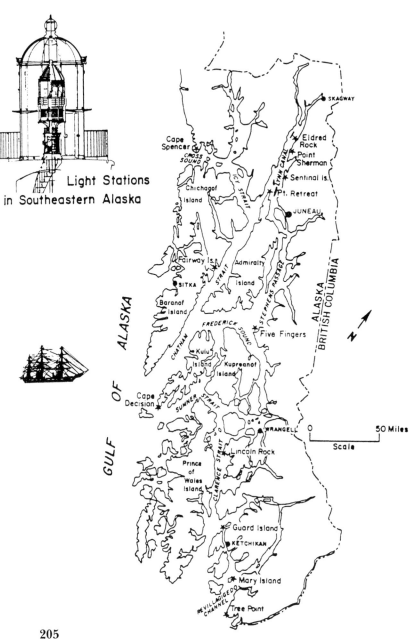

Light Stations in Southeastern Alaska

solons in Washington, D.C., to consider the cost and dangers associated with manning and supplying isolated Alaska light stations. He cited inclement weather and perilous waters and urged the increased use of unmanned acetylene buoys and beacons over costly, fully-manned lighthouses. In the long run tht far-sighted individual proved his point, for such equipment could and did operate for months without servicing and was widely used in sections of Alaska. But in all fairness, it should be pointed out that resident stations before the advent of "miracle navigation aids" were responsible for saving the lives of many victims of shipwreck who otherwise might have succumbed to the terrible rigors of a harsh seacoast.

Lahaina Lighthouse as it appears today. It is near the site of the first lighthouse in the islands, and antedated any on the Pacific Coast or Alaska. The first lighthouse at Lahaina was built in 1840 and rebuilt several times thereafter. The one pictured here was built of concrete in 1916 and abuts the old Pioneer Inn.

An early photo of Honolulu Harbor in the day of the sailing vessel, showing one of the few pictures of the pioneer lighthouse. It was established under the old Hawaiian Monarchy August 2, 1869, resting on piling in the middle of the harbor. It stood 26 feet above the water and displayed a fourth order French lens. It was known as the Honolulu Harbor Lighthouse, or "the harbor wink."

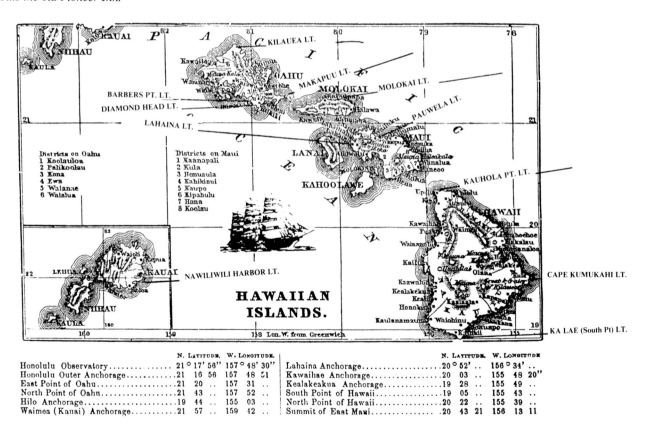

	N. LATITUDE.	W. LONGITUDE.		N. LATITUDE.	W. LONGITUDE.
Honolulu Observatory	21° 17' 56"	157° 48' 30"	Lahaina Anchorage	20° 52' ..	156° 34' ..
Honolulu Outer Anchorage	21 16 56	157 48 51	Kawaihae Anchorage	20 03 ..	155 48 20"
East Point of Oahu	21 20 ..	157 31 ..	Kealakeakua Anchorage	19 28 ..	155 49 ..
North Point of Oahu	21 43 ..	157 52 ..	South Point of Hawaii	19 05 ..	155 43 ..
Hilo Anchorage	19 44 ..	155 03 ..	North Point of Hawaii	20 22 ..	155 39 ..
Waimea (Kauai) Anchorage	21 57 ..	159 42 ..	Summit of East Maui	20 43 21	156 13 11

MAP OF THE HAWAIIAN ISLANDS
Circa 1875

Locations of major Hawaiian lighthouses are super-imposed, most of which were non-existent when this map was published.

Lighthouses of Hawaii

Even in paradise isles there is a need
for light to shine out of dark places.
.....JAG

No longer the drowsy, tropical haven of yesteryear, the State of Hawaii stands out in sharp contrast with the past. When Captain James Cook discovered Hawaii in 1778, the Sandwich Islanders cared nothing about lighthouses and undoubtedly were unaware that such things existed. The closest they came to navigation aids was the placement of torches when an errant fishing craft or war canoe was overdue by nightfall.

Cook found Hawaii was a congeries of wholly feudalistic local societies in which all social, political and economic power was concentrated in the local chiefs who owned all the land in their districts and had complete power of life and death over their subjects. In the late 18th and 19th centuries, one chief, Kamehameha I, succeeded, largely by conquest, achieving totality of absolute power over the entire Hawaiian chain and all of its people.

During the balance of the 19th century, the absolute power and exclusive land ownership of the Monarchy were gradually diluted. A constitution was proclaimed, a legislative body and judicial system were constituted, and the King districted the lands of Hawaii among himself personally, the Crown and the people.

The Hawaiian Kingdom's ultimate alliance with the United States was determined in 1875 when the Reciprocity Treaty was concluded, permitting Hawaiian sugar to enter America duty free.

The Monarchy was overthrown in 1893, a provincial government and Republic followed, and in 1898, the Hawaiian Islands were annexed by and became a territory of the United States.

When Cook initially dropped anchor in Hawaii he estimated the population at about 300,000, but the Polynesians whose protracted isolation had left them with little, if any, resistance to Western diseases, despite the medical work of the missionaries, the government, and others, dropped to less then 60,000 in the following century.

Though the British explorer is credited with the official discovery, the claim still remains that the actual discovery was by a Spanish navigator named Gaetano, who allegedly sighted the islands while en route to the Philippines from New Spain (Mexico) in 1542. Though his claim is debatable, the true discoverers were of course the incredible Polynesians, who without chart or compass challenged the sea, guided by the stars, and came to the Paradise Isles, centuries before the white man ever knew they existed. Motivated by their pagan gods, perhaps as a result of some long forgotten chaos, their quest finally ended.

Anthropologists tell us that the first Polynesians to land in Hawaii probably came ashore near South Point, now officially named Ka Lae, at the southern tip of the Big Island around 750 AD. Some historians claim they arrived considerably prior to that date, but migration to the other islands came in natural process and the bountiful land caused the population to flourish.

When a brisk fur trade developed between the Pacific Northwest and China in the early 1800's, Hawaiian portals served as supply and rest stops for the weary crewmen. Next came the sandlewood spree, the islands' first sought after export. From 1791 till 1820 the Hawaiian mountainsides were raped ruthlessly and the timber sold for handsome prices in the Oriental markets. Trees were quickly depleted, and the kings and chiefs who claimed ownership soon found they were in debt to foreign investors.

The Hawaiian capital was eventually moved from the Kona (Kailua) coast of Hawaii, near where Cook met his tragic death at Kealakakua, to Lahaina, on the island of Maui. Shortly after, the whaling era, with rough and tumble intervention by rugged men of the sea, arrived. They came on like thunder finding Hawaii an oasis in a wide ocean and a natural stopping off place for supplies and recreation—their slogan—"There is no God west of Cape Horn."

The gullible natives' only defense against them were the early missionaries that arrived almost simultaneously with the first whaling ships. With little conscience or morality, the Yankee and British whalermen, weary from long months at sea, distasteful working conditions and poor diet, found the islands offered their most favored things in life—food and women.

On the other hand, what the *Mayflower* was to New England, the little brig *Thaddeus* was to Hawaii when she dropped her hook off Kohala, Hawaii in March 1820, 160 days out from Boston with the first small contingent of missionaries.

There was mounting competition between the ports of Honolulu, Lahaina and Hilo to gain the lion's share of the American and British whaleships. The first capital city of the unified Hawaiian government was at historic Lahaina. Lele, was the name the ancient Polynesians first applied to the roadstead town. That name originated from one tragic day on which the original village was completely wiped out by the forces of Kamehameha I in his conquest of Maui. Atoning for that day of destruction by his predecessor, Kamehameha II established Lahaina as the capital of the Hawaiian Kingdom and it was there that the original constitution was drawn up in 1840. Five years later, the capital was moved to Honolulu.

From the 1820's to the 1860's the whaling industry was perhaps the foremost economic factor of the islands. Lahaina gained the nod for the whaleships as a wintering port due to "excessive port charges and the outrageous cost of provisions at Honolulu." The little village by the sea began to prosper, boasting the first newspaper, published in the islands, in 1834, and the first school established west of the Rockies.

It was amid all that activity that Hawaii's first official lighthouse came to fruition. Vague records, and some historians have stated that the initial beacon in the islands was constructed as Keawaiki, described as Lahaina's Road to Tahiti, in 1866. However, according to an article in the Interior Department archives there is an account of a correspondence—J. Kapena to P. Kanoa—translated from Hawaiian). November-December 1840, that the original lighthouse at Keawaiki (Lahaina) dated from November 1840. Kapena was allegedly J. M, Kapena, later governor of Maui and a minister of the cabinet under King Kalakaua.

The lighthouse is described in that account as being in the form of a "tall looking box-like structure, about nine feet high and one foot wide, so was all sides; built on a suitable position facing the landing." It was built in order that the landing might be visible to "those vessels, boats and canoes that may come in port at night; because there were quite a number of boats wrecked by the waves."

The report continued: "Therefore was this lighthouse erected with two lights projecting one above the other and having two glass windows on the eastern and two on the southern sides, in a position facing the landing. Two openings on the western and two on the northern sides were doors with real wooden enclosures, where the lights are inserted to their positions. This was the way this news is described; on the 4th day of November 1840 the light was turned on, and it is burning every night. I believe the reign of King Kamehameha III will/not/ terminate or may still be in existence, the continual burning of these lamps are not supposed to go off at nights; as prescribed by the chiefs. The salary that will be paid to the keeper of this lighthouse is $20 a year."

The Lahaina Light of 1866 must have either been rebuilt from the original, updated or re-established, as it stood, according to the records of that date, "26 feet above the water, and could be seen across Lanai Channel."

Again, the *Hawaiian Almanac* of 1884, reads: "a lighthouse has been erected at the landing, port of Lahaina. The window on the sea side of the lightroom is of 20 x 40 inch glass, with glass at the northwest and southwest ends. The colored glass stands at equal angles side and front and a vessel in ten fathoms of water will have two bright lights for about half a mile each way directly in front of the lighthouse. At a greater distance it will show a colored light until the lights almost appear like one, or the red light like a reflection from the other light. The light towards Molokai is the brightest so that the lights now have the appearance of a large and small light close together."

The latter mentioned navigation aid was evidently in use until 1905 when funds provided by the government gave the Lighthouse Service the green light to update existing Hawaiian beacons. In that year the new Lahaina light structure was erected. Eleven years later; (1916) it too was replaced, this time by a 39 foot high narrow, pyramidal concrete tower which is still in use today supporting a modern beacon with a flashing red characteristic.

It would seem that the advent of the whaling vessels in Hawaii would have stimulated the placing of lighted beacons in the islands, but it was not to be, and even the missionaries were so busy trying to turn on the spiritual lights that they found no time to spearhead an effort for navigation lights. The original Lahaina beacon which undoubtedly was an outright native effort, was built out of sheer necessity. Strange indeed, that New Englanders who came from shores polka dotted with lighthouses were not more conscious of the need for navigation aids in the islands. Perhaps it was the almost complete absence of fog and the frequent starlit nights that diverted any such consideration.

The sea has always been both Hawaii's barrier and highway. In the day of the commercial sailing vessel, unpredictable winds, swift currents and jagged reefs made inter-island voyages uncertain and on occasion dangerous. Sometimes schooners required as many as 11 days to make the 90 mile passage from Honolulu to Lahaina when the winds and seas were contrary.

Honolulu (Honoruru) Harbor was discovered on November 21, 1784 by Captain Brown of the British ship *Butterworth.* At least five different expeditions passed the islands, including those of Cook and Vancouver before the port was discovered. With the dwindling whaling industry after 1865, most Pacific commerce made Honolulu their port of call. King Kamehameha II moved there with his royal family and administration officials. Thus it was in Honolulu Harbor that the second official Hawaiian lighthouse was commissioned. The light was first displayed on August 2, 1869, shining from a pyramidal-shaped lighthouse erected on a pier of piling, 47 feet above the harbor. The navigation aid and the pier on which it stood were built in the center of the harbor allowing ships to pass on either side. The lighting apparatus was a fourth order Fresnel, illuminated by whale oil lamps, and was visible nine miles. Erected under the King Kalakaua reign, the sentinel was faithfully administered to by natives, a rare

occupation for Hawaiians at that point in history. Locals referred to the lighthouse as the "Harbor Wink," and appeared none too impressed by its presence.

As increasingly larger ships called at Honolulu, the lighthouse ironically became somewhat of a hazard to navigation in the restricted channel, which prompted the establishment of a new lighthouse on Sand Island, which partly encloses the harbor on the seaward side. That lighthouse guided ships until the construction of the 193 foot buff-colored Aloha Tower at the foot of Fort Street, completed in 1926. It was to become one of Honolulu's major landmarks, carrying four clock dials and the lighted word Aloha, above the dock where the big liners berthed. Once the city's tallest structure, it is now dwarfed by many high rise buildings along the shoreline.

In years past there was also a navigation light on the old Custom House tower. After Honolulu was electrified, that light was given a green characteristic so it would not be confused with city lights.

In the early years, Honolulu had a waterfront similar to San Francisco's Barbary Coast—a haven of whiskey, disorderly sailors, easy women and houses of ill-repute. Just as at Lahaina, there was a constant agitation between Christian and heathen, and sometimes the clergy were blamed for extinguishing makeshift navigation lights in order to prevent whaleships from coming in to anchor at night.

When the United States government accepted responsibility for Hawaiian aids to navigation in 1904, the total in all of the islands was 75, and of that number most were unlighted and some only crude day markers. At best, the system was described as "highly inadequate" and in many cases "downright crude."

President Theodore Roosevelt transferred Hawaii's navigation aids from the territorial government to the Lighthouse Board on January 1, 1904 at which time it became a subdistrict of the 12th Lighthouse District to which an inspector and engineer were appointed. Broken down into categories, there were 19 lighthouses, 20 buoys and 20 daymarks plus 16 private aids maintained by the Inter-Island Steam Navigation Company, the principal mover of passengers and freight among the islands.

Of the more than 100 sophisticated lighted aids to navigation in the islands today, only five were established before the turn of the century. These, in addition to Lahaina Light and Diamond Point, (as the Diamond Head Light was originally labled) were at Laau Point on Molokai, built in 1882; Barbers Point, near Honolulu built in 1888, and Laupahoehoe, on Hawaii Island, constructed in 1890. Other lights in existence before the U. S. Lighthouse Service took over were either discontinued or re-established.

An inspector's report summed up the situation with lachrymose: "The lighthouses are generally of a very crude character. The one on top of the customhouse in Honolulu being a lantern of a kind with a crimson cloth tied around it to give it a red glow. There is not a revolving light on any coast. On the island of Hawaii, there are but six lights and they are all fixed, so called, two small colored and four white ones, all very cheap and of short range. The keepers of the lighthouses are generally paid from $25 to $30 per month."

Under the old Hawaiian lighthouse system some of the navigation aids were pitiful. The average lighthouse was a wooden skeleton affair, with a small square room at the top into which a lamp was placed. At one outcrop on the south coast of Maui, "two ordinary kitchen lamps" marked the dreaded basalt reef that had snagged several ships. The light marking Maalaea Bay, near the spot where McGregor Point Light stands today, displayed an "ordinary red lantern hung from a post." One of the better aids was at Paukaa Point near the entrance to Hilo Harbor composed of three small reflector lights.

Barbers Point is a statuesque tower built in 1933 replacing a coral stone tower built in 1888 under the monarchy. The 72 foot lighthouse is situated on the southwest point of Oahu.

Under the old Hawaiian Monarchy, a fee was levied against all commercial vessels using island ports to pay for the operation of the lighthouses. The regulation read:

> There shall be levied upon all vessels arriving from abroad at any port of the Kingdom where a lighthouse may be established, the sum of $3, which shall be paid before departure to Collector of General Customs. All vessels engaged in the coasting trade shall pay 10 cents per ton as light dues, in consideration that they may be entitled to visit all ports where a lighthouse may be established, for a term of one year without further charge.

When the U. S. Lighthouse Board assumed responsibility for the Hawaiian lights, they attacked the problem three-fold. First, they installed Fresnels, mostly fourth order lenses at the already established stations, and lens-lanterns at others. Next, it went about rebuilding and improving the towers and keepers dwellings. Then, the inspector conducted a survey to determine where new lights were the most urgently needed to safeguard the waterways.

Barbers Point Light, established in 1888 on the southwest point of Oahu, was replaced by a stately tower built of concrete in 1933. That was back in the depression years, and the great tower lifted its lofty bulk in comparative solitude. Today the fast sprawling city and military counterparts have greatly altered the one-time picturesque setting of the lighthouse. The 72 foot structure is visible for 15 miles and at its prime was considered secondary in importance only to Kilauea, Makapuu and Molokai lights. A radio direction finder calibration facility is attached to the station today.

The original lighthouse at Barbers Point (Laeloa), one of the better efforts of the monarchy, was built of coral stone, and the light was 43 feet above the sea, visible for ten miles. The lens and lighting apparatus were of the fourth order of Fresnel, displaying a fixed white light.

Barbers Point was named many years before the lighthouse became a reality. In October 1796, when the brig *Arthur* was outbound from Honolulu for Canton laden with sea otter skins, she ran hard aground. Her master was Captain Henry Barber, and he and 16 of his 22 man crew managed to escape and reach a point of land nearby. That spot eventually was given Barber's name.

John Young (kidnapped Yankee boatswain of the snow *Eleanora*) who had been given the status of a chief among the Hawaiians, managed to salvage the cargo from the *Arthur* and return most of the recovered goods to the British skipper, but his overseer, King Kamehameha, demanded possession of the wreck's ten cannon which were promptly placed about the monarch's palace.

Sitting below the timeless slopes of long dormant Diamond Head, is a lighthouse known to seafaring men around the world. Commissioned in 1899, the coral masonry tower was declared unstable in 1916 when the rock began to crumble. By the following year the imperfections were altered after a "metamorphosis" took place. The tower was raised to 55 feet and the focal plane was 147 feet above the blue Pacific. With a concrete face and a filled out image the structure was far more formidable in appearance.

The old keeper's dwelling in recent years was taken over by the Commandant of the 14th Coast Guard District, affording him one of the prime seascape settings on Oahu. The red and white occulting beams of light are still seen today by just about every ship and airplane coming into Honolulu.

By 1906, the Lighthouse Service was making considerable strides in improving Hawaiian aids. It maintained 19 lighthouses from Kauai to Hawaii, but shipwrecks and strandings occurred with dismaying frequency. The previous year, the Lighthouse Board declared, "All deepsea commerce between Honolulu and Puget Sound, the Pacific Coast of the United States, Mexico, Central America, including Panama, passes Makapuu Head.. and not a single light on the whole northern coast of the Hawaiian Islands to guide ships on their approach to land after a voyage of several thousand miles."

Congress responded with an appropriation of $60,000. That money was targeted for Makapuu, but the tower and the outbuildings were not completed and in operation until October 1, 1909. Since that day, its big "bulging eye" has been one of the premier lights in the Pacific. The rugged 46 foot lighthouse astride the lofty black sea cliffs is some 420 feet above the ocean, its light visible 28 miles. The hyper-radiant lens measures eight and three quarters feet in diameter, is 13 feet high and is composed of 1,140 prisms of French-made polished glass. Ironically Makapuu in the Hawaiian language means, "bulging eye," and that is exactly what the light appears to be. It is one of the world's more brilliant in the classic lighting category.

A rather rare and unfortunate accident occurred at Makapuu on April 9, 1925. An explosion in the lighthouse watch room claimed the life of the first assistant keeper and seriously injured the second assistant. The incandescent oil vapor lamp with three 55 mm mantles were being trimmed at 3 a. m. The cylindrical tank containing alcohol was filled to overflowing. Unaware that the room was filled with fumes, the keeper lit a match resulting in an explosion that took his life and knocked the assistant flat on his back. Fortunately the lens escaped damage being on the deck above the watch room.

There is much history and legend in the timeless walls of Makapuu. From the lighthouse it is said that the early morning rays put the Koolau pali into sharp relief and the waters turn emerald in color. Behind the lighthouse up the cliff is a rock, shaped like a face, said to be that of Malei, and according to the ancient Hawaiians, she was demi-goddess, guardian of the waterways.

Samuel A. Amalu, perhaps the best known of the former Hawaiian light keepers, put in several years at Makapuu starting in 1920 at a salary of $200 a month.

Lighthouse beams are good for more than just guiding ships. It was Kauai's Kilauea Point Light that brought airplane pilots Maitland and Hegenberger back onto their course after overshooting Oahu on the first transpacific flight in 1927. Hegenberger picked up the beam 90 miles off Kauai and was able to navigate back to Oahu's Hickam Field.

The 52 foot reinforced concrete tower was built in 1913 and commands prime position 216 feet above the sea at the northerly tip of the island. When the tower was commissioned it was fitted with a fantastic creation of glass and metal in its crown, namely two double panels making a complete revolution in 20 seconds, giving a double flash every ten seconds. The moving parts weighed nearly four tons and the entire apparatus turned on a mercury float. The mammoth first order (Barbier) French-made lens, something in the shape of a modified clamshell, reputedly cost $12,000, and was one of the largest lens of its type in the Pacific, affording a brilliant flash providing a landfall for ships bound to Honolulu from the Orient or on the general transpacific passage. With an oil lamp, the lens afforded a flash of 240,000 candlepower, a spectacular light in 1913, but in later years when the Coast Guard utilized a 1,000 or 1,500 quartz-iodine electric bulb, it was estimated that the lens was capable of putting out 4.5 million candlepower per flash.

Kilauea was one of the last Hawaiian lighthouses to be automated. Its final official keeper was a colorful Samoan named Emilia A. Kellsall, who with considerable regret padlocked the door in December 1974.

Much to the chagrin of many, the classic tower and light, have been put out to pasture, and since 1976 the Coast Guard has marked the point with a modern revolving beacon atop a ten foot concrete pole.

Kilauea Point is one of the most visited spots on Kauai, and most deep-sea ships bound to and from the Far East on the southerly route in years past were totally dependent on its piercing flash. The lighthouse at this writing was not open to the general public but the

grounds are accessible and viewers are usually greeted by the clown-like booby birds that nest on the cliffs, plus a seascape that is breathless.

At the very opposite end of the Hawaiian chain, the most southerly tip of the islands, as well as the most southerly point of the United States, is Ka Lae or South Point. Allegedly, the first Polynesians landed on Hawaiian soil there after rigorous months in their great canoes. Historians believe that event took place sometime between 500 and 750 A.D.

The location was in later years deemed worthy of a navigation light, but perhaps because it was sacred ground to the Hawaiians, the Monarchy never placed a beacon there. Centuries ago the natives may have lit torches to guide their double canoes home safely by nightfall. At any rate, the Lighthouse Service established the first navigation aid on the point in 1906. Though strategically located, it was never considered a primary beacon, as ship traffic off the southern tip of the island chain has always been relatively light compared to the more

One of the early lighthouses built on the island of Oahu was Diamond Head. This is the original structure on completion in 1899. In 1916-17 the Lighthouse Service rebuilt and strengthened it. It still stands today, landmark and seamark known to mariners the world over. The Commandant of the Coast Guard's 14th District, Honolulu, resides in the keepers former dwelling.

Colorful Diamond Head Lighthouse on the island of Oahu has served as the greeter light for maritime traffic inbound for Honolulu since 1899.

northerly routes. As a result, many different towers have marked the location and a variety of lighting systems, the present one being a white concrete pole with a flashing light and a diamond shaped daymark. Nominal range of the light is eight miles seaward above the lava outcrops of the point.

Even today, the elder Hawaiians insist the entire area is filled with mana spirits of those long departed. Directly below the navigation aid lie the decaying ruins of Kalalea Heiau which local natives consider so potent with mana spirits, they refuse to enter, and advise others to do the same. It was an important fishing shrine of the past, and offerings are still made at a large stone, presumably deified. Hawaiians allowed the government to build a navigation aid there in 1906 only because, in their opinion, it was for humanitarian purposes, allowing an exception.

Fickle currents run concurrently and high breakers slam into the nearby perpendicular lava walls of Ka Lae, an area of bountiful fishing for native Hawaiians for centuries. The cliffs are pockmarked with small holes chiseled out with ancient tools where the natives secured their canoes in ages past. It is a fascinating place to visit.

Modern lighthouses sometimes get mixed up with aerial beacons. Cape Kumukahi Light was established in 1929, but was rebuilt five years later and nobody was able to figure out whether it was aerial or marine oriented. Originally intended as a dual primary light to guide airplanes from the mainland and to act as a landfall light for ship traffic from the Panama Canal and Latin American ports, its true

Makapuu Lighthouse, established in 1909, following shipwrecks on the main searoad to Honolulu is very much intact today. It has been the backdrop for several TV programs.

Amid lush growth in an idyllic setting. Diamond Head Lighthouse lives on as greater Honolulu grows up around it. U.S. Coast Guard photo.

purpose has always been somewhat of a mystery. The tall 124 foot skeleton structure displays a 1.7 million candlepower revolving beacon 165 feet above the sea and is picked up by ships 23 miles out.

Cape Kumukahi is the easternmost point of the most easterly Hawaiian island. Hot, glowing lava often rolls like a fiery dragon down the slopes of Mauna Loa's Kilauea crater toward the coast, and on occasion it will reach Cape Kumukahi sending up great billows of steam as it comes in contact with the ocean. As the lava cools, the cape is enlarged, and today the lighthouse is considerably farther from the sea then at its inception, and the island a bit closer to California.

A miracle saved the lighthouse in 1960 when a molten lava river divided at the base of the structure, after crushing the station outbuildings. In its devastating path it had consumed forests, villages, farms and houses. Had it rolled any closer, the tower would have crashed in tangled wreckage. Since that day, it has been tabbed, "the lucky lighthouse."

When the lava encircled the light tower it covered an ancient Hawaiian graveyard located nearby, and the natives of the area claimed Pele's outburst was guided by evil spirits.

Automated today like the other island lights, Cape Kumukahi has weathered both lava flows and seismic tidal waves, the latter having left many scars along the shoreline.

Hawaii's past is often submerged in seafare lore, and is a potpurri of events, colored with myths, volcanoes and tsunamis. Devastating seismic tidal waves have had a profound effect on the port city of Hilo.

Ready for shipment to Makapuu Lighthouse, one can see the size of the giant apparatus manufactured in France specially for the Makapuu tower. It is one of the largest of its type in the Pacific. Old U.S. Lighthouse Service photo.

Often termed the "bulging eye," Makapuu Lighthouse at the southeast point of Oahu Island is situated 420 feet above the Pacific. Courtesy U.S. Coast Guard.

As a result of the 1960 killer waves, 61 persons died, 282 were injured and 308 business firms washed away including some of those rebuilt after the 1946 tsunami.

Secondary lighthouses north of Cape Kumukahi were threatened by the 1960 wave—Paukaa, Pepeekeo, Laupahoehoe and Kukuihaele—were all on the fringes of the watery onslaught but managed to escape destruction. The contour of Hilo Bay, however, has been changed many times and one small concrete lighthouse has stood empty on its shores for years because of changes in the harbor prompted by the seismic tidal waves.

The earlier mentioned Paukaa Point Light has probably flirted with more seismic waves than any other lighthouse. Located on the point immediately north of Hilo, its history goes back to the 1880's under the Monarchy, and though it is usually in the path of the watery avalanches, its height above the water, 145 feet, has allowed it to escape major destruction. Uncle Sam placed a light there in 1907, and in 1929 replaced it with a small pyramidal concrete structure which today displays a flashing green light. Its companion light, north of Hilo, Pepeekeo, has also had some close shaves with waves. That light was also established in 1907 and today is atop a skeleton tower. Laupahoehoe Light on the northeast shore of the Big Island was

Kilauea Lighthouse on the northern tip of the island of Kauai was built in 1913 and fitted with one of the most powerful beacons in the Pacific, seen by both maritime and air traffic for many miles. Today, the grand old lighthouse has been superseded by a light on a concrete pole, though the tower remains as a popular tourist attraction. U.S. Coast Guard photo.

A Coast Guard aerial photo of Kilauea Light Station when it was still manned with radio beacon in use.

Upper left, South Point (Ka Lae), the most southerly point of the United States, landing place of the first Hawaiians, first lighted in 1906. Lower left, abandoned harbor light at Hilo, seismic wave victim; Upper right, McGregor Point Light on Maui, and lower right, Kailua Light on Kukailimoku Point at the north entrance to Kailua Bay, established in 1909.

Since 1929, a beacon light has marked lonely Cape Kumukahi on the Big Island. At one time it was considerably nearer the water than it is presently, the lava from Kilauea crater having pushed the land mass seaward via its rivers of molten lava that hardened after solidifying in the seawater. Courtesy 14th District Coast Guard.

One of the tallest structures on the island of Hawaii is Cape Kumukahi Lighthouse. The 124 foot high skeleton tower which serves as both an aid to navigation for ships and airplanes sits in a field of lava on the easternmost point of the island. Labled the "lucky lighthouse" it was the only structure in the area that escaped destruction by a devastating lava flow from fiery Kilauea Crater in 1960. Photo courtesy, U.S. Coast Guard 14th District Honolulu.

Pauwela Point Light, appearing more like an aerial beacon, casts its beams over the waters on the eastern approach to Kahului Harbor on Maui Island. The point has been lighted since 1910. U.S. Coast Guard photo.

Upper left, Kauiki Light, established 1908, the present tower built of concrete in 1914 located on Puu Kii, a small rocky outcrop near Hana, a place of historical significance. Lower left, Pauwela Light, east side approach to Kahului Harbor, established 1910, the reflecting beacon installed in 1937. Photos at right are of the Kauhola Lighthouse on the northern part of the Big Island, an 85 foot cylindrical concrete tower built in 1933, replacing the 1912 tower. The lantern house has been removed and the lighting apparatus is an air-way beacon.

As brooding clouds fringe the pali, noble Mokokai Lighthouse, the tallest aid to navigation in the Hawaiian Islands maintains its important vigil as it has since 1909. U.S. Coast Guard photo, courtesy 14th District.

The giant lighting apparatus manufactured in France for Molokai Lighthouse is pictured here before being taken to the site. Old Lighthouse Service photo.

commissioned in 1890, and has shouldered some watery fusillades. Today it is marked by a pole structure.

Another lighthouse of importance on the Big Island is situated at Kauhola Point, on the northern shore, five miles east of Upolu Point. The navigation aid was funded in 1912, but was updated in 1932 with a formidable 85 foot cylindrical, concrete tower, one of the last major light towers constructed in Hawaii under the old Lighthouse Service.

Prior to the annexation of Hawaii by the United States, the Monarchy maintained a lighthouse in the 1880's, one half mile due south of Mahukona Anchorage, nine miles from the existing Kawaihae Harbor Light. It was a stone tower painted white and displayed its light 75 feet above the sea.

When the Lighthouse Service established the Kawaihae Harbor Light in 1906, it gave serious consideration to a light at Kauhola but it was not built until six years later. After automation, in recent years the lantern house was removed from the tall tower and replaced by an aero marine type beacon. The tower windows were cemented over and much of the eye appeal vanished from what had previously been considered one of Hawaii's most attractive lighthouses.

Molokai Lighthouse is the tallest and most costly of all Hawaiian Island sentinels, lifting its octagonal, pyramidal concrete bulk gracefully skyward for 138 feet. The reputed cost of the structure was $60,000, at least that was what was budgeted for the station, but there were several hidden costs that surfaced before the project was completed. Its brilliant flashing light, after it was electrified in later years, produced two million candlepower, and mariners claimed that it was visible under ideal conditions 28 miles at sea from an elevation of 213 feet above the water.

Located on the Makanalua Peninsula, the lighthouse borders on the infamous leper colony of Kalaupapa, which once gave the 260 square mile Molokai the title of "the forbidden island."

Built in 1909, much difficulty was experienced in landing building materials and supplies, all of which had to be lightered to the beach and then transported a considerable distance to the lighthouse site. Much of the credit for the landside labor must go to the so-called "Kona Nightingale," the name affectionately applied to the Hawaiian donkey. They were invaluable in hauling equipment over the rough terrain during the construction of the lighthouse.

One of the major problems in the project was piping in fresh water from a source other than that utilized at the leper colony. To draw on a good supply, it had to be brought in from distant Waikolu Valley. By using the gravity flow principal, pipe fashioned of native hardwood was fitted tightly against the steep face of the pali to flow properly down to the lighthouse reservation.

Congress at first tried to sidestep or oppose the construction of a first class lighthouse on Molokai, especially when they learned that the most feasible location was right next to the leper colony. An ancient Hawaiian "Kapu" had long been applied to the miserable little settlement, described in decades past as "one of the bleakest hellholes on the face of the earth." Wretched souls infected with the then incurable disease were transported to the peninsula by ship and often shoved overboard to struggle through the surf to a world of bitterness and isolation.

Today, the Kalaupapa leper colony is no longer feared, and tourists visit in increasing numbers, coming in by plane or down the switchback pali cliffs via the donkey express (Kona nightingales).

Nawiliwili Lighthouse at Ninini Point on Kauai Island is pictured here a few years back near a large pineapple field. The original lens and lantern were replaced by a double drum exposed beacon. The light is a guide to the island's main seaport. Courtesy U.S. Coast Guard 14th District.

Only about 200 patients remain in the neatly maintained village, modern sulfa drugs having virtually controlled the once dreaded malady, permitting the colony to be gradually phased out. Many of the patients, though pronounced cured, have elected to live out their lives there. Once walled off from the remainder of the island by the massive pali cliffs, the leprosarium took a turn for the better several decades ago with better management in the wake of a missionary priest, Father Damien, who came to the incubus-like colony in 1866 and gave of his best to the people until he too, contracted the disease and died.

Under the Hawaiian Monarchy in the 1882-84 period there was a major lighthouse located on the southwest point of Molokai, known as Lae o Ka Laau. It was situated 50 feet above the water and displayed a fixed white fourth order light, visible 11 miles. It had the reputation of being twofold—one to guide ships and the other to warn people away from the leper colony. Today, that point is still lighted but the name has been shortened to Laau Point. In the old days it was the one notable light on the island until the advent of the great Molokai tower.

There was a period of apprehension and adjustment for the first keepers assigned to Molokai Lighthouse. After all, in 1909, there was still no cure for the disease and only a fence separated them from the perimeter of the colony. A mutual respect, however, created a sort of no-mans land and no problems resulted.

The vulnerability of the peninsula to seismic tidal waves was evident in 1946 when giant seas created by an undersea eruption in Alaska hit the island. Four voluminous seas slammed into the pali cliff, rising more than 50 feet, snatching out the old water pipes at a level never before attained in the memory of the oldest Hawaiians.

When automation came to Molokai Lighthouse in 1970, the tower which had had very few visitors had even fewer. Not very many persons have had the privilege of climbing the 187 step spiral staircase. The flight of steps are traversed today only by an occasional Coast Guard lighthouse maintenance crew or an inspector, but the powerful flashing light shines on.

In 1910, a guiding approach light for Maui's Kahului Harbor was established nine miles east northeast of the port. Despite the many years of port activity no light had marked the point till that year. Sugar packets were frequent visitors and the portal was dangerous, in fact, there were strandings and wrecks on several occasions, especially frustrating to those working in the sugar mill town of Spreckelsville. In later years the harbor was improved and jetty rock controlled the depths.

The former lighthouse at Pauwela was replaced in 1937 with a 47 foot skeleton tower with a powerful exposed rotating beacon at an elevation 169 feet above the Pacific.

Another prominent lighthouse is situated on the island of Kauai. Though it doesn't have the notoriety of the old Kilauea Point Light, it nevertheless is one of the finest structures of its kind in the islands. Nawiliwili Harbor Light on Ninini Point is a towering 86 footer, but like its counterpart at Kauhola Point on the Big Island it too has had its lantern house removed in favor of an exposed beacon. Built very similar to the Kauhola tower, Nawiliwili Light was commissioned in the same year, 1932—a cylindrical, reinforced concrete tower, buff colored, flashing twin rotary aero beacons of more than one million candles.

The original lighthouse at the point was commissioned by the Lighthouse Board in 1906 and was located 20 feet from its successor. Until recent years the sentinel was bordered on the landside by pineapple fields but new construction is crowding in on the graceful tower.

The name Nawilwili is taken from the nearby mountains which afford a silhouette profile of Queen Victoria shaking an admonishing forefinger. According to ancient tradition, it depicts the famous queen reminding her unpredictable nephew, Kaiser Wilhelm to behave himself, "Now Willi Willi!"

A strange submarine islet exists a few miles west of Kauai. Its existence was secretly guarded until 1923 when it was found to be not only a bountiful fishing area but also a possible hazard to navigation. Ancient Polynesians handed down many legends of its existence, but because of their gods, they guarded the secret wall.

Informed of the mysterious island in 1923, the government delayed action until a few years later when the Coast Guard cutter *Mojave* was ordered to make a survey. Results showed the inundated island just off the main shipping lanes at Latitude 21 degrees 40′ 45″ N. Longitude 160 degrees 35′ 45″W. The depth of water over the obstruction was sounded at 39 feet below the surface and found to be of no immediate concern to commerce. The increasing displacement of modern day superships may sometime in the future demand second thoughts on marking the underwater obstruction. Kauai Rock, as it has been named, may yet find a slot in the official *Light List.*

No history of marine lighting in the Hawaiian Islands could be written without mention of Kaula. Many years ago, this unusual natural marine bastion demanded the placement of an automatic gas beacon. Kaula is the westerly islet of the immediate Hawaiian archipelago, lying 180 miles from Honolulu and 19 miles from the island of Niihau. Tablelike and lofty, it is composed of only 100 acres, uninhabited and anything but a paradise, fit only for seabirds. The geographic hazards of access kept human beings away from Kaula down through the centuries and the birds of the sea lived in undisturbed tranquility, nesting by the thousands on the high plateau. The rare intruder could hardly walk about without crushing eggs during the nesting season. It was once an entertaining passtime for steamers to heave to off the island, blast their whistles and treat the passengers in watching the aroused birds take off in cloud of feathers, so great it would hide the sun.

Encompassing about a mile in length, it is almost bare of vegetation. Kaula was not designed for man, nor man for Kaula, and before the advent of the helicopter, and by then it was too late, the light on the islet had been lopped off the *Light List.*

The challenge was accepted by the Lighthouse Service in 1924 to place an automatic gas light atop the 550 foot high fortress-like islet, and what a challenge it was. Landings were only possible in the summer months and once getting to the sheer base of the isle there were only two possible places to even consider an ascent, as most of the cliffs could not be scaled. At the chosen landing, a trail 600 feet long had to be chiseled out before climbing to the upper ledge. Bronze handholds had to literally be grouted into the walls of overhanging cliffs for the workers to follow the trail, sometimes within reach of the breakers. A ladder and chains were additionally utilized in the climb, and at a still higher level a derrick would eventually be placed for both hoisting and lowering a boat with supplies and workers.

After the initial surveys, the lighthouse tender *Kukui* was assigned as the mothership for the project. Under the guidance of assistant superintendent F. A. Edgecomb the work got underway. As far as is known, no white man had ever gained the summit of the isle, and only one Hawaiian, who when contacted afforded so little information that his claim was doubted. Hawaiians considered the place to be sacred and at the same time insurmountable.

One can understand the difficulty of gaining the summit of Kaula Island (19 miles southwest of Niihau) let alone the problems of placing an automatic gas light at its summit, 550 feet above the sea. That was the challenge facing the workers that came there in 1924 aboard the **Kukui.** *Photo by Dr. H.S. Palmer.*

After two unsuccessful landings in a small boat, a third was attempted and ended in immersion for all when the boat capsized. When at last the party gained a foothold they managed to climb to the 200 foot level but were unable to go any higher. So down they went, discouraged but not defeated. They rowed their surfboat to another ledge on Kaula's southwestern extreme. Again, by using handholds and footholds they ascended to within 60 feet of the summit, but there the going got tougher. Using blasting powder and scaling ladders they finally gained the top, the effort culminating in three days of exhausting effort. After a period of rest, they surveyed the table land seeking the best position for the beacon.

Traversing land the ancient Hawaiians believed to be haunted by mana spirits, Edgecomb and his party shared the conquered islet with masses of screaming birds. The invaders soon learned the reason the Hawaiians considered it sacred ground when on the northwest side a great sea cave was discovered, broad and high enough for a small schooner or sampan to enter. The cathedral-like cavern was said to be the home of Kuhaimoana, deified king of all the sharks in the Hawaiian Islands. The old natives would enter the cave and pray before casting fishing lines or dropping nets. An evil curse was upon any who failed to follow the practice. They adhered strictly to the belief, for fish abounded in that well secreted area, respect of the god assuring a good catch. According to the legend, Kuhaimoana came there to live after he had outgrown his former abode at Lanai Island. Later he grew so enormous that he turned into coral.

Descendents of the ancients continued to both believe in and fear the shark god. Ironically, a young Hawaiian who was a crew member aboard the *Kukui* in 1924 could not understand why no accidents befell the caucasian invaders of the islet when they failed to offer prayers to Kuhaimoana. He finally concluded that the god was satisfied because of the humanitarian purpose of the endeavor.

After the difficult erection of the light standard and the light, it was illuminated by acetylene gas which was piped up the cliffside from a small supply house high above the landing well out of the reach of the seas. To guard against failure of the light, a duplicate gas cylinder was afforded allowing the light to burn for a year without refueling. It was somewhat amazing that there were no causalties during the construction period although on several occasions men were washed off the precipitous cliffs. It would have been a test for the most seasoned mountain climbers, in fact, just getting to the rock was a dangerous undertaking. One had to stand in the stern of the surfboat, grab a free hanging rope coming down from the overhang of the cliff, then swing to the base of the rock and let go at the right time. If the person happened to be of Hawaiian extraction he would additionally have to be wondering if the shark god would approve.

Placing the heavy gas cylinders below the summit made it easier for the resupply crews to make exchanges.

Today, the plateau of Kaula is without an aid to navigation but the birds are disturbed by an even greater evil, one that should certainly have disturbed the shark god. The military uses the islet for occasional strafing and bombing practice. The sea acres surrounding the lonely habitat have been declared a danger zone to the public and though men no longer have to risk the danger of servicing the light, the sea birds are most unhappy with the disturbing element brought on by mankind.

When innovative navigation aids came into being, Kaula Light was no longer considered essential to navigation.

Another automatic gas light installation was placed at Lehua Island in 1931, at the highest elevation of any similar installation in America. Lehua, about one sixth of a mile off the north end of Niihau, is a small, crescent-shaped rocky islet with the crescent open to the northward. It gradually rises to 700 feet where the Lighthouse Service erected a small skeleton tower, mounting a gas light with a focal plane 709 feet above the sea. The almost total absence of fog or low hanging clouds

One of the better known U.S. Lighthouse tenders to serve the islands was the **Kukui.**

in the general area made such a lofty position feasible.

It is of interest that the two most difficult places in the islands to install navigation lights—Lehua and Kaula—were only in service about two decades before their discontinuance. The wider range of radio beacons and radar allowed their demise.

Another tiny uninhabited islet, Molokini, actually the crater rim of an undersea, extinct volcano, is also the location of a navigation light. The crescent of land that rises above the channel 2½ miles westward of Maui is crowned by a skeleton tower with a flashing light, 188 feet above the water. The first light on the islet placed there in 1911 was an unattended gas acetylene fixture which set an all-time record burning without failure for two decades, flashing over 200 million times without a miss. During that period only the gas cylinders had to be replaced by refills. The present tower erected in 1947 is still in use displaying a flashing light.

Kahoolawe Southwest Point Light has shared its role with an island bombing range for decades. Despite a continuously running public outcry, the Navy has retained jurisdiction there peppering the major portion of the island with aerial bombs, and strafing from surface vessels. Unexploded ordnance litters the 45 mile square island. Somehow numerous wild goats and scrawny rabbits have managed to forage out an existence amidst the devastation. What might have been a lovely tourist isle is tantamount to a scarred battlefield.

The State of Hawaii has endeavored to get the island relinquished for more useful purposes, but Uncle Sam turns a deaf ear.

The light, at the southwest point of the isle between Maui and Lanai, shines from a 40 foot skeleton tower, 140 feet above the sea, and Coast Guardsmen go there on occasion the service it, but only when the bombs aren't dropping. Though the Navy tries to give the light a wide berth, the blockbusters often rattle the tower, and there have been some near misses. During night practice flares are dropped to light up the target range.

Ancient Hawaiians infrequently visited Kahoolawe. Some grazed their sheep there or planted melons and sweet potatoes but lack of fresh water was a nagging problem. There were only three permanent residents on Kahoolawe when the 1875 census of the islands was taken.

A navigation light was first placed on the island in 1928 and updated in 1952.

Several minor navigation aids dot the shores of the archipelago. Most fail to captivate the viewers imagination, but there is one pint-sized lighthouse on the island of Maui that forms a virtual plug

*The U.S. Lighthouse tender **Columbine** which performed stellar service in the Hawaiian Islands. This Lighthouse Service photo was taken in 1910.*

over an ancient volcano. Kauiki Head on Puu Kii at the entrance to Hana Bay sits atop a wee islet separated from a bold headland. To reach it by land one must walk along the base of a 390 foot monolith, cross a narrow rock bridge, then climb a wooden staircase to reach the 14 foot concrete tower standing at an elevation 85 feet above the water.

Established in 1908, the little tower was rebuilt of reinforced concrete in 1914 and is still in use today. It cradles a flashing white light, with a nominal range of seven miles.

There are two caves at the base of Kauiki Head (Puu Kii). One was the birthplace of Kaahumanu, the favorite wife of King Kamehameha. It was nearby that the great Hawaiian leader and his warriors tangled with the army of the King of Maui in a bloody fracas.

Captain James Cook anchored in Hana Bay on his exploration of the islands in 1778, and it was there that the missionaries came in 1820 and planted, in addition to God's word, the districts's first sugar cane. Above the town of Hana rises 10,000 foot Haleakala, which ancient Hawaiians labeled the "House of the Sun." Amid its scenic and historical surroundings the little lighthouse is a prime attraction for painters and photographers.

Hawaii has come a long way in updating aids to navigation since the Kingdom era. If a ship sought entry to Honolulu in 1875 the Pilot Book read:

> The Channel, which ought never be taken, even by a war vessel, without a pilot, is a narrow passage through the coral reef, averaging 550 feet in width by three-quarters of a mile in length, from the spar buoy to the lighthouse. This light may be seen from a steamer's deck eight miles off. There are 22 feet of water off the bar at mid-tide, the fall being about 30 inches a day."

Nakalele Point has been lighted since 1908. The above marker was placed there in 1970, marking the northernmost point of Maui Island. The late lighthouse keeper Oswald Allik stands alongside, amazed at the unfortunate change in navigation aids.

A typical minor navigation aid seen in many parts of the Hawaiian Islands. This is Kukii Point Light on Kauai Island, a concrete structure built in 1916.

A century later, Honolulu Harbor became the crossroads of the Pacific, and adjoining Pearl Harbor, one of America's most important naval bases, unfortunately, the prime target of the Japanese during the devastating attack on December 7, 1941, the day of imfamy.

Honolulu is headquarters of the 14th Coast Guard District which is responsible for all the aids to navigation in Hawaii and other Pacific isles—more than 700 lighthouses, radio beacons, channel markers and other signals.

Before the advent of complex and innovative navigation aids numerous shipwrecks were recorded around the islands. The waters are very deceptive, the winds and currents sometimes unpredictable, and coral reefs have been the bane of many swept there by contrary konas or even tradewinds. It was actually the stranding of the Pacific Mail passenger liner *Manchuria,* August 22, 1906, that spurred action for the badly needed light at Makapuu. She ran afoul of the reef at Waimanalo while hugging the shore too closely. She had aboard a large passenger list and considerable general cargo, including numerous sacks of flour. Initially her plight appeared hopeless and as a precaution all the passengers were evacuated. The wreck created considerable drama as scores of islanders flocked to the shore to see the big liner struggling for her life. Salvage crews were rushed to the scene and work went on around the clock. Cargo was jettisoned, temporary hull repairs were made and a fleet of tugs stood by should they get the ship afloat. All the while the local residents were picking up the sacks of flour from the beaches, wet but still usable. The all-out effort paid off many days later when after several failures the ship was finally towed free by a host of snorting tugs, and ushered off to the nearest repair yard for a costly overhaul.

There have been some outstanding lighthouse personnel who have manned Hawaii's lighthouses in years past. Manuel Ferreira, for instance spent three decades in the service and continued on with the Coast Guard after 1939. In 1927, while keeper of the Barbers Point Light, he spotted the five-masted schooner *Bianca* in trouble in storm-tossed seas. The vessel was outbound from Honolulu for the Far East when driving winds tore her canvas to ribbons. Helpless in the heavy seas, the unwieldly windjammer was driven steadily toward the reef. In desparation, her master ordered the anchors dropped and all hands prayed they would hold.

Though Ferreira was unable to launch the station skiff through the high surf, and without a telephone or radio available at the lighthouse, he did the next best thing. He began running through the driving rain setting some kind of unrecorded track record. Three miles later, puffing and drenched, he reached the nearest telephone and summoned authorities. Within a short time the USS *Sunadin* steamed out of Honolulu, reached the wallowing schooner, got a line aboard and towed her to safety. Ferreira's quick action undoubtedly saved the wooden-hulled *Bianca* from certain destruction on the dreaded reef.

Another well known Hawaiian lighthouse keeper was Samuel Apool Amalu. He put in 33 years of duty, including several at Makapuu, but bowed out when the Coast Guard took over the Lighthouse Service in 1939.

Captain Manyon of the lighthouse tender *Columbine* and the members of his crew received a special commendation from President Woodrow Wilson for their heroic work in pulling a large disabled bark from certain destruction while stranded in the breakers in a severe storm off Kauai. His answer, "It was no big thing. It's all in the line of duty." Already to his credit was a gold lifesaving medal for the rescue of a patrol craft in Puerto Rico.

Automation of lights in the islands, as on the mainland, has reduced the drama and romance of the old days when the human element was far more involved. The islands are marked with many empty foundations where little lighthouses once stood such as the one on Lanai, near Shipwreck Bay. Nobody seems to remember when it was established or the extent of its usage. Nearby is a shallow bay where the hulks of derelict ships that have outlived their usefulness have been purposely run aground to rot away, including many of the former steamers of the Inter Island Steam Navigation Company, vessels that were the lifeline between island ports for many years until the advent of the airliner. The old skippers depended heavily on the island navigation aids when the pace of living in Hawaii was much slower than it is today. There were colorful landings on all the islands from whence sugar cane and pineapple were shipped. Aloha means both hello and goodbye, and time marches on. Gone forever are the days when the oil of whales provided the illuminant for the old lamps that lighted the way for those who made their living on the island seas, but the Hawaiian word for light, "Kukui," will never flicker out.

Race Rocks Lighthouse is British Columbia's oldest active sentinel, and one of the finest stone block towers on the entire Pacific. It has warned ships away from the reef on which it stands since 1860-61. It is in mint condition and at this writing still has keepers on duty. On the Strait of Juan de Fuca, near Victoria, it is a mile and a half off the mainland. Photo courtesy T.E. Morrison.

Debris scattered about at the Race Rocks station after a gale. A section of the tower and keepers dwelling is pictured.

A giant oil drilling rig being towed to sea by Canadian tugs passes historic Fisgard Lighthouse in the 1960s. Bill Halkett photo.

Fisgard Lighthouse, the first in British Columbia, went into operation in 1860 on Fisgard Island, west side of the entrance to Esquimalt Harbor. The splendid masonry structure was bugled out of active service in recent years, replaced by the Fisgard Sector Light, a minor aid to navigation. The old keepers dwelling is now a lighthouse museum. It is flanked by old Fort Rodd both of which were integrated into a single national park as of 1962. Scores of visitors roam the grounds annually.

The 26,000 ton Canadian Pacific liner **Empress of Canada** trying to stay clear of Race Rocks in 1929 in a heavy fog, instead ran hard aground at Albert Head. It took a fleet of tugs to pull her free and there was considerable damage to her hull. A few months later an aid to navigation was placed on Albert Head.

British Columbia Lighthouses

*Steadfast, serene, immovable, the same
year after year, through all the silent night
Burns on forevermore that quenchless flame,
Shines on that inextinguishable light!
...Henry Wadsworth Longfellow*

Though automation slowly dribbles into the British Columbia lighthouse picture, the province is far behind the progress attained by its American counterparts. This is not because of backwardness, but basically because of the extremely intricate waterways and sparse population among the myriad of islands, islets and waterways which from the air appear like a giant jigsaw puzzle of green, blue and aqua with all the parts waiting to be pieced together. Thus a large number of the lighthouses under the Canadian Coast Guard in both the Victoria and Prince Rupert Districts still retain keepers. They are men and women of high caliber, for the most part totally dedicated to their roles, which even in the present day of communications and fast transport can be extremely lonely and isolated from the world at large. And certainly the personal touch, aside from the financial outlay by the Canadian government, makes the stations more interesting and free from vandalism.

In recent years many Canadians have been shocked by the sudden disappearance of several historic lighthouses, mostly of the frame variety, but like the U. S. Coast Guard, Transport Canada under which the Canadian Coast Guard functions, has no time for historic preservation or nostalgic compassion. Their job is to get on with the best and most economical way to maintain aids to navigation for those who go down to the sea in ships.

No coastline in all the world is quite like that of British Columbia which might be described as barbarous, scraggy, vandalic, delicate, beautiful, scenic, malformed or misshapen, depending in what sector one might find himself. Thousands of islands, islets, rocks, reefs, straits, bays and channels form a never ending fairyland of intrigue and adventure. Much of it is pristine, uncluttered and void of human habitation, colorful little fishing villages and occasionally a metropolis featuring a bustling seaport. Angling through the labyrinth of waterways one could become totally confused if not endowed with the intelligence of a navigator or aided by the many and varied navigation aids that mark the way, especially along the Inside Passage that separates British Columbia from greater Puget Sound to the south and the border of southeastern Alaska to the north. Some areas along the passage are just the same as they were thousands of years ago.

Then there is the Canadian side of the Strait of Juan de Fuca and on up the west coast of Vancouver Island and the so-called Outside Passage with its intricacies, outcrops and danger areas, much of it marked to warn the seafarer of the dangers, especially necessary under adverse weather conditions.

To put it mildly, the Canadian Coast Guard in British Columbia has its hands full, not only in protecting life and property, but with maintaining hundreds of aids to navigation, including several lighthouses.

In the old days, lighthouse stations were supplied once every two to three months and even then, resupply was never certain during protracted stormy periods. A ship's workboat laden with supplies or personnel had to be hoisted by derrick or sling, a difficult task at best, particularly under stressful sea conditions, while the lighthouse tenders held their ground well off the station. To get through extended periods of no outside supply, keepers and their families sometimes

B.C. WEST COAST LIGHTHOUSES

PRINCE RUPERT DISTRICT BASE

LANGARA POINT	DRYAD POINT	IVORY ISLAND
GREEN ISLAND	ADDENBROKE ISLAND	POINTER ISLAND
LUCY ISLAND	TRIPLE ISLAND	EGG ISLAND
BONILLA ISLAND	LAWYER ISLAND	
McINNES ISLAND	BOAT BLUFF	

VICTORIA COAST GUARD DISTRICT

PINE ISLAND	SHERINGHAM	GALLOWS POINT
PULTNEY POINT	PACHENA POINT	PORLIER PASS
CAPE MUDGE	AMPHITRITE POINT	SATURNA ISLAND
CHROME ISLAND	ESTEVAN POINT	TRIAL ISLAND
BALLENAS ISLAND	QUATSINO	RACE ROCKS
ENTRANCE ISLAND	SCARLETT POINT	CARMANAH
SANDHEADS	CHATHAM POINT	CAPE BEALE
ACTIVE PASS	SISTERS ISLAND	LENNARD ISLAND
DISCOVERY ISLAND	MERRY ISLAND	NOOTKA
ALBERT HEAD	POINT ATKINSON	CAPE SCOTT

had to rely on survival techniques by setting trap lines, putting out fish nets and growing their own vegetables.

While certain delays still occur, lighthouse keepers can usually count on a visit at least every two weeks and a major resupply at least once a month, which keeps the Canadian Coast Guard aids to navigation vessels moving the better part of the time, not to mention the legions of unmanned navigation aids that need servicing. The vessels employed at this writing are the *Sir James Douglas, Wolfe* and *Camsell,* or one of six Coast Guard helicopters which bring everything needed at the stations—food, fuel, machinery, mail and such specialty items as pigs, cows, goats, and even a piano has been transported by sea to a lighthouse.

Despite technological changes over the past 20 years and the automation of equipment, the role of the British Columbia light keeper continues as an important link in the overall program of the Canadian Coast Guard, and though subject to change it adds a special dimension to the service. Though radio beacons and other electronic navigational gear have changed the role somewhat, the human element has proven essential in solving the unpredictable problems of weather, in aiding search and rescue operations and in providing a necessary service to mariners.

Long live manned lighthouses!

For many years the western Canadian shores have been considered dangerous for deep-sea ships, local commercial vessels and pleasure craft seeking safe harbor. Among the many navigation safeguards are 43 light stations in British Columbia, from the southern tip of Vancouver Island to the Alaskan border.

Canadians are well acquainted with lighthouses. The first recognized light tower was built by the French at Louisbourg, Cape Breton Island in 1740. It was lit by a circle of oil fed wicks carried in a glazed wooden chamber (lamphouse) atop a 66 foot column. The structure, 22 feet in diameter was damaged during the second seige of Louisbourg in 1758 and not replaced until 1842.

By 1910, Canada had 952 lighthouses along its shores on both coasts and had earned a national reputation as a leader in lighthouse design. Colonel W. P. Anderson, a Canadian architect and engineer, pioneered the technique of using reinforced ferro-concrete in construction of the towers and then added "flying buttresses" which rendered amazing strength by withstanding the strongest winds in Mother Nature's book of destruction, especially those on British Columbias' exposed Pacific rim.

The responsibility for management of Canada's marine aids was incorporated into the overall mandate of Transport Canada, headquartered in Ottawa, when the department was formed in 1936. At first it was known as the Department of Transport. In 1983, the Marine Administration of Transport Canada, better known as the Canadian Coast Guard was operating 20,000 lights, buoys, lighthouses, radio beacons and other marine markers from coast to coast, including 1,880 on the west coast, a tremendous responsibility for any government agency.

A typical British Columbia light station provides a number of navigational aids for the mariner. Its conspicuous shape and color by day and light characteristic by night provide a geographic reference to confirm a landfall location or radar position. The tower and light afford a reference for a visual line position to assist the mariner in determining a precise position. The radio beacon provides another bearing line that extends beyond the horizon, while the foghorn serves as a warning or homing reference in periods of low visibility.

Light keepers serve a vital role in assisting mariners. They operate and maintain mechanical and electrical equipment such as the fog alarm, generators, air compressors, and fog detectors in addition to the light beacon. In addition to keeping the machinery in working order, sea conditions and weather observations are taken several times a day and are used in weather broadcasts. An on-going radio contact with the Canadian Coast Guard VHF radio safety communications system provides essential service in relaying urgent messages and distress signals.

Numerous times a light keeper is called on to assist in a search and rescue operation, aid hikers who are lost or hungry, or to supply pleasure craft with emergency fuel. Sometimes lighthouse keeping is a

family tradition, passed on from father to son, from generation to generation. The motivation for a family or an individual to move to a lighthouse is summed up in the words of Jean Beaudet who served at the Bonilla Island station:

"The search for something fresh and worth living for and a natural inclination toward adventure...my wife and I found everything we longed for...hard work for a tangible reason, peace of mind and togetherness."

Station attendants usually take pride in their dwellings, with mowed lawns and productive gardens producing bright flowers and plump vegetables. Hours are often irregular, the access to a station may be difficult and the keeper is restricted to remaining at the site. Isolation is sometimes frustrating. When searching for suitable light keepers, the Canadian Coast Guard looks for qualities which indicate stability, reliability, and compatability with the living and working environment.

It is comforting to know that keepers are still very much a part of the overall function of Canadian lighthouses, for they have become a vanishing breed in the United States. Time may well make the above treatise on light keepers pass, but it is obvious that American lighthouses have never been quite the same since the advent of widespread automation. Many hope that the transition in British Columbia will be indeed slow in coming to pass.

Canadian West Coast lighthouses are divided into two districts—the Victoria Coast Guard District and the Prince Rupert District. There is also the Hay River, Northwest Territories under the Western Region, but it has no lighthouses, only buoys and minor lights. As of this writing, the Victoria District includes the following manned lighthouses: Pine Island, Pultney Point, Cape Mudge, Chrome (Yellow) Island, Ballenas Island, Entrance Island, Sand Heads, Active Pass, Discovery Island, (Albert Head, automated 1984) Sheringham Point, Pachena Point, Amphitrite Point, Estevan Point, Quatsino, Scarlett Point, Chatham Point, Sisters Island, Merry Island, Point Atkinson, Gallows Point, Porlier Pass, Saturna Island, Trial Island, Race Rocks, Carmanah, Cape Beale, Lennard Island, Nootka and Cape Scott.

The Prince Rupert District oversees the following lighthouses: Langara Point, Green Island, Lucy Island, Bonilla Island, McInnes Island, Dryad Point, Addenbroke Island, Triple Island, Lawyer Island, Boat Bluff, Ivory Island, Pointer Island and Egg Island.

Most of the classic lighting systems, namely Fresnels, have been removed from Canadian lighthouses in favor of more modern beacons, but at this writing they remain in two important lighthouses in the Victoria District—Point Atkinson on the searoad to Vancouver, B. C. and at Pachena Point on the west coast of Vancouver Island. In a marked departure from the classic systems. AGA PRB 21 fixtures have been installed at Estevan and Cape Scott. They are revolving arrays of high powered sealed beam lamps, eight beams per panel, and in essence are a 20th century adapation of the ancient clusters of parabolic reflectors each lighted by a single candle or oil flame. The new beacons are extremely powerful, effective and relatively easy to maintain.

When one thinks of British Columbia lighthouses one thinks first of Race Rocks. That lighthouse, located west of Victoria, B.C. is the finest stone block structure of its kind anywhere in the Pacific. Great blocks of granite, some six feet thick were cut, dressed and marked in Scotland and then shipped around the Horn by sailing vessel in 1859. Discharged by lighter at the site, the stone was placed by skilled masons to form a monumental 105 foot conical, shaped tower. The oil light in the tower lantern was lit in 1861, and has sent its friendly glow seaward since that date. There is only one older lighthouse in the province and that is the inactive Fisgard Lighthouse which became operative on November 16, 1860. Both lighthouses were under construction at the same time.

*Sand Heads Lightship No. 16 stood guard at the mouth of the Fraser River from 1913 until 1956 when replaced by the Sand Heads Lighthouse, lower left. No. 16, built as a sailing schooner in 1880 with the name **Thomas F. Bayard**, was the second lightship to serve the Fraser post. The first, was anchored there in 1866 and was withdrawn in 1879 in favor of a lighthouse. With the course of the river changing, a lightship again resumed the position in 1913, and she was replaced by the present lighthouse. Long time master, Captain E.L. Janes, was sad when the No. 16 was withdrawn, he having stuck with her through thick and thin including a few strandings when she parted her cables.*

George Davies who arrived with the supply vessel, was appointed initial keeper at Fisgard and was later transferred to Race Rocks.

Fisgard Light took its name from the British frigate that was utilized in the survey of Esquimpalt Harbor in 1847. Several years ago, the pioneer lighthouse, and nearby Fort Rodd became part of the Canadian National Park System. The light was cancelled in 1969, and the former keeper's dwelling converted to a lighthouse museum. Minor harbor lights have replaced the Fisgard beacon, but the lighthouse, designed by Herman Otto Tiedemann, German engineer and architect, stands as a cherished trophy of another day. Race Rocks on the other hand is very much alive, and enthusiastically maintained by its keepers. (C. Redhead assisted by L. W. Kennedy at this writing). The light, foghorn and radio beacon associated with the station warn ships away from a smattering of wave-washed obstructions.

Captain Kellett, performing survey work aboard the HMS *Herald,* in 1846 applied the name Race Rocks, suggested four years earlier by officials of the Hudson's Bay Company, evidently guided in their decision from the swift tidal sweep, nearly six miles an hour around the barrier.

Kellett was quoted as saying: "This dangerous ground is appropriately named, for the tide makes a perfect race around it." Thus, the name was officially retained.

On Christmas eve in 1865, London-born lighthouse keeper George Davies anxiously awaited the arrival of his sister, brother-in-law and three friends who were going to spend the holidays at the lighthouse. As their small boat neared the station, cross seas and a swirling eddy flipped it over, and before the eyes of the keeper all five occupants were thrown into the rough waters. Davies watched in horror. (A few days earlier the station skiff had been carried away by a storm and had not been replaced by the surveyor general.) One of the occupants of the boat drifted to within 20 feet of the landing, but there was no conveyance available to Davies, not even a lifering, so the swift currents carried the victim away. All five persons drowned. The shock weighed so heavily on the keeper that 11 months later he died.

The original funding allotted for Race Rocks and Fisgard lighthouses was $35,000, which today seems like a pittance for two such

The former Fiddle Reef Lighthouse, 1895-1979, was a prominent fixture near Victoria. It was replaced by a small light on a circular tower known as Fiddle Reef Sector. Old Department of Transport photo.

Vintage photo of the old Saturna Island Lighthouse at East Point in the Canadian San Juans. Built in 1888, it was replaced by Saturna Island Sector Light atop a red skeleton tower in 1978.

sturdy towers. Most records allege that Race Rocks Light was officially commissioned on February 7, 1861, including those of the Department of Transport, (Transport Canada) but other sources claim it sent out its first rays of light on December 26, 1860, shortly after the ill-fated bark *Nanette* approached the fog-shrouded rocks and crashed on the outcrops. Inbound for Esquimalt, 174 days out from England, the crew of the vessel struggled to safety with only the clothes on their backs, the cargo and the ship becoming a total loss, being valued at $160,000.

Somewhat on the reverse side, during the previous year, the ship *Morning Glory,* outbound for Valparaiso became waterlogged and had to be purposely grounded on Race Rocks to prevent her from going down in deep water.

Many vessels of many descriptions have encountered trouble off the troublesome barrier which lies just 1.5 miles from Vancouver Island. As recently as January 23, 1950, a keeper lost his life leaving the lighthouse in the station skiff to get his monthly allotment of supplies. The craft was found empty the next day after gale-force winds had raked the strait, but his body was never recovered.

A freak gale claimed the steamer *Sechelt* on March 24, 1911. As the vessel, on the Victoria-Sooke run, passed near the lighthouse she attempted to put about in the midst of the storm. Caught in the trough, succeeding waves swamped her decks, over she rolled and went down like a rock taking 30 souls to a watery grave.

A drama of another kind took place off Race Rocks on October 15, 1925 when the Dutch cargo vessel *Eemdyk* stranded on nearby Bentinck Island, known for its leper colony. Two days later, the tug *Hope* in attempting to refloat the freighter, capsized drowning seven persons.

Four years later, on a foggy October 13, 1929, the sleek three-stack passenger liner *Empress of Canada* endeavoring to keep clear of Race Rocks grounded on nearby Albert Head. The story got prime front

A sight to behold, Point Atkinson Lighthouse at the north point of the entrance to Burrard Inlet is a regal, hexagonal-shaped tower with six buttresses. The station was established in 1875, and continues its role with light, foghorn and radio beacon.

page news coverage, and though the 26,000 ton, 24-knot ship was freed eventually on a floodtide with the assistance of a fleet of tugs, Lloyd's of London was most unhappy when presented with a bill for $100,000. Within a year of the stranding, Albert Head was marked by a light and foghorn and was a manned station until recent years.

The topographical formation of Race Rocks created a zone of silence for years, mariners insisting the foghorn was inaudible. Not until somebody came up with the suggestion of raising the elevation of the signal by some 30 feet was the dilemma solved. Under all weather conditions navigators are warned to remain at least a mile off Race Rocks, the tall tower, on Great Race Rock, easily recognizable with broad black and white bands. The warning includes a wide berth for Rosedale Reef, a ship killer in its own right, named for the British ship *Rosedale* that grounded there in 1862.

To better facilitate shipping on the Canadian side of the Strait of Juan de Fuca, the Canadian government established a lighthouse at Sheringham Point in 1912, 16 miles northwest of Race Rocks. In a picturesque setting, the station stands out with its 64 foot hexagonal, reinforced concrete tower and red circular lantern house, passed by a continual parade of deep-sea ships and commercial fishing vessels.

Named by Captain Kellett during his survey for British vice Admiral William Louis Sheringham R. N. in 1846, the title stuck, negating the name Punta de San Eusivio, placed on the nob of land by Spanish navigator Quimper in 1790.

The keeper at Sheringham often hears military hardware from his lofty perch, for in the vicinity of Sheringham Point and San Simon Point, Canadian armed forces use the area for sea-oriented gunnery practice.

Space does not permit coverage of the many manned and unmanned light stations in British Columbia waters, but in the following lines are some gleanings and highlights concerning the more important Canadian sentinels on that nation's Pacific side. The larger

One of the long time keepers of Point Atkinson was Gordon Odlum, seen tending the needs of the big Fresnel in the lantern house in the 1960s. Vancouver Province photo.

229

Sheringham Point Lighthouse, on the Strait of Juan de Fuca was commissioned in 1912 and has been little altered, although the light and fog signal have been updated. It is one of many manned British Columbia lighthouses. This Department of Transport photo was taken in the 1930s.

percentage are located in the southern half of the province where most of the major seaports are located, but the rugged northern coast, along the Inside and Outside passages is the location of some of the lesser known but nevertheless splendid sentinels of light where drama and isolation sometimes go hand in hand. Some of the lighthouses have been reduced in status, automated or discontinued in recent years, but the majority still have keepers on duty.

Situated at Sand Heads at the mouth of the Fraser River on a platform supported by piling driven deep into the river bed stands an unorthodox lighthouse built in 1956-57 to replace the veteran *Sand Heads Lightship No. 16.* The foundation, a modern adaptation of the pile screw principal was employed—hollow steel pile being filled with concrete. The first floor of the aluminum structure contains an engine room, kitchen, living room, bathroom, and store rooms; the second floor has four bedrooms and a radio and radio beacon room. Designed for two men rotationally, for two week periods, the station has its own boat used to effect crew changeovers from Steveston, six miles upriver. The beacon is a DCB 10 rotating beacon. Total cost of the station was $238,000, and though to the casual viewer it is anything but appealing to the eye, it has proven itself highly efficient for its purpose.

Marking the gateway to the Fraser, where upriver lies the port of New Westminster, there exists an on-again off-again chapter of marine history. Sand Heads was the location of the first lightship on either the U. S. or Canadian Pacific shoreline. In 1866, the pioneer Fraser River Lightship took up its station, but by 1884, due to dry rot and neglect, the old vessel had to be replaced by the North Sand Heads Lighthouse. The frame structure was mounted on iron piles driven into the sand and braced with stringers and heavy strength bolts. The two-story affair, with lantern and clockwork fogbell was in service for only two decades, its demise being forced before its time by the changing of the river channel, leaving the lighthouse sitting like a stranded porpoise a mile out of the main shipping lanes.

"Tear it down," ordered the Canadian government, and so the brief career of the North Sands Head Lighthouse came to a screeching halt in 1911. A plan was then put forth to re-establish the beacon on Rose Spit on the eastern side of Graham Island. The CGS *Newington* towed a derrick scow to the site to aid in the dismantling, but after exhaustive efforts with little success it was decided that the wooden structure would have to be burned down to the steel piling. The *Newington's* mate, Oscar Hallgren, affectionately known as Long Bill, scattered coal oil liberally about the structures' interior and then put a match to

it, but he had not considered his escape and found himself on the top floor engulfed in flames. Dashing frantically about from window to window, he finally, from sheer desperation, hurled himself from the raging inferno to the river waters below where his shipmates rushed to his rescue. Of his own admission, he was a wetter but wiser man.

Lightship No. 16 assumed her post at the river entrance in 1913 and rendered tenacious service until 1955, but not without incident. Before becoming a lightship, the vessel had several aliases—a pilot vessel, cargo-passenger sailer and a sealing vessel all under the name *Thomas F. Bayard,* American built, on the east coast in 1880. As a lightship she was fitted out with quarters for a three man crew, and within her 86 by 21 foot frame was a light and a fog signal.

While on station in February 1947, a furious storm lashed the river mouth, causing the vessel to slip her anchor cables and drift ashore. Her one man crew at that time, Captain Len James, managed to walk to safety along the north arm of the jetty.

Pulled free and repaired, the aging ship returned to her station. Then on November 11, 1955, history repeated itself. Gale-lashed seas ripped her from her anchorage and drove her hard on the rocks, doing considerable damage to her hull planking. It was that incident that prompted the Department of Transport to terminate the services of the overaged vessel, after which plans were made for the existing lighthouse at the mouth of the Fraser. The vessel was sold to private interests and pushed around from pillar to post for several years until finally a plan was devised to restore the vessel as a sailing schooner under a $50,000 government grant, and she remains afloat after more than a century.

So, Sand Heads has been the location of two lighthouses and two lightships, a rather unusual circumstance in the history of Canadian pharology.

No lighthouse is better known in the province than Point Atkinson Light, passed by all the ships moving in and out of busy Vancouver B. C. Harbor. Located on the north point of the entrance to Burrard Inlet, the 60 foot tower has been a land and seamark since 1912, although the station was established in 1875. The hexagonal concrete reinforced tower, with six buttresses, shines its light 108 feet above the water and features a powerful fog signal and radio beacon.

One of the traditional old-time light keepers who tended Atkinson for many years, was Gordon Odlum. His long tenure of service went back to the day when the lamps were lit with kerosene and the lenses were turned by counterweights much like a grandfather clock. Regularly he wound the weights and timed the sequence with his stopwatch to be certain the light characteristic was precisely correct.

In 1963, an electric motor was installed to revolve the big Fresnel, but the former hand gear was retained in case of power outages. Since that date, Point Atkinson has been an experimental point for electronic systems, but as of 1985, the station still retained its classic lighting fixture.

Odlum earned his papers as a radio operator when he shifted into the new era, but vividly recalled how he and his assistant until 1963 each climbed steps equivalent to 150,000 feet per year to keep the light in proper operation. The grandfather clock mechanism which revolved the lens had a suspended 500 pound weight that dropped 50 feet down a shaft (or trunk) every 2½ hours. It took ten minutes to rewind and each keeper made four trips a day or climbed 400 feet.

Former district marine agent for the Department of Transport, Thomas Morrison, got his start at Point Atkinson helping pack 50 tons of coal from a small lighter to the foghorn house where it was used as fuel to generate steam for the fog whistle.

One of the keepers of the light at this writing, D. R. Graham, is putting the finishing touches on a voluminous book on the history of British Columbia lighthouses.

Many of B. C.'s most colorful and isolated light stations are in the northern sector. Take Langara Point Light for instance. Built in 1913, it is the most northerly major beacon in the province between Puget Sound and Alaska, the light, fog signal and radio beacon being the only buildings on a tiny islet off the northwest tip of Graham Island in the Queen Charlotte chain. At the southern end, on an even smaller islet is Cape St. James Light Station, dating from 1914. Marking the north and the south points of the Queen Charlottes, they were built a year apart, one hexagonal in shape, the other octagonal, and both of reinforced concrete. Though kin under their thick skins, they are miles apart and for the most part separated from the rest of the world.

Except for being the home of the Haida Indians and where the rare jade totems come from, the Queen Charlottes are relatively unknown to most, one of the charming secrets of the modern world. Sparsely populated and separated from the mainland by 75 miles of frequently rough water, known as the Hecate Strait, the island chain is about 175 miles long tapering down like a conch shell at the southern extremity. Graham and Moresby are the two largest islands, separated by Skidegate Channel, all of which are away from the tourist rush.

It was Juan Perez, a Spanish naval officer who discovered the island chain in his corvette *Santiago* July 18, 1774. Reputedly the Haidas had never before seen white men. He dropped anchor off Langara Island and named it for Admiral Langara of the Spanish Navy. Little did he know that someday it would become the natural location of a lighthouse. It was unfortunate that it took so many years to establish lighthouses at either end of the chain. The west coast of the Queen Charlottes are virtually isolated and except for lighthouse keepers, radio operators and their families, Langara and St. James, so far apart, are like two bookends with the land mass in between.

Some of the sting of the intolerable loneliness of bygone years at the two stations has been improved by more frequent visits from the lighthouse tenders and in an emergency, a helicopter.

A modern radio beacon was installed at the St. James station in 1958. Its big revolving light sends warnings out from a lofty elevation 318 feet above the Pacific. Its distant cousin at the other end of the chain is strengthened by six buttresses of the Anderson design, and is situated 100 feet above the water.

Quatsino Light at the southeast end of Kains Island on the British Columbia west coast was established in 1907 and has been an important guiding beacon since that date.

A rather unusual situation occurred there in October 1971. The eating habits of a wild cougar became crucial to two couples who tended the beacon. The lively creature swam 800 feet to the small island evidently in search of a meal of venison. Little did he realize the wee bit of terra firma had no deer population to satisfy his hunger pangs.

One of the keepers sent out a radio message inquiring about the behavior of a hungry cougar. Back came the "reassuring" word from the provincial wildlife branch that animals of the breed are reasonably well behaved but that there was "a remote possibility it could attack a human. Its like playing Russian roulette with a 10,000 shot revolver," the authority said, "You never know what an individual animal will do."

Meanwhile the somewhat perplexed attendants kept hoping the cougar would just desist. Finally they got their wish. He suddenly vanished, probably swimming back to Vancouver Island where the pickings weren't quite so slim.

Green Island Lighthouse in Chatham Sound, established in 1906, was the locale of a tragic occurrence in June of 1963. Two lighthouse keepers disappeared mysteriously from the island much to the horror of their wives. They had set out from the station on a Sunday afternoon in a 14 foot skiff with an outboard motor to recover some creosoted timbers that had washed away from the helicopter landing pad. Their wives kept a lookout until it grew dark and then lit a bonfire on the beach and put the light into operation.

One of the splendid reinforced concrete towers in the northern district is Langara in the Queen Charlottes. Fortified with six buttresses it was commissioned in 1913 and fitted with a first order lens. The tower remains with a new lighting apparatus. Department of Transport photo.

When the missing men failed to return by the next day, their spouses sent out a message for urgent assistance which launched an extensive sea and air search from the Prince Rupert District, 30 miles away. An exhaustive effort turned up nothing.

To this day, the disappearance of the two keepers remains a mystery, mostly due to the fact that the sea was not rough when they launched out on their mission.

In February of 1967, a Department of Transport emergency crew was rushed north to begin salvaging equipment at Pine Island Light Station after it was struck by what was believed a 50 foot seismic tidal wave. More than $50,000 in damage was caused when a wall of water crushed the powerhouse, foghorn house and radio beacon. The light tower escaped serious damage.

Lighthouse keeper Rex (Pen) Brown, his wife and two children were asleep when the wave struck. Their home, only a few yards from the ruined powerhouse was providentially spared after the wave took a strange twist.

Pictured here is Green Island Lighthouse built in 1906, on an isle in Chatham Sound. The photo was taken in the 1940s. Courtesy, Department of Transport.

Cape St. James, one of the very isolated lighthouses in the Queen Charlottes, is located on St. James Island and was solidly built of reinforced concrete in 1914. The photo shows the uniformed keepers and the wife of the head keeper, taken in the 1920s. The tower is still very much in use today. Photo courtesy Department of Transport, northern district.

As a safeguard, Brown (who has been with the Victoria District Office for the past several years) took his family to higher ground for safety, but the sea recoiled from its furious attack.

The lighthouse tender *Camsell* made knots to the island to assist with repairs and cleanup. The station radio beacon had been bent 35 degrees by the power of the onrushing sea.

Nearby Egg Island Lighthouse also received damage from the onslaught. And certainly there was concern there, because in 1948, the former lighthouse at that location had been washed into the sea by a similar Act of God.

Solitary Cape Mudge Lighthouse stands sentinel on the southern tip of Quadra Island on the main shipping channel. Treacherous Seymour Narrows is located eight miles north of the lighthouse. Until 1958 the narrows was famous for Ripple Rock, one of the most feared ship hazards in Pacific coastal waters. After a half century of futile efforts to eradicate the obstruction, men finally succeeded in constructing a tunnel underneath the rock and implanting underwater explosives. The result was the world's largest non-nuclear blast to that date, an awesome explosion that gained world-wide attention. Now

there is deep water where the rock once broke the surface. Deep-sea ships pass in safety despite an extremely swift tidal surge through the narrows.

Ripple Rock is gone, but stalwart, concrete Cape Mudge Lighthouse continues its vigil as it has since 1915 when it replaced the original lighthouse which dated from 1898.

Typical of those vanishing Canadian lighthouses was the First Narrows sentinel. In February 1969, the 79 year old structure, long a fixture at the mouth of Vancouver's Capilano River off Ambleside Beach was terminated by inferno.

The Vancouver Pile Driving and Contracting Company held a contract to burn and remove the wooden structure, and nary a voice of protest was lifted. Suddenly one day the historic building, painted white with red trim, perched like a happy clam on a piling supported platform, was no longer there. It rated a big picture in the *Vancouver Province*, engulfed in flames, and that was its obituary.

Problems of another nature involving modern lighthouse keepers occurred at Cape Scott at the northern tip of Vancouver Island. On April 7, 1969, time, expense and poor weather were against the three attendants at the station who were eligible to vote in the general election in the Comox-Alberni district".

"There's just no way we can get a ballot box to them," local authorities insisted. "The only way to reach the trio at Cape Scott would be to hire a helicopter."

Colin Wilson from the district office said, "If I were to put in a request to fly a ballot box there, the wires between here and Ottawa would burn out."

He estimated the cost would be $3,500, or $350 per hour for ten hours flying time, and then went on to say the tip of the island had just been battered by a storm.

Lighthouse keeper J. A. Pulley and his two assistants were three of 41,600 persons in the district eligible to vote, but their isolated station which was supplied by ship once a month, was miles away from any other habitation. On that occasion they were unable to vote, but being strong individuals used to their isolation, took it all in stride.

A violent storm struck the area between Cape Scott and Cape St. James (from northern Vancouver Island to the Queen Charlottes) in late April 1985. Two commercial fishermen drowned, four halibut vessels foundered, and 17 persons were rescued by a joint effort of both American and Canadian helicopters. Seas of 30 feet and winds exceeding 65 knots made rescue work hazardous on April 25-26. All

The old Quatsino (Kains Island) Lighthouse on the southeast end of the island, built in 1907, was replaced by a modern, white circular tower in 1977. Photo taken in 1918.

Egg Island Lighthouse was built in 1898, and is pictured here in the year 1913. Located on the island summit in Queen Charlotte Sound, a lattice tower replaced the aging structure in recent years. From Department of Transport files, (now Transport Canada).

beacon was established there in 1900 at a strategic position in the Gulf of Georgia, east of Parksville on Vancouver Island. The station has been updated several times and the light is presently displayed from a white circular tower.

The place might be referred to as a "whale of an island," for the name is of Spanish origin, Isles de las Ballenas (Islands of the Whales) a title applied by the 1791 expedition of Lieutenant Francisco Eliza exploring in the Spanish armed ships *San Carlos* and *Santa Saturnina,* the latter vessel in command of Jose Maria Narvaez.

Evidently the British paid little attention to the Spanish language, for the Admiralty charts carried the islands with the name "Ballinas" until the Geographic Board of Canada made a correction in 1905.

Chrome Island Light Station on Denman Island was formerly called Yellow Island Light Station by local inhabitants. Yellow Island was officially adapted by the Admiralty surveyors in 1860, the name originating from the unusual light colored rock that covers much of the isle's terrain, the east end marked with numerous ancient Indian hieroglyphics.

Sophistication must have set in when the island's name was changed in recent years from Yellow to Chrome, or else someone was trying to prove a point with a color chart. At any rate, the "colorful" island is rich in history and lore. Perhaps the real reason for the name change was confusion with Yellow Island in Discovery Passage.

During a heavy southeast gale on December 16, 1900, the British steamer *Alpha,* bound for Union Bay for bunker coal, before departure for Japan, ran hard on the rocks at the east end of the island and foundered with her captain and eight crewmen. The tragedy was revived in recent years when Vancouver B. C. scuba diver Al Rogers recovered the barnacle-encrusted bell, still bearing the ship's name.

Cape Mudge Lighthouse, near Campbell River on the inside route, is a stately octagonal reinforced concrete lighthouse built in 1915, replacing the 1898 structure. This photo was taken in 1965.

the Canadian lighthouses in the general area kept operating throughout the storm.

In recent years a new lighting fixture was placed at Cape Scott, one of the powerful AGA PRB 21 models, consisting of panels of sealed beams, eight to a panel.

One does not usually view lighthouse keepers as a discontented breed of workmen, but in our age of protest marches, civil strife and automation they sometimes climb on the bandwagon. In the spring of 1966, the Department of Transport was confronted by a problem when the lighthouse keepers in the British Columbia and the Yukon Territory requested the federal government to make revision in their duties. Requests included that they not be required to do any painting and maintenance work above 30 feet and that the work hours be shortened, with safety gear provided. The requests were taken under advisement at the biennial convention of the B. C. branch of the Civil Service Association held in Vancouver B. C. The 32 delegates complained that most lighthouses in the province were staffed by only two keepers, meaning each man was on duty for 12 hours a day. The membership at that time included about 100 lighthouse keepers in B. C. and the Yukon.

Some of the requests were granted, some denied, but it appeared that a mutual meeting of the minds was gained, with always the overshadowing thought that someday their jobs might be curtailed by automation.

A touch of the Spanish influence surrounds Ballenas Islands Lighthouse on the north point of North Ballenas Island. The first

Lights have marked Chrome Island since 1890, and today it is referred to as Chrome (Yellow) Island Range, a yellow flashing light and a yellow and a white fixed range light, the former shown from a red skeleton tower. A fog signal has been on the island since 1908.

Another interesting British Columbia lighthouse is Dryad Point, located on the northeast coast of Campbell Island. Following its establishment in 1899 it was in the charge of a Bella Bella Indian known as Captain Carpenter, the title conveyed upon him because his given name translated into English was "Rainbow," hardly an appropriate handle for a robust Indian. His squaw was a descendant of an old chief of high rank named Kaiete who, in 1805 reputedly inspired an attack on the Boston ship *Atahualpa,* trading for pelts on Millbank Sound, which resulted in the death of Captain Oliver Porter, his chief mate and nine crewmen out of the complement of 23. Nine others were wounded in the bloody melee but they fought bravely on and not only thwarted the capture of their ship, but fatally shot Kaiete.

Dryad Point was named for the Hudson's Bay brig *Dryad,* which played a major role in the early maritime history of British Columbia. Originally named Turn Point by the Admiralty surveyors, it was later changed by the Geographic Board of Canada to avoid any conflict with the United States lighthouse located at Turn Point on Stuart Island in the San Juan Archipelago.

In 1980, the former Dryad Point Lighthouse was replaced by a white square structure and recorded in the Canadian *Pacific Coast List of Lights* as the Dryad Point Sector.

Atop the summit of San Rafael Island just inside Yuquot Point, at Friendly Cove stands Nootka Lighthouse. Most of the early explorers and traders were familiar with the Nootka Sound area, and for countless years it has been the habitation of a segment of the Indian nation. History abounds in that cozy corner of picturesque British Columbia.

A tablet affixed to a monument at the entrance to Nootka Sound reads:

"Discovered by Captain James Cook in March 1778. In June 1789, Spain took possession and established and maintained a settlement there until 1795. The capture of British vessels in 1789, almost led to war between the two countries prevented only by the Nootka Convention the following year. Vancouver and Quadra met there in August 1792 to determine the land to be restored under that convention."

Cape Scott at the extreme northwest tip of Vancouver Island has been lighted since 1927. The structure here holds a DCB 36 beacon with a long range. In the 1980s, it was replaced with an AGA PRB 21 fixture—a host of parabolic sealed beams in tiers.

Dryad Point Lighthouse was constructed in 1899, near Bella Bella, a colorful little station in the northern district. Located at the north entrance of the main passage, Seaforth Channel, it is referred to today as Dryad Point Sector. Joe Williamson photo.

*Chrome (Yellow) Island Light was established in 1890 on the extemity of the island in Baynes Sound. The structue was updated in 1898, 1922 and 1977. The Canadian **Light List** presently lables it, Chrome Island Range involving two lights on the island.*

Upper photo, the old Cape Beale Lighthouse, dating from 1874, was replaced by a new structure in March 1958 (lower photo). Again in 1979, the name was changed to Cape Beale Sector, a red square skeleton tower with white slatwork. The beacon is located on the southeast point of Barkley Sound entrance.

The initial lighthouse was not placed there till 1911, a rather late date on the calendar considering the marine activity connected with the locale. The sentinel was a square, wooden dwelling surmounted by an iron lantern house rising 37 feet above the ground, with a focal plane 103 feet above the water. The station was updated in 1958 and is presently listed as a red, square skeleton tower with white slatwork. A fog signal has been on the premises since 1928.

There are sections of the west coast of Vancouver Island that have never been fully explored. The deep ravines, tree-forested hills and rocky, sea front bastions have formed a backdrop for a cemetery of ships down through history. The ill-reputed coast has claimed a wreck for every mile of shore from Port Renfrew to Barclay Sound; the sailors of old referring to that area as the "Graveyard of Ships." From Amphitrite Point to Estevan Point the same situation exists. Prevailing northerly currents, pea soup fogs and fickle winds have swept many vessels on the tentacle-like outcrops of Vancouver Island's western ramparts totalling most of them out, and in several cases causing loss of life.

Recognizing the urgent need for aids to navigation, the Canadian government around the turn of the century was forced to take more aggressive measures in providing safeguards. Until 1891, the only lighthouse along that bizarre coast was at lonely Cape Beale. It was erected in 1874, and due to the difficulty of bringing in building materials, the tower, foghorn house and dwelling had to be fashioned of virgin timber felled at the site. The station was completed July 1, 1874, and the light, a first order catoptric revolving lens, was displayed that night. That pioneer structure was in service till 1958 when it was replaced by a more modern slatwork-surrounded circular tower with cast aluminum lantern house.

Today it is listed as Cape Beale Sector Light, flashing white and red from a red square skeleton tower with white slatwork. Two foghorns sound in unison and a radio beacon is attached to the station. The tower stands on the southeast point of the Barkley Sound entrance.

To tempest-tossed sailors, old Cape Beale Light was like a rose among thorns, for when night closed in, or wet fogs dropped their mantle blotting out the natural landmarks, danger lurked with a capital D. With no other lights or fog signals in the vicinity, no radio-telephone, radar, radio beacons or direction finders the lighthouse was heavily depended upon for guidance.

A dramatic chapter in British Columbia lighthouse history unfolded in the early part of the century. A gale was whipping the North Pacific December 6, 1906 as the bark *Coloma* commenced her voyage to Australia from Puget Sound laden with lumber. Captain J. Allison and his crew of nine scurried about the decks as they moved out of the Strait of Juan de Fuca into the Pacific. Velocity of the wind was such that it began ripping the canvas to ribbons, until under bare poles the vessel was carried unceremoneously toward the dreaded coast of lost ships. Low scudding clouds brought waves of rain so heavy that it blotted out the shoreline.

An alert Captain Thomas Paterson, keeper of the Cape Beale Light peered out on the troubled ocean when suddenly in the din his trained eye caught the blurry outline of the troubled ship. Winds had blown down the single telephone line which was the station's only contact with the outside world. It appeared but a matter of time until the vessel would be on top of the rocky reef.

Caught in a dilemma, the station keeper could not leave his post, having to stay nearby the fires burning in the boiler to keep the steam foghorn activated to prevent other vessels from nearing the dangerous shore. The lighthouse tender *Quadra* lay at anchor at Bamfield, six miles away, but how could he alert its commanding officer of the ship in distress.

Realizing her husband's predicament, brave Minnie Paterson volunteered to go for help. Night was coming on with a furor, fallen trees were everywhere, the still standing forest, dark and thick, divided by rocky barriers and deep ravines. Still, the frail woman hesitated not, and though grave concern was expressed by her husband, she began her perilous journey.

After several rigorous hours, tired, battered and bruised, with almost superhuman endurance, she half walked, half crawled to the home of Mrs. Annie McKay, daughter of the previous keeper at Cape Beale, who lived near the village of Bamfield. Hardly stopping to rest, she and her friend hurried to the beach, launched a skiff into turbulent waters and rowed out to the anchored government tender where astounded crewmen pulled the two aboard and escorted them to Captain Hackett's cabin.

Within a short time, the *Quadra* was steaming up, and after debarking the women, headed out into the teeth of the gale. Oil skin-clad lookouts scanning the inky coastline soon spotted the hazy outline of the disabled vessel, tugging at her anchor cables. The watch sang out, "Wreck dead ahead!"

The *Coloma* was on the verge of holing her wooden hull on the sharp rocks, so close to the dreaded barrier that the rescue vessel could not move in for fear of going aground. Volunteers were called to man the ship's boat and take a line to the floundering square-rigger. Several stepped forward and with great difficulty the craft was launched on the lee side of the *Quadra*. Exercising some expert small boat handling, the oarsmen risking life and limb came alongside the imperiled vessel and managed to rescue the crew, one at a time jumping into the confines of the pulsating craft. Constant baling was necessary to keep from swamping. Finally they got clear of the *Coloma* and headed back to the *Quadra* reaching their destination none too soon, for shortly after, the distressed sailing vessel slipped her chains and was dashed to pieces on the rocks.

The survivors owed their lives to the indomitable Minnie Paterson, who after a long rest made her way back to the lighthouse and a grand reunion with her husband. When word reached the outside, Minnie was acclaimed as British Columbia's 'Grace Darling.' Due to overexertion, from that ordeal she died five years later bringing great sadness to her husband and five children.

The first keeper assigned to Cape Beale in 1874, was Irish-born Emmanuel Cox, who arrived by steam tug with his wife, three daughters and two sons. He transferred from Berens Island Lighthouse near Victoria. The family had a rigorous existence at the station, and the keeper after several years died at his lonely post.

Carmanah Lighthouse, southeast of Cape Beale, was the second major navigation aid funded and constructed by the Canadian government on Vancouver Island's west coast. Erected in a pristine sector, the new lighthouse appeared so much by day like the Cape Beale sentinel that it was decided to paint the lantern house red as opposed to the black lantern house at the other station. (Today virtually all the lantern houses on British Columbia lighthouses are painted red).

Commissioned in 1891, its presence was a much appreciated addition to the maritime scene especially to masters of sailing vessels awaiting favorable sailing conditions for entering the strait. The growing importance of the lighthouse was recognized to the point that the original frame structure was replaced by a more durable 56 foot concrete reinforced tower just three decades later.

Before the turn of the century, the attendants at both Carmanah and Cape Beale learned how to tolerate loneliness and privation, often waiting many weeks for supplies and mail to arrive by sea. They were resourceful enough to raise their own vegetables, hunt wild game and fish from virgin streams and ocean rocks. Often their survival depended on their resourcefulness.

In the interim, the rash of ship disasters along the western rim of Vancouver Island prompted the Canadian government to establish lifesaving huts at certain points where a shipwreck trail of sorts led castaways to temporary shelter and supplies of imperishable foods. From there, they usually made their way to one of the lighthouses where they were guests until a rescue vessel arrived.

Despite the efforts of the two lighthouses at the turn of the century, shipwrecks increased and public demand was for more and better safeguards. Limited funds prevented further input until the shocking disaster on January 23, 1906. The passenger liner *Valencia,* bound for Puget Sound from San Francisco, overran her course while seeking out the entrance to the Strait of Juan de Fuca, and in the thickening maw was driven into an inescapable gunk hole near Pachena Point. What had begun as an uneventful voyage north ended in a nightmare. Before dawn on that miserable winter day, a pitiful band of survivors stood shivering around a small beach fire gazing with stinging eyes toward the scene of the wreck. The *Valencia,* her hull ripped open like a tin can had gone down, claiming 117 lives, and there was not a woman or child among the 37 survivors. From the standpoint of loss of life, it was the worst disaster along that coastal graveyard of ships.

As a result of that terrible tragedy, the Canadian government was forced into the construction of Pachena Point Lighthouse which was established in 1907, a 66 foot octagonal frame tower, one of two in the Victoria District that at this date retains its classic lighting system. Its Fresnel is visible 20 miles at sea from a lofty perch, 200 feet above the sea. The lighthouse had the distinction of being pictorially featured in the 1910 *Encyclopedia Britannica* as an example of a typical modern lighthouse. By todays standards it is outmoded, and a few years back there was discussion of replacing it with a modern tower and lighting fixture. Thus far, that endeavor has been delayed, and the shingle-covered tower continues its proud vigil.

Some other notable wrecks in the vicinity of Pachena Point in addition to the *Valencia,* were the bark *Sarah* wrecked in November 1891, and the schooner *Laura Pike* in March of the same year. On December 31, 1895, the British iron-hulled bark *Janet Cowan,* a lofty 2,497 ton square-rigger out of Greenock, crashed ashore four miles east of Pachena, 108 days out of Capetown. Seven of her crew, including the skipper perished of exposure after reaching the hostile shores.

Though Vancouver Island's maritime graveyard doesn't have as many victims as it once did, an occasional cargo ship becomes a twisted mass of steel from running afoul of its outer clutches of rock.

By 1940, the government of Canada had 50 navigation aids in service between Carmanah and Cape Scott compared to only two before the turn of the century.

Aged sea charts labled the area as highly dangerous to navigation and old salts told tales of shipwreck and of hostile natives along its shores from the time of Spanish exploration. Fragile records, Indian legends or relics from wrecked ships gave mute evidence of the stark drama of the yesteryears. Such happenings of the past are revived every time an old barnacle-encrusted anchor, cannon or other piece of wreckage is raised from the offshore waters or is uncovered from the sands along the shore.

The native Indians of the British Columbia coast in pre-discovery times were not navigators, and unlike the early Polynesians were unable to plot a course by the stars, but few could equal them in the building or handling of their canoes, anywhere from a dugout to a large war canoe. They generally remained within sight of the land using as their aids to navigation, the headlands, mountain peaks and tall trees along the coastal routes. Sometimes they paddled their large canoes several hundreds of miles, either to barter or carry out hit-and-run raids, much in the style of the Vikings.

Amphitrite Point was named by Captain Richards of the British survey vessel *Plumper* in 1859, to honor the HMS *Amphitrite,* a 24 gun frigate, of 1,064 tons which served in British Columbia waters for six years. The name Amphitrite comes from Greek mythology, she being the wife of Poseidon or King Neptune, goddess of the seas.

The lighthouse, marking the point at the entrance to Ucluelet Harbor on the west coast of Vancouver Island, is a unique rectangular tower built of concrete with a rounded front and a red octagonal iron lantern. The structure stands on a concrete base 11 feet high with a rounded front. A lighthouse was first placed at the location in 1905, but the present structure is more modern and able to withstand the punishment from the cruel pranks of the rugged weather pattern in the area. There is also an important radio beacon at the site.

Lennard Island has been marked by a lighthouse since 1904 at the southwest point of the island on the west side of Templar Channel, south of Wickaninnish Island. Named in honor of Edward Barrett-Lennard who in 1869 circumnavigated Vancouver Island in his cutter-yacht *Templar,* the place is pivotal for navigators. On his island voyage, Lennard was accompanied by his friend, Captain N. Fitz Stubbs, who brought him out from England aboard his ship *Athelstan.* Captain Richards of the British survey ship *Hecate* applied Lennard's name to the isle in 1861.

Near Wickaninnish Island, named for the great chief of the Clayoquot tribe, is the alleged site of a terrible tragedy where in 1811 John J. Astor's ship *Tonquin,* while trading for sea otter skins became the scene of a bloody fracas after the natives attempted to take over the ship and massacre its crew. The vessel was blown to pieces when the one remaining crewman set off the powder magazine killing great numbers of natives who in turn had killed all the other white men on the vessel, including Captain Jonathan Thorn.

The original Lennard Island lighthouse was an octagonal wooden tower, 80 feet high, standing 108 feet above the sea, and displaying a first order dioptric light, visible 16 nautical miles. It has been replaced by a pencil thin circular tower with a red band at the top and an exposed revolving beacon, highly practical but with none of the charm of its predecessor.

Estevan Lighthouse was the only aid to navigation in Canada to encounter enemy shellfire during World War II. A Japanese submarine surfaced at night and fired shells at the tower. The light must have impressed the skipper of the submersible, for it evidently was his target. The alert station attendant had the good sense to quickly extinguish the beacon's glow as well as all other lights at the station, thus saving the tower from serious damage. Shells whizzed over the premises and landed harmlessly in the fields and forest beyond. Further survey showed that 30 rounds of shells hit the area but none of the buildings sustained serious damage. The submarine vanished into the night never to return, though a sharp vigil was maintained for months thereafter.

Carmanah, on the point two miles from Bonilla Point on Vancouver Island's west coast, is a prime example of an octagonal, reinforced concrete tower, rising 56 feet and situated 175 feet above the Pacific. The station was first established in 1891 following a rash of shipwrecks. The photo was taken by her former keeper H.C. Pearce. The radio beacon is pictured near the tower.

The keepers can be seen at work on the lantern dome at Pachena Lighthouse on the west coast of Vancouver Island. This charming old tower dating from 1907, warns ships away from a coast of lost ships, where it is claimed, over a 40 mile stretch, that there is one wreck for each mile. At this writing, Pachena maintains its dignity, still utilizing its big Fresnel. It also has the distinction of having had its picture in the **Encyclopedia Britannica** *as an example of a fine lighthouse. The wooden tower, 66 feet high is flanked by two comfortable keepers dwellings.*

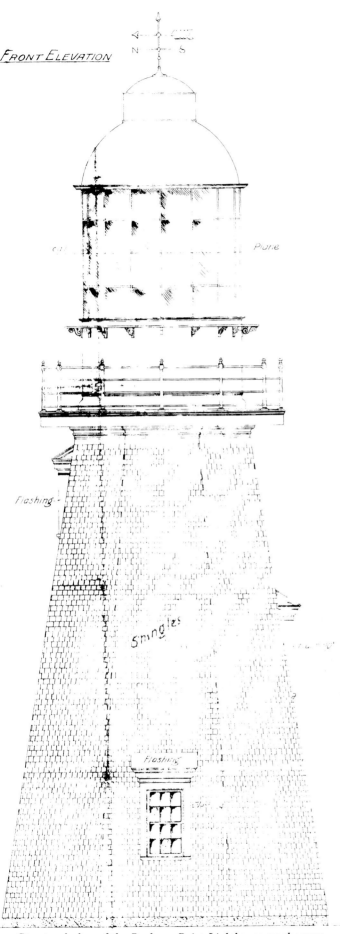

E. T. Redford, then chief wireless operator at Estevan Point, afforded the following eyewitness report of the June 20, 1942 incident:

The submarine surfaced about two miles offshore and was plainly visible. Shelling commenced at approximately 9:40 p.m. and continued for about 40 minutes. The first shells landed on the beach about 100 yards in front of the lighthouse. Mr. Lally, who was the light keeper at the time, immediately put out the light. The sub apparently then raised its sights, for from then on the shells went overhead. Approximately 25 shells were fired and, except for a few buildings hit by shell fragments, no damage was caused either to the lighthouse or radio station. With the exception of the men on shift, who tapped out word of the shelling to Pacific Command, all others gave a hand getting the women and children away from the settlement. The submarine pulled out on the surface and everyone could see and hear the diesel engines quite clearly. While naturally there was some nervousness, everyone, including the women and children, took the whole incident in their stride, then spent the following day souvenir hunting.

Structural plan of the Pachena Point Lighthouse on the west coast of Vancouver Island, circa 1906-07. Courtesy Canadian Coast Guard, Victoria District.

One of the great lighthouses certainly has to be Estevan, located at the southwest extremity of Estevan Point at Hole-in-the-Wall on the west coast of Vancouver Island. Built of reinforced concrete with six flying buttresses for additional strength, the Anderson-design has gained world renown. Department of Transport photo.

Estevan Lighthouse was one of the few targets fired on by a Japanese submarine in the Pacific Northwest during World War II. The keeper extinguished the light and no damage was inflicted. Estevan's big prismatic lens was replaced by an AGA PRB 21 beacon recently.

The 5.9 caliber, 80 pound shells were large projectiles, many landing in the vicinity of Hesquiat village, three miles behind the lighthouse.

Several months later, a Japanese submarine was sunk off the the coast of New Zealand by the allied forces, and a survivor confessed that he was a crew member aboard the submersible that had shelled a lighthouse off Canada's west coast.

Estevan Lighthouse, erected in 1907, and upgraded three years later, is an impressive 127 foot high octagonal, reinforced concrete tower, the tallest in the province, resplendent in appearance. It stands guard at Hole-in-the-Wall, on the extremity of Estevan Point, and is one of Colonel W.P. Anderson's greatest design triumphs on any Canadian coast. The tower is virtually invincible, designed to sway in high intensity winds or earthquakes, afforded extra strength with its flying buttresses. It has been shaken so severely by earthquakes that all the mercury has slopped out of the bath which formerly floated the lens, but the tower showed no signs of stress.

The former Fresnel has been replaced by a PRB-21, an AGA product with revolving arrays of high powered sealed beam lamps, eight to a panel, designed for modern high intensity lighthouse installations. The station as of 1985 was also utilizing a powerful diaphone fog signal and an important radio beacon.

Captain James Cook in 1778 called the location Breakers Point, and though Vancouver retained that name, future charts adopted Estevan. Little did any of those early navigators realize it would be well over a century and a quarter before the point would be marked by a lighthouse, one of the most important in all of Canada. Even after all those years, the construction crew had to literally carve the place out of pristine wilderness. The landing of supplies and provisions was extremely difficult, all materials coming by water. There were ravines, ridges, rocks and tall timber that had to be cleared before the great tower could rise skyward.

Estevan Point has an historical background. It was there that the Hesquiat Indians, (related to the Nootkas), had their first contact with a ship manned by caucasians. In the early summer of 1774. Captain Juan Perez of the Spanish Navy sailed in the *Santiago* from Monterey with instructions from the Viceroy of Mexico to examine the coast as far north as 60 degrees N. Latitude and to take possession of the lands for Spain; to further plant bottles containing the evidence. The naval party, along with their priest, landed and made an unsuccessful attempt to convert the Hesquiats to Roman Catholicism. Perez's second lieutenant, Estevan Jose Martinez, was the nephew of Don Manuel Antonio Flores, the viceroy of Mexico and it was the former who started the trouble with England by seizing at Nootka, in 1789, the British vessels *Iphigenia, Northwest America, Princess Royal* and *Argonaut.*

Canadian lighthouse authorities have never forgotten their greatest white elephant. The drama unfolded at Triangle Island, 25 miles west

A classic example of a frame lighthouse is found at Lennard Island. The graceful 80 foot tower surmounted by an iron lantern house with an umbrella dome, was built in 1904. It was replaced in 1980 by a white, circular tower with a red band at top. Department of Transport photo.

of Cape Scott, shown on the Admiralty chart of 1849 as an island with reefs around it, in the shape of a triangle—thus the name.

Government authorities decided in 1908 to place a lofty experimental marine beacon atop 700 foot Triangle Island. The station which was activated in 1910 along with a wireless station, lasted but one decade. The lighthouse was then shifted to Cape Scott and the wireless station to Bull Harbor.

Chance Brothers, of Birmingham, England, a firm internationally recognized in the marine optic field, and the contractor for lighthouses in many parts of the world, was chosen to set up the experimental station 500 feet higher than the elevation of any other Canadian primary lighthouse. The 46 foot tower at the summit was said by some navigators to be "out of this world." It was to have been the answer to all marine traffic moving through the outside passage to Alaska and northern B. C. ports as well as a landfall light for transpacific vessels. But alas, though the light was brilliant in clear weather, fog, murk, mist and rain virtually muzzled its glow. Even low hanging clouds frequently engulfed its presence. From the island's narrow beach to the lighthouse there was a climb of 1,000 steps. A fog signal was considered but never installed. The station was costly to construct, costly to maintain and a costly mistake.

After the lighthouse and wireless station were abandoned, the lantern, lens, lighting apparatus and reflectors were removed and placed in storage at the Department of Transport's ship depot on Victoria's inner harbor.

Winds that sweep the lofty island are sometimes fierce. Two years after the lighthouse was commissioned, a hurricane blew down the wireless towers and damaged station buildings. Windows were blown out and doors torn from their hinges. All of the clothing and personal effects in the wireless station dwelling were sucked out and blown

Entrance Island Lighthouse built in 1876, was a proud antique edifice on an island at the northern approach to Nanaimo. It has been replaced by a modern circular tower.

Holland Rock Lighthouse, constructed and commissioned in 1908, became a victim of a devastating fire that completely consumed the structure in 1946. Today Holland Rock is marked by a white skeleton tower on the southern extremity of the rock, on the northern inside channel. Department of Transport photos, Prince Rupert District.

away. The lantern had to have special bracing built on its interior to hold the heavy plate glass panes from blowing out of their iron frames. The station houses swayed so badly in heavy winds that personnel claimed they sometimes felt seasick.

Supply was also a problem, for hazardous weather conditions sometimes forced a wait of two months before a ship arrived. The lighthouse and the wireless crew bemoaned their isolated duty and complained bitterly when food ran short between visits of the lighthouse tender.

The initial keeper of the experimental light station was James W. Davies, who previously served aboard the lighthouse tenders *Sir James Douglas* and *Quadra* as well as the lighthouses at Scarlett Point, Carmanah, Pachena and Egg Island. He retired in 1930 after 38 years in the service. When assigned to Triangle Island, Davies, the son of B. C.'s first lighthouse keeper, George Davies, arrived aboard the chartered freight boat *Leebro* with his wife, and three daughters, all of school age. Being placed on an intolerably lonely island open to the full fury of the Pacific was an experience never forgotten. No correspondence courses were available so the teaching chores fell to the bachelor wireless men at the station who were somewhat pleased with the extra curricular activities.

In November 1918, the fisheries patrol vessel *Galiano,* doing extra duty as a fill-in lighthouse tender called at Triangle with supplies. She was to pick up two passengers, a Miss Brunton, who had been hired for a year as a housekeeper for the bachelor wireless crew, and Sidney Elliott, one of the operators. Elliott's baggage was sitting on the beach. He waited for the ship's boat to come in with the lighthouse supplies, but before his departure, a wireless message cancelled his leave. Dejectedly he ascended the 1,000 steps back to his domicile.

With startling suddeness, leaden clouds dropped a canopy of gloom over the scene as the rain began to pelt down and the seas mounted in fury. The workboat crew in a hurry to get back to their vessel, dumped the lighthouse freight on the small section of beach, lifted the departing housekeeper into the boat's confines and hastened back to the *Galiano* which was struggling to hold her position. The storm struck with fury as they weighed anchor and set a course for Ikeda Head wireless station in the Queen Charolettes. The vessel never reached her destination. The wireless operator on Triangle received a message from the *Galiano's* master, Captain Pope, a terse message of only three words, "We are sinking!" The vessel vanished into the depths with her crew of 26, and Miss Brunton, their passenger. Suddenly those 1,000 weary steps seemed to Elliott some kind of a miracle, for had it not have been for the last minute order cancelling his leave he would have been asleep in the deep.

Two years later, Triangle Island Light Station was turned back to Mother Nature, and the sea birds, seals and sea lions got back the rocky climes they possessed before the intruders came.

Another veteran lighthouse replaced by a modern counterpart is at Entrance Island, a two acre plot off Gabriola Island, near Nansimo. The Minister of Transport had termed it right for automation, but public protest over having the important station without the human element has at least for the present postponed any such plans, and the facility continues to be faithfully attended.

The first Entrance Island Lighthouse was established in 1876 when ships came up the Strait of Georgia to collect coal from Nanaimo mines. For many years seafaring men have depended heavily on services rendered by the keepers residing on the small islet. The premises are so restricted that families assigned there often board their children on Gabriola Island during the school season.

Winter storms often rake the barren piece of terra firma, and in one incident a few years back one of the station attendants was almost blown off the boat landing ten feet above the water. The new 63 foot circular concrete tower withstands the storms much better than did its frame predecessor, although enough praises can not be heaped on the old facility, a 50 foot square frame tower attached to a dwelling which was the apex of the rocky isle for nearly a century.

Two families are usually attached to the station, 12 hours a day, seven days a week, 11 months in the year. As a rule they are compatible but do not tend to over socialize in such restricted surroundings.

Egg Island Lighthouse, established in 1898, on a small islet in Queen Charlotte Sound was destroyed by what was believed to be a seismic tidal wave on November 3, 1948. Fortunately the keeper, Mr. Wilkens, his wife and son were the only ones at the station and they miraculously escaped death when the wave washed the station dwelling from its foundation, smashing it to kindling and depositing the remains in the gully behind. The alert keeper had taken his family to a safer place just before the awesome wave plowed into their home. Earlier warning waves alerted Wilkens to the unusual sea conditions, and the same wave that smashed their dwelling, lifted out the footbridge they had just crossed while seeking higher ground. Only the foghorn house escaped the rape by the savage seas.

After the ocean moderated, the CGS *Birnie,* under Captain Norman MacKay, was dispatched to remove the cold and hungry survivors. The damage was surveyed and a temporary light installed until a new lighthouse could be built. The replacement building was a rectangular concrete dwelling surmounted by a 52 foot tower on the summit at the west end of the island. Today the tower has lattice work around it and there is a fog signal and radio beacon at the station.

A disaster of another kind struck Holland Rock Lighthouse. In late 1946, an overheated cook stove set the edifice on fire. Inasmuch as the building was very confined and the rooms small, the blaze got out of control and the keeper had no choice but to launch the station skiff, saving only the clothes on his back and his pet cat. The lighthouse occupied virtually the entire rock and when the CGS *Alberni* arrived on the scene, Captain J. Peterson, her master, reported it as a total disaster, not even a single piece of salvageable equipment.

Today the rock is marked by a white skeleton tower in use since 1959. The destroyed lighthouse was established in 1908.

An engineering triumph was a way to describe the construction of 76 foot Triple Island Lighthouse in 1920. The reinforced concrete tower rising from the corner of a huge concrete building, contained spacious quarters for the keepers and fog signal equipment, and from a distance, appeared more like a castle rising from the sea than a lighthouse. It replaced a structure of inferior quality displaying a gas light, built seven years earlier.

All building supplies and materials had to be freighted in by water, and during the construction period, the contractor's scow capsized in rough waters and a derrick had to be barged in to right it. Built on the northwesterly rock of the Triple Islets group, the three-story structure was one of the most ambitious undertakings of the Department of Transport during that decade, in fact, District Marine Agent E. Harris described it as one of Canada's finest lighthouses, the walls of the tower varying from 18 inches on the first floor to 15 inches on the third, with an overall average of 12 inches on all walls, of reinforced concrete throughout. Fastened deeply in a natural rock formation, the fortress-like sentinel is able to withstand earthquake, and tidal wave and is virtually fireproof.

Today, the station attendants mind the light, diaphone fog signal and radio beacon, important factors on the Pacific coast sealanes of British Columbia. In 1965, D. Robinson Construction Ltd. was

Construction of Triple Islands Lighthouse tower in September 1920. The station was established in 1913, and is one of the formidable lighthouses in British Columbia. The concrete reinforced tower is 76 feet high and was fitted with a third order dioptric Fresnel. Department of Transport photo, northern district.

awarded a subtrade contract for construction of a combined dwelling and light tower alteration project valued at $54,848, implemented under the Federal Department of Transport.

Sisters Island Light commissioned in 1898 on the Strait of Georgia is situated on the easterly and largest of a group of rocks known as Sisters Islets. It was the site of a $124,000 rebuilding and modernization program in 1979 by D. Robinson Construction, at which time a 55 foot concrete circular lighthouse, outbuildings and helicopter pad were erected. The final result was a prime example of what a modern Canadian lighthouse should look like, at least that was the opinion of the Canadian postal service which featured the new Sisters Lighthouse on one of its postage stamps, which has now become a collector's item.

Merry Island Lighthouse on the southeast extremity of the island, at the southeast entrance to Welcome Passage, was established in 1903. The isle was named in 1860 by Captain Richards of the HMS *Plumper,* honoring a Mr. Merry who was a wealthy iron master and race horse owner.

There has been confusion from time to time with the Merry Island Lighthouse in Canada and the Mary Island Lighthouse in Alaska, even though they are a considerable distance apart.

The completed Triple Islands Light, a monument to its builders. A small boat is landing supplies on the rocky outcrops. Department of Transport photo, northern district.

Sisters Lighthouse (Sisters Islets) was established in 1898 and for several decades appeared just as the photo depicts. Then, like so many of the colorful old sentinels, it outlived its usefulness and was replaced by a modern circular concrete tower. In October 1985, Sisters Light was the subject on a series of four Canadian postage stamps, an example of a modern lighthouse. Four other lighthouses were also in the elite league, including historic Fisgard. Department of Transport photo, Victoria district.

Scarlett Point Lighthouse at the entrance to Christie Passage was established in 1905. Since 1978, a red skeleton tower has marked the point.

The original lighthouse was replaced in recent years by a modern concrete counterpart. The pioneer was a rectangular frame structure with an octagonal wooden lantern, and shared its roost with Radio Coast Station VCU. The light and foghorn today are of modern manufacture.

One of the grand old men of the Canadian lighthouse service was Captain Arthur Broughton Gurney who died in 1963 at the age of 85. He had been in charge of the Active Pass Lighthouse at Georgina Point on Mayne Island for 23 years when he retired in 1945. Born in Middlesex, England, he began his lighthouse duties in British Columbia in 1905 at the Pine Island Lighthouse in Queen Charlotte Sound. He then transferred to Ballenas Lighthouse in 1912 and finally moved to Active Pass in 1921 where he rounded out four decades of lighthouse service.

Active Pass today is marked by a modern circular tower, but the station was commissioned back in 1885, and has been an important aid to navigation since that date.

A skeleton tower cradles the light at the Boat Bluff Station today, the original lighthouse of 1907, merely a memory. Still very active at this writing, there in recent years, an old custom, often practiced in the past, was revived. Cruise ships on the Alaska run during the tourist season, in answer to a letter from the light keeper's daughter blast their whistles when passing the station, much to her delight.

Other colorful Canadian light stations are found at Lucy Island, established in 1907; at Ivory Island on Robb Point, Milbanke Sound, since 1898, now the site of a skeleton navigation aid; Pointer Island, south of the east entrance to Lama Passage, marked since 1899; Dryad Point, since 1899, at the north entrance to the passage into Seaforth Channel, now known as Dryad Point Sector; McInnes Island, at the north entrance to Milbanke Sound, established in 1921, plus a continuing list of other navigation aids in the northern district.

Some lesser known light stations in the Victoria District include Chatham Point on Johnstone Strait, dating from 1908 and now marked with a white circular tower with a black band at the top; Portlock Point on Prevost Island in the Strait of Georgia where in 1985 one of the last of the old frame towers, dating from 1895, is still in service; Porlier Pass, marked since 1902; Trial Islands on the southeast side of that southern most isle on the fringes of the Strait of Juan de Fuca, displaying a light and fog signal since 1906; Gallows Point, lighted since 1923, now marked by a circular tower etc.

Needless to say, British Columbia sealanes virtually bristle with navigation aids.

Nor should we leave the subject without tribute to some of the faithful old lighthouse tenders that served the province in the past. One especially stands out—the lighthouse tender *Quadra* which afforded yoeman service from 1892 till 1917. She has a successor today bearing her name, as does another old tender, the *Sir James Douglas* which also put in a quarter century of service to B. C. lights. The old *Quadra* was commanded by a colorful gentleman known to all as Captain John T. Walbran. He kept his vessel spit and polished at all times, his crew properly attired and a sword frequently displayed with his uniform. Replacing the original *Sir James Douglas*, the *Quadra* was the dependable life source to the lonely lighthouse keepers, and in many cases their only link with the outside world. Her master was a well trained merchant naval officer and a history buff as well. He wrote the treasured *Walbran's Place Names,* a compendium of geographic features and how they came to be named, and by whom. The salty individual had overseen the construction of the *Quadra* in Paisley, Scotland in 1891, and brought her west via the Strait of Magellan, arriving at Esquimalt 69 days later. The vessel hoisted canvas along the way to conserve fuel. Measuring 175 feet in length, the 265 ton steamer had a top speed of 11 knots.

In May 1892, while en route to the Bering Sea, the *Quadra* rammed into a ledge of uncharted rock in the Queen Charlottes, and

This photo of Addenbroke Lighthouse was taken in 1928. The 1914 structure seen here has been replaced by a skeleton tower in recent years. It is located on the west point of the island in Queen Charlotte Sound. Department of Transport photo.

Lawyer Islands Lighthouse, built in 1901, is pictured here several years ago with the keeper standing on the wooden walkway. Unfortunately, this fine structure was replaced by a skeleton tower on the summit of the northernmost island. Department of Transport photo.

Pointer Island Lighthouse, the original of 1899, pictured here, was replaced by an aluminum skeleton tower in 1975. The photo was taken in 1935. The lighthouse is located at the east entrance to Lama Passage. Department of Transport photo.

Lucy Island Lighthouse on an island along the searoad to Prince Rupert Harbor, was established in 1907 and was typical of the little Canadian sentinels on the intricate channels of British Columbia— frame, hipped roof with square lantern house at the peak. The location is marked today with a flashing red light on a small tower. Old Department of Transport photo, northern district.

the obstruction carries her name to this day. Though scarred from the stranding, she was soon back in service.

In 1909, the *Newington* was purchased to assist the *Quadra*, and in 1913, the *Estevan* was built. Other tenders joining the fleet in those early years were the *Berens, Alberni* and *Alexander Mackenzie*.

After a collision with the steamer *Charmer* on February 26, 1917, at the entrance to Nanaimo Harbor, the *Quadra*, under Captain Edmund C. LeBlanc, had to be beached to prevent her sinking. Unfortunately, LeBlanc was pilot on the ill-fated SS *Islander* when she went down with 42 souls in Lynn Canal after striking an iceberg in 1901.

Badly damaged, but later refloated, the *Quadra* was sold by the government to Britannia Mines and coverted to an ore carrier. In 1924, she was sold again and this time became an infamous rumrunner, slowly going from riches to rags, during the American prohibition years.

Ivory Island Lighthouse, on Robb Point, Milbanke Sound, was a frame structure built in 1898; Note the square lantern house. The picture was taken in 1917. The oldtimer has been replaced by a red skeleton tower in recent years. Department of Transport photo.

On March 14, 1972, the MS **Valene,** a Panamanian-registered freighter was wrecked on the rocks at the edge of Austin Island off the west coast of Vancouver Island. She was typical of scores of vessels that have come to grief along the rugged B.C. coastline, just one more reason why so many navigation aids are needed in those waters. Photo by E.A. Delanty.

One of the few wooden oldtimers remaining in British Columbia is Portlock Point, built in 1895. The lighthouse is pictured several years back with the tender **Berens** standing offshore, and the frame bell tower in the foreground. Photo courtesy Pen Brown, Victoria District.

Solander Island, a humpy sea-girt piece of rock off the western shores of Vancouver Island was not marked by an aid to navigation until 1929. The difficulty of servicing the unmanned light can be seen in the pictures below, the Canadian aids to navigation vessel **Camsell** at anchor below the light structure, one of the highest marine aids in B.C. The former beacon at the 305 foot elevation site is now utilized at Cleft of the Rock Lighthouse. Photos (1964), courtesy Pen Brown, Victoria District office Canadian Coast Guard (Transport Canada).

Old Discovery Island Lighthouse, built in 1886, is shown here in the 1920s, a one-of-a-kind lighthouse, all contained in one unit. It was replaced by a circular concrete tower in 1978. Location is the eastern extremity of the island on Haro Strait. Department of Transport photo.

*Crowds gather at the end of the breakwater, crowned by Ogden Point Light, in Victoria Harbor to watch the sailing yacht **Kialoa** cross the finish line. A light was first placed there in 1917.*

The original Prospect Point Lighthouse built in 1898, with square lantern house, large fog bell and keepers quarters all in one structure, atop stone blocks at the base of the cliff. The old building was raised many years ago, from under the Lion's Gate Bridge.

The present Prospect Point Light atop a solid concrete tower has been in use since 1948, an eye-catcher with its prominent red band. Photo taken 1968.

Lighthouse on legs—Brockton Point on the extremity of the point inside the First Narrows, Vancouver Harbor, was established in 1890 and has always been a favorite viewing spot for locals and tourists as well. Present structure, circa 1924.

First Narrows Lighthouse in Burrard Inlet, Vancouver, B.C., a landmark for several decades, is there no more. The old wooden structure with a square lantern house is pictured here as it looked in 1944.

*Thomas and Minnie Paterson. He was keeper of Cape Beale Lighthouse 1895-1908. She became British Columbia's 'Grace Darling' for her part in saving the crew of the imperiled bark **Coloma** in 1906.*

Burnaby Shoal is an interesting example of a minor light near Vancouver. The concrete pillar established in 1912, houses a light and fog bell in this photo taken in the 1950s. The bell was still there in the 1980s, but a new light and a radar reflector has been added.

The steam whistle warning ships off the Columbia River was silent on the Columbia River Lightship **No. 50** after she was driven ashore in a storm in November 1899. After several unsuccessful attempts to refloat her, an epic overland salvage effort was undertaken. Months later, the battered vessel was relaunched into Bakers Bay, the better part of a mile away from where she went aground on exposed McKenzie Head. A jubilant crowd poses here as the **No. 50** is readied for relaunching on June 2, 1901.

Foghorn trumpets on a typical government lightship called out their warnings in all four directions. U.S. Lighthouse Service photo.

U.S. Lighthouse tender **Manzanita,** named for the former **Manzanita,** was built in 1908 and performed yoeman service for four decades at all of the lighthouses in the Pacific Northwest waters.

Ode to the Foghorn

Fog, the ghostly wraith that haunts
the sea and shore in mystic silence.
.....JAG

What better way to terminate a writing on lighthouses than to pay tribute to the ugly, least featured, least romantic aspect of the light station—the fog signal. Such mechanisms have been the bane of lighthouse keepers, an irritation to the general public and the target of more profanity, more frustration and more resignations than could ever be recorded.

If automation was ever an accepted word to the traditional old-time lighthouse keeper, it had to involve fog signals. Few living today suffered the physical pain involved in their upkeep and maintenance, such as packing sacks of coal or wood on their backs, dumping tons of gritty, black lumps into a chute, or rolling in drums of fuel oil for storage. And how about shoveling fuel into the boiler to raise a head of steam to sound the whistle or horn, or even worse, cleaning the boiler? All such chores demanded sweat, grit, grime and more sweat.

The curse of the fogbell has been mentioned, and certainly it became a nightmare when the striking mechanisms failed or the weights got stuck, demanding manual operation around the clock. It was a flashback to the day of the world's first known fog device—the gong. They were mounted on shore standards or on the forecastle of ships in ages past, bonged by hand till the sand ran out of the hour glass, watch upon watch.

But with all the negativism, fog signals have saved countless lives of those imperiled on shrouded seas. Over and above the saving qualities of the old foghorn, certain persons found they also had romantic qualities, in fact, there is something warming and melancholy on a still, fog-filled morn when one is listening to the symphony of strange noises rising out of a mystic fog. Lest the reader think the writer a bit light in the head, let it be said that there was a song written based on the dreary sound of foghorns. Donald Capon, a former school principal in Vancouver B. C., composed what he labled the "Foghorn Song," by listening to the ships and shore signals in and around the bustling Canadian harbor during befogged hours. A musician at heart, he picked up on the various notes and added a few of his own, the finished version, a very acceptable rendition that was taught to his high school students and eventually sung before the student body, with great enthusiasm.

As the elite Colonel Anderson was instrumental in the design and engineering of the ferro concrete, reinforced lighthouse for Canadian shorelines, so was another Canadian credited with a big breakthrough in fog signals several years ago. Going back to the mid-1850's, Robert Foulis was much troubled by a local shipwreck with a heavy loss of life. He felt it could have been prevented had a proper warning signal been in operation.

Canadians seem to have an ear for making the most out of music, and while Foulis was listening to his daughter practice on the piano he found his answer. Like any proud father, he enjoyed seeing his offspring faithfully putting in her hour on the ivorys each day. But one sound, a deep tone, low in bass, seemed to haunt this St. John, New Brunswick, music teacher and inventor. Its tone lasted longer than did any other. If he could somehow capture that one sound and magnify it he might be able to make fog-bound navigators sit up and take notice. As his daughter zeroed in on that note again and again he went to his shop and put his genius to work assembling a devise that sounded loudly when connected to a crude boiler. The steam pressure was built up and then released through a horn, producing with great gusto the exact sound he heard his daughter play on the piano.

Like all Rube Goldberg-type inventors he got his share of criticism, laughter and ridicule, but he was persistent enough to finally get the Canadian government to give his invention a trial. What did the Crown have to lose by letting him hook up his contraption on a small island in the harbor? This he did, and then went home to wait for the next thick fog to drop its curtain over the harbor.

It happened three weeks later, in fact, it was so thick that he was unable to leave his residence. A sympathetic guardian on the island had the foresight to stoke up the boiler, realizing that the inventor would be delayed by the pea-souper. Somewhat discourged by his inability to get there, Foulis hoped the islander would give his invention a try. When he opened his window, to his delight he heard the piercing sound wafting across the harbor, music to his ears. He had proven his point and from that day on, the steam operated foghorn became the standard for Canada and several other maritime countries as well.

May it be duly recorded that foghorns and music can go hand-in-hand.

Meanwhile, back across the border, the old Yankee ingenuity also was at work. It was during the same time period that the man C. L. Daboll was urging the Lighthouse Board to consider his experiments with whistles and trumpets operated by compressed air. Daboll thought in big terms, very big, in fact the largest model of Daboll's signal trumpet was 17 feet long, with a gaping mouth 38 inches across. The sound was produced from compressed air vibrating a reed ten inches long and 2½ inches wide, an exaggerated adaptation of holding a blade of grass over one's mouth and blowing hard into it to produce a weird sound. For some unknown reason the Lighthouse Board did not immediately adopt the Daboll principal, and several years passed before the effectiveness of the system was fully realized. When it finally did catch on, hundreds of American lighthouses were equipped with Daboll fog signals and they proved highly successful.

The invention is not to be compared with the fog signal mentioned earlier, that Major Hartman Bache had placed over a natural blowhole at Farallon Light Station in 1859. That brick structure acted as a support and an air conductor. Economy-minded, the inspector had a locomotive steam whistle inserted at the top of the brick chimney. When the surf was high, the device afforded a reasonable sound, but when needed the most during foggy periods, when the ocean was usually the calmest, the whistle sounded like an under-nourished popcorn wagon. Finally, in 1871, as tremendous seas crashed into the island fissure that contained the blowhole, the rush of air was so great that it completely shattered the chimney and blew the whistle sky-high. A more efficient fog signal was installed within the decade.

Old Bob Gerloff, the legend of Tillamook Rock, the man who never wanted to leave his islet abode when his turn came for leave, was undaunted by the protracted periods when the foghorn droaned endlessly on. When he was forced into retirement he made a formal request to the lighthouse authorities to live on at the rock at no expense to the government, but his request was denied. Every night after his retirement he would be standing at the sea wall in Seaside, Oregon from where he could observe the lighthouse, just to be sure the light came on at sunset. When the fog rolled in, he would stroll the beach listening for the mournful cry of the fog trumpets.

A large percentage of shipwrecks and collisions, before the advent of miracle navigation aids, were fog-related. Familiarity with certain sounds was a necessity to navigators. Ironically, when radar first came into wide usage, there was a rash of ship collisions, for man soon learned that just having such equipment aboard ship was no safeguard. A device of such nature, it was soon discovered, was no better than the trained eye watching the screen or an operator understanding the keys.

The day of the fog signal is not yet over. The latest equipment comprises a number of vertically arranged glass-reinforced plastic housings containing coding devices. Housing contains a diaphragm assembly drive unit and amplifier equipment. The sound units are spaced to give maximum efficiency with narrow vertical distribution, and though each is self-contained, all are electronically synchronized. Then there are directional sound signals of modular construction, applied in single or multiple arrays, the horn and emitter units assembled in stacks for wider horizontal angles of coverage. They are a far cry from their predecessors, but the name of the game remains the same.

On file with the former U. S. Lighthouse Service, and in several incidents with the Coast Guard, are scores of irate letters from disturbed civilians describing the fog signal sounds in nasty terms. One eastern newspaper writer likened a New England foghorn to "a screech like an army of panthers, wierd and prolonged, gradually lowering in note until after a half minute it becomes the roars of a thousand mad bulls, with intermediate voices suggestive of the wail of a lost soul, the moan of the bottomless pit and the groan of a disabled elevator."

So dear reader, the next time you are near a harbor or on the seashore when fog rolls in, listen to the beeps, boofs and brrrrumphs and remember your impressions are all in the mind. Is it irritating or is it music?

We are told by color experts that there are some 38,000 shades of gray. There are those of the opinion that all those shades are associated with fog and its melancholy. A story is told of a commercial fisherman who made his living from the sea. He lived with his wife in a beach shack on a sandy finger of land, and did much of his commercial trolling immediately off the shore where he resided. His wife, who he often accused of talking too much, had a type of operatic voice, and when fog rolled in while he was at sea she would periodically go out on the sandspit and hit a high note which in turn would alert her husband of his distance from the shore. She was faithful to her task until one foggy day after he had been at sea a few days she came down with a bad case of laryngitis. No notes would come forth from her voice box, and as a result, the frustrated fisherman ran his vessel hard aground on the rocks at the end of the sandspit.

Though that feminine "foghorn" was silent for awhile, it took the loss of the man's boat to make him realize that without her vocal chords he was in big trouble. He never again accused her of talking too much.

Index